# Solving business problems by simulation

Second Edition

# Solving business problems by simulation

Second Edition

Jan Szymankiewicz
James McDonald
Keith Turner

McGRAW-HILL BOOK COMPANY

**London** · New York · St Louis · San Francisco · Auckland
Bogotá · Guatemala · Hamburg · Lisbon · Madrid · Mexico
Montreal · New Delhi · Panama · Paris · San Juan
São Paulo · Singapore · Sydney · Tokyo · Toronto

Published by
McGRAW-HILL Book Company (UK) Limited
MAIDENHEAD · BERKSHIRE · ENGLAND

**British Library Cataloguing in Publication Data**

Szymankiewicz, Jan
    Solving business problems by simulation.
    ——2nd ed.
    1. Digital computer simulation
    I. Title   II. McDonald, James   III. Turner, Keith
    IV. Poole, T. G.
    Using simulation to solve problems
    001.4′2      QA76.9.C65
    ISBN 0-07-084946-3


**Library of Congress Cataloging-in-Publication Data**

    Solving business problems by simulation
    Jan Szymankiewicz, James McDonald, Keith Turner
    Rev. ed. of: Using simulation to solve problems
    T. G. Poole, J. Z. Szymankiewicz. c1977.
        Bibliography: p.
        Includes index.
        ISBN 0-07-084946-3
    1. Digital computer simulation.   I. McDonald, James.
    II. Turner, Keith.   III. Poole, T. G. (Tom G.)
    Using simulation to solve problems.   IV. Title.
    T57.62.S99 1988
    001.4′34—dc19      87-26630

1234  WL  898

Typeset by Bath Typesetting Ltd.
Printed in Great Britain by Whitstable Litho Ltd.,
and bound by Skyline Bookbinders Ltd.

# Contents

# Preface

In the first edition of this book—*Using Simulation to Solve Problems* written by Tom Poole and Jan Szymankiewicz—the preface began thus:

> Simulation is a practical and widely used problem-solving technique, and yet there is surprisingly little practical or case study literature available to guide those interested in the subject. Books published to date have been mostly of a review nature which, while offering a necessary academic dimension to the subject, are of no great assistance to the practical problem solver.
>
> The great strength of simulation is that it allows a model of a problem to be developed from first principles and an understanding of its behaviour acquired by a simple question and answer approach.
>
> Unfortunately, simulation has not been fully exploited as a problem-solving technique, for two reasons. Firstly, managers and problem solvers consider simulation to be the domain of the specialist well versed in the precise prose of a computer language. This has resulted in simulation projects being viewed from the computer's point of view—which, for the purposes of understanding a problem, is rather like looking at it the wrong way down a telescope. Secondly, training establishments offer a syllabus which all too often leans towards the academically stimulating subjects. This results in, for example, queueing theory—which is rarely used in solving real problems—being allocated much more time than simulation, which is treated as one of those techniques which you pick up as and when you need it.
>
> The purpose of our book is to bridge the gap by concentrating on the basic principles of simulation and teaching the reader to build and operate models of real-life problems. The ability to construct simple flow diagrams and to follow a set of rules for operating a model are the only skills required.

These statements are just as valid today as they were then (1977). However, during the past decade the number of 'practical problem solvers' interested in using simulation techniques has grown considerably.

In 1977 serious simulations could only be undertaken by organizations who owned or had access to large mainframe computers. The relentless pace of technological advance has changed all this. Today the same simulations, which ten years ago needed those large mainframes, now can be carried out on mini and micro computers. It is truly amazing that suitable hardware is now available for less than £5000.

Not only is the hardware cheaper, but also the software is far more powerful and sophisticated. Today, users have very high expectations about what software will do for them. They take it for granted that a system will be highly user-friendly, fully interactive and have sophisticated colour graphics. These high expectations have come about mainly from the explosion of visually exciting computer games. Of course, the reader will appreciate that most of these games are themselves simulations—war games, treasure hunts, moon-landings, etc.

Using the latest developments in computer colour graphics, simulation software is now also highly visual and therefore very exciting to 'play'. These major developments in both hardware and software have resulted in the demand for simulation increasing by at least a factor of ten.

Despite the technological advances and the increased interest in the subject there are still no truly practical and up-to-date books on simulation aimed at the typical 'problem solver'. We have therefore produced this substantially revised second edition.

The book is a complete and up-to-date treatment of the subject. We describe in detail how simulation models using the principles described. The modelling approach is presented in the form of a 'teach yourself' text.

Many simulation systems exist for running models on computers and the ease with which this can be done depends on the system used. Most require the use of computer specialists. However, the system which is featured in the book, HOCUS*, requires no knowledge of computer programming as it utilizes a suite of standard programs.

In addition to having built several hundreds of simulation models personally, the authors have presented papers, given seminars and run training courses throughout the world. We have trained many hundreds of managers, engineers, designers and students to build simulation models using the principles described. The modelling approach is presented in the form of a 'teach yourself' text.

The book covers the simulation of both discrete and continuous processes and therefore provides the guidelines for modelling most types of problems.

Part One of the book describes the steps in building informal simulation models and hand simulation. A step-by-step instruction text is provided with examples and exercises. This takes the reader to the point of building a model and operating it by hand.

Part Two describes building formal models for hand and computer simulation. We separate the tasks of model building and computer operation and provide a simple discipline to ensure that both may be accurately and quickly completed. The approach is designed to produce hand simulation models which are transferred directly to the computer without the assistance of a programmer. It is an approach which can be learnt by managers, designers, industrial engineers and students of most disciplines.

Part Three explains how models are run on a computer. We describe how information is extracted and presented for maximum impact and how results are displayed using animated colour graphics. We present criteria for selecting a simulation language and describe in some detail how one major multi-national corporation set about this task.

Part Four discusses the key elements of experimentation, and sets out guidelines for the management of simulation projects. These were designed to ensure that maximum benefits are achieved and that the end result is a successful implementation.

Part Five looks into the future and discusses developments that are likely to take place in the next five to ten years—developments that will ensure that the dramatic growth in demand for simulation over the past decade will continue at an even faster rate. We consider the

---

* Registered trade mark of P-E International plc, Park House, Egham, Surrey, United Kingdom.

impact of new generations of computers and languages, man–machine interfaces (touch-sensitive screens, voice recognition and speech synthesis), Very Large Scale Integration (VLSI), Intelligent Knowledge Based Systems (Expert Systems) and Artificial Intelligence. Some of the developments may take longer than ten years and some of our forecasts are highly speculative. It will be interesting to see how accurate we have been when we produce the third edition of this book!

Finally, in Part Six a number of new and up-to-date case studies are included which set out the method and experience of the project teams involved, together with a measure of the costs and benefits achieved. They have been specially chosen to cover a range of organizations, types of model and project team background. They are intended to illustrate the factors which result in the successful use of simulation.

Readers wishing for an overview of simulation should concentrate on reading the following: Chapters 1, 2, 3, 4 (first four pages), 8 (first five pages), 9 (first two pages), 10 (first two pages), 11, 12, 13, 14 and all the Case Studies. This is a total of around 140 pages, and gives a very good appreciation of the simulation approach to solving problems, and its role as a powerful management tool. Having read this we are sure you will want to return to the other pages later, to learn about more of the detail.

JAN SZYMANKIEWICZ
JAMES MCDONALD
KEITH TURNER

# Acknowledgements

The authors gratefully acknowledge the contribution made by Tom Poole, as a co-author of the first edition of this book.

We record our thanks to Adrian Haughton, Rod Pugh, Peter Sparkes and other colleagues in P-E who have assisted us in various ways by contributing valuable information, checking drafts and helping coordinate the case studies. Special thanks are also due to Marian Hammond for typing the draft of this edition.

Finally, we acknowledge the contribution made by Robin Hills to the original development of the HOCUS system, by our colleagues in P-E for the subsequent development of the system, and by Humphrey Holme formerly of ICI Plastics Division for the development of some of the facilities described in Chapter 7.

# Part One

Informal models for hand simulation

# 1.

## What is simulation?

### Solving problems

Simulation is one of the most powerful techniques available for solving problems. It involves the construction of a replica or *model* of the problem on which we experiment and test alternative courses of action. This gives us a greater insight into the problem and places us in a better position from which to seek a solution.

Let us consider where simulation fits in the problem-solving spectrum, by categorizing the process by which we make a decision as being *intuitive, analytical* or *numerical*.

*Intuitive* The majority of problems with which we are confronted in our everyday life require a decision within seconds or minutes. In the time available we balance in our 'mind's eye' the factors involved and the implications of alternative courses of action. We make a decision based on our past experience and a quick review of the alternatives. The approach does not require a great deal of time, and is justified when a good answer now is better than the best possible answer after lengthy deliberation. Most line managers live in an environment where they have to give quick answers to questions and they are judged on their ability to make good intuitive decisions. These tend to be the day-to-day operational decisions falling within the range of past experience and all concerned hope that the penalty for making a mistake is not too painful.

*Analytical* Some problems are less restricted by time. These tend to be strategic problems where mistakes are potentially expensive. The time available must be used as effectively as possible to improve confidence that the correct decision has been made.

The analytical approach is used when the behaviour of the factors involved and the relationships between them can be fully described. The problem is defined in mathematical terms—such as simultaneous equations—which are then solved to give the optimum answer. This approach normally requires mathematicians, programmers and a computer to perform the analysis.

We can illustrate the analytical approach by taking as an example the Marketing Director of a brewery who, following a survey of customers, believes he has identified a market for a new type of beer. He specifies the characteristics of this new product in terms of colour, strength, taste, etc., and from these are calculated the raw materials and processes to be used. For this approach to succeed it must be presumed that the chemistry of beer is well understood and that clear instructions can be given to the Head Brewer. When feasible, this approach is the cheapest and quickest way of reaching the optimum solution.

However, in the majority of cases we are not in the fortunate position of being able either to describe our problem with the precision required, or to solve the mathematical equations. We are therefore reduced to using a numerical or simulation approach in order to solve our problem.

*Numerical*  In most cases the lack of time is not our greatest difficulty, but the lack of suitable information, understanding of the problem and the capacity to describe it in a structured way. Most people have difficulty in describing their problems formally and they distrust specialists who claim to be able to generate the optimum answer by using a computer. In the numerical approach we experiment with alternatives and, with the better understanding this gives, 'home in' on an answer.

In the case of the new beer example the simulation approach is to take, say, four possible raw material mixes and process each of them in four possible ways. This produces 16 (4 × 4) products which are then tested. If one of the 16 products satisfies the Marketing Director's specification, we are lucky and our task is complete. More likely we take those products closest to the requirement as a starting point around which further experimentation is conducted. This continues until an acceptable product is produced.

We conduct experiments in a systematic way until we either get a satisfactory answer or give up through lack of progress. The greater our understanding of the problem the quicker we are able to produce an answer. We start from the point of present understanding of the problem and proceed, according to ability and application, to search for the best possible solution in the time available. This means that we cannot be certain of what answers we will produce. It is pretty certain that none of them will be the optimum. Indeed we will have no idea what the optimum is. However, as we will see in later chapters, the solutions we produce are usually very acceptable to management because we can prove they will work.

Simulation forces us into observing and understanding the behaviour of the problem by identifying those factors which are important. This results in an appreciation of the dynamics of the total system under study, and helps avoid bias towards solving special mathematical problems relating to one aspect of the system, which is a danger inherent in the analytical approach.

*Simulation is a 'trial and error' approach which allows us to describe a problem and gain understanding of the factors involved, by asking questions and observing the answers.*

## A simulation model

Simulation is used to understand and solve problems either by experimenting with the real world, as in the brewery example, or by representing the problem by means of a replica or model. In most cases, experimenting in the real world is not practical as it results in 'trial and disaster' rather than 'trial and error'. It is much cheaper for a project team to correct a mistake on a piece of paper or a blueprint than it is for a management team to make expensive changes to an operational system.

The problem solver constructs a model on which to experiment. A model is a grossly simplified representation of real life, which only incorporates those features thought to be important. The use of simulation models goes back many centuries and like most problem-solving techniques evolved, or at least their use was first recorded, in a military environment where experimentation in the real world can be disastrous.

Chess is an example of a simulation model. It is probably one of the oldest games of skill, and is thought to have been derived from an Indian war game in which the different pieces were given a certain freedom of movement or firepower. The game represents a miniature battle in which success is measured simply by the capturing of the opponent's king. Similar in concept were the Prussian war games (Kriegspiels), in which squares on the map were given terrain characteristics and fighting units varying firepower. From these beginnings war games and management games have evolved.

The game of 'Monopoly' is probably one of the most popular examples of a simulation model. It is a greatly simplifed representation of property dealing in which the measure of performance is money. Uncertainty and the advance of time is introduced by means of dice and two sets of cards. The model is drawn on a board and the property tycoons are represented by tokens which move around the board. During different games players can evaluate the effect of alternative strategies and the extent to which they are sensitive to chance events or particular combinations of circumstances. For example, is it better to concentrate on the low-, medium- or high-price properties; accumulate the railway stations; purchase houses on all properties; or speed the development of hotels on particular sites? The attractive features of Monopoly are that it is simple, easily learnt, visual and exciting. A simple story and set of rules have been built up from first principles so that it can be understood and operated by anyone.

*A simulation model is a simplified representation of real life which allows the understanding and solution of a problem to be achieved by a trial and error approach.*

## Understanding the problem

The first objective in building a simulation model is to gain understanding of the problem. In the case of an airport we may build a replica of the runway and imitate the typical arrival and departure times of planes in order to see what interference occurs and measure waiting time. By observing this behaviour, the causes of the delays become apparent and alternative ways of operating are suggested. These can then be tested in the model.

To gain understanding of a problem everyone who can contribute to its definition should be able to communicate their knowledge in a simple and disciplined way. They will have various skills and view the problem from differing angles. Their contributions must be harnessed in such a way that the model satisfies the following criteria:

— It is *accurate*. The contributors agree that the model accurately represents a simplified description of the real-life problem.

— It is *acceptable*. The model incorporates what are believed to be the essential factors of the real-life problem. As understanding grows the model will be modified. Acceptability to management is particularly important in those cases where the model produces solutions which are contrary to their intuition. If they accept the model description, the search is then to discover where and why their intuition has let them down. Where opinions are strongly held this can be a difficult task but acceptance of the model and its recommendations are prerequisites for successful implementation.

— It is done *quickly*. The quicker the problem is understood the greater the time to find a solution.

In order to satisfy these criteria it is necessary to have a logic language which allows all concerned to contribute effectively. Let us consider the different ways in which the models in the 'mind's eye' of each of the contributors can be communicated.

## The communication chain

The fact that many people usually contribute to the description of a model means that we have difficulties in communication. If the model is to be defined in a specialist computer language another dimension is added to this difficulty. Let us consider the normal sequence of events in the building of a simulation model—or other types of computer model for that matter.

We start with the man who has the problem (Fig. 1.1). He may be a line manager or a designer. He thinks of the problem in terms of day-to-day detail and describes his understanding of the situation as a series of statements of what normally occurs, punctuated by instances of recent exceptions which come to mind as he relates the story. Aware that he has a problem he seeks, or is directed, to someone who can help him—usually someone from a Management Services unit. The adviser is experienced in recognizing the form of a problem but usually has limited knowledge of operational detail. His strength is his ability to set down the skeleton of the problem on which to hang the detail prior to determining the appropriate method of solution. They discuss the problem and, if a simulation model is thought to be appropriate, the discussion then usually proceeds to the writing of a computer program.

At this point the adviser specifies the model, but not necessarily correctly. The problem may not have been accurately described and this fact may not have been recognized or checked, or the adviser may have misunderstood the nature of the problem.

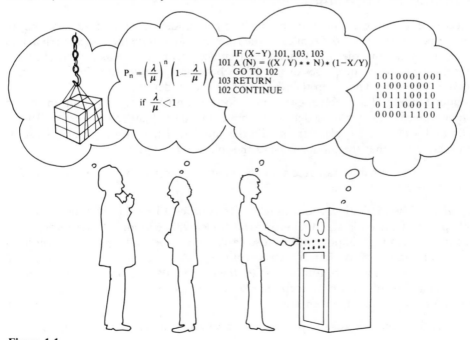

$$P_n = \left(\frac{\lambda}{\mu}\right)^n \left(1 - \frac{\lambda}{\mu}\right)$$

$$\text{if } \frac{\lambda}{\mu} < 1$$

```
    IF (X−Y) 101, 103, 103
101 A (N) = ((X / Y) ∗ ∗ N) ∗ (1−X/Y)
    GO TO 102
103 RETURN
102 CONTINUE
```

```
1 0 1 0 0 0 1 0 0 1
0 1 0 0 1 0 0 0 1
1 0 1 1 1 0 0 1 0
0 1 1 1 0 0 0 1 1 1
0 0 0 0 1 1 1 0 0
```

**Figure 1.1**

The specification may be a detailed flow chart, precisely defining the problem logic, which is then taken by a programmer who endeavours to express it in one of the many available computer languages. The only discretion allowed to the programmer is the way he describes the logic to the computer.

The danger is that the programmer is given a loose specification which he misinterprets and punctuates with programming errors. The temptation for the programmer to embellish the specification with some technical additions of personal interest is another potential source of error. The program will be keyed into the computer with every likelihood of keying errors. The final link in the communication chain is the computer which may involve compiler and operating system errors.

What are the hard facts of such a situation?

- The model which arrives at the computer does not represent the problem to be solved, having been re-interpreted a number of times during its journey to the computer.
  *Observation*: it is not accurate.
- The model is represented by a computer listing in which the interacting components are shown as a series of program statements. This description is unlikely to generate confidence and acceptance by those who described the problem originally and who will be responsible for implementing any recommendations.
  *Observation*: it is not acceptable.
- Errors made at each step in the communications chain have been mixed up and when the computer stops, the painful process of unravelling them begins. Correcting this hierarchy of mistakes is usually a lengthy exercise, consuming valuable project time.
  *Observation*: it is overdue.

This rather gloomy view shows that there is a great danger that the model will fail to satisfy the criteria of accuracy, acceptability and speed of development. The communications chain is analogous to resistances in a circuit, which when placed in series give the maximum impedance to any flow of electricity. Alternatively, it may be compared with the old soldier's tale of the message 'send reinforcements we're going to advance' being corrupted as it passes through the communications network and eventually reaching headquarters as 'send three and fourpence we're going to a dance'. Playing the whispering game is a luxury that model builders cannot afford.

The justification for the long communications chain was that the model must be operated on a computer. From the moment that assumption was made attention has been directed towards expressing the problem in computer terminology rather than describing it in a form which everyone can recognize and confirm as the one to be solved. This very assumption has seriously limited the effective use of simulation as a problem-solving technique, and has been a major cause of simulation projects failing to be completed within the limitations of time and cost.

How do we overcome the dangers inherent in getting the problem to a computer along this communications chain? One answer is to separate the task of building the model from that of running it on a computer, as shown in Fig. 1.2.

We must first describe the problem accurately and confirm the resulting model with everyone concerned. This is achieved by using a simple flow diagram as a hand simulation model, to represent the problem in a manner similar to the game of Monopoly.

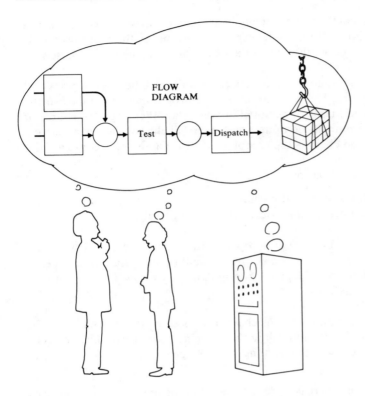

**Figure 1.2**

The flow diagram acts as the most up-to-date description of the problem against which all contributors discuss their experience, provide data and confirm the extent to which the model mirrors reality. As understanding of the problem increases the flow diagram is modified. New aspects are introduced, others amplified and some are dropped.

## Informal and formal models

The building of an accurate, acceptable model is an evolutionary process for which good communication with line management, a simple method of producing flow diagrams and a systematic questioning procedure are essential. The flow diagram can be operated as a hand model to test the logic, to gain understanding and to record the results of changing the parameters. If the problem can be solved manually then an informal model is adequate.

In an *informal* model the modeller writes information, conditions, constraints and instructions on the flow diagram as an *aide mémoire* to guide him when he is running the simulation. As long as the notes are logical, consistent and the modeller can understand them, this is a perfectly valid and flexible approach to describing a personal model.

A disadvantage is that the terminology or shorthand he uses may not be understood by anyone else, or even possibly by himself should he return to it at some future date. However, when a problem requires immediate solution and we have to solve it manually, an informal modelling approach offers considerable flexibility.

If the model is large or needs to be run over a long period then hand simulation can be extremely time-consuming and operating the model on a computer becomes an attractive proposition. If a computer is to be used then we can embark on a second task, that of describing the hand simulation model in a form suited to the computer. In this case there are advantages in building a formal model.

In a *formal* model a standard notation and set of rules are used by the modeller. He abides by the rules, which impose a discipline so that other people (or computers) who also understand the rules, can operate the model. The advantages are that many people can be involved in building and using the model and the task of transferring it to a computer is simplified. A disadvantage is that rules may be restrictive in terms of the descriptive freedom they allow.

While simple models requiring a few hours' work can usually be tackled using an informal approach, the advantages of building a formal model far outweigh the disadvantages. However, in this book we give examples of both types of model, and let the reader choose.

# 2.

## The flow diagram

### The basic framework

To build a model of a problem we need a logic language which will enable us to represent the problem on paper in the form of a flow diagram. The preparation of this diagram, as stressed in Chapter 1, is the first essential step in simulation model building. It is the means by which we discover just how much, or how little, is known about the problem.

We have chosen a procedure which naturally complements the thought processes and the narrative normally used by a designer, engineer or manager when describing a problem. It is the *activity based* approach which defines a problem in terms of *entities* being *active* or *idle*.

*Entities*. These are simply resources. The principal ones are men, machines, materials, and money.

A profit-oriented organization is concerned with converting its available resources into more valuable resources. The greater its ability to bring about this conversion the greater the profit achieved.

A service-oriented organization is concerned with providing the best possible service using its available resources. For example, an ambulance service will endeavour to organize its available ambulances in such a way that the maximum number of calls can be satisfied within a stated time.

Entities are the resources in the model, such as a gang of men, a ship, an aeroplane, a doctor, a hospital bed, or a machine. An entity may have *attributes* which are used to describe it in greater detail. They are numerical properties which may be fixed or variable. Consider as an example:

Entity: A London double-decker bus
Attributes – *fixed*:    length
                         height
                         maximum carrying capacity
                         fuel tank capacity
      – *variable*:  route
                         driver
                         fuel in tank
                         number of passengers

If we conduct a simulation involving a London bus we would certainly need the entity Bus. How many of the attributes we would need to include in the model would depend upon the extent to which they were required to describe the behaviour of the bus. We shall develop this point later in Chapter 7 when we deal with complex models.

A simulation model is a flow diagram which shows the active and idle states of the entities. When an entity is active it is involved in an *activity* and when it is idle it is waiting in a *queue*. Therefore, an entity spends its life in a sequence of activities (active state) and queues (idle state). The characteristics of an activity and a queue are as follows:

– *Activity*   An activity is the state in which an entity remains, either on its own, or with other entities, while a specified operation takes place over a period of time. The time may be constant or variable. It is calculated beforehand and once the activity has started it will continue for this duration unless the logic of the model allows it to be interrupted. For example, a machine, an operator, and a piece of steel are involved for a period of time in the activity of machining a component. If interruptions occur, because of a machine breakdown or a tea break, for instance, the model logic should reflect this.

– *Queue*   A queue is the state in which an entity waits to start an activity.

At this point we should ask a very important question. Why are resources ever in idle states? Let us consider the situation where a production unit produces goods and customers consume them at the rate at which they are produced. This is shown in Fig. 2.1.

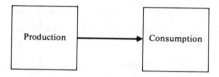

**Figure 2.1**

There is no need to hold any finished stock at the end of the production line. The production unit and the consumer are completely interdependent. If the unit stops producing the consumer stops consuming and vice versa.

However, normally consumers are separated from the production unit both by distance and time and therefore it is necessary to hold an inventory of finished stock as shown in Fig. 2.2.

**Figure 2.2**

The purpose of this inventory, or idle resource, is to decouple the production unit from the consumer. In the theoretical case where infinite stock is held the production unit and the consumer are completely independent of one another. Establishing an inventory policy is a matter of deciding where and how much this decoupling should be. This is done by balancing the benefits and penalties of holding idle resources in a system.

Many simulation exercises are concerned with deciding what levels of idle resources are required in order to give a certain flexibility of operation. An example is the number of service engineers to have on duty, so that there is a certain level of confidence of dealing with the likely pattern of calls for assistance.

It is the movement of entities through a system, from active state (activity) to idle state (queue), that is represented in a simulation model. When building a simulation model we have to decide:

— what entities to include;
— what attributes each entity should have;
— where the model starts and ends;
— how detailed the model description should be.

## A simple example

We illustrate this by considering a simple model of a man drinking beer in a bar (see Plate 1, top). Three types of entity are involved—a Man, a Glass and a Barmaid. If we find that additional entities are needed to describe the problem more realistically, we will introduce them later. Similarly, if the Man, Glass or Barmaid proves to be superfluous to the description we will eliminate it. The model will only deal with the Man drinking his beer and the Barmaid filling his Glass. The first step is to list the entities separately and decide the degree of detail required.

First we consider the Barmaid. The simplest description of her actions is:

| Entity | States |
|--------|--------|
| Barmaid | fill glass (A) |
| | idle (Q) |

The second entity, the Glass, is described as follows:

| Entity | States |
|--------|--------|
| Glass | being drunk from (A) |
| | wait empty (Q) |
| | being filled (A) |
| | wait full (Q) |

Note that activities and queues alternate. This is a feature which we will use to advantage in our hand simulation exercises in later chapters.

Finally, we describe the third entity in the model—the Man:

| Entity | States |
|--------|--------|
| Man | drink (A) |
| | wait (Q) |

Our attention is concentrated on what happens to the Man and no mention is made at this point of the conditions that must be satisfied before he can drink. This will come later.

We have considered the three entities separately and recorded what happens to them individually. Only when we are confident that these three descriptions are accurate can we contemplate describing, in a meaningful way, how these entities interact with one another.

Symbols are used to convert the words into a simple flow diagram. An activity is represented by □ and a queue by ○.

The life cycles of the Barmaid, Glass and Man can now be drawn as shown in Fig. 2.3.

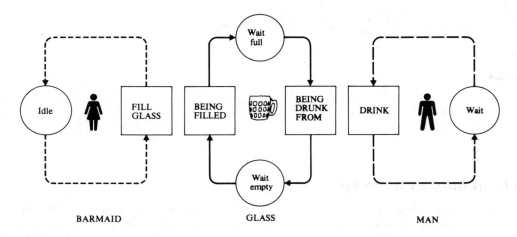

**Figure 2.3**

These life cycles are known as *activity life cycles*. The arrows indicate the direction to be followed when reading the story and can be clockwise or anticlockwise. All that matters is that the story unfolds correctly as we follow the arrows through the successive active and idle states. The drawing of accurate individual life cycles is one of the most difficult tasks in simulation modelling. Obviously there is little hope of describing a complex interacting system if the individual cycles cannot be described accurately and agreed.

In order to show the interrelationship between the entities, the second step is to join the activity life cycles along those parts of their cycles where interaction takes place. In this example the activity of 'drink' for the Man and 'being drunk from' for the Glass are one and the same activity. The activity requires the entities Man and Glass and lasts from the time the Man picks up the glass full until he puts it down empty. Therefore, the activity life cycles for the Man and the Glass can be joined by combining these activities into a single activity of 'drink beer'.

Similarly, the life cycles for the Barmaid and the Glass can be joined for the activities of 'fill glass' and 'being filled'. The interaction between the three entities is shown in the flow diagram (Fig. 2.4 and Plate 1, centre and bottom).

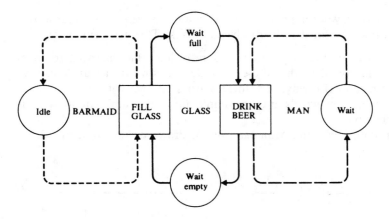

**Figure 2.4**

## The boundary of a model

The diagram briefly describes in terms of activities and queues what happens when one Barmaid spends all her time serving one Man with one Glass. The boundary of our model is restricted to the action that takes place across the bar. It might be suggested that the model would be more realistic if the Barmaid could undertake another task—that of serving in the off-licence, say. We need to describe this in terms of additional entities, activities and queues.

The Barmaid will serve customers in the off-licence in an activity which we call 'serve customer'. We have a new entity, Customer, whose behaviour is described as follows:

| Entity | States |
|--------|--------|
| Customer | wait in outside world (Q) |
| | generate customer (A) |
| | wait to be served (Q) |
| | being served (A) |

The barmaid now has two life cycles described as follows:

| Entity | States |
|--------|--------|
| Barmaid | 1. fill glass (A) |
| | idle (Q) |
| | 2. serve customer (A) |
| | idle (Q) |

The idle states can be combined into one queue and the flow diagram in Fig. 2.5 shows how the activity life cycles of Man, Glass, Barmaid, and Customer are linked together.

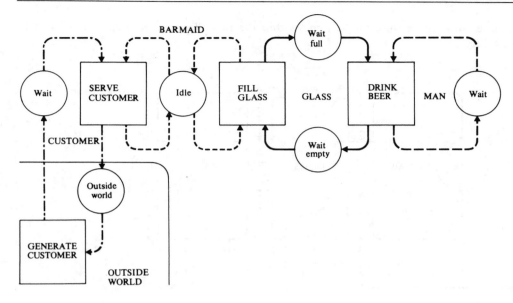

**Figure 2.5**

Two important features have been introduced in this example. The first is that the Barmaid can go from being idle to either 'fill glass' or 'serve customer'. If she can start either at the same time, a decision has to be made as to which activity takes priority. This is done by numbering the activities so that the lowest number takes priority. This will be explained in later chapters.

The second important feature is the way we describe the arrival pattern of Customers at the off-licence. We are not concerned with where the Customers come from or what they do when they leave the off-licence, and we have no need to know their identity. All that is required is that Customers arrive in a pattern similar to the real world. This is the boundary of our model and it can be represented by means of one queue (outside world) and one activity which *generates* Customers in a representative manner. The use of a queue and an activity to describe the interface of a model with the outside world is used extensively in simulation. Examples include patients arriving at a hospital, planes at an airport, ships at a port, breakdowns on a machine.

## Extending a model

The models described in Figs 2.4 and 2.5 make many assumptions, one of which is that beer is always available. The logic allows the activity of 'fill glass' to take place as long as there is an empty Glass and an idle Barmaid. If there is no limitation of beer supply then we do not actually need beer in our model. If it is limited and this may stop the 'fill glass' activity from starting, then we need to include beer as an entity in the model.

The ease with which this can be done within the modelling framework can be seen by studying Fig. 2.6.

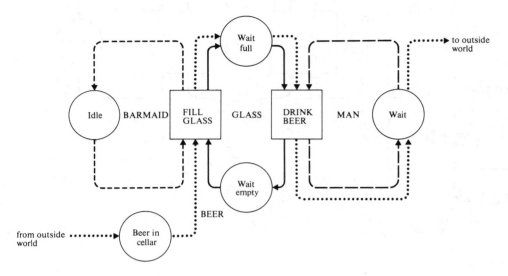

**Figure 2.6**

The Beer travels from the cellar into the Glass and, hopefully, all or most of it into the Man. The rest of the Beer's life cycle is outside the carefully restricted scope of this model. It passes into an outside world and we are not interested in the return cycle, although simulators who are also beer drinkers have been known on occasions to speculate.

## Model details

Let us now return to the beer drinking example shown in Fig. 2.4, and enter the details which will enable us to hand simulate (see Fig. 2.7). We give each queue and activity a distinctive name, to help us relate the model to the real world. We give each queue a reference number to simplify the task of saying where entities come from and go to.

The outline flow diagram now requires information on the conditions for starting and ending activities. We can see, by examining the activity life cycles entering each activity, which entities need to be available before the activity can start. In the case of 'fill glass' a Glass needs to be available in queue 4 and a Barmaid in queue 1. If these two conditions are not satisfied the activity of 'fill glass' cannot start. Similarly, the activity 'drink beer' requires a Glass in queue 2 and a Man in queue 3. We list the entities required in each activity together with where they come from (*source queue*) which is written to the left of the entity name, and where they go to (*destination queue*), which is written to the right of the entity name.

In Chapter 3 we use this model as the basis of the first example of a hand-operated simulation model. However, before describing how we introduce the passage of time into a model let us recapitulate the main points of this chapter.

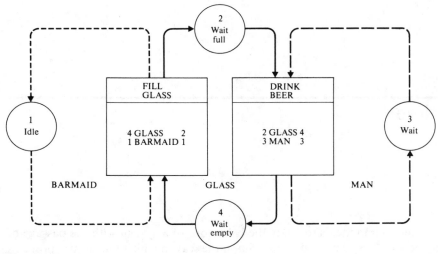

**Figure 2.7**

## Summary

– Problems are described in terms of entities (resources) being active (engaged in an activity) or idle (waiting in a queue).
– An activity is an operation for which we can predict a duration—either known or estimated, constant or variable.
– A queue is where entities wait between activities. We normally cannot predict how long an entity will remain in a queue, but in Chapter 4 we will see how to monitor waiting times in queues.
– When building a model we have to decide what entities to include. Start with the fewest possible and only add if absolutely necessary.
– Consider where the model starts and ends. If necessary use a queue and an activity to represent arrivals from the outside world.
– Determine how much detail is needed for each entity. Keep it as simple as possible and only add detail if it proves necessary.
– Drawing a flow diagram:
*Step 1* Draw the activity life cycle for each entity separately. This is probably the most difficult part of simulation modelling but it is essential to get an accurate description of what happens to each entity. We often get conflicting descriptions. These must be resolved as quickly as possible because accurate activity life cycles are the foundation stones upon which the whole simulation model is built.
*Step 2* Combine activity life cycles to represent the interaction between entities. This will often show that the degree of detail differs between the life cycles of entities and will result in some modifications. Confirm that any modified activity life cycles are accurate.
*Step 3* Enter information describing the activities and queues and the entities involved.

# 3.

## Handling time

The purpose of a simulation model is to study the behaviour of a system with the passage of time. The performance of the system will depend upon the way in which the entities progress around their activity life cycles. Therefore, the next important step after describing a model is to organize the advance of time.

### Specifying activity durations

We recall from Chapter 2 that the time an entity waits in a queue depends upon a number of conditions being satisfied before its next activity can start. As a result, waiting times in a queue depend upon the state of a system. One of the objectives of a simulation exercise may be to measure not only the length of queues but also the time entities wait in the queues.

An activity brings together entities and holds them for a period of time before dispatching them to their next queue. As such, activities drive the entities around their activity life cycles. The duration of an activity is calculated at the time when the activity starts, and its end time is thus predicted. The only circumstance which can change this end time is when the logic allows an activity to be interrupted. In this and later chapters there is a series of examples and exercises which takes the reader through the ways in which activity times are used to advance a model.

One of the simplest types of simulation model is a *bar chart* on which time is marked and the active and idle states of an entity are recorded. Consider the case of an operator carrying out an assembly task on a conveyor which is advanced by a motor at regular intervals. The passage of time may be depicted as shown in Fig. 3.1.

The bar chart model shows the operator's life for five minutes as a succession of active and idle states of 50 seconds and 10 seconds respectively. By contrast the motor advancing the conveyor is active for 10 seconds and idle for 50 seconds.

Using the procedure described in Chapter 2 we can describe this same model as shown in Fig. 3.2.

If the motor and operator are always available in queues 1 and 4 respectively, the conveyor will go around its life cycle in one minute spending zero time in queues 2 and 3.

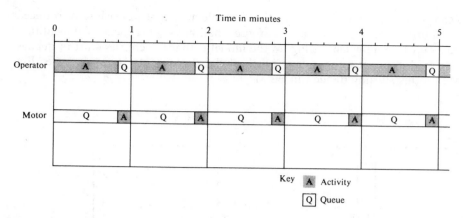

**Figure 3.1**

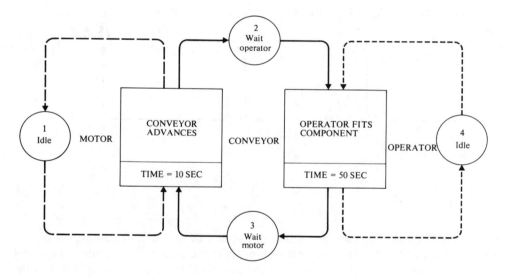

**Figure 3.2**

## Advancing a model through time

Let us return to the beer-drinking example and describe the steps by which we advance it through time. We have to define the time for the 'fill glass' and 'drink beer' activities. For simplicity let it take three minutes to fill the glass (activity 1) and seven minutes to drink (activity 2). The model is now complete and we are ready to start the hand simulation. As in Monopoly all we need now is something to represent an entity as it moves around its activity life cycle. This can be a counter, coin, or any other suitable article. If we wish to introduce a little reality and improve communication, we can use small physical replicas of the entities.

An important point to note when setting up the model is that the entities start in queues. We place the Barmaid in her starting queue, which obviously can only be queue 1 (see Fig. 3.3), and the Man in his starting queue (queue 3).

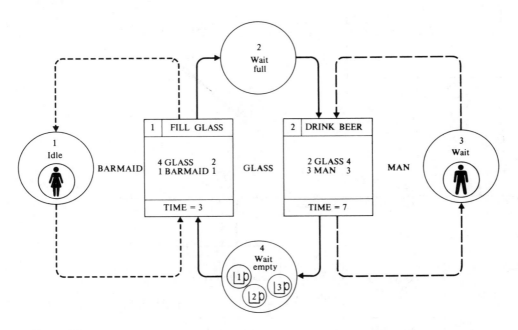

**Figure 3.3**

If we have three Glasses, they can start either in queue 4 or queue 2, depending on how we wish to start the simulation. In this example we start with the three Glasses empty in queue 4.

To advance the model through time we need to use a *clock* and follow a simple set of rules. These are set out below and if you hand simulate using the flow diagram and complete the record sheet as instructed you will learn the basic steps of hand simulation.

*Step 1*   Select coloured counters to represent:
        the Barmaid,
        the three Glasses,
        the Man.
        Number the glasses 1, 2 and 3.
*Step 2*   Put the Barmaid in queue 1,
        the three Glasses in queue 4,
        the Man in queue 3.
*Step 3*   Prepare a Simulation Record Sheet (see Fig. 3.4), entering a simulation clock time of 0.
*Step 4*   Simulate as instructed below using the three phases of start—time—end. You can check your final results against Fig. 3.5.

| Simulation Record Sheet | | | |
|---|---|---|---|
| Time | End | Start | Simulation clock time |
| ╳ | | | 0 |
| | | | |
| | | | |
| | | | |
| | | | |
| | | | |
| | | | |
| | | | |
| | | | |
| | | | |
| | | | |
| | | | |
| | | | |
| | | | |
| | | | |
| | | | |
| | | | |

**Figure 3.4**

*START phase*  Test each activity in number order to see if it can start.
- Activity 1  Fill glass
  - Is there a Glass in queue 4?—Yes (use Glass 1).
  - Is there a Barmaid in queue 1?—Yes.
  - All conditions satisfied so activity can start.
  - Move Glass 1 and Barmaid into the activity.
  - When will activity end?—At time 0 + 3 = 3—write 3 by side of activity.
- Activity 2  Drink beer.
  - Is there a Glass in queue 2?—No.
  - Activity cannot start.

All activities have been tested and started where possible, so tick the Start column next to time 0.

*TIME phase*  Nothing will change in the model until an activity comes to an end. Therefore, we can advance the clock to the earliest activity end time which is 3—that of activity 1 (fill glass). Enter 3 in the next row of the Simulation Clock Time column. Tick the Time column in the same row to indicate that we have advanced the clock.

*END phase*  We end all activities which have time 3 and send the entities to their destination queues.
- Activity 1  Send Glass 1 to queue 2 and the Barmaid to queue 1. Cross out the time (3) by the side of activity.
- Activity 2  Not in progress.

All possible activities have been ended, so tick the End column.

*START phase*   We now return to the Start phase at time 3. Test each activity in number order.
- Activity 1   Fill glass.
        Is there a Glass in queue 4?—Yes (use Glass 2).
        Is there a Barmaid in queue 1?—Yes.
        All conditions satisfied so activity can start.
        When will activity end?—At time $3 + 3 = 6$—write 6 by side of activity (under crossed out $\cancel{3}$).
- Activity 2   Drink beer.
        Is there a Glass in queue 2?—Yes (use Glass 1).
        Is there a Man in queue 3?—Yes.
        All conditions satisfied so activity can start.
        When will activity end?—At time $3 + 7 = 10$—write 10 by side of activity.
All activities have been tested and started where possible, so tick the Start column next to time 3.

*TIME phase*   Look for the earliest end time which is 6 (end time for activity 1 is 6 and for activity 2 is 10). Advance clock time by entering 6 in the Simulation Clock Time column and tick the Time column.

*END phase*   End all activities with time 6.
- Activity 1   Send Glass 2 to queue 2 and Barmaid to queue 1. Cross out 6 by side of activity.
- Activity 2   In progress until time 10.
Tick the End column.

*START phase*   Start all activities possible at time 6.
- Activity 1   Is there a Glass in queue 4?—Yes (use Glass 3).
        Is there a Barmaid in queue 1?—Yes.
        All conditions satisfied so activity can start.
        When will activity end?—At time $6 + 3 = 9$—write 9 by side of activity (under crossed out $\cancel{6}$).
- Activity 2   In progress until time 10.
Tick the Start column at time 6.

*TIME phase*   Activity 1 is earliest to finish with time 9, so advance clock to this time. Enter 9 in the Simulation Clock Time column and tick the Time column.

*END phase*   End all activities with time 9.
- Activity 1   Send Glass 3 to queue 2 and Barmaid to queue 1.
        Cross out 9 by side of activity.
- Activity 2   In progress until time 10.
Tick the End column.

*START phase*   Start all activities possible at time 9.
- Activity 1   Is there a Glass in queue 4?—No.
        Activity cannot start.
- Activity 2   In progress until time 10.
Although no activities can start, tick the Start column. It often happens that when an activity ends no other activities can start until later activities come to an end so we just keep advancing the clock.

*TIME phase*   Activity 2 will end at time 10. We enter this in the Simulation Clock Time column and tick the Time column.

*END phase*   End all activities with time 10.
- Activity 1   Not in progress.
- Activity 2   Send Glass 1 to queue 4 and Man to queue 3.
        Cross out 10 by side of activity.
Tick the End column.

*START phase*   Start all activities possible.
– Activity 1   Can start, with Glass 1 and Barmaid.
                Activity will end at 10 + 3 = 13.
                Write 13 by side of activity.
– Activity 2   Can start with Man and Glass 2.
                Activity will end at 10 + 7 = 17.
                Write 17 by side of activity.
Tick the Start column.

*TIME phase*   Move clock to earliest end time of 13 and tick the Time column.

*END phase*
– Activity 1   Send Glass 1 and Barmaid to destination queues.
– Activity 2   In progress until time 17.
Tick the End column.

*START phase*   No activities can start at time 13. Tick the Start column.

*TIME phase*   Move to earliest end time (17) and tick the Time column.

*END phase*
– Activity 1   Not in progress.
– Activity 2   Send Glass 2 to queue 4 and Man to queue 3.
                Cross out 17.
Tick the End Column.

*START phase*
– Activity 1   End time = 17 + 3 = 20.
– Activity 2   End time = 17 + 7 = 24.
Tick the Start column.

*TIME phase*   Advance clock to 20.

*END phase*
– Activity 1   Send Glass 2 to queue 2 and Barmaid to queue 1.
                Cross out end time.
– Activity 2   In progress until time 24.
Tick the End column.


EXERCISE 3.1

Carry on simulating until time 40 and check the position of the entities, the end times by the side of activities, and the record sheet with that shown in Fig. 3.5. If it differs go back and start again until you discover where you made your mistake.

If you followed the instructions successfully and your model entries match those of Fig. 3.5 you have mastered the method of advancing time in a simulation model.

You will have noted the repetitive three phases START—TIME—END used to run the model. The purpose of this is to separate the starting and ending of activities so as to simplify hand simulation and minimize the possibility of making an error. This simplicity is also necessary when instructing a computer and this three-phase approach is used by a number of computer simulation languages.

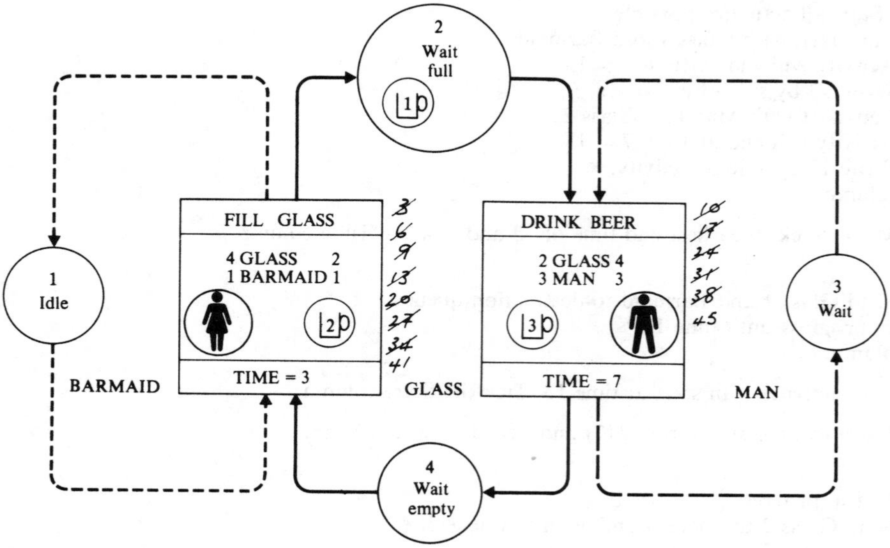
2
Wait
full
1p
1
Idle
FILL GLASS
4 GLASS 2
1 BARMAID 1
2p
TIME = 3
3
6
9
13
20
27
34
41
BARMAID
GLASS
DRINK BEER
2 GLASS 4
3 MAN 3
3p
TIME = 7
10
17
24
31
38
45
MAN
3
Wait
4
Wait
empty

| Simulation Record Sheet | | | |
|---|---|---|---|
| Time | End | Start | Simulation clock time |
| X | X | ✓ | 0 |
| ✓ | ✓ | ✓ | 3 |
| ✓ | ✓ | ✓ | 6 |
| ✓ | ✓ | ✓ | 9 |
| ✓ | ✓ | ✓ | 10 |
| ✓ | ✓ | ✓ | 13 |
| ✓ | ✓ | ✓ | 17 |
| ✓ | ✓ | ✓ | 20 |
| ✓ | ✓ | ✓ | 24 |
| ✓ | ✓ | ✓ | 27 |
| ✓ | ✓ | ✓ | 31 |
| ✓ | ✓ | ✓ | 34 |
| ✓ | ✓ | ✓ | 38 |
| | | | |
| | | | |
| | | | |
| | | | |
| | | | |
| | | | |
| | | | |

**Figure 3.5**

The technical terminology for this simple procedure is 'Three-phase discrete time advance simulation'. It sounds complicated but really is as easy as has been demonstrated. Having now established ourselves as 'experts' in this field, let us move on to the next major hurdle—that of building models where the time for an activity varies according to some defined pattern.

## Timetables

Perhaps the simplest example of the variation of an activity time is the sequence of times of a traffic light which shows red, amber, and green for 21, 3, and 15 seconds respectively. In a simulation of the traffic light, the flow of traffic in one direction is controlled by a timetable of 21, 3, 15 if the time units are seconds. If the time units are of 3 seconds duration the timetable is $\frac{21}{3}$, $\frac{3}{3}$, $\frac{15}{3}$ or 7, 1, 5.

During simulation the values are used in sequence. When the list is used up the first value is taken again.

*Example—Train inter-arrival times*   The schedule for the arrival times of trains is given below in the left-hand column. The activity for generating trains uses the timetable given in the right-hand column, assuming the simulation starts at 05.30. One train is in the queue waiting to enter the station and the next train will be put in this queue 105 minutes later.

| Arrival times | Inter-arrival times (minutes) |
|---|---|
| 05.30 | |
| | 105 |
| 07.15 | |
| | 42 |
| 07.57 | |
| | 75 |
| 09.12 | |
| | 63 |
| 10.15 | |
| | 193 |
| 13.28 | |
| | 167 |
| 16.15 | |
| | 115 |
| 18.10 | |
| | 100 |
| 19.50 | |
| | 180 |
| 22.50 | |
| | 400 |

If all days are similar and we wish to simulate a number of days, we simply cycle round the timetable.

*Example—Working day*  The activities controlling the time when employees are working use the following timetable, assuming that the simulation starts at 08.00.

| Working day | | Timetable (minutes) |
|---|---|---|
| Start work | 08.00 | 135 at work |
| Morning break | 10.15–10.30 | 15 off work |
| | | 135 at work |
| Lunch | 12.45–13.30 | 45 off work |
| | | 105 at work |
| Afternoon break | 15.15–15.30 | 15 off work |
| | | 90 at work |
| Finish work | 17.00 | 900 off work |

*Example—Working week*  Employees work for eight hours and entertain themselves for the other 16 hours in the day. For a five-day simulation, starting at the commencement of work on Monday morning, the timetable for working and not working is 8, 16, 8, 16, 8, 16, 8, 16, 8, if the time units are hours. If we wish to extend the simulation for a number of weeks in which a five-day week is worked followed by a weekend, the timetable is 8, 16, 8, 16, 8, 16, 8, 16, 8, 64. The 64-hour weekend is the end of the timetable and the simulation returns to the first reading of 8. One way of cross-checking figures is to add all the entries in the timetable and confirm that they total 168 hours ($7 \times 24$).

EXERCISE 3.2

Prepare the timetable in hours, starting at the commencement of work at 08.00 on Monday morning, for a man working four hours, having a lunch break of one hour, working four hours, for a five-day week and a weekend.

EXERCISE 3.3

Prepare the timetable in minutes, starting at midday, for the arrival of trains at a station according to the following daily schedule:

00.42, 03.12, 06.48, 07.06, 08.00, 10.00, 11.00,
12.00, 15.24, 16.24, 18.00, 20.54, 22.00, 23.30.

## Distributions

A timetable is used when the activity times can be represented by a predetermined sequence of constant times. Where activity times are not predetermined and vary between known limits their behaviour can be observed, recorded, and plotted as a cumulative distribution. Using the cumulative distribution and a table of random numbers, we are able to reproduce a similar pattern of behaviour in the simulation. The precise method of doing this is described in the following three steps:

*Step 1: Data collection*  We collect a number of samples of the time the real activity takes. The size of the sample will be governed by the accuracy required in the simulation, but in the first instance a small sample of say 30 values is often sufficient.

*Step 2: Distribution construction*  We compile the values sampled into a cumulative distribution. A simple way of doing this is to display the data in, say, 10 intervals of equal width. To determine the interval size we divide the difference between the largest and smallest value by 10. We count the number of values which fall into the first interval, the number which fall into the first two intervals, and continue until finally we count the number which fall into all the intervals. This number will be equal to the sample size.

We plot the numbers as percentages of the total sample size, against the upper value of each interval.

*Example*  The following times for an activity have been observed:

15, 23, 25, 27, 32, 16, 48, 31, 17, 15, 9, 28, 32, 37, 28, 12, 16, 18, 41, 45, 18, 20, 20, 44, 10, 28, 31, 38, 47, 19.

The largest value is 48.
The smallest value is 9.
The difference is 39.
Hence the interval size is $39/10 = 3.9$.
Take this to be 4 for convenience.
The upper values of the intervals are 13, 17, 21, etc.

We construct a table showing the number of observations less than or equal to the upper value of each interval, and express this as a percentage of the total sample size.

| Interval upper value (Time) | 13 | 17 | 21 | 25 | 29 | 33 | 37 | 41 | 45 | 49 |
|---|---|---|---|---|---|---|---|---|---|---|
| Number of observations less than or equal to upper value | 3 | 8 | 13 | 15 | 19 | 23 | 24 | 26 | 28 | 30 |
| Percentage of total (Probability) | 10 | 27 | 43 | 50 | 63 | 77 | 80 | 87 | 93 | 100 |

We plot a graph of percentage (probability) against time and join the points by straight lines, as shown in Fig. 3.6.

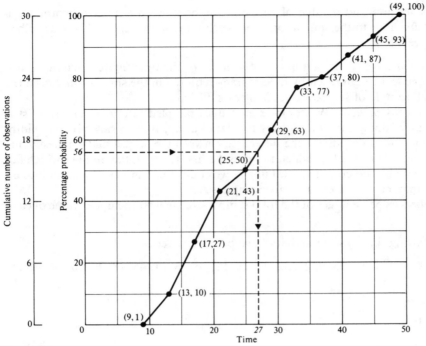

**Figure 3.6**

The coordinates are (9,1), (13,10), (17,27), (21,43), (25,50), (29,63), (33,77), (37,80), (41,87), (45,93) and (49,100). The cumulative distribution is constructed by connecting these 11 points with straight lines. While we could interpolate the curvature between the points, this is open to personal interpretation. To keep the method consistent and reproducible on the computer we prefer straight lines drawn between the points. If it is felt that this does not describe the distribution accurately enough then more points can be included.

If we are in doubt about the number of observations taken, we can always add to the sample size and see whether the shape of the distribution changes. Where the curve is irregular (as in Fig. 3.6), we either have too small a sample or have observed times which do not come from the same source. In either case we must investigate more closely. We increase the number of observations. If the curve remains the same this could be due to factors which are not catered for in the model logic. For example, in a maintenance model it is possible that an annual overhaul of two weeks has been included. If the model does not cover such a situation the observation should be excluded.

*Step 3: Sampling*   During simulation, we sample from the distribution using the following procedure.

We use a random number table giving numbers between 1 and 100, selecting systematically to avoid any element of choice.

For each random number we read from the vertical axis across to the curve and then down to the horizontal axis to give the time, as shown in Fig. 3.6. A random number of 56 gives an activity time of 27. Every value on the vertical scale has an equal chance of being used and therefore the curve groups the resultant activity times into a similar pattern to that from which the curve was drawn. Where the curve is steep there is a high frequency of occurrence and where it is nearly flat there is a very low frequency.

Random behaviour can be created in many ways. For example tossing an unbiased coin can be used to generate numbers in the range 1–2, throwing a die to generate numbers in the range 1–6, and spinning a roulette wheel to generate numbers in the range 0–36. In order to generate a value which can be related easily to probability a random number scale of 1–100 is used. Tables of such numbers are given in Appendix 1.

EXERCISE 3.4

In preparation for a simulation exercise in Chapter 6 plot the cumulative distribution of the following 200 machine repair times.

| Interval (min) | Frequency of occurrence | Cumulative frequency of occurrence |
|---|---|---|
| 11–20 | 2 | 2 |
| 21–30 | 6 | 8 |
| 31–40 | 16 | 24 |
| 41–50 | 24 | 48 |
| 51–60 | 32 | 80 |
| 61–70 | 24 | 104 |
| 71–80 | 38 | 142 |
| 81–90 | 16 | 158 |
| 91–100 | 12 | 170 |
| 101–110 | 14 | 184 |
| 111–120 | 10 | 194 |
| 121–130 | 6 | 200 |

EXERCISE 3.5

For the same exercise complete the following table and plot the cumulative distribution of the following 200 machine running times.

| Interval (min) | Frequency of occurrence | Cumulative frequency of occurrence |
|---|---|---|
| 51–100 | 8 | |
| 101–150 | 18 | |
| 151–200 | 32 | |
| 201–250 | 30 | |
| 251–300 | 28 | |
| 301–350 | 20 | |
| 351–400 | 16 | |
| 401–450 | 14 | |
| 451–500 | 10 | |
| 501–550 | 8 | |
| 551–600 | 8 | |
| 601–650 | 4 | |
| 651–700 | 2 | |
| 701–750 | 2 | |

EXERCISE 3.6
Using random number Table 1 in Appendix 1 and reading from left to right along successive rows, generate the first 25 repair times. Similarly, using random number Table 2, generate the first 25 machine running times. Round off all times to the nearest minute.

Many simulations have foundered due to the faulty recording and reading of distribution times, even though the basic model was correct. The key to success is to measure carefully, check, prepare cumulative distributions, generate times using random numbers, and check back against the original distribution.

There are many textbooks which describe the characteristics of classical statistical distributions and the different ways of deriving random numbers; some are listed in the Bibliography. In practice we should examine and validate the activity times collected. Where the activity times can be adequately described by one of the classical statistical distributions it may be possible to solve the problem mathematically using queueing theory. However, because of the mathematical complexities, this approach is very seldom applied. Where a simulation model is used, it is simpler and safer to describe the observed or possible behaviour as a cumulative distribution.

If we are in any doubt regarding the accuracy of a distribution, we can check to see how any recommendations will be affected by varying the distribution through the likely limits. We then know how sensitive the recommendations are to the activity time assumptions.

## Factors influencing activity durations

In addition to the duration of an activity being a constant, a value from a timetable or a sample from a distribution, it can also be:

- a value related to the attributes of the entities engaged in the activity;
- a value calculated by observing the present or past state of the model (e.g., the time required to reheat an ingot of steel depends on how long it has been cooling);
- related to a rate of flow.

These more complex time components are described in greater detail in Chapters 5 and 7.

## Interrupting activities

The logic of a model may require an activity to be interrupted if certain circumstances arise. For example, consider a vessel being emptied and the liquid pumped through a filter. The time taken to empty the vessel can be calculated from the volume of liquid and the rate of flow. However, should the pump break down during this period it will be necessary to interrupt the activity and delay the further transfer of liquid until the pump has been repaired. Alternatively, the filter characteristics may change, in which case the activity must be interrupted to recalculate the new flow rate and the activity end time. If the filter is changed or cleaned this will mean stopping the activity for a time before restarting, possibly at a new rate of flow.

This type of activity is called a *continuous* activity which consumes material at a steady rate unless interrupted. The interruption may delay the activity until conditions allow it to start again, or it may be an instantaneous break used to re-adjust the flow rate. Examples of this type of activity are described in Chapter 7.

Now that we have some feeling for handling time in a simulation model we can put this into practice, using the examples and exercises in the following chapters.

## Solutions to exercises

SOLUTION 3.2
4, 1, 4, 15, 4, 1, 4, 15, 4, 1, 4, 15, 4, 1, 4, 15, 4, 1, 4, 63.

SOLUTION 3.3
204, 60, 96, 174, 66, 90, 72, 150, 216, 18, 54, 120, 60, 60. Note that the start is at midday. A train will be waiting to enter the station and the next one will arrive at 15.24 or 204 minutes later. Check that you have 14 entries in your timetable and that the entries total 1440 minutes (24 hours).

SOLUTION 3.4

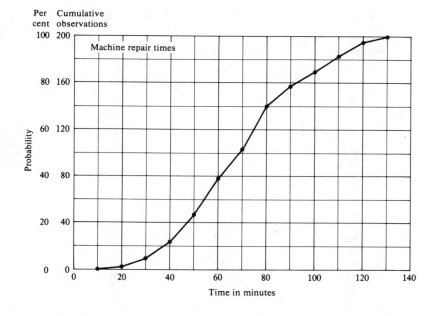

SOLUTION 3.5

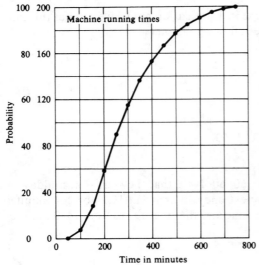

| Interval (min) | Cum. freq. of occ. |
|---|---|
| 0–50 | 0 |
| 51–100 | 8 |
| 101–150 | 26 |
| 151–200 | 58 |
| 201–250 | 88 |
| 251–300 | 116 |
| 301–350 | 136 |
| 351–400 | 152 |
| 401–450 | 166 |
| 451–500 | 176 |
| 501–550 | 184 |
| 551–600 | 192 |
| 601–650 | 196 |
| 651–700 | 198 |
| 701–750 | 200 |

SOLUTION 3.6

| Random no. Table 1 and Repair times | | Random no. Table 2 and Running times | |
|---|---|---|---|
| *Random no.* | *Repair time* | *Random no.* | *Running time* |
| 89 | 106 | 43 | 247 |
| 42 | 62 | 78 | 414 |
| 85 | 100 | 84 | 460 |
| 26 | 51 | 33 | 213 |
| 53 | 71 | 72 | 375 |
| 66 | 77 | 91 | 538 |
| 49 | 68 | 44 | 250 |
| 13 | 41 | 2 | 75 |
| 97 | 120 | 56 | 293 |
| 13 | 41 | 38 | 230 |
| 20 | 47 | 40 | 237 |
| 21 | 48 | 33 | 213 |
| 5 | 31 | 4 | 100 |
| 5 | 31 | 69 | 356 |
| 34 | 56 | 89 | 513 |
| 60 | 74 | 50 | 271 |
| 70 | 79 | 67 | 345 |
| 49 | 68 | 71 | 369 |
| 68 | 78 | 33 | 213 |
| 82 | 95 | 67 | 345 |
| 43 | 63 | 12 | 144 |
| 52 | 70 | 69 | 356 |
| 61 | 75 | 62 | 320 |
| 93 | 112 | 40 | 237 |
| 33 | 56 | 12 | 144 |

# 4.

## Model building

The most practical way of building a simulation model is to use, where possible, items from real life such as planning boards, job cards, control sheets and ledgers. Let us consider three application areas which may be amenable to this approach.

## Application 1—Scheduling a delivery fleet

The weekly schedule for a vehicle fleet delivering goods to retail outlets can be represented on a planning board.

The first column shows the type of vehicle and its capacity. The next five columns show the day of the week divided into hours. The final column is for recording weekly statistics on load carried, mileage covered, hours driven, costs, etc. If a magnetic board is used, the journey is represented by a magnetic strip whose length reflects the total journey time. The delivery points and load carried are written on the strip.

If we want to explore the effect of less frequent deliveries, night drops, larger vehicles, mechanical aids for unloading, moving the depot, or shorter driving hours, it is easy to introduce the changes and show the implications on the planning board.

The authors have involved the vehicle route planners of companies in the simulation of proposed changes in distribution methods. Projected changes in sales by product group, types of customer, or region are converted into an expected number and size of delivery in the region for a particular period. These are then converted into typical orders and handed to the vehicle scheduler.

If the organization has a vehicle fleet of less than 20 then vehicle scheduling is likely to be entirely manual and the scheduler will produce vehicle trips using his considerable experience. Many organizations with larger fleets use computer-based vehicle scheduling simply to handle the volume of data. However, they all have experienced schedulers who modify the computer solution to make the schedules 'more practical'. And, of course, if the scheduler says the goods can be delivered, then they almost certainly will be delivered.

## Application 2—Designing a stock control system

In an effort to improve customer service or sales revenue, or reduce money tied up in stocks, an organization may consider a number of alternative forecasting methods and ways of controlling its stocks. This can be done using existing or redesigned stock cards, as the model on which to measure the effects of change.

The demand is created by taking typical past periods and using random numbers to create a desired pattern. The stock control rules are noted on the top of the stock cards and the demands deducted, re-order levels broken and replenishment orders placed. The lead time for replenishment can be taken from historical data or generated by random numbers.

For each change the following information can be recorded:

— accuracy of the forecasting system;
— frequency and duration of stock-outs;
— customer service level;
— number of orders placed;
— amount of money tied up in stock.

By repeated use of the model the most important factors influencing the performance of the system can be identified and often a very simple solution can be developed. For example, a few exceptionally large orders among many small ones may cause a forecasting system to swing wildly. If this is recognized then rather than develop a sophisticated forecasting system it may be better to separate the few freak demands and treat them as special cases.

Similarly, by using such a model the merits of controlling stocks by fixed order quantity, fixed period review or some other set of rules can be explored. The results can be displayed on forms and cards familiar to management and much of the clerical effort of modelling can be done by those responsible for the day-to-day administration of the existing system.

## Application 3—Modifying a chemical plant

A process diagram of a chemical plant can be used as the basis for a simulation model. The batches to be scheduled are taken from a previous period, or generated to represent the forecast throughput. The work is progressed on a bar chart or work schedule. Typical patterns of breakdown, processing times, repair times, set-up, cleaning, etc., are introduced using historical or estimated data. In this way the effect of proposed design changes can be studied and the cost benefit evaluated.

Such exercises are particularly valuable where bottlenecks have occurred in a system and it is proposed to introduce additional plant or support facilities to remove them. The simulation may demonstrate that the expected benefits will indeed accrue. However, often we find that the bottleneck moves somewhere else and all our expenditure has achieved is to move the queue to another part of the plant. Change is usually both costly and painful. It is much better to quantify the effects of change before pursuing it.

## Informal models

Many simple problems can be tackled using existing planning boards and documents. Where these are not available, or are unsuitable, we have to construct our own.

We now demonstrate how to construct an informal model using several examples in which a number of products are scheduled through a number of machines. If you want to ensure that you have fully understood the examples you should set up the models as shown and follow the instructions given.

*Example—Production scheduling* Three products A, B and C are processed on three machines 1, 2 and 3. The processing times, in hours, are as follows:

| Product  Machine | A | B | C |
|---|---|---|---|
| 1 | 8 | 3 | 2 |
| 2 | 2 | 9 | 7 |
| 3 | 3 | 5 | 6 |

We will construct a model and schedule five products in the sequence A, A, B, B and C, recording the delivery times, and noting the time jobs wait and machines stand idle.

The first step is to prepare a flow diagram together with activity times and operating rules, as shown in Fig. 4.1.

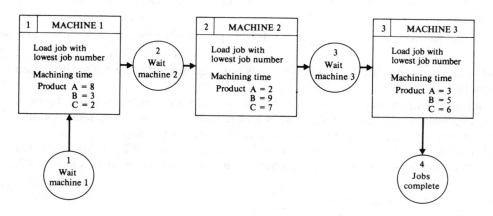

**Figure 4.1**

This model is drawn on a large sheet of paper (newsprint is particularly suitable) with the machining time for each product in each activity, together with an unambiguous statement of which job should be selected from the preceding queue. For reference each queue and activity is numbered. The products themselves are represented by pieces of card on which is written the job number, the product type, and any other information relevant to the simulation.

The five products are placed in queue 1 as shown in Fig. 4.2.

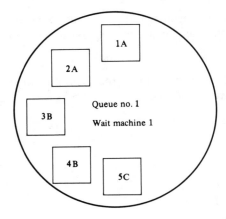

**Figure 4.2**

Jobs are placed in queue 1 in the order of loading on machine 1. Job 1 is at the head of the queue with successive jobs placed behind in an anticlockwise direction. In this way we can easily add to, or take from the queue without moving all the jobs in the queue. There are three ways in which we can record information about the behaviour of the model:

*Method 1* is to use the job card to record information on its progress through the machines. This method is particularly suited to simulations where actual job cards are used. The model may be a scale drawing of the production unit, around which the job cards are moved. Such models help those concerned with the everyday operation to understand the model and the results produced.

*Method 2* is to record the information on the flow diagram by the side of each activity and queue.

*Method 3* is to use a separate sheet which records both the time advance of the simulation and information.

We favour a combination of Methods 2 and 3 for two reasons. Firstly, each step taken in advancing the model is recorded and therefore can be retraced if required. Secondly, it allows us to link the time advance of the model to the recording of information.

We will advance the model through time using the three phases START—TIME—END as described in Chapter 3, but first we prepare a Simulation Record Sheet as shown in Fig. 4.3.

Simulation Record Sheet

| | | | SIM. CLOCK TIME | IDLE TIME ON MACHINES | | | | | | | | | NUMBER OF JOBS IN QUEUES | | | |
|---|---|---|---|---|---|---|---|---|---|---|---|---|---|---|---|---|
| | | | | MACHINE 1 | | | MACHINE 2 | | | MACHINE 3 | | | | | | |
| TIME | END | START | | ON | OFF | DUR | ON | OFF | DUR | ON | OFF | DUR | Q1 | Q2 | Q3 | Q4 |
| | | | 0 | | | | | | | | | | | | | |
| | | | | | | | | | | | | | | | | |
| | | | | | | | | | | | | | | | | |
| | | | | | | | | | | | | | | | | |
| | | | | | | | | | | | | | | | | |
| | | | | | | | | | | | | | | | | |
| | | | | | | | | | | | | | | | | |

**Figure 4.3**

The simulation starts at time zero, and this is written in the first row of the Simulation Clock Time column. The idle time for each machine is recorded by putting a tick in the On or Off column for each machine whenever it starts or stops being idle. The duration of any machine idle time is the difference between successive On and Off times. All machines are idle at time zero and so we tick their On columns. The number of jobs in each queue will be recorded after each Start phase when all activities possible have been started.

*START phase*   Test each activity in number order to see if it can start.
– Activity 1   Can start.
  Move job with lowest job number (Job 1, product A).
  When will job end?—at time 8 (0 + 8)—write 8 by side of activity.
  Machine 1 stops being idle. Tick Off column in time 0 row. Idle time = 0(0 − 0).
– Activity 2   Cannot start.
– Activity 3   Cannot start.
For information note the number of jobs waiting in queues 1, 2, 3 and 4. These will be 4, 0, 0, 0. We have now started all activities possible at time 0 and recorded information, so we tick the Start column.

*TIME phase*   Find the activity with the earliest end time and advance the simulation clock to this time. This is time 8. Write 8 in the next row of the Simulation Clock Time column. Tick the Time column in the same row to note that the instruction has been carried out.

*END phase*   We end all activities with time 8 and send the jobs to their destination queues.
– Activity 1   Send Job 1 to queue 2.
  Note that Machine 1 becomes idle by ticking the On column in the same row as time 8.
  Cross out time 8 by the side of the activity (clearly enough to show it has finished but do not obliterate it as we may wish to retrace our steps later).
– Activity 2   Not in progress.
– Activity 3   Not in progress.
Tick the End column in the same row as time 8.

*START phase*   Start all activities possible at time 8.
– Activity 1   Can start.
  Move Job 2 (product A).
  When will job end?—at time 16(8 + 8)—write 16 by side of activity (under 8).
  Machine 1 stops being idle. Tick Off column in time 8 row.
  Idle time = 0(8 − 8).
– Activity 2   Can start.
  Move Job 1 (product A).
  When will job end?—at time 10(8 + 2)—write 10 by side of activity.
  Machine 2 stops being idle. Tick Off column in time 8 row.
  Idle time = 0(8 − 0).
– Activity 3   Cannot start.
For information note the queue lengths as 3, 0, 0, 0.
Tick the Start column at time 8.

*TIME phase*   Look for earliest end time. This is activity 2 at time 10.
Advance simulation clock to time 10. Tick the Time column.

*END phase*   End activities with time 10.
– Activity 1   In progress until time 16.
– Activity 2   Move Job 1 to queue 3.
  Machine 2 becomes idle. Tick On column against time 10.
  Cross out time 10 by side of activity.

– Activity 3  Not in progress.
Tick the End column at time 10.

*START phase*
– Activity 1  In progress until time 16.
– Activity 2  Cannot start.
– Activity 3  Can start.
          Move Job 1 (product A).
          When will job end?—at time 13(10 + 3)—write 13 by side of activity.
          Machine 3 has stopped being idle. Tick Off column at time 10. Idle time was 10(10 − 0).
Note queue lengths as 3, 0, 0, 0 and tick the Start column at time 10.

*TIME phase*  Advance the clock to 13 and tick the Time column.

*END phase*
– Activity 1  In progress until time 16.
– Activity 2  Not in progress.
– Activity 3  Move Job 1 into queue 4.
          Machine 3 becomes idle. Tick the On column at time 13.
          Cross out time 13 by side of activity 3.
Tick the End column at time 13.

*START phase*
– Activity 1  In progress until time 16.
– Activity 2  Cannot start.
– Activity 3  Cannot start.
Note queue lengths as 3, 0, 0, 1 and tick the Start column at time 13.

EXERCISE 4.1

Continue simulating until all five jobs have been machined.

Your model and record sheet should now resemble Figs 4.4 and 4.5. If they do not, check where you made a mistake and start again from the point in time before the error.

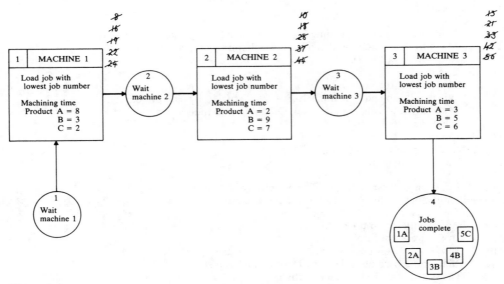

**Figure 4.4**

**Simulation Record Sheet**

| TIME | END | START | SIM. CLOCK TIME | MACHINE 1 | | | MACHINE 2 | | | MACHINE 3 | | | Q1 | Q2 | Q3 | Q4 |
|---|---|---|---|---|---|---|---|---|---|---|---|---|---|---|---|---|
| | | | | ON | OFF | DUR | ON | OFF | DUR | ON | OFF | DUR | | | | |
| ✕ | ✕ | ✓ | 0 | ⊘ | ✓ | 0 | ⊘ | | | ⊘ | | | 4 | 0 | 0 | 0 |
| ✓ | ✓ | ✓ | 8 | ✓ | ✓ | 0 | | ✓ | 8 | | | | 3 | 0 | 0 | 0 |
| ✓ | ✓ | ✓ | 10 | | | | ✓ | | | | ✓ | 10 | 3 | 0 | 0 | 0 |
| ✓ | ✓ | ✓ | 13 | | | | | | | ✓ | | | 3 | 0 | 0 | 1 |
| ✓ | ✓ | ✓ | 16 | ✓ | ✓ | 0 | | ✓ | 6 | | | | 2 | 0 | 0 | 1 |
| ✓ | ✓ | ✓ | 18 | | | | ✓ | | | | ✓ | 5 | 1 | 0 | 0 | 1 |
| ✓ | ✓ | ✓ | 19 | ✓ | ✓ | 0 | | ✓ | 1 | | | | 1 | 0 | 0 | 1 |
| ✓ | ✓ | ✓ | 21 | | | | ✓ | | | | | | 1 | 0 | 0 | 2 |
| ✓ | ✓ | ✓ | 22 | ✓ | ✓ | 0 | | | | | | | 0 | 1 | 0 | 2 |
| ✓ | ✓ | ✓ | 24 | ✓ | | | | | | | | | 0 | 2 | 0 | 2 |
| ✓ | ✓ | ✓ | 28 | | | | ✓ | ✓ | 0 | | ✓ | 7 | 0 | 1 | 0 | 2 |
| ✓ | ✓ | ✓ | 33 | | | | | | | ✓ | | | 0 | 1 | 0 | 3 |
| ✓ | ✓ | ✓ | 37 | | | | ✓ | ✓ | 0 | | ✓ | 4 | 0 | 0 | 0 | 3 |
| ✓ | ✓ | ✓ | 42 | | | | | ✓ | | | | | 0 | 0 | 0 | 4 |
| ✓ | ✓ | ✓ | 44 | | | | ✓ | | | | ✓ | 2 | 0 | 0 | 0 | 4 |
| ✓ | ✓ | ✓ | 50 | | ✓ | 26 | ✓ | ✓ | 6 | ✓ | ✓ | 0 | 0 | 0 | 0 | 5 |

**Figure 4.5**

You will find that the final job was completed at time 50 and that queues built up and disappeared again during the simulation. The model and record sheet have recorded each step and these can easily be retraced. Machine 1 was working continuously until time 24 and was idle for the last 26 hours. There were always one or two jobs waiting in queue 2 between times 22 and 33. On no occasion did a job wait in queue 3 for loading on Machine 3.

EXERCISE 4.2
Schedule the products in reverse order (starting with job 5 in queue 1) to see what effect this has on the time required to complete the last job and on the pattern of queuing. The model and record sheet for this exercise are shown in Fig. 4.6.

By loading the jobs in reverse order the total time for completing the five jobs is reduced from 50 to 38. Jobs wait in queue 2 between time 5 and 27 and in queue 3 between time 29 and 32. The variations between Exercises 4.1 and 4.2 can be attributed to the sequence in which the jobs are loaded on Machine 1 and the pattern of times for the jobs on the three machines. This is a very simple example, and yet merely changing the sequence has significantly reduced the total time and the pattern of jobs waiting in queues.

Sequencing problems are usually sensitive to what may appear to be insignificant changes in starting conditions and operating rules.

If other factors are included, such as set-up times, machine breakdown, inspections and rejected work, it is easy to appreciate why the dynamics of scheduling problems are not easily understood. By using a simulation model the factors which most influence the behaviour of a system can be identified and possible operating rules studied.

We have now carried out a very simple exercise scheduling just five jobs through three machines. We have also reminded ourselves of the procedures for advancing time in a model and for recording information. Let us now consolidate this with further exercises.

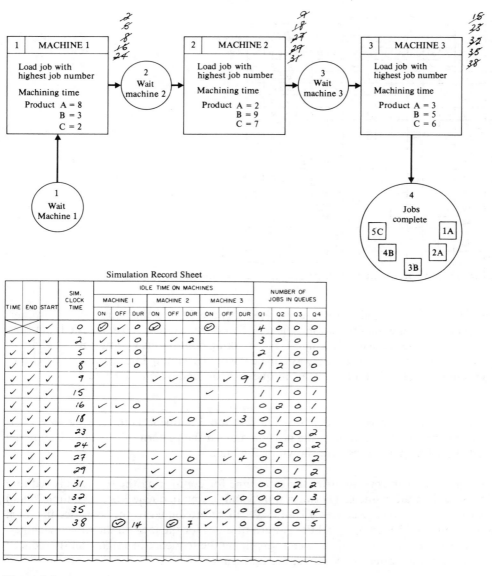

**Figure 4.6**

EXERCISE 4.3
Using the model shown in Fig. 4.1 schedule the following 15 jobs in the sequence A, A, B, C, A, B, B, A, C, C, B, A, A, C, B.

EXERCISE 4.4
Add an inspection operation after Machine 3, which requires four hours on product A and seven hours on products B and C. Note the pattern of idle time of the inspector.

EXERCISE 4.5

Twenty per cent of jobs are rejected by the inspector. When a job is rejected an additional product has to be manufactured. The pattern of rejection is found to be random. We can reject 20 per cent of jobs when the inspection activity ends by using random number tables to decide whether the product goes into the queue of completed jobs or returns to the tail of queue 1 as a rescheduled job.

Using Table 3 (Appendix 1) take the first 15 random numbers and determine which jobs are rejected. If the random number is 1–20 the job is rejected, if 21–100 it passes inspection.

EXERCISE 4.6

The rejection rates are random but differ for the three products. Product A has a rejection rate of 35 per cent, product B of 14 per cent and product C of 8 per cent. Using the same random numbers determine which jobs are rejected, using the following criteria:

Product A:  1–35—reject;  36–100—pass.
Product B:  1–14—reject;  15–100—pass.
Product C:  1–8 —reject;  9–100—pass.

EXERCISE 4.7

We will now embark on a larger scheduling exercise with a number of products being processed on four machines. In addition to different processing times the products have other attributes which influence the scheduling decision and which we wish to record.

A factory makes four products, A, B, C and D, which are processed sequentially on four machines (1, 2, 3 and 4). The processing times, in hours, for each product on each machine are as follows:

| Machine \ Product | A | B | C | D |
|---|---|---|---|---|
| 1 | 8 | 1 | 4 | 5 |
| 2 | 5 | 4 | 2 | 4 |
| 3 | 8 | 1 | 5 | 3 |
| 4 | 1 | 6 | 4 | 4 |
| Total processing time | 22 | 12 | 15 | 16 |

There are 35 orders waiting to be processed. The product mix is:

| Product | A | B | C | D |
|---|---|---|---|---|
| | 10% | 20% | 29% | 41% |

The profit per product is:

| Product | A | B | C | D |
|---|---|---|---|---|
| | £40 | £15 | £30 | £10 |

The due dates for all products are evenly distributed between 31 and 131 hours from the start of the simulation (a rectangular or uniform distribution).

*Simulate* 120 hours of factory operation using each of the following five scheduling rules for loading on each of the four machines:

1. Job number order.
2. Shortest operation (earliest due date first if more than one product with similar time).
3. Highest profit per job (earliest due date first if more than one product with similar profit).
4. Highest profit per machine hour (earliest due date first if more than one product with similar profit per machine hour). This is calculated by dividing the profit on the product by the total number of process hours for its manufacture. This gives a notional profit per process hour.
5. Earliest due date.

*Answers required.* For each rule:

– Determine the number of jobs completed, in progress and waiting to start.
– Calculate the total profit for completed jobs.
– Produce a histogram of customer service.
– What is the pattern of queues of jobs in the factory and how do these change with time? What is the reason for this?

*Comment on*:

– What effect does the scheduling rule have on the operation of the factory?
– Which rule gives the best machine utilization, profit and customer service?
– Profit and customer service are considered to be important. Which of the five rules do you recommend?

*The model*    The first step is to draw the model on a large sheet of paper as shown in Fig. 4.7, and write the machine times for each product in the activities.

The product proportions can be related to random numbers as follows:

| Product | Proportion (%) | Random number |
|---------|----------------|---------------|
| A | 10 | 1–10 |
| B | 20 | 11–30 |
| C | 29 | 31–59 |
| D | 41 | 60–100 |

Take the first 35 random numbers from Table 1 (Appendix 1)—starting with 89—and determine the product type for each job.

Take the next 35 random numbers—starting with 40—and determine the due date for each job by adding 30 to the number read. This gives an evenly distributed pattern of due dates between 31 and 131.

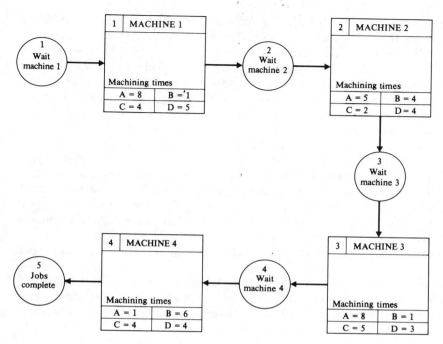

**Figure 4.7**

The product type and delivery date of the 35 jobs are recorded as shown:

| Job number | Random number | Product type | Random number | Due date | Delivery date | Early (−) | Late (+) |
|---|---|---|---|---|---|---|---|
| 1 | 89 | D | 40 | 70 | | | |
| 2 | 42 | C | 94 | 124 | | | |
| 3 | 85 | D | 19 | 49 | | | |
| 4 | 26 | B | 9 | 39 | | | |
| 5 | 53 | C | 31 | 61 | | | |
| 6 | 66 | D | 100 | 130 | | | |
| 7 | 49 | C | 100 | 130 | | | |
| 8 | 13 | B | 24 | 54 | | | |
| 9 | 97 | D | 96 | 126 | | | |
| 10 | 13 | B | 1 | 31 | | | |
| 11 | 20 | B | 69 | 99 | | | |
| 12 | 21 | B | . | . | | | |
| . | . | . | . | . | | | |
| . | . | . | . | . | | | |
| . | . | . | . | . | | | |

Complete the table and compare with the results at the end of the chapter. However logical the model description is, any mistakes in the creation of data will cause errors. Take great care to ensure that the patterns being duplicated are accurate.

The final three columns of the table are for recording the time at which each job is delivered. By comparing this with its due date the difference, early or late, can be derived.

Five scheduling rules are to be considered, so this means five separate hand simulations with jobs being selected from the queues according to the priority rule that applies.

Run the first simulation for 120 hours, loading the job with the lowest job number. Record the number of jobs in the queues at the end of each START phase. At the end of the simulation count the number of jobs completed, in progress, and waiting to start, and calculate the profit on the completed jobs. Prepare a histogram of customer service, showing whether jobs are late or early. Compare your model and results with those given at the end of the chapter. If there are any differences try to locate the source of the error by checking your job list, due dates and activity times. It is easy to make mistakes so take great care. We have prepared the model in such a way that every step in the hand simulation can be retraced. Check and discipline yourself to follow the rules for advancing the model. They may appear simple and you may foresee what will happen next, but instill in yourself the discipline of checking each activity in number sequence. It is slow but sure.

Simulate using the five rules and compare your results and comments with those at the end of the chapter.

For those concerned with teaching simulation, this exercise provides a useful basis for a half-day course where the class is divided into teams of two or three, with each team taking one of the scheduling rules. If there are more than five teams you can add other scheduling rules, change the product mix or machining times. The results for each team can be compared, comments solicited and the benefits of experimentation demonstrated.

If we have to tackle a real-life scheduling problem we develop a model along the lines described. Where possible we set out the activities on a plant layout diagram, with actual job cards and process sheets showing activity times. This increases the reality of the model.

The results of the experiments can be entered on the normal management control reports (if they exist and are suitable). Additional features which we may wish to include are machine set-ups, inspection, rework, transport between machines, operator availability or machine breakdown. The ways of handling such situations are described in later chapters.

## Solving production scheduling problems

Even the simple exercises we have just completed illustrate the dynamics of production scheduling problems in which quite small changes in the product mix and priorities can cause significant changes in the results.

Production scheduling has been a graveyard for practising management scientists and problem solvers for many years. One reason is the complexity of the task and another is that they try to satisfy too many objectives at once with an 'all singing–all dancing' system which they do not fully understand and which the user is unable to use with confidence. There are many objectives to be achieved, such as maximum machine and operator utilization, profit and throughput; minimum work-in-progress and lead time and the best possible customer service. All have to be satisfied by scheduling rules flexible enough to respond to the whims of the market and to the performance of management and employees.

The scheduling packages are generally designed on the principle of satisfying everybody's needs to some degree and operating elegantly on the computer. So often they fail to give the customer the 'bespoke' features he needs.

What is the solution? It is to be able to specify what you want from a scheduling system, and then be able to check the extent to which the alternatives you are offered match your requirements. The great difficulty is to specify the requirements of your particular product range, manufacturing methods and management style, in a way that permits the alternatives to be checked.

This presupposes that you have some appreciation of the dynamics of the problem. One way of achieving this is to observe the real world: the other is to simulate. For manufacturing organizations intent on improving their scheduling efficiency we commend simulation as a first step in the understanding and specifying process. You may well be lucky and find an 'off-the-shelf' package that will suit your needs. More often than not you will have either to modify an existing package or to write your own from scratch.

Whatever the outcome take care to avoid choosing the wrong scheduling system as the penalties of failure can be catastrophic.

This is a problem area where the 'slow but sure' approach is needed and simulation is one way of checking the next step.

EXERCISE 4.8

We now consider a problem confronting a public service, which has to organize its limited resources to give the best possible service. One such organization which would be called to public account, should it fail, is the ambulance service. Let us take a simple example and study the pattern of demand on three ambulances attached to a hospital. If emergency calls have been recorded and found to be random in behaviour, this can be expressed as an expected number of calls in any period, say one hour.

This rate will probably vary during the day and the week, but for this exercise let us presume that the calls are random in nature at an average rate of five calls per hour. Using the cumulative distributions given in Appendix 2, together with random numbers, we can duplicate this pattern of calls.

Find the cumulative distribution representing $\lambda = 5/60$ (Fig. A2.2, Appendix 2) and use random numbers from Table 4 (Appendix 1).

The first random number is 52; locate this on the vertical axis of the distribution. Read across to the line $\lambda = 5/60$, and then down to the time scale to give 9 minutes (round off to the nearest minute). The first call will arrive 9 minutes after the start of the simulation. Take the next random number (50), repeat the procedure to get 8 minutes. The second call will arrive 8 minutes after the first at time 17. Generate the arrival time of the first 10 calls and check your results with the following:

| Call number | 1 | 2 | 3 | 4 | 5 | 6 | 7 | 8 | 9 | 10 |
|---|---|---|---|---|---|---|---|---|---|---|
| Random number stream 4 | 52 | 50 | 83 | 48 | 8 | 41 | 33 | 80 | 73 | 89 |
| Inter-arrival time | 9 | 8 | 22 | 8 | 1 | 6 | 5 | 19 | 16 | 27 |

Prepare the flow diagram as shown in Fig. 4.8 using small cards to represent each call and the ambulances.

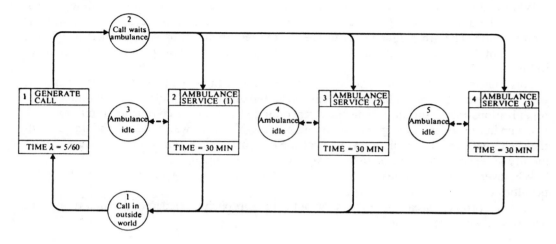

**Figure 4.8**

If available, Ambulance 1 is used in preference to 2 and 3. Similarly, Ambulance 2 is used in preference to 3. For simplicity we presume that all three ambulances take a constant time of 30 minutes to service a call.

Simulate for 620 minutes starting with all ambulances idle and the first call arriving at time 9. Record the time that calls wait for an ambulance and the time ambulances are idle.

Compare your results with the solution at the end of the chapter.

If you have successfully completed the exercises in this chapter you will have had plenty of practice in hand simulation. To build larger models and tackle other types of problem, you will need to develop your ability to draw flow diagrams.

With an informal model it is possible to record detailed instructions in each queue and activity, and to set up a data collection procedure as the situation requires. In this way a hand simulation model of a complex problem can be built within a few hours or days. Hand simulation is hard work and monotonous but it is instructive and profitable. In spite of its simplicity you will obtain greater satisfaction in return for your efforts than by clutching at pseudo-scientific formulae which may solve the general case but seldom match the requirements of the real-life situation. Informal simulation models are the refuge of those who put more store in finding the simplest practical solution quickly, rather than those who prefer to wallow in the imagined glory of having explored the boundaries of science.

However, in spite of their flexibility there are disadvantages in using informal models. These are discussed in Chapter 5 where a case is made for adopting a simple formal model building procedure.

## Solutions to exercises

SOLUTION 4.3

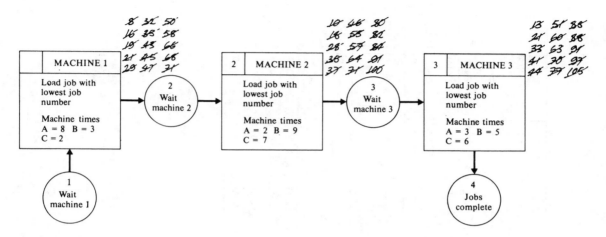

After time 19 Machine 2 was continuously busy and up to four Jobs were waiting to be loaded. Improved throughput and machine utilization could be achieved by reducing the times on Machine 2 or possibly by rescheduling the Jobs. Machine 2 is the bottleneck on this run, but if the machining time for products B and C were reduced from 9 and 7 to 7 and 5 respectively, what would be the effect?

SOLUTION 4.4

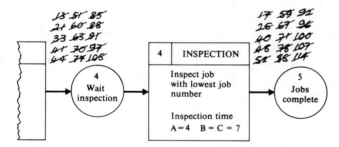

The Inspector was idle in time intervals 0–13, 17–21, 25–33, 40–41 and 59–60. He completed work at time 114.

SOLUTION 4.5
Jobs 2, 6, 9 and 13 are rejected.

SOLUTION 4.6
Jobs 2(A) and 13(A) are rejected.

## SOLUTION 4.3
(continued)

Simulation Record Sheet

| TIME | END | START | SIM. CLOCK TIME | MACHINE 1 | | | MACHINE 2 | | | MACHINE 3 | | | Q1 | Q2 | Q3 | Q4 |
|---|---|---|---|---|---|---|---|---|---|---|---|---|---|---|---|---|
| | | | | ON | OFF | DUR | ON | OFF | DUR | ON | OFF | DUR | | | | |
| ✗ | ✗ | ✓ | 0 | ⊘ | ✓ | 0 | ⊘ | | | ⊘ | | | 14 | 0 | 0 | 0 |
| ✓ | ✓ | ✓ | 8 | ✓ | ✓ | 0 | | ✓ | 8 | | | | 13 | 0 | 0 | 0 |
| ✓ | ✓ | ✓ | 10 | | | | ✓ | | | | ✓ | 10 | 13 | 0 | 0 | 0 |
| ✓ | ✓ | ✓ | 13 | | | | | | | ✓ | | | 13 | 0 | 0 | 1 |
| ✓ | ✓ | ✓ | 16 | ✓ | ✓ | 0 | | ✓ | 6 | | | | 12 | 0 | 0 | 1 |
| ✓ | ✓ | ✓ | 18 | | | | ✓ | | | | ✓ | 5 | 12 | 0 | 0 | 1 |
| ✓ | ✓ | ✓ | 19 | ✓ | ✓ | 0 | | ✓ | 1 | | | | 11 | 0 | 0 | 1 |
| ✓ | ✓ | ✓ | 21 | ✓ | ✓ | 0 | | | | ✓ | | | 10 | 1 | 0 | 2 |
| ✓ | ✓ | ✓ | 28 | | | | ✓ | ✓ | 0 | | ✓ | 7 | 10 | 0 | 0 | 2 |
| ✓ | ✓ | ✓ | 29 | ✓ | ✓ | 0 | | | | | | | 9 | 1 | 0 | 2 |
| ✓ | ✓ | ✓ | 32 | ✓ | ✓ | 0 | | | | | | | 8 | 2 | 0 | 2 |
| ✓ | ✓ | ✓ | 33 | | | | | ✓ | | | | | 8 | 2 | 0 | 3 |
| ✓ | ✓ | ✓ | 35 | ✓ | ✓ | 0 | ✓ | ✓ | 0 | | ✓ | 2 | 7 | 2 | 0 | 3 |
| ✓ | ✓ | ✓ | 37 | | | | ✓ | ✓ | 0 | | | | 7 | 1 | 1 | 3 |
| ✓ | ✓ | ✓ | 41 | | | | | | | ✓ | ✓ | 0 | 7 | 1 | 0 | 4 |
| ✓ | ✓ | ✓ | 43 | ✓ | ✓ | 0 | | | | | | | 6 | 2 | 0 | 4 |
| ✓ | ✓ | ✓ | 44 | | | | | | | ✓ | | | 6 | 2 | 0 | 5 |
| ✓ | ✓ | ✓ | 45 | ✓ | ✓ | 0 | | | | | | | 5 | 3 | 0 | 5 |
| ✓ | ✓ | ✓ | 46 | | | | ✓ | ✓ | 0 | | ✓ | 2 | 5 | 2 | 0 | 5 |
| ✓ | ✓ | ✓ | 47 | ✓ | ✓ | 0 | | | | | | | 4 | 3 | 0 | 5 |
| ✓ | ✓ | ✓ | 50 | ✓ | ✓ | 0 | | | | | | | 3 | 4 | 0 | 5 |
| ✓ | ✓ | ✓ | 51 | | | | | ✓ | | | | | 3 | 4 | 0 | 6 |
| ✓ | ✓ | ✓ | 55 | | | | ✓ | ✓ | 0 | | ✓ | 4 | 3 | 3 | 0 | 6 |
| ✓ | ✓ | ✓ | 57 | | | | ✓ | ✓ | 0 | | | | 3 | 2 | 1 | 6 |
| ✓ | ✓ | ✓ | 58 | ✓ | ✓ | 0 | | | | | | | 2 | 3 | 1 | 6 |
| ✓ | ✓ | ✓ | 60 | | | | | | | ✓ | ✓ | 0 | 2 | 3 | 0 | 7 |
| ✓ | ✓ | ✓ | 63 | | | | | ✓ | | | | | 2 | 3 | 0 | 8 |
| ✓ | ✓ | ✓ | 64 | | | | ✓ | ✓ | 0 | | ✓ | 1 | 2 | 2 | 0 | 8 |
| ✓ | ✓ | ✓ | 66 | ✓ | ✓ | 0 | | | | | | | 1 | 3 | 0 | 8 |
| ✓ | ✓ | ✓ | 68 | ✓ | ✓ | 0 | | | | | | | 0 | 4 | 0 | 8 |
| ✓ | ✓ | ✓ | 70 | | | | | ✓ | | | | | 0 | 4 | 0 | 9 |
| ✓ | ✓ | ✓ | 71 | ✓ | | | ✓ | ✓ | 0 | | ✓ | 7 | 0 | 4 | 0 | 9 |
| ✓ | ✓ | ✓ | 77 | | | | | ✓ | | | | | 0 | 4 | 0 | 10 |
| ✓ | ✓ | ✓ | 80 | | | | ✓ | ✓ | 0 | | ✓ | 3 | 0 | 3 | 0 | 10 |
| ✓ | ✓ | ✓ | 82 | | | | ✓ | ✓ | 0 | | | | 0 | 2 | 1 | 10 |
| ✓ | ✓ | ✓ | 84 | | | | ✓ | ✓ | 0 | | | | 0 | 1 | 2 | 10 |
| ✓ | ✓ | ✓ | 85 | | | | | | | ✓ | ✓ | 0 | 0 | 1 | 1 | 11 |
| ✓ | ✓ | ✓ | 88 | | | | | | | ✓ | ✓ | 0 | 0 | 1 | 0 | 12 |
| ✓ | ✓ | ✓ | 91 | | | | ✓ | ✓ | 0 | ✓ | ✓ | 0 | 0 | 0 | 0 | 13 |
| ✓ | ✓ | ✓ | 97 | | | | | ✓ | | | | | 0 | 0 | 0 | 14 |
| ✓ | ✓ | ✓ | 100 | | | | ✓ | | | | ✓ | 3 | 0 | 0 | 0 | 14 |
| ✓ | ✓ | ✓ | 105 | | ⊘ | 34 | | ⊘ | 5 | ✓ | ⊘ | 0 | 0 | 0 | 0 | 15 |

SOLUTION 4.7

Table of products and due dates

| Job number | Random number | Product type | Random number | Due date (random number + 30) | Delivery date | Early (−) | Late (+) |
|---|---|---|---|---|---|---|---|
| 1 | 89 | D | 40 | 70 | | | |
| 2 | 42 | C | 94 | 124 | | | |
| 3 | 85 | D | 19 | 49 | | | |
| 4 | 26 | B | 9 | 39 | | | |
| 5 | 53 | C | 31 | 61 | | | |
| 6 | 66 | D | 100 | 130 | | | |
| 7 | 49 | C | 100 | 130 | | | |
| 8 | 13 | B | 24 | 54 | | | |
| 9 | 97 | D | 96 | 126 | | | |
| 10 | 13 | B | 1 | 31 | | | |
| 11 | 20 | B | 69 | 99 | | | |
| 12 | 21 | B | 11 | 41 | | | |
| 13 | 5 | A | 70 | 100 | | | |
| 14 | 5 | A | 37 | 67 | | | |
| 15 | 34 | C | 70 | 100 | | | |
| 16 | 60 | D | 82 | 112 | | | |
| 17 | 70 | D | 9 | 39 | | | |
| 18 | 49 | C | 47 | 77 | | | |
| 19 | 68 | D | 76 | 106 | | | |
| 20 | 82 | D | 75 | 105 | | | |
| 21 | 43 | C | 98 | 128 | | | |
| 22 | 52 | C | 17 | 47 | | | |
| 23 | 61 | D | 12 | 42 | | | |
| 24 | 93 | D | 81 | 111 | | | |
| 25 | 33 | C | 60 | 90 | | | |
| 26 | 57 | C | 40 | 70 | | | |
| 27 | 66 | D | 46 | 76 | | | |
| 28 | 4 | A | 53 | 83 | | | |
| 29 | 98 | D | 4 | 34 | | | |
| 30 | 27 | B | 93 | 123 | | | |
| 31 | 45 | C | 48 | 78 | | | |
| 32 | 61 | D | 70 | 100 | | | |
| 33 | 9 | A | 21 | 51 | | | |
| 34 | 33 | C | 93 | 123 | | | |
| 35 | 27 | B | 7 | 37 | | | |

*Scheduling rule 1*  Lowest job number

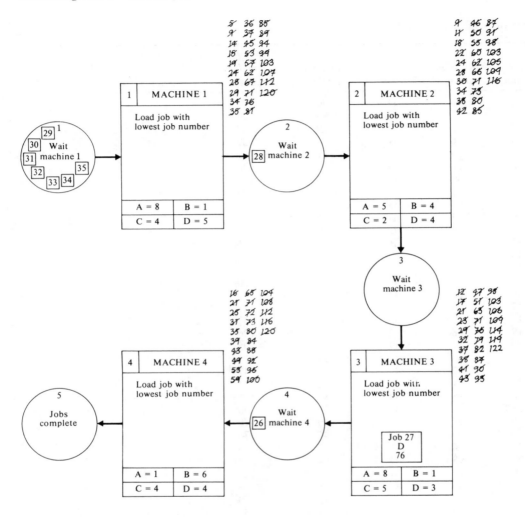

*Comments*  No large queues developed. The alternating of product types resulting from loading by job number helped to balance the short and long operation times of different products on different machines. After Machine 3 started work at time 9 on Job 1 it was occupied for 97 of the available 111 hours. By examining the queues and machine utilizations the scope for improvement by reducing machining times, adding machines or working overtime can be assessed and then checked by simulating the proposed change.

This is a simple rule which takes no notice of the customer due date, and the histogram of the differences between delivery date and due date shows variations between − 103 and + 70, a range of 173.

| SIM CLOCK TIME | NO. OF JOBS WAITING | | |
|---|---|---|---|
| | Q2 | Q3 | Q4 |
| 0 | | | |
| 5 | | | |
| 9 | | | |
| 11 | | 1 | |
| 12 | | | |
| 14 | | | |
| 15 | 1 | | |
| 16 | 1 | | |
| 17 | 1 | | |
| 18 | | | |
| 19 | 1 | | |
| 21 | 1 | | |
| 22 | | | |
| 23 | | | 1 |
| 24 | | | 1 |
| 25 | | | |
| 28 | | 1 | |
| 29 | 1 | | 1 |
| 30 | | 1 | 1 |
| 31 | | 1 | |
| 32 | | | 1 |
| 34 | | 1 | 1 |
| 35 | 1 | 1 | |
| 36 | 2 | 1 | |
| 37 | 3 | | 1 |
| 38 | 2 | | 2 |
| 39 | 2 | | 1 |
| 41 | 2 | | 2 |

| SIM CLOCK TIME | NO. OF JOBS WAITING | | |
|---|---|---|---|
| | Q2 | Q3 | Q4 |
| 41 | 2 | | 2 |
| 42 | 1 | | 2 |
| 43 | 1 | | 2 |
| 45 | 2 | | 2 |
| 46 | 1 | | 2 |
| 47 | 1 | | 3 |
| 49 | 1 | | 2 |
| 50 | | | 2 |
| 51 | | | 3 |
| 53 | 1 | | 2 |
| 55 | | | 2 |
| 57 | 1 | | 2 |
| 59 | 1 | | 1 |
| 60 | | 1 | 1 |
| 62 | | 2 | 1 |
| 63 | | 1 | 2 |
| 65 | | 1 | 1 |
| 66 | | 2 | 1 |
| 67 | | 2 | 1 |
| 71 | | 2 | 1 |
| 72 | | 2 | |
| 73 | | 3 | |
| 76 | | 2 | |
| 79 | | 1 | 1 |
| 80 | | 2 | |
| 81 | | 2 | |
| 82 | | 1 | 1 |
| 84 | | 1 | |

| SIM CLOCK TIME | NO. OF JOBS WAITING | | |
|---|---|---|---|
| | Q2 | Q3 | Q4 |
| 84 | | 1 | |
| 85 | 2 | | |
| 87 | 2 | | 1 |
| 88 | 2 | | |
| 89 | 2 | | |
| 90 | | 1 | 1 |
| 91 | 2 | | |
| 92 | 2 | | |
| 93 | | 1 | 1 |
| 94 | | 1 | 1 |
| 96 | | 1 | |
| 98 | | 1 | 1 |
| 99 | | 1 | 1 |
| 100 | | 1 | |
| 103 | | 1 | 1 |
| 104 | | 1 | |
| 105 | 2 | | |
| 106 | | 1 | 1 |
| 107 | | 1 | 1 |
| 108 | | 1 | |
| 109 | | 1 | 1 |
| 112 | | 1 | |
| 114 | | | 1 |
| 116 | | 1 | |
| 119 | | | 1 |
| 120 | | | |
| | | | |

Products completed = 25
In process = 3
Wait load (Q1) = 7

Profit on products completed
A – 2 × 40 = £ 80
B – 5 × 15 = £ 75
C – 8 × 30 = £240
D –10 × 10 = £100
£495

| Job no. | Prod. type | Due date | Delivery date | Early (−) | Late (+) |
|---|---|---|---|---|---|
| 1 | D | 70 | 16 | 54 | |
| 2 | C | 124 | 21 | 103 | |
| 3 | D | 49 | 25 | 24 | |
| 4 | B | 39 | 31 | 8 | |
| 5 | C | 61 | 35 | 26 | |
| 6 | D | 130 | 39 | 91 | |
| 7 | C | 130 | 43 | 87 | |
| 8 | B | 54 | 49 | 5 | |
| 9 | D | 126 | 53 | 73 | |
| 10 | B | 31 | 59 | | 28 |
| 11 | B | 99 | 65 | 34 | |
| 12 | B | 41 | 71 | | 30 |
| 13 | A | 100 | 72 | 28 | |
| 14 | A | 67 | 73 | | 6 |
| 15 | C | 100 | 80 | 20 | |
| 16 | D | 112 | 84 | 28 | |
| 17 | D | 39 | 88 | | 49 |
| 18 | C | 77 | 92 | | 15 |
| 19 | D | 106 | 96 | 10 | |
| 20 | D | 105 | 100 | 5 | |
| 21 | C | 128 | 104 | 24 | |
| 22 | C | 47 | 108 | | 61 |
| 23 | D | 42 | 112 | | 70 |
| 24 | D | 111 | 116 | | 5 |
| 25 | C | 90 | 120 | | 30 |

*Scheduling rule 2* Shortest operation

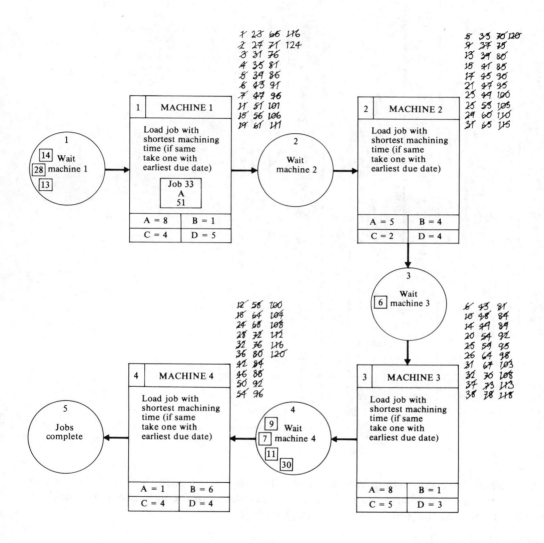

| SIM CLOCK TIME | Q2 | Q3 | Q4 |
|---|---|---|---|
| 0 | | | |
| 1 | | | |
| 2 | 1 | | |
| 3 | 2 | | |
| 4 | 3 | | |
| 5 | 3 | | |
| 6 | 4 | | |
| 7 | 5 | | |
| 9 | 4 | | |
| 10 | 4 | | 1 |
| 11 | 5 | | 1 |
| 12 | 5 | | |
| 13 | 4 | | |
| 14 | 4 | | 1 |
| 15 | 4 | | 1 |
| 17 | 3 | 1 | 1 |
| 18 | 3 | 1 | |
| 19 | 4 | 1 | |
| 20 | 4 | | 1 |
| 21 | 3 | 1 | 1 |
| 23 | 3 | 2 | 1 |
| 24 | 3 | 2 | |
| 25 | 2 | 2 | 1 |
| 26 | 2 | 1 | 2 |
| 27 | 3 | 1 | 2 |
| 28 | 3 | 1 | 1 |
| 29 | 2 | 2 | 1 |
| 31 | 2 | 2 | 2 |
| 32 | 2 | 1 | 2 |
| 33 | 1 | 2 | 2 |
| 35 | 2 | 2 | 2 |
| 36 | 2 | 2 | 1 |

| SIM CLOCK TIME | Q2 | Q3 | Q4 |
|---|---|---|---|
| 36 | 2 | 2 | 1 |
| 37 | 1 | 2 | 2 |
| 38 | 1 | 1 | 3 |
| 39 | 1 | 2 | 3 |
| 41 | | 3 | 3 |
| 42 | | 3 | 2 |
| 43 | 1 | 2 | 3 |
| 45 | | 3 | 3 |
| 46 | | 3 | 2 |
| 47 | | 4 | 2 |
| 48 | | 3 | 3 |
| 49 | | 3 | 4 |
| 50 | | 3 | 3 |
| 51 | | 3 | 3 |
| 53 | | 4 | 3 |
| 54 | | 3 | 3 |
| 56 | | 3 | 3 |
| 58 | | 3 | 2 |
| 59 | | 2 | 3 |
| 60 | | 3 | 3 |
| 61 | | 3 | 3 |
| 64 | | 2 | 3 |
| 65 | | 3 | 3 |
| 66 | | 3 | 3 |
| 67 | | 2 | 4 |
| 68 | | 2 | 3 |
| 70 | | 2 | 4 |
| 71 | | 2 | 4 |
| 72 | | 2 | 3 |
| 73 | | 1 | 4 |
| 75 | | 2 | 4 |
| 76 | | 2 | 3 |

| SIM CLOCK TIME | Q2 | Q3 | Q4 |
|---|---|---|---|
| 76 | | 2 | 3 |
| 78 | | 1 | 4 |
| 80 | | 2 | 3 |
| 81 | | 1 | 4 |
| 84 | | | 4 |
| 85 | | 1 | 4 |
| 86 | | 1 | 4 |
| 88 | | 1 | 3 |
| 89 | | | 4 |
| 90 | | 1 | 4 |
| 91 | | 1 | 4 |
| 92 | | | 4 |
| 95 | | | 5 |
| 96 | | | 4 |
| 98 | | | 5 |
| 100 | | | 4 |
| 101 | | | 4 |
| 103 | | | 5 |
| 104 | | | 4 |
| 105 | | | 4 |
| 106 | | | 4 |
| 108 | | | 4 |
| 110 | | | 4 |
| 111 | | | 4 |
| 112 | | | 3 |
| 113 | | | 4 |
| 115 | | | 4 |
| 116 | | | 3 |
| 118 | | | 4 |
| 120 | | | 3 |

Products completed = 26
In process = 6
Wait loading (Q1) = 3

Profit on products completed
A – 0 × 40 = £ 0
B – 5 × 15 = £ 75
C – 10 × 30 = £300
D – 11 × 10 = £110
£485

*Comments* The shortest operation scheduling rule always ensures that the maximum number of jobs are loaded on to each machine and placed in the next queue as quickly as possible. It streams the jobs in product groups as follows:

Machine 1—B, C, D, A
Machine 2—C, B or D, A
Machine 3—B, D, C, A
Machine 4—A, C or D, B

This resulted in queues building up quickly and products overtaking one another. In spite of Jobs 30 and 11 (both product B) finishing on Machine 1 at times 6 and 7 respectively, they were still sitting in queue 4 at time 120 having been overtaken by 10 product C jobs and 11 product D jobs.

| Job no. | Prod. type | Due date | Del. date | Early (−) | Late (+) |
|---------|-----------|----------|-----------|-----------|----------|
| 10 | B | 31 | 12 | 19 | |
| 35 | B | 37 | 18 | 19 | |
| 4 | B | 39 | 24 | 15 | |
| 22 | C | 47 | 28 | 19 | |
| 5 | C | 61 | 32 | 29 | |
| 26 | C | 70 | 36 | 34 | |
| 12 | B | 41 | 42 | | 1 |
| 18 | C | 77 | 46 | 33 | |
| 31 | C | 78 | 50 | 28 | |
| 25 | C | 90 | 54 | 36 | |
| 15 | C | 100 | 58 | 42 | |
| 8 | B | 54 | 64 | | 10 |
| 34 | C | 123 | 68 | 55 | |
| 29 | D | 34 | 72 | | 38 |
| 17 | D | 39 | 76 | | 37 |
| 23 | D | 42 | 80 | | 38 |
| 2 | C | 124 | 84 | | 40 |
| 3 | D | 49 | 88 | | 39 |
| 1 | D | 70 | 92 | | 22 |
| 27 | D | 76 | 96 | | 20 |
| 32 | D | 100 | 100 | 0 | |
| 20 | D | 105 | 104 | 1 | |
| 19 | D | 106 | 108 | | 2 |
| 24 | D | 111 | 112 | | 1 |
| 21 | C | 128 | 116 | 12 | |
| 16 | D | 112 | 120 | | 8 |

Examination of queue sizes shows how Jobs were held up in queue 2 (time 2–43), queue 3 (time 17–92), and queue 4 (time 10–120). While 26 Jobs were completed, which is one more than by the previous rule, the profit is less. Neither rule takes any account of profit.

Where Jobs in a queue had similar machining times, however, the one with the earliest due date was selected. The effect this had on delivery variation is shown in the table above. Compared with the previous rule it had some effect in reducing the range to 95 (−55 to +40). This is a significant improvement, but is not the best result. On this occasion the secondary objective of due date has had a beneficial result.

*Scheduling rule 3*   Highest profit per job

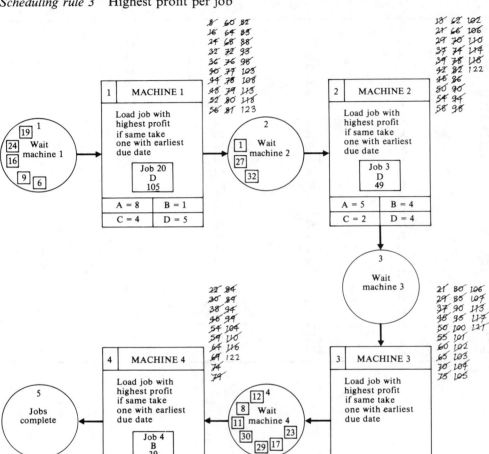

*Comments*   This rule looks only at the total profit of the job regardless of the processing time. As such it is a simple rule with a financial objective (presuming there is no difficulty in measuring profit or contribution). It has the effect of scheduling the jobs in product groups in the order A, C, B, D. The differences in machining times for each product on each machine cause queues to build up quite rapidly in the system. Queue 3 built up steadily to 5 at time 94 but then rapidly ran down again from 5 to nil between times 99 and 105. About this time queue 4 built up rapidly from nil to 6. This was caused by a stream of product B passing quickly through Machine 3.

Only 17 products were completed and 7 were waiting in queue 4. However, the profit was £520 due to the concentration on the highest profit lines. While fewer products are produced customer service is quite poor, with a range of 133 ($-54$ to $+79$). This example illustrates the situation where rules are quoted as satisfying two or more objectives—the extent to which the secondary objectives are satisfied is often less than people expect, and is very sensitive to the dynamics of the system itself.

| SIM CLOCK TIME | Q2 | Q3 | Q4 |
|---|---|---|---|
| 0 | | | |
| 8 | | | |
| 13 | | | |
| 16 | | | |
| 21 | | | |
| 22 | | | |
| 24 | | | |
| 29 | | | |
| 30 | | | |
| 32 | | | |
| 36 | | | |
| 37 | | | |
| 38 | | | |
| 39 | | 1 | |
| 40 | | 1 | |
| 42 | 2 | | |
| 44 | 2 | | |
| 45 | | 1 | |
| 46 | 2 | | |
| 48 | 2 | | |
| 50 | 2 | | |
| 52 | 2 | | |
| 54 | 3 | | |
| 55 | 2 | | |
| 56 | 2 | | |

| SIM CLOCK TIME | Q2 | Q3 | Q4 |
|---|---|---|---|
| 56 | | 2 | |
| 58 | | 3 | |
| 59 | | 3 | |
| 60 | | 2 | |
| 62 | | 3 | |
| 64 | | 3 | |
| 65 | | 2 | |
| 66 | | 3 | |
| 68 | | 3 | |
| 69 | | 3 | |
| 70 | | 3 | |
| 72 | | 2 | |
| 74 | | 4 | |
| 75 | | 3 | |
| 76 | | 3 | |
| 77 | 1 | 3 | |
| 78 | 1 | 4 | |
| 79 | 2 | 4 | |
| 80 | 3 | 3 | |
| 81 | 4 | 3 | |
| 82 | 4 | 4 | |
| 83 | 5 | 4 | |
| 84 | 5 | 4 | |
| 85 | 5 | 3 | |
| 86 | 4 | 4 | |

| SIM CLOCK TIME | Q2 | Q3 | Q4 |
|---|---|---|---|
| 86 | 4 | 4 | |
| 88 | 5 | 4 | |
| 89 | 5 | 4 | |
| 90 | 4 | 4 | |
| 93 | 5 | 4 | |
| 94 | 4 | 5 | |
| 95 | 4 | 4 | |
| 98 | 4 | 5 | |
| 99 | 4 | 5 | |
| 100 | 4 | 4 | |
| 101 | 4 | 3 | 1 |
| 102 | 3 | 3 | 2 |
| 103 | 4 | 2 | 3 |
| 104 | 4 | 1 | 3 |
| 105 | 4 | | 4 |
| 106 | 3 | | 5 |
| 107 | 3 | | 6 |
| 108 | 4 | | 6 |
| 110 | 3 | | 5 |
| 113 | 4 | | 6 |
| 114 | 3 | | 6 |
| 116 | 3 | | 5 |
| 117 | 3 | | 6 |
| 118 | 3 | | 6 |
| 121 | 3 | | 7 |

Products completed = 17
In process = 13
Wait load (Q1) = 5

Profit on products completed
A — 4 × 40 = £160
B — 2 × 15 = £ 30
C — 11 × 30 = £330
$$\underline{\underline{£520}}$$

| Job no. | Prod. type | Due date | Del. date | Early (−) | Late (+) |
|---|---|---|---|---|---|
| 33 | A | 51 | 22 | 29 | |
| 14 | A | 67 | 30 | 37 | |
| 28 | A | 83 | 38 | 45 | |
| 13 | A | 100 | 46 | 54 | |
| 22 | C | 47 | 54 | | 7 |
| 5 | C | 61 | 59 | | 2 |
| 26 | C | 70 | 64 | 6 | |
| 18 | C | 77 | 69 | 8 | |
| 31 | C | 78 | 74 | 4 | |
| 25 | C | 90 | 79 | 11 | |
| 15 | C | 100 | 84 | 16 | |
| 34 | C | 123 | 89 | 34 | |
| 2 | C | 124 | 94 | 30 | |
| 21 | C | 128 | 99 | 29 | |
| 7 | C | 130 | 104 | 26 | |
| 10 | B | 31 | 110 | | 79 |
| 35 | B | 37 | 116 | | 79 |

*Scheduling rule 4*   Highest profit per process hour

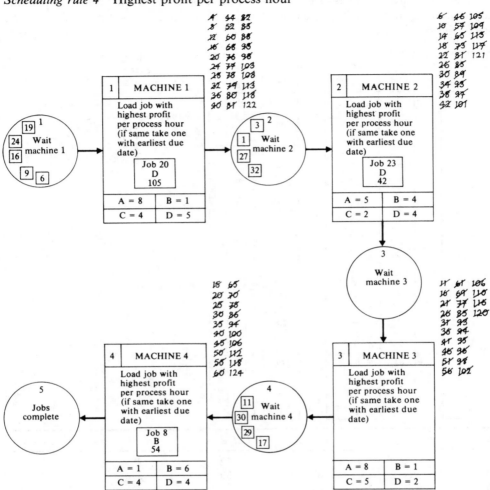

*Comments*   This rule endeavours to improve on rule 3 by making allowance for the processing time on the machines. Profit per hour is calculated as follows:

Products: A £$\frac{40}{22}$ = £1.82,   B £$\frac{15}{12}$ = £1.25,   C £$\frac{30}{15}$ = £2.00,   D £$\frac{10}{16}$ = £0.625

The Jobs are therefore streamed in product groups as follows: C, A, B, D. (Note the highest profit rule (rule 3) streamed in order A, C, B, D.) The queue behaviour is similar to rule 3 with queues building up quickly. The number of jobs completed is 19 which is much lower than the 26 achieved using the shortest operation rule.

The profit is £550 which is a significant improvement and reflects the effect of improving the financial measure used to select the jobs for loading.

The customer service is poor even though the rule again takes due date as a secondary criterion. The range of 150 (−73 to +77) is little better than rule 1.

| SIM CLOCK TIME | Q2 | Q3 | Q4 |
|---|---|---|---|
| 0 | | | |
| 4 | | | |
| 6 | | | |
| 8 | | | |
| 10 | | 1 | |
| 11 | | | |
| 12 | | | |
| 14 | | 1 | |
| 15 | | 1 | |
| 16 | | | |
| 18 | | 1 | |
| 20 | | 1 | |
| 21 | | | |
| 22 | | 1 | |
| 24 | | 1 | |
| 25 | | 1 | |
| 26 | | 1 | |
| 28 | | 1 | |
| 30 | | 2 | |
| 31 | | 1 | |
| 32 | | 1 | |
| 34 | | 2 | |
| 35 | | 2 | |
| 36 | | 1 | |
| 38 | | 2 | |
| 40 | | 2 | |

| SIM CLOCK TIME | Q2 | Q3 | Q4 |
|---|---|---|---|
| 40 | | 2 | |
| 41 | | 1 | |
| 42 | | 2 | |
| 44 | | 2 | |
| 45 | | 2 | |
| 46 | | 2 | |
| 50 | | 2 | |
| 51 | | 1 | |
| 52 | | 1 | |
| 55 | | 1 | |
| 56 | | | |
| 57 | | 1 | |
| 60 | | 1 | |
| 61 | | | |
| 65 | | 1 | |
| 68 | | 1 | |
| 69 | | | |
| 70 | | | |
| 73 | | 1 | |
| 76 | | 1 | |
| 77 | 1 | | |
| 78 | 2 | | |
| 79 | 3 | | |
| 80 | 4 | | |
| 81 | 4 | 1 | |
| 82 | 5 | 1 | |

| SIM CLOCK TIME | Q2 | Q3 | Q4 |
|---|---|---|---|
| 82 | 5 | 1 | |
| 83 | 6 | 1 | |
| 85 | 8 | 1 | |
| 86 | 8 | 1 | |
| 88 | 6 | 1 | |
| 89 | 5 | 2 | |
| 93 | 5 | 2 | |
| 94 | 5 | 1 | |
| 95 | 8 | | 1 |
| 96 | 5 | | 2 |
| 97 | 4 | | 2 |
| 98 | 5 | | 3 |
| 100 | 6 | | 2 |
| 101 | 4 | | 2 |
| 102 | 4 | | 3 |
| 103 | 5 | | 3 |
| 105 | 4 | | 3 |
| 106 | 4 | | 3 |
| 108 | 5 | | 3 |
| 109 | 4 | | 3 |
| 110 | 4 | | 4 |
| 112 | 4 | | 3 |
| 113 | 4 | | 3 |
| 116 | 4 | | 4 |
| 117 | 3 | | 4 |
| 118 | 4 | | 3 |
| 120 | 4 | | 4 |

Products completed = 19
In process = 11
Wait load (Q1) = 5

Profit on products completed
A – 4 × 40 = £160
B – 4 × 15 = £ 60
C – 11 × 30 = £330
                £550

| Job no. | Prod. type | Due date | Del. date | Early (−) | Late (+) |
|---|---|---|---|---|---|
| 22 | C | 47 | 15 | 32 | |
| 5 | C | 61 | 20 | 41 | |
| 26 | C | 70 | 25 | 45 | |
| 18 | C | 77 | 30 | 47 | |
| 31 | C | 78 | 35 | 43 | |
| 25 | C | 90 | 40 | 50 | |
| 15 | C | 100 | 45 | 55 | |
| 34 | C | 123 | 50 | 73 | |
| 2 | C | 124 | 55 | 69 | |
| 21 | C | 128 | 60 | 68 | |
| 7 | C | 130 | 65 | 65 | |
| 33 | A | 51 | 70 | | 19 |
| 14 | A | 67 | 78 | | 11 |
| 28 | A | 83 | 86 | | 3 |
| 13 | A | 100 | 94 | 6 | |
| 10 | B | 31 | 100 | | 69 |
| 35 | B | 37 | 106 | | 69 |
| 4 | B | 39 | 112 | | 73 |
| 12 | B | 41 | 118 | | 77 |

*Scheduling rule 5*  Earliest due date

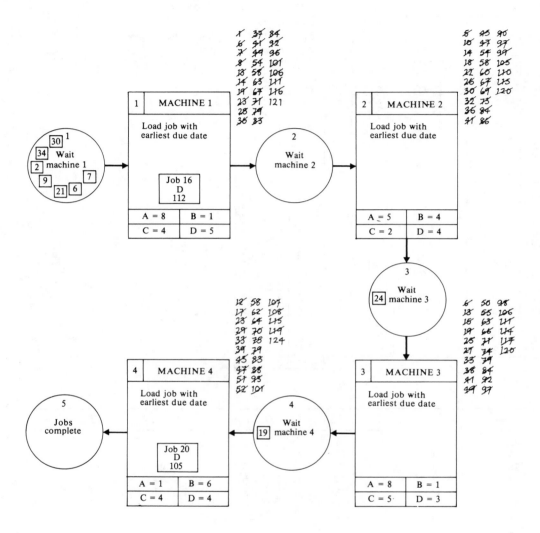

| SIM CLOCK TIME | JOBS IN QUEUE | | |
|---|---|---|---|
| | Q2 | Q3 | Q4 |
| 0 | | | |
| 1 | | | |
| 5 | | | |
| 6 | | | |
| 7 | 1 | | |
| 8 | 2 | | |
| 10 | 1 | | |
| 12 | 1 | | |
| 13 | 2 | | |
| 14 | 2 | | |
| 15 | 2 | | 1 |
| 17 | 2 | | |
| 18 | 1 | | |
| 19 | 2 | | 1 |
| 22 | 1 | | 1 |
| 23 | 2 | | |
| 25 | 2 | | 1 |
| 26 | 1 | | 1 |
| 27 | 1 | | 2 |
| 28 | 2 | | 2 |
| 29 | 2 | | 1 |
| 30 | 1 | | 1 |
| 32 | | 1 | 1 |
| 33 | | | 1 |
| 36 | | 1 | 1 |
| 37 | 1 | 1 | 1 |
| 38 | 1 | | 2 |
| 39 | 1 | | 1 |

| SIM CLOCK TIME | JOBS IN QUEUE | | |
|---|---|---|---|
| | Q2 | Q3 | Q4 |
| 39 | 1 | | 1 |
| 41 | 1 | | 2 |
| 43 | 1 | | 1 |
| 45 | | 1 | 1 |
| 47 | | 2 | |
| 49 | | 1 | 1 |
| 50 | | | 2 |
| 51 | | | 1 |
| 52 | | | |
| 54 | | 1 | |
| 56 | | | 1 |
| 58 | | 1 | |
| 60 | | 2 | |
| 61 | | 2 | |
| 63 | | 1 | |
| 64 | | 1 | |
| 66 | | | |
| 67 | | 1 | |
| 69 | | 2 | |
| 70 | | 2 | |
| 71 | | 1 | |
| 73 | | 2 | |
| 74 | | 1 | 1 |
| 75 | | 1 | |
| 79 | | | |
| 83 | 1 | | |
| 84 | 1 | | |
| 86 | | 1 | |

| SIM CLOCK TIME | JOBS IN QUEUE | | |
|---|---|---|---|
| | Q2 | Q3 | Q4 |
| 86 | | 1 | |
| 88 | | 1 | |
| 90 | | 2 | |
| 92 | | 1 | |
| 93 | | 1 | |
| 96 | 1 | 1 | |
| 97 | | 1 | |
| 98 | | | 1 |
| 99 | 1 | | 1 |
| 101 | | 1 | |
| 105 | | 2 | |
| 106 | 1 | | 1 |
| 107 | | 1 | |
| 108 | | 1 | |
| 110 | | 2 | |
| 111 | 1 | | |
| 112 | | | 1 |
| 115 | 1 | | |
| 116 | | 1 | |
| 117 | | | 1 |
| 119 | | | |
| 120 | | | 1 |

Products completed = 24
In process = 4
Wait load (Q1) = 7

Profit on products completed
A − 4 × 40 = £160
B − 6 × 15 = £ 90
C − 7 × 30 = £210
D − 7 × 10 = £ 70
£530

*Comments* The sole objective of this rule is to deliver goods as early as possible and consistent with a delivery schedule. The Jobs are not scheduled in product groups and this has the effect of mixing the long and short machine times as in rule 1. Few queues occurred and 24 Jobs were completed.

Profit at £530 was better than the £520 of rule 3 (highest profit per job). This was pure chance as no note was taken of this when loading machines, although the mixing of the products helped.

Customer service was the prime objective and the effect can be seen in the histogram with the delivery time range of 38 (− 19 to + 19). As all Jobs went through the same four machines and the total process time for each product only varied between 12 and 22 hours the use of a final due date was successful.

However, where jobs differ greatly in the number of operations that have to be performed and in the processing time involved, this rule will not be effective.

One possible improvement is to schedule on due date for each operation by working back from the due date and allowing the time for each operation. The jobs in each queue are then scheduled on the basis of the due date of the next operation—this is an ordered queue of work (see Chapter 7).

| Job no. | Prod. type | Due date | Del. date | Early (−) | Late (+) |
|---|---|---|---|---|---|
| 10 | B | 31 | 12 | 19 | |
| 29 | D | 34 | 17 | 17 | |
| 35 | B | 37 | 23 | 14 | |
| 4 | B | 39 | 29 | 10 | |
| 17 | D | 39 | 33 | 6 | |
| 12 | B | 41 | 39 | 2 | |
| 23 | D | 42 | 43 | | 1 |
| 22 | C | 47 | 47 | 0 | |
| 3 | D | 49 | 51 | | 2 |
| 33 | A | 51 | 52 | | 1 |
| 8 | B | 54 | 58 | | 4 |
| 5 | C | 61 | 62 | | 1 |
| 14 | A | 67 | 64 | 3 | |
| 1 | D | 70 | 70 | 0 | |
| 26 | C | 70 | 75 | | 5 |
| 27 | D | 76 | 79 | | 3 |
| 18 | C | 77 | 83 | | 6 |
| 31 | C | 78 | 88 | | 10 |
| 28 | A | 83 | 93 | | 10 |
| 25 | C | 90 | 101 | | 11 |
| 11 | B | 99 | 107 | | 8 |
| 13 | A | 100 | 108 | | 8 |
| 15 | C | 100 | 115 | | 15 |
| 32 | D | 100 | 119 | | 19 |

Summary of statistics at time 120

| Measure of performance | Scheduling rule: Job no. | Shortest operation | Highest profit per job | Highest profit per process hour | Earliest due date |
|---|---|---|---|---|---|
| **Production** | | | | | |
| No. of jobs completed: | 25 | 26 | 17 | 19 | 24 |
| Work in progress: | 3 | 6 | 13 | 11 | 4 |
| Jobs waiting start: | 7 | 3 | 5 | 5 | 7 |
| **Financial** | | | | | |
| Profit on completed jobs: | £495 | £485 | £520 | £550 | £530 |
| **Customer service** | | | | | |
| Earliest delivery | −103 | −55 | −54 | −73 | −19 |
| to | to | to | to | to | to |
| latest delivery | +70 | +40 | +79 | +77 | +20 |

## Histograms of delivery time variations

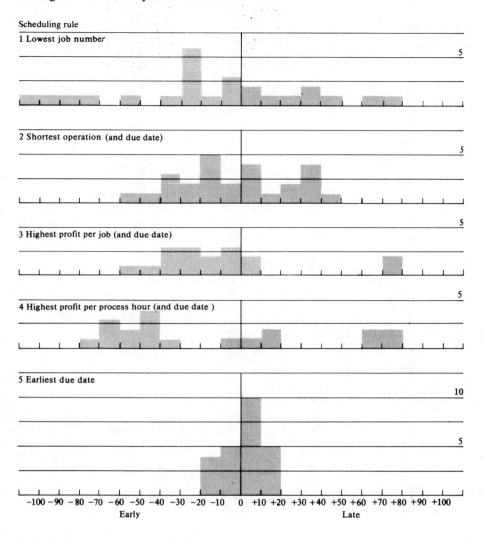

SOLUTION 4.8

Inter-arrival times for calls—random at average rate of five per hour (see next page).

| Call number | Random no. (stream 4) | Inter-arrival time | Cumulative time | |
|---|---|---|---|---|
| 1 | 52 | 9 | 9 | |
| 2 | 50 | 8 | 17 | |
| 3 | 83 | 22 | 39 | |
| 4 | 48 | 8 | 47 | |
| 5 | 8 | 1 | 48 | |
| 6 | 41 | 6 | 54 | |
| 7 | 33 | 5 | 59 | 7 calls in 1st hour |
| 8 | 80 | 19 | 78 | |
| 9 | 73 | 16 | 94 | 2 calls in 2nd hour |
| 10 | 89 | 27 | 121 | |
| 11 | 82 | 20 | 141 | |
| 12 | 57 | 10 | 151 | |
| 13 | 1 | 0 | 151 | 4 calls in 3rd hour |
| 14 | 96 | 38 | 189 | |
| 15 | 98 | 48 | 237 | 2 calls in 4th hour |
| 16 | 30 | 4 | 241 | |
| 17 | 61 | 11 | 252 | |
| 18 | 16 | 2 | 254 | |
| 19 | 64 | 12 | 266 | |
| 20 | 37 | 6 | 272 | |
| 21 | 50 | 8 | 280 | |
| 22 | 2 | 0 | 280 | |
| 23 | 64 | 12 | 292 | |
| 24 | 33 | 5 | 297 | 9 calls in 5th hour |
| 25 | 70 | 15 | 312 | |
| 26 | 27 | 4 | 316 | |
| 27 | 24 | 3 | 319 | |
| 28 | 17 | 2 | 321 | |
| 29 | 44 | 7 | 328 | |
| 30 | 34 | 5 | 333 | |
| 31 | 10 | 1 | 334 | |
| 32 | 88 | 26 | 360 | 8 calls in 6th hour |
| 33 | 89 | 27 | 387 | |
| 34 | 75 | 17 | 404 | |
| 35 | 26 | 4 | 408 | 3 calls in 7th hour |
| 36 | 91 | 29 | 437 | |
| 37 | 87 | 25 | 462 | 2 calls in 8th hour |
| 38 | 89 | 27 | 489 | |
| 39 | 86 | 24 | 513 | |
| 40 | 36 | 5 | 518 | |
| 41 | 76 | 17 | 535 | |
| 42 | 36 | 5 | 540 | 5 calls in 9th hour |
| 43 | 14 | 2 | 542 | |
| 44 | 57 | 10 | 552 | |
| 45 | 54 | 9 | 561 | |
| 46 | 30 | 4 | 565 | |
| 47 | 93 | 32 | 597 | 5 calls in 10th hour |
| 48 | 93 | 32 | 629 | |
| 49 | 9 | 1 | 630 | |
| 50 | 86 | 24 | 654 | |

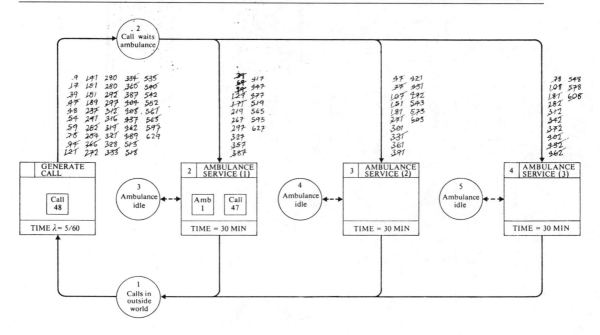

*Comments*  Up to time 620 a total of 47 Calls had been received. The activity times are arranged in groups of ten so that it is easy to read the number of occasions on which an activity has taken place. This is known as the 'activity run count' with which you will become familiar in later chapters.

Ambulances 1, 2 and 3 completed 17, 16 and 13 Calls respectively. The time Calls waited for an Ambulance is shown in the final column of the simulation record sheet.

Of the 47 Calls received 20 were answered immediately and the other 27 waited anything up to 57 minutes. This figure sounds alarming, and an average waiting time for all calls of 12.8 minutes is not particularly comforting.

Ambulance 1 was idle for 87 minutes, Ambulance 2 for 140 minutes and Ambulance 3 for 220 minutes. This example illustrates that where a fixed number of resources have to service a random pattern of demand it is impossible to expect both good service and high utilization. Above a 70 per cent level of utilization queues start to build up rapidly. It is a help to all concerned in interpreting results to show how the results are distributed, so that they can judge the implications of the proportion of occurrences which exceed a particular value. This can be done using histograms, or tables showing the frequency of occurrence in each time band.

The effect of adding another ambulance to the fleet, or of being able to reduce the time taken to service the call, can easily be simulated and the results compared.

Should the frequency of random calls vary during the simulation this can be handled by moving to the appropriate cumulative distribution in Appendix 2. If the work of the ambulance also includes some scheduled (non-random) calls these can be introduced by means of another generator.

| TIME | END | START | SIM CLOCK TIME | AMB 1 ON | AMB 1 OFF | AMB 1 DUR | AMB 2 ON | AMB 2 OFF | AMB 2 DUR | AMB 3 ON | AMB 3 OFF | AMB 3 DUR | CALL NO | ON | OFF | DUR |
|---|---|---|---|---|---|---|---|---|---|---|---|---|---|---|---|---|
| | | ✓ | ① | ② | | | ② | | | ② | | | 1 | | | |
| ✓ | ✓ | ✓ | 9 | | ✓ | 9 | | | | | | | 1 | ✓ | ✓ | 0 |
| ✓ | ✓ | ✓ | 17 | | | | | ✓ | 17 | | | | 2 | ✓ | ✓ | 0 |
| ✓ | ✓ | ✓ | 39 | ✓ | ✓ | 0 | | | | | | | 3 | ✓ | ✓ | 0 |
| ✓ | ✓ | ✓ | 47 | | | | ✓ | ✓ | 0 | | | | 4 | ✓ | ✓ | 0 |
| ✓ | ✓ | ✓ | 48 | | | | | | | ✓ | | 48 | 5 | ✓ | ✓ | 0 |
| ✓ | ✓ | ✓ | 54 | | | | | | | | | | 6 | ✓ | | |
| ✓ | ✓ | ✓ | 59 | | | | | | | | | | 7 | ✓ | | |
| ✓ | ✓ | ✓ | 69 | ✓ | ✓ | 0 | | | | | | | 6 | | ✓ | 15 |
| ✓ | ✓ | ✓ | 77 | | | | ✓ | ✓ | 0 | | | | 7 | | ✓ | 18 |
| ✓ | ✓ | ✓ | 78 | | | | | | | ✓ | ✓ | 0 | 8 | ✓ | ✓ | 0 |
| ✓ | ✓ | ✓ | 94 | | | | | | | | | | 9 | ✓ | | |
| ✓ | ✓ | ✓ | 99 | ✓ | ✓ | 0 | | | | | | | 9 | | ✓ | 5 |
| ✓ | ✓ | ✓ | 107 | ✓ | | | | | | | | | | | | |
| ✓ | ✓ | ✓ | 108 | | | | | | | ✓ | | | | | | |
| ✓ | ✓ | ✓ | 121 | | | | ✓ | | 14 | | | | 10 | ✓ | ✓ | 0 |
| ✓ | ✓ | ✓ | 129 | ✓ | | | | | | | | | | | | |
| ✓ | ✓ | ✓ | 141 | | ✓ | 12 | | | | | | | 11 | ✓ | ✓ | 0 |
| ✓ | ✓ | ✓ | 151 | | | | ✓ | ✓ | 0 | | | | 12 | ✓ | ✓ | 0 |
| ✓ | ✓ | ✓ | 151 | | | | | | | ✓ | | 43 | 13 | ✓ | ✓ | 0 |
| ✓ | ✓ | ✓ | 171 | ✓ | | | | | | | | | | | | |
| ✓ | ✓ | ✓ | 181 | | | | ✓ | | | ✓ | | | | | | |
| ✓ | ✓ | ✓ | 189 | | ✓ | 18 | | | | | | | 14 | ✓ | ✓ | 0 |
| ✓ | ✓ | ✓ | 219 | ✓ | | | | | | | | | | | | |
| ✓ | ✓ | ✓ | 237 | | ✓ | 18 | | | | | | | 15 | ✓ | ✓ | 0 |
| ✓ | ✓ | ✓ | 241 | | | | ✓ | | 60 | | | | 16 | ✓ | ✓ | 0 |
| ✓ | ✓ | ✓ | 252 | | | | | | | ✓ | | 61 | 17 | ✓ | ✓ | 0 |
| ✓ | ✓ | ✓ | 254 | | | | | | | | | | 18 | ✓ | | |
| ✓ | ✓ | ✓ | 266 | | | | | | | | | | 19 | ✓ | | |
| ✓ | ✓ | ✓ | 267 | ✓ | ✓ | 0 | | | | | | | 18 | | ✓ | 13 |
| ✓ | ✓ | ✓ | 271 | | | | ✓ | ✓ | 0 | | | | 19 | | ✓ | 5 |
| ✓ | ✓ | ✓ | 272 | | | | | | | | | | 20 | ✓ | | |
| ✓ | ✓ | ✓ | 280 | | | | | | | | | | 21 | ✓ | | |
| ✓ | ✓ | ✓ | 280 | | | | | | | | | | 22 | ✓ | | |
| ✓ | ✓ | ✓ | 282 | | | | | | | ✓ | ✓ | 0 | 20 | | ✓ | 10 |
| ✓ | ✓ | ✓ | 292 | | | | | | | | | | 23 | ✓ | | |
| ✓ | ✓ | ✓ | 297 | ✓ | | | | | | | | | 24 | ✓ | | |
| | | | 297 | | ✓ | 0 | | | | | | | 21 | | ✓ | 17 |
| ✓ | ✓ | ✓ | 301 | | | | ✓ | ✓ | 0 | | | | 22 | | ✓ | 21 |
| ✓ | ✓ | ✓ | 312 | | | | | | | ✓ | | | 25 | ✓ | | |
| | | | 312 | | | | | | | | ✓ | 0 | 23 | | ✓ | 20 |
| ✓ | ✓ | ✓ | 316 | | | | | | | | | | 26 | ✓ | | |
| ✓ | ✓ | ✓ | 319 | | | | | | | | | | 27 | ✓ | | |
| ✓ | ✓ | ✓ | 321 | | | | | | | | | | 28 | ✓ | | |
| ✓ | ✓ | ✓ | 327 | ✓ | ✓ | 0 | | | | | | | 24 | | ✓ | 30 |

| | | | | | | | | | | | | | | | | |
|---|---|---|---|---|---|---|---|---|---|---|---|---|---|---|---|---|
| ✓ | ✓ | ✓ | 327 | ✓ | ✓ | | 0 | | | | | | 24 | | ✓ | 30 |
| ✓ | ✓ | ✓ | 328 | | | | | | | | | | 29 | ✓ | | |
| ✓ | ✓ | ✓ | 331 | | | | ✓ | ✓ | 0 | | | | 25 | | ✓ | 19 |
| ✓ | ✓ | ✓ | 333 | | | | | | | | | | 30 | ✓ | | |
| ✓ | ✓ | ✓ | 334 | | | | | | | | | | 31 | ✓ | | |
| ✓ | ✓ | ✓ | 342 | | | | | | | ✓ | ✓ | 0 | 26 | | ✓ | 26 |
| ✓ | ✓ | ✓ | 357 | ✓ | ✓ | 0 | | | | | | | 27 | | ✓ | 38 |
| ✓ | ✓ | ✓ | 360 | | | | | | | | | | 32 | ✓ | | |
| ✓ | ✓ | ✓ | 361 | | | | ✓ | ✓ | 0 | | | | 28 | | ✓ | 40 |
| ✓ | ✓ | ✓ | 372 | | | | | | | ✓ | ✓ | 0 | 29 | | ✓ | 44 |
| ✓ | ✓ | ✓ | 387 | ✓ | | | | | | | | | 33 | ✓ | | |
| | | | 387 | | ✓ | 0 | | | | | | | 30 | | ✓ | 54 |
| ✓ | ✓ | ✓ | 391 | | | | ✓ | ✓ | 0 | | | | 31 | | ✓ | 57 |
| ✓ | ✓ | ✓ | 402 | | | | | | | ✓ | ✓ | 0 | 32 | | ✓ | 42 |
| ✓ | ✓ | ✓ | 404 | | | | | | | | | | 34 | ✓ | | |
| ✓ | ✓ | ✓ | 408 | | | | | | | | | | 35 | ✓ | | |
| ✓ | ✓ | ✓ | 417 | ✓ | ✓ | 0 | | | | | | | 33 | | ✓ | 30 |
| ✓ | ✓ | ✓ | 421 | | | | ✓ | ✓ | 0 | | | | 34 | | ✓ | 17 |
| ✓ | ✓ | ✓ | 432 | | | | | | | ✓ | ✓ | 0 | 35 | | ✓ | 24 |
| ✓ | ✓ | ✓ | 437 | | | | | | | | | | 36 | ✓ | | |
| ✓ | ✓ | ✓ | 447 | ✓ | ✓ | 0 | | | | | | | 36 | | ✓ | 10 |
| ✓ | ✓ | ✓ | 451 | | | | ✓ | | | | | | | | | |
| ✓ | ✓ | ✓ | 462 | | | | | ✓ | 11 | ✓ | | | 37 | ✓ | ✓ | 0 |
| ✓ | ✓ | ✓ | 477 | ✓ | | | | | | | | | | | | |
| ✓ | ✓ | ✓ | 489 | | ✓ | 12 | | | | | | | 38 | ✓ | ✓ | 0 |
| ✓ | ✓ | ✓ | 492 | | | | ✓ | | | | | | | | | |
| ✓ | ✓ | ✓ | 513 | | | | | ✓ | 21 | | | | 39 | ✓ | ✓ | 0 |
| ✓ | ✓ | ✓ | 518 | | | | | | | | ✓ | 56 | 40 | ✓ | ✓ | 0 |
| ✓ | ✓ | ✓ | 519 | ✓ | | | | | | | | | | | | |
| ✓ | ✓ | ✓ | 535 | | ✓ | 16 | | | | | | | 41 | ✓ | ✓ | 0 |
| ✓ | ✓ | ✓ | 540 | | | | | | | | | | 42 | ✓ | | |
| ✓ | ✓ | ✓ | 542 | | | | | | | | | | 43 | ✓ | | |
| ✓ | ✓ | ✓ | 543 | | | | ✓ | ✓ | 0 | | | | 42 | | ✓ | 3 |
| ✓ | ✓ | ✓ | 548 | | | | | | | ✓ | ✓ | 0 | 43 | | ✓ | 6 |
| ✓ | ✓ | ✓ | 552 | | | | | | | | | | 44 | ✓ | | |
| ✓ | ✓ | ✓ | 561 | | | | | | | | | | 45 | ✓ | | |
| ✓ | ✓ | ✓ | 565 | ✓ | | | | | | | | | 46 | ✓ | | |
| | | | 565 | | ✓ | 0 | | | | | | | 44 | | ✓ | 13 |
| ✓ | ✓ | ✓ | 573 | | | | ✓ | ✓ | 0 | | | | 45 | | ✓ | 12 |
| ✓ | ✓ | ✓ | 578 | | | | | | | ✓ | ✓ | 0 | 46 | | ✓ | 13 |
| ✓ | ✓ | ✓ | 595 | ✓ | | | | | | | | | | | | |
| ✓ | ✓ | ✓ | 597 | | ✓ | 2 | | | | | | | 47 | ✓ | ✓ | 0 |
| ✓ | ✓ | ✓ | 603 | | | | ✓ | | | | | | | | | |
| ✓ | ✓ | ✓ | 608 | | | | | | | ✓ | | | | | | |
| ✓ | ✓ | | 620 | | | | ⓥ | 17 | | ⓥ | 12 | No calls – Pues 2 | | | | |

# Part Two

Formal models for hand and
computer simulation

# 5.

## Building a simple formal model

We have now seen how to build informal models using the concept of entities which have life cycles consisting of queues and activities. By building a model in such a visual way, we can demonstrate to all concerned how it operates by hand simulation. Because it is easy to understand, even non-experts can respond by pointing out errors or inconsistencies and, even more important, indicate whether all relevant factors have been incorporated. In this way we are sure that an accurate, acceptable model is built quickly.

However, unless we have already solved the problem by the better understanding we have gained from building the model, we will want to simulate for long periods and perform a number of experiments. We do this either by continuing with hand simulation, or by transferring the model to a computer. In both cases there are considerable advantages in formalizing the model building procedures.

Hand simulation is time consuming, and therefore we may need help. It will be much easier to communicate the rules for operating the model if they are formally laid down.

Running the model on a computer involves using a program. We can either write our own or use a standard program. In writing our own we must select a suitable simulation programming language, and use the model as the specification. To do this quickly depends on whether:

- we know the simulation language well;
- we have sufficient time to write and test the program;
- the program is easy to modify;
- the language is well proven;
- the language is available on the computer we propose to use.

If we are not capable of writing the program ourselves, we can of course seek assistance. If we have access to a programmer, he will find his task much easier and will make fewer mistakes if the model has been built using clearly defined rules.

If we use a standard program, we will not be involved in any programming at all, but then the model must be built using rules acceptable to the program. In this second part of the book we describe how to build such models using the rules of the HOCUS system.

In this chapter we limit the models to ones involving entities which do not have attributes, and this enables us to simulate simple discrete processes. Attributes are introduced in Chapter 7 where we describe how they are used to model complex problems involving discrete and continuous processes.

Many examples and exercises are given and the only way you can assure yourself that you understand the examples is to complete the exercises and compare your solutions with those given at the end of the chapter. If you cannot reconcile the two you should return to the appropriate point in the text.

In the examples we refer to two formats—one to represent a queue and the other an activity—and they are reproduced in Fig. 5.1.

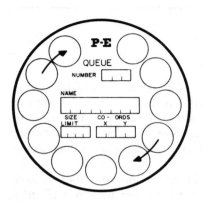

**Figure 5.1**

In order to make the diagrams clearer, full formats are not used in the flow charts. Squares and circles are used instead, but the information is written in positions appropriate to the formats. When necessary, details of how to enter the information on to the formats are given at the end of the example.

## Simple activity diagram

With any simulation problem we begin with a simple model. It usually becomes more complex as further details are uncovered and we gain understanding of the problem.

Our first example concerns the maintenance of a machine. When the machine breaks down it is repaired by a mechanic. After repair the machine runs until it breaks down again.

The first step in building a model, as we have already seen in Chapter 2, is to list the entities involved and describe their life cycles in terms of queues and activities. In most problems it is unlikely that all the entities can be confidently listed at this stage. The ones that have been omitted will become apparent as the model is developed, and these can be added later. In this example the life cycles of the machine and mechanic are as follows:

| Entity | States |
|--------|--------|
| Machine | run (A) |
| | wait repair (Q) |
| | being repaired (A) |
| | wait run (Q) |
| Mechanic | repair (A) |
| | idle (Q) |

We draw the life cycles of the Machine and Mechanic using the formats and observe that the two are linked together in the 'repair' activity, as shown in Fig. 5.2.

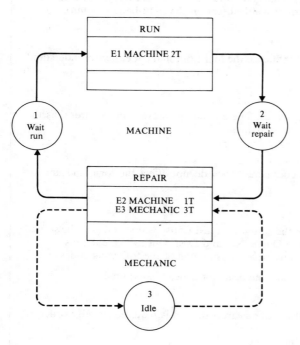

**Figure 5.2**

## Format details

The details of a model are entered in the formats as follows. All names are left justified (start in the left-hand column) and all numbers are right justified (end in the right-hand column).

### Queue names

Give each queue a name. The names do not influence the logic, but make it easier to understand the model and interpret results.

### Queue numbers

Number the queues consecutively from 1 upwards. There is no significance in the order, as the numbers are used only as identifiers within the activities.

### Activity names

Give each activity a name. As with the queue names, they do not affect the logic and are for descriptive purposes only.

### Activity conditions

For each activity, list the entities required in the column headed Entity Name and give the source and destination queue numbers in the Source Queue No. and Dest. Queue No. columns.
Specify the position of the entity in the source queue, using one of the following codes:

- E, if it has only to exist in the queue, and the one nearest the head is required.
- H, if it must be at the head of the queue.
- T, if it must be at the tail of the queue.
- I, if it has only to exist in the queue, and the one nearest the tail is required (inverse order of search).
- Z, if it is to be selected at random from the queue.

Write the letter E, H, T, I or Z in the Source Queue Pos. column.
You are recommended to use E in all cases, unless the logic specifically requires H, T, I or Z. Remember that there can only be one entity at the head (or tail) of a queue and that entities are not moved from a queue until all the conditions of an activity are satisfied.
In a similar way, specify the position in the destination queue to which an entity is to be sent, using one of the following codes:

- H, to the head of the queue.
- T, to the tail of the queue.

Write the letter H or T in the Dest. Queue Pos. column.

### Number of conditions

State the number of conditions listed in the activity, in the top right-hand corner of the format.

EXERCISE 5.1

Draw a flow diagram of a machine which runs until it breaks down, when it is repaired by a mechanic. After repair it is checked by an inspector before running again.

## Duplicated activities

In many models we find that instead of a single resource, there are several similar resources which follow similar life cycles. For example, in the machine maintenance problem, the mechanic may have to maintain three similar machines. In this case each machine runs independently of the others but follows the same sequence of operations. When a machine breaks down it joins the queue of broken down machines and waits for the mechanic to repair it.

The flow diagram has to be extended to allow for up to three machines to run simultaneously, as shown in Fig. 5.3.

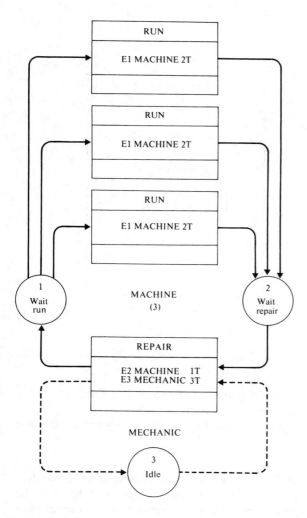

**Figure 5.3**

If there is more than one Machine waiting for repair, the Mechanic has to decide which one to repair first. In Fig. 5.3 he repairs the one nearest the head of the queue, that is the one which has broken down first.

This model can be represented more simply by either drawing the three 'run' activities as an echelon, or writing ' × 3' near the top right-hand corner of the format, as shown in Fig. 5.4.

It should be noted that there is still only one 'repair' activity, because at any instant in time, only one repair can be performed by the single Mechanic.

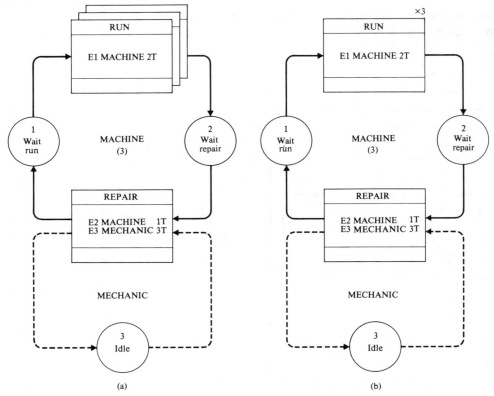

Figure 5.4

EXERCISE 5.2
(a) What modifications are necessary to Fig. 5.4 if two mechanics are available?
(b) Draw a flow diagram for 13 similar machines and three mechanics.
(c) What modifications are necessary to Fig. 5.4 if the machine most recently broken down is to be repaired first?

## Extending a model

Having started with a simple model, we usually find that some parts have to be expanded. This is because certain areas are critical to the overall performance and have to be investigated more closely. Also, with a better understanding of the problem, further relevant information may have to be included. Aspects which were initially overlooked or considered unimportant are revealed as being of consequence.

Suppose that in our machine maintenance example we discover that the time taken to repair is critical to the overall utilization of the machines, and decide that it is necessary to investigate this more closely. We observe that the original 'repair' activity can be broken down into the following work elements:

- an electrician disconnects the power supply;
- a heavy gang pulls out the machine from its mounting;
- a fitter removes the fittings;
- a mechanic repairs the machine;
- a fitter replaces the fittings;
- a heavy gang puts back the machine on to its mounting;
- an electrician reconnects the power supply.

If there are three machines, one mechanic, one electrician, one heavy gang and one fitter, our original model is extended as shown in Fig. 5.5.

The flow diagram raises two interesting points:

(a) *Model layout* Most models contain a mainstream entity—one which is fundamental to the model. Examples are aeroplanes in an airport, jobs in a production unit and patients in a hospital. Careful layout can ensure a neat and logical model, and this can often be achieved if the life cycle of the mainstream entity is drawn around the edge of the paper with the service entities, such as electricians and fitters, in the middle. In Fig. 5.5 we have also taken advantage of the fact that there is a mirror image of some of the operations. Each entity should be colour coded so that the separate life cycles are easily distinguished. In our diagrams we use different types of line to represent the various entities.

(b) *Priorities* In the start phase of hand simulation (see Chapter 3) activities are checked in the order in which they are numbered and so if activities share entities, an activity with a lower number has priority.

Figure 5.5 shows several examples of this, where 'reconnect' (A4) has priority over 'disconnect' (A10), 'put back' (A5) has priority over 'pull out' (A9), and 'replace fittings' (A6) has priority over 'remove fittings' (A8).

---

**Format details**

Activity numbers

Number the activities consecutively from 1 upwards. Unlike the queue numbers, the numbering of activities is important as the number implies a priority. Activities are checked in numerical order and so if two or more activities require the same entity from the same queue, the activity with the lower number will be given priority.

---

EXERCISE 5.3

What modifications would you make to Fig. 5.5 if:

- 'reconnect' has priority over 'disconnect';
- 'pull out' has priority over 'put back';
- 'remove fittings' has priority over 'replace fittings';
- there are two mechanics?

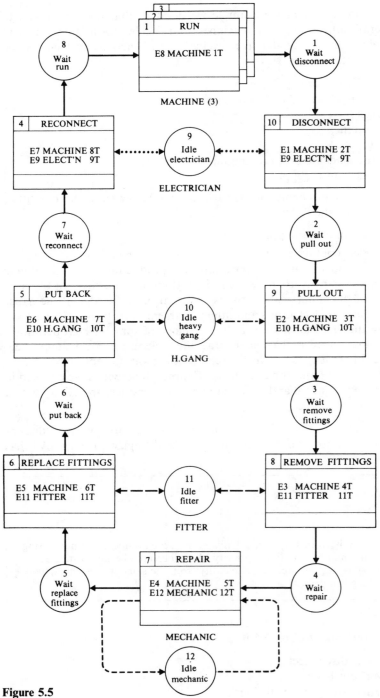

**Figure 5.5**

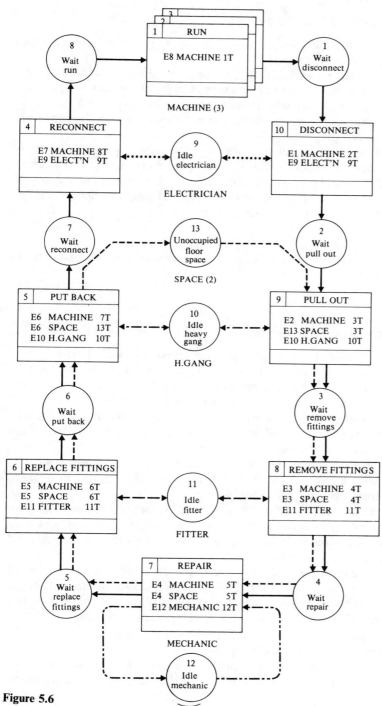

**Figure 5.6**

## Limiting entities in part of a model

There are occasions when we need to limit the number of entities in part of a system, because of a shortage of space or some other constraint.

Suppose in the machine maintenance example, that although there are three machines, not more than two can be off their mountings at any one time because of the lack of space.

We model this by introducing an entity which represents the new scarce resource—floor space—called Space. We have two of these, and in order to pull a machine out, Space must be available in addition to the heavy gang being idle.

This is shown in Fig. 5.6 where the 'pull out' activity (A9) now requires Space to be available in the unoccupied floor space queue (Q13). The Space remains with the Machine until the Machine is put back by the Heavy gang (A5) when it is released into the unoccupied floor space queue (Q13) and so is available for the next Machine. Having two Spaces restricts the number of Machines off their mountings at any time to two.

EXERCISE 5.4
What modification would you make to Fig. 5.6 if there is room for only one machine to be off its mountings at any one time?

## Boundaries of a model—generators

In every model we must give careful thought to the problem of what to include and what to leave out. We cannot model the whole world, although there is always a temptation to move in that direction. For example, when building a model to investigate the operation of a port we may not want to include details of what happens to ships before they arrive or after they leave. The only relevant information is the time when ships arrive and certain details of each ship, for example, its size and type of cargo. All we have to model is the arrival pattern of the ships as they approach the port from the high seas or 'outside world'.

A simple example of entities entering a system is a one-man barber's shop where customers arrive every 15 minutes to have a haircut. The barber deals with each customer in order of arrival, taking 10 to 20 minutes (distribution 1) for each.

The first step is to model the arrival pattern of the customers. As we are not concerned with where customers come from, how they travel to the barber's shop or even the length of their hair, we can have a number of customers in a queue called 'outside world' and a 'generate' activity that lasts for 15 minutes as shown in Fig. 5.7.

A Customer is taken from the outside world (Q1), held in the 'generate' activity (A1) for 15 minutes and is then released into the barber's shop (Q2) where he waits for his haircut. At the same time, the next Customer is taken from the outside world and held for 15 minutes. In this way a Customer arrives every 15 minutes, which is precisely the pattern required.

All customers eventually get their hair cut. They then leave and are put back into the outside world, to be generated again! This technique of re-cycling entities is common in simulation and is used to keep the total number of entities in a model to a minimum. All we have to ensure is that the arrival pattern is not disrupted by running out of entities in the outside world.

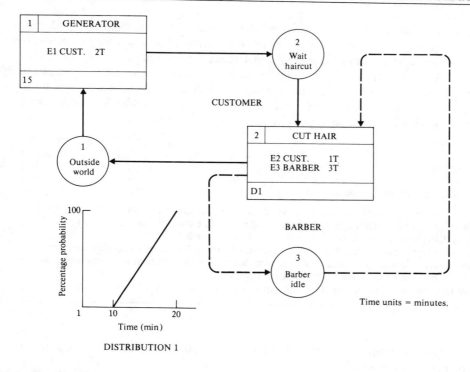

Figure 5.7

An alternative to re-cycling would be to put all customers who have had a haircut into a new queue, say queue 4. We would then have to start with a large number of Customers in queue 1, the number depending on the length of simulation. As the simulation progressed, Customers would gradually move from queue 1 and accumulate in queue 4, never to be used again. Why not combine queues 1 and 4 and re-cycle the Customers?

The technique of using generators is very common. It is worth emphasizing that generators are ordinary activities. The appropriate entities are taken from their source queues and held for the specified time before being released. This means that to model a particular arrival pattern, the time for the generate activity is the time between arrivals—the inter-arrival time.

Take as an example trains arriving at a station. If they arrive at 07.30, 07.45, 07.55, 08.12, 08.18, 08.29, 08,56 . . . . . . , and if we start simulating at 0.700, the times for the 'generate trains' activity come from a timetable (see Chapter 3) with entries 30, 15, 10, 17, 6, 11, 27 . . . . . . , assuming the time units to be minutes.

As with the time for any activity it is better where possible to use observed data for a 'generate' activity, and to compile a distribution or timetable, rather than assume statistical distributions.

However, in many cases it is known or assumed that a number of entities arrive randomly during a period of time—for example, 40 vehicles per hour arrive at a garage for petrol, or 10 patients per hour arrive at a hospital casualty department for treatment. If they do arrive randomly, the inter-arrival time of such entities can be assumed to follow a negative exponential distribution, with an appropriate rate of arrival. A number of these distributions have been plotted for various arrival rates and can be found in Appendix 2 together with details of how to use them. An example of their use is given in Exercise 4.8.

---

**Format details**

Activity duration—constant and data field

The duration of an activity can include a constant time and a data field time. The data field component is either a sample from a distribution or the next value from a timetable. The methods of constructing distributions and timetables are given in Chapter 3.

Distributions and timetables are numbered consecutively from 1 upwards and this number is entered on the activity format. In order to distinguish between a distribution and timetable, the letter D or T can be written in front of the data field number.

In choosing the time units remember that the times are rounded to the nearest integer.

---

EXERCISE 5.5
(a) If an activity has a timetable with the five values 18, 6, 20, 18, 2, what are the activity times on the first 12 occasions?
(b) Plot the distribution for the 'cut hair' activity at the barber's shop (see Fig. 5.7). What are the first six observations using random numbers from Table 1 in Appendix 1?
(c) Draw a flow diagram of a single-runway airport. Aircraft are not given permission to land until the runway is clear. Aircraft waiting to take off must also wait until the runway is clear. Air traffic control always gives priority to aircraft waiting to land.
(d) What modifications are necessary to the diagram if there are two runways, and
    (i) either is used for taking off or landing;
    (ii) one is used for taking off and the other for landing?

## Restricting the size of a queue

We have seen in this chapter how to limit the number of entities in part of a model by introducing an entity to represent the scarce resource. However, if we wish to restrict the length of a single queue it may be more convenient to specify a queue size limit. In doing this we should make provision for subsequent arrivals if the queue becomes full, by specifying an alternative destination queue for the entities.

If we return to the barber's shop example we can now include the restriction that the shop has room for only four Customers to wait for a haircut. If Customers arrive and find that the shop is full, they leave immediately and their custom is lost.

A model of this is shown in Fig. 5.8, where the 'wait haircut' queue (Q2) is restricted to four entities and an alternative queue is specified in the 'generate' activity (A1). If the barber's shop is full, the Customer goes back to the outside world.

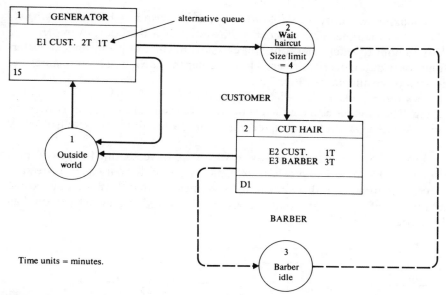

Time units = minutes.

**Figure 5.8**

---

### Format details

Queue restriction

The number of entities in a queue can be restricted by specifying a *queue size limit* on the queue format. However, there is no need to specify a limit if the size is automatically limited by the number of entities in the model—which is usually the case.

Alternative destination queue

If a queue size is limited, entities which are normally sent to the queue can be sent to an alternative queue by entering the alternative queue number and position in the Alt Queue No. and Alt Queue Pos. column. As with the destination queue, the position can be the head or the tail (H or T).

If a queue size limit is specified and no alternative queue is given, entities are put into the restricted queue, even if this violates the limit.

---

## Entities available for intermittent periods

There are situations where resources are available only during certain periods of time. Examples of these are:

— men available for work;
— doctors treating patients during surgery hours;
— shops open for business or deliveries;
— ships entering a port during high water.

We model these by making an entity available for a specified period and then blocking its availability for the rest of the time. This concept is illustrated by a tidal port example.

A Ship takes half an hour to enter a harbour, but can start to enter only during high water, which lasts for four hours out of every thirteen. Thus to enter the harbour a Ship requires the Tide, which is not always available (see Fig. 5.9).

When the tide goes out we place a Block at the head of queue 3 preventing the 'enter' activity from starting. The Block is removed when the tide comes in and ships can now enter. In this way the Block acts as a shutter on queue 3, being up for four hours out of every thirteen.

This is the first example we have come across in which we have specified the head of a queue. It is worth noting that in all the previous examples we could have used 'H' instead of 'E' as the source queue position—but there are dangers. Remember that there can only be one entity at the head (or tail) of a queue and that entities are not moved into an activity until all the conditions have been satisfied.

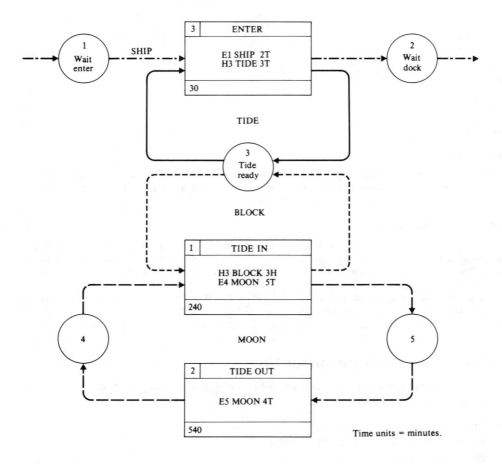

**Figure 5.9**

## Measuring waiting time

In most models, we want to know how long entities wait in certain parts of the system. These times can help us to decide whether a modification is acceptable or not. For example we can measure the effect that:

- an appointments system has on the time patients wait for treatment;
- the mechanical handling of goods has on the time lorries spend at a warehouse;
- an additional mechanic has on the time that machines wait for repair.

Waiting times are measured with clocks. Each entity has up to 20 clocks, referred to by the letters ABCDFGJKLMNPQRSUVWXY. (The reason for omitting EHTIO and Z is given in Chapter 7, Ordered queues.)

We switch on a clock by specifying the clock letter followed by a plus sign (e.g., A+), and switch it off by the clock letter followed by a minus sign (e.g., A−). If we record the times when an entity clock is switched on and when it is switched off, the difference will give the time the entity has been in that part of the system.

Clocks can be switched on or off at the start or end of any activity. Figure 5.10 shows part of the life cycle of Patients in the casualty department of a hospital. Patients are checked in at reception, seen by a doctor and then treated. The A-clock of the patient measures how long they wait to be seen by the doctor and the B-clock measures how long they wait for treatment.

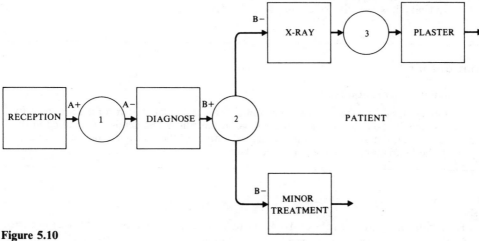

**Figure 5.10**

---

### Format details

Clock switches

Clocks switched on or off at the beginning of an activity are entered in the In Switch column to the left of the entity name, and clocks switched on or off at the end of an activity are entered in the Out Switch column to the right of the entity name.

EXERCISE 5.6

(a) In Fig. 5.7, how would you measure the time customers wait for a haircut, and the amount of time the barber is idle?
(b) In Fig. 5.7, how would you measure the total time a customer spends in the barber's shop?

## Relating activity duration to some property of an entity—correlation term

On occasions the duration of an activity is affected by the time one of the entities spends in some part of the system. For example, the longer we have to wait for a pint of beer on a hot day, the faster we drink it when it arrives.

We model such a situation by first measuring the waiting time with a clock, and then using this time to influence the duration of an activity. We illustrate this by the following example.

A gang of men normally work an eight-hour day. They do jobs which last 1–2 hours each (distribution 1). If they are still working at the end of their normal day, they complete the job during overtime before going home. They arrive for work at the same start time each day.

In Fig. 5.11 the Shift moves round its life cycle every 24 hours. The A-clock of Shift measures the extent of the overtime, and the amount of time off work is 16 hours less the overtime. This is included in the model by using the correlation term in activity 2. Note that the 'off shift' activity has priority over the 'work' activity.

---

### Format details

Activity duration—correlation term

The correlation component of the activity duration uses the last clock time recorded for an entity engaged in the activity, and is taken as a percentage of that time. The details are entered in the areas marked Percent, Att and Entity name. If several entities of the specified type are used in the activity, then the first is taken for the correlation term.

---

EXERCISE 5.7

Patients arrive randomly at the rate of 10 an hour at a doctor's surgery. The waiting room opens half-an-hour before the doctor arrives and is open for three hours in total. All patients that enter the waiting room are treated. Draw a flow diagram to describe this logic and show how you would measure the amount of time worked by the doctor. Plot the distribution of patient inter-arrival times from the graphs given in Appendix 2.

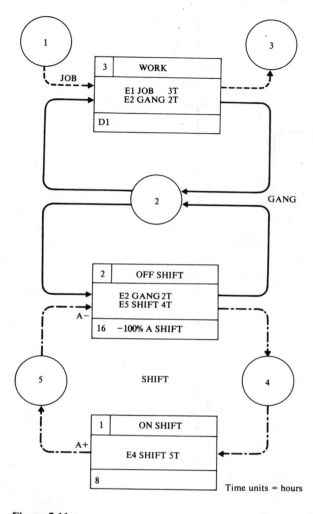

**Figure 5.11**

## Entities with a fixed life cycle

We have already seen some entities which have a fixed life cycle. The Shift in Fig. 5.11 must go through its activities in the order 'on shift', 'off shift', 'on shift'. On the other hand, the gang does not go through its activities in any predetermined order. It will go into the 'work' activity a number of times depending on the arrival pattern of the jobs and then into the 'off shift' activity.

We now look at another example, this time concerning the movements of a lift in a pit shaft. A lift, capable of carrying one wagon, moves up and down a pit shaft taking full wagons from the bottom to the top, and empty wagons from the top to the bottom, as shown in Fig. 5.12.

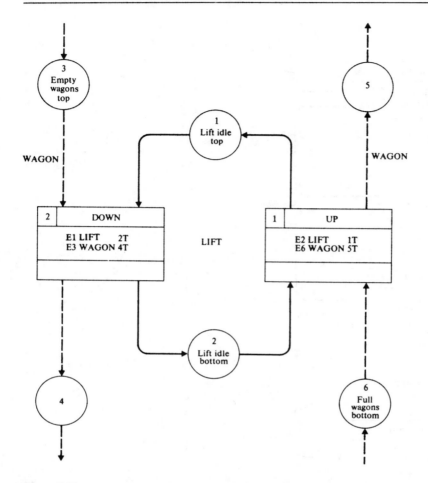

**Figure 5.12**

The Lift can only travel up when there is a Wagon at the bottom and travel down when there is a Wagon at the top. How might we modify the logic to allow the Lift to move down if there is no Wagon at the top, but there is one at the bottom? You may like to consider ways of doing this before reading the next section.

## Alternative conditions, non-compulsory conditions and condition sets

Sometimes we need to specify a number of conditions as alternatives. In the lift example we want to allow the Lift to travel down to pick up a full Wagon if there is no empty Wagon at the top. Thus to move down there must be an empty Wagon at the top, or alternatively, a full Wagon at the bottom. Figure 5.13 shows this, together with the case where the Lift can travel up to pick up an empty Wagon if there is no full Wagon at the bottom.

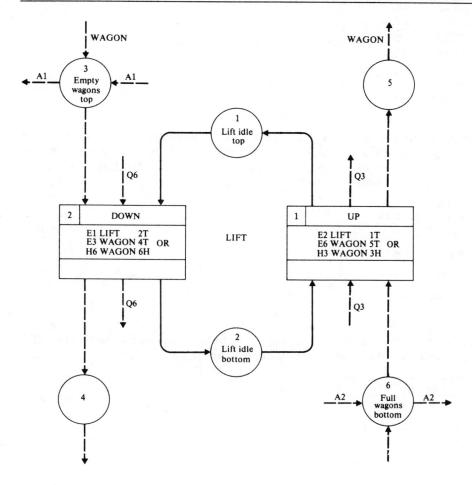

**Figure 5.13**

The conditions of the 'down' activity say that in order to start there must be a Lift in queue 1 *and* a Wagon in queue 3 *or* a Wagon in queue 6. If a Wagon is taken from queue 6 it is put back to the head of queue 6 when the activity ends because, of course, physically it does not move.

It should be noted that the order in which the alternatives are listed implies a preference. In this example to move down we take an empty Wagon at the top in preference to a full Wagon from the bottom.

In some circumstances an entity is used in an activity only if one is available. Its absence does not cause the activity to fail. Figure 5.14 shows an activity which moves a Pallet from queue 7 to queue 10. It starts whether the Pallet is loaded with a Part or not, i.e., the condition 'Part' is non-compulsory (NC).

| 4 | MOVE PALLET | | |
|---|---|---|---|
| E7 | PALLET | 10T | |
| E7 | PART | 10T | NC |
| | | | |

**Figure 5.14**

It is frequently desirable to specify several entities in a set of alternative conditions. In Fig. 5.15 Pallets with Parts are moved to queue 10, but empty Pallets are put to queue 11. The first two conditions in this example form an optional 'condition set' (OE,ES) which is the preferred alternative to the third condition.

| 7 | MOVE PALLET | | |
|---|---|---|---|
| E7 | PALLET | 10T | OS |
| E7 | PART | 10T | ES |
| E7 | PALLET | 11T | |
| | | | |

**Figure 5.15**

The activity in Fig. 5.16 shows a task which could be done by a Man or two Boys. Here, if the Man is not available then the condition set is compulsory (CS,ES).

| 12 | DO JOB | | |
|---|---|---|---|
| E10 | JOB | 7T | |
| E11 | MAN | 11T | OR |
| E12 | BOY | 12T | CS |
| E12 | BOY | 12T | ES |
| | | | |

**Figure 5.16**

## Format details

### Alternative conditions

Normally conditions are taken to be concurrent, but if OR is written in the Alt Cond column the condition in that row and the following condition are treated as alternatives. Any number of alternative conditions can be specified. The order in which alternatives are written implies a preference.

Should a single entity be non-compulsory it is denoted by NC in the Alt Cond column.

Sets of entities can be defined by putting OS (alternative set), CS (compulsory set) or NS (non-compulsory set) in the Alt Cond column of the first condition in the set. The end of a set is denoted by ES.

EXERCISE 5.8

(a) Lorries and vans arrive at a depot and form a queue. Both take the same time to unload and require a man and a fork lift truck. What are the details of an activity entitled 'unload vehicle', if vehicles are unloaded in order of arrival?

(b) You have the unlikely task of simulating a ship sinking. The captain gives the order to abandon ship. Passengers enter the life boat in the order children, women, men. The crew follow and the captain is the last to leave. What are the details of an activity entitled 'enter life boat'?

## Using part of an entity

On occasions an activity requires only part of a physical resource. For example two cranes on a single track, each uses a different part of the track as it moves. In modelling this we must prevent them from colliding.

The approach used in Fig. 5.17 is to divide the track into a number of elements called Track. Each Crane occupies one Track element. Queue 3 contains the empty Tracks to the left of Crane X, queue 4 contains the empty Tracks between the Cranes, and queue 5 contains the empty Tracks to the right of Crane Y. The Cranes are either idle in queues 1 and 2, together with the Tracks which they occupy, or are moving along the track from one element to the next.

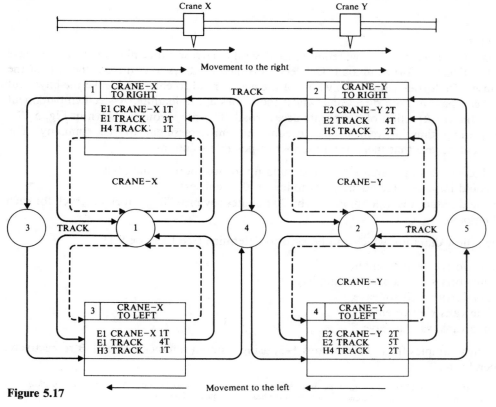

**Figure 5.17**

Movement of Crane X to the right (A1) takes a Track from queue 4 and puts the Track it was occupying into queue 3. Movement of Crane Y to the right (A2) takes a Track from queue 5 and puts the Track it was occupying into queue 4. Activities 3 and 4 control movement to the left reversing the flow of the Tracks. The Cranes are next to one another when queue 4 is empty.

EXERCISE 5.9
What modification would you make to Fig. 5.17 if the cranes must remain at least two track elements apart?

## Summary

We have now developed some basic techniques for modelling simple discrete processes. In Chapter 7 we extend these to model more complex problems involving both discrete and continuous processes.

Before moving on, you are strongly urged to tackle the following three exercises as they incorporate the majority of ideas that have been developed in this chapter. You are asked to produce the flow diagrams which will be used as hand simulation exercises at the end of Chapter 6.

EXERCISE 5.10
*Warehouse unloading bays*    A warehouse situated off a narrow public highway has three bays at which articulated lorries unload. Delivery vans pass the bays to and from the rear of the warehouse. The lorries require the whole of the access road to enter and leave the bays, but the vans can pass in both directions, whilst the lorries are unloading. A steep embankment precludes the construction of a separate access road. The site layout is shown in Fig. 5.18.

The queuing time of vehicles has become an embarrassment to the company. The management believe that there are a number of possible solutions:

- by reducing the stores area they could build up to two more loading bays;
- they could impose some queuing discipline on the vehicles*;
- they could reduce the unloading time by 20 minutes (by providing a fork lift truck for each loading bay).

Draw a flow diagram, which can be used to determine (see Exercise 9.1):

- the time lorries wait to enter;
- the time lorries spend at a loading bay;
- the time lorries wait to leave;
- the time vans wait to enter;
- the time vans wait to leave.

Take twenty samples from distributions 1–3, using random number Tables 1–3 respectively, in Appendix 1.

---

* At the moment, only the vehicle at the head of the queue on the public highway is allowed to enter. An alternative is to allow a van to enter, irrespective of its position in the queue, if a lorry at the head of the queue cannot enter.

*Times*:

| | |
|---|---|
| Articulated lorries entering: | 6 minutes |
| Articulated lorries leaving: | 4 minutes |
| Vans entering: | 2 minutes |
| Vans leaving: | 2 minutes |
| Articulated lorries unloading: | 90–160 minutes (distribution 1) |
| Inter-arrival time of articulated lorries: | 3–55 minutes (distribution 2) |
| Inter-arrival time of vans entering: | 1–30 minutes (distribution 3) |
| Inter-arrival times of vans leaving: | 1–30 minutes (distribution 3) |

*Distributions*:

| Percentage points | | 1 | 5 | 15 | 60 | 90 | 100 |
|---|---|---|---|---|---|---|---|
| Dist. 1, | minutes: | 90 | 95 | 100 | 115 | 130 | 160 |
| Dist. 2, | minutes: | 3 | 5 | 20 | 40 | 50 | 55 |
| Dist. 3, | minutes: | 1 | 3 | 9 | 17 | 25 | 30 |

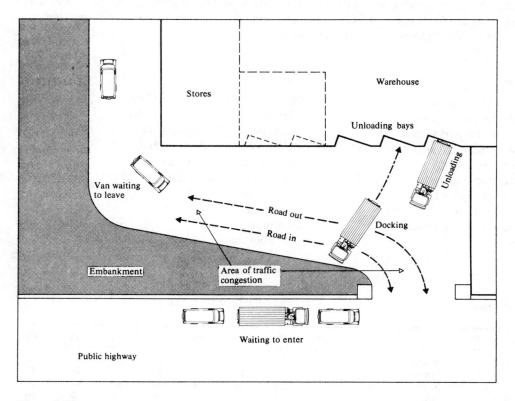

**Figure 5.18**

EXERCISE 5.11

*Tidal port* A tidal port handles three types of ships: tankers, coasters and a passenger ferry. There are berths in the harbour for two tankers, three coasters and the ferry. The coasters and the ferry can enter harbour at any state of the tide, but tankers only in a period two hours either side of high tide.

No ship is allowed to enter unless there is an appropriate berth available; there is ample room for ships to queue outside when necessary.

The tables below give the timings of the various activities. The ferry is due to arrive and depart at the times shown. Any delay caused by waiting to enter or leave harbour is made up either by reducing the time at the berth, or the time away from the harbour. A priority system is in operation for ships waiting to enter or leave the harbour. The passenger ferry takes priority, entering or leaving, over the tankers; the tankers have priority, entering or leaving, over the coasters. Only one ship may enter or leave at a time.

Draw a flow diagram, which can be used to determine (see Exercise 9.2):

– how long each type of ship waits to enter and leave;
– the effect of changing the entering and leaving priority rules;
– the effect of reducing the tanker unloading time by 20 per cent.

Assume that the simulation starts at 05.00 hours at the beginning of high tide. Take twenty samples from distributions 1–4, using random number Tables 1–4 respectively, in Appendix 1. *Note*: Do not forget to define your time units.

*Times*:

| | |
|---|---|
| Ferry arrival times: | 00.30 hr  10.15 hr  17.45 hr |
| Ferry departure times: | 05.00 hr  12.15 hr  19.45 hr |
| Tanker inter-arrival time: | 11–36 hours (distribution 1) |
| Coaster inter-arrival time: | 2–48 hours (distribution 2) |
| Tankers unloading: | 18–50 hours (distribution 3) |
| Coasters unloading: | 1–10 hours (distribution 4) |
| Ferry entering or leaving: | 30 minutes |
| Tankers entering or leaving: | 60 minutes |
| Coasters entering or leaving: | 40 minutes |
| Tides: | One high tide is 13 hours after the last |

*Distributions*:

| Percentage points | | 1 | 5 | 25 | 50 | 75 | 90 | 95 | 100 |
|---|---|---|---|---|---|---|---|---|---|
| Dist. 1, | hours: | 11 | 14 | 16 | 20 | 24 | 28 | 32 | 36 |
| Dist. 2, | hours: | 2 | 3 | 11 | 18 | 24 | 32 | 40 | 48 |
| Dist. 3, | hours: | 18 | 24 | 28 | 34 | 38 | 40 | 42 | 50 |
| Dist. 4, | hours: | 1 | 2 | 4 | 5 | 6 | 7 | 8 | 10 |

EXERCISE 5.12

*Steel mill*   A steel slab production plant has the following processes:

*Melting*   A load of steel, enough for one batch of slabs, is prepared and melted in the furnace.

*Teeming*   The steel is poured into a set of moulds so emptying the furnace.

*Setting*   Ingots are allowed to solidify in the moulds.

*Stripping*   The moulds are broken open and the ingots dislodged by a gang of men.

*Mould cleaning*   The moulds are cleaned and re-assembled by the same gang of men. Cleaning and re-assembly has priority over stripping.

*Loading*   The batch of ingots is loaded into soaking (reheating) pits by a crane.

*Soaking*   The batch of ingots is held at a high temperature in a soaking pit until they are ready for folling. (This time must be increased if the ingots are cool on arrival at the pits.).

*Unloading*   The batch of ingots is unloaded without interruption into the rolling mill.

*Rolling*   The batch of ingots is rolled into slabs.

The following resources are available:
- one furnace;
- seven sets of moulds;
- three setting locations (room for three batches of ingots to form);
- one gang of men (who do both stripping and mould cleaning);
- two cranes (which can both do loading and unloading);
- ten soaking pits;
- one rolling mill.

The performance of the resources cannot be improved, but their numbers can be changed to increase throughput. It is possible to change the number of moulds, setting locations, gangs of men and cranes. Draw a flow diagram which can be used (see Exercise 9.3) to examine the utilization of resources and ways of overcoming bottlenecks. Take 20 samples from distributions 1 and 2, using random number Tables 1 and 2 respectively in Appendix 1.

*Times*:

| | |
|---|---|
| Melting: | 45–85 minutes (distribution 1) |
| Teeming: | 10 minutes |
| Setting: | 75 minutes |
| Stripping: | 6–19 minutes (distribution 2) |
| Mould cleaning: | 10 minutes |
| Loading: | 18 minutes |
| Soaking: | 120 minutes + cooling time, where cooling time is the time taken by the batch of ingots from teeming to be ready to soak. |
| Unloading: | 18 minutes |
| Rolling: | 45 minutes |

*Distributions*:

| Percentage points | | 1 | 5 | 10 | 20 | 40 | 60 | 80 | 90 | 95 | 100 |
|---|---|---|---|---|---|---|---|---|---|---|---|
| Dist. 1, | minutes: | 45 | 48 | 53 | 58 | 63 | 67 | 73 | 79 | 83 | 85 |
| Dist. 2, | minutes: | 6 | 8 | 9 | 10 | 11 | 12 | 13 | 15 | 16 | 19 |

## Solutions to exercises

SOLUTION 5.1

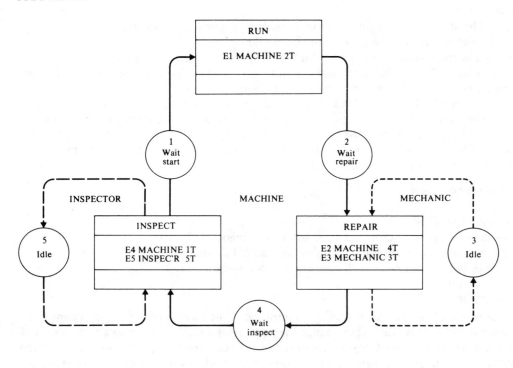

SOLUTION 5.2
(a) See diagram on page 97.
(b) As for (a) above but with 13 'run' activities and 3 'repair' activities.
(c) There are two possible solutions. The first is shown in diagram on page 97. In the 'repair' activity the machines are taken from the tail of queue 2 (i.e., source queue position is T). The second solution is to put the machine to the head of queue 2 in the 'run' activity, and to take the machine from the head of queue 2 in the 'repair' activity.

SOLUTION 5.3
Modifications are as follows:

- 'reconnect' has lower activity number than 'disconnect';
- 'pull out' has lower activity number than 'put back';
- 'remove fittings' has lower activity number than 'replace fittings';
- there are two 'repair' activities in addition to the two mechanics.

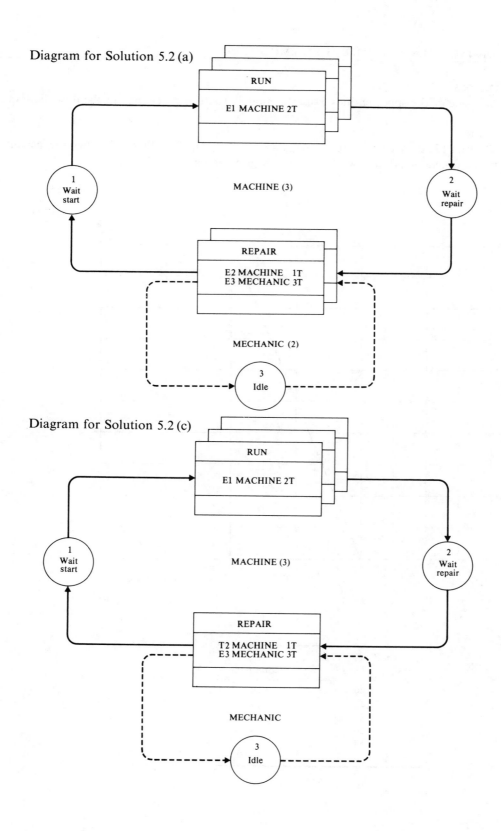

Diagram for Solution 5.2 (a)

RUN

E1 MACHINE 2T

MACHINE (3)

1
Wait
start

2
Wait
repair

REPAIR

E2 MACHINE   1T
E3 MECHANIC 3T

MECHANIC (2)

3
Idle

Diagram for Solution 5.2 (c)

RUN

E1 MACHINE 2T

MACHINE (3)

1
Wait
start

2
Wait
repair

REPAIR

T2 MACHINE   1T
E3 MECHANIC 3T

MECHANIC

3
Idle

SOLUTION 5.4

Remove one of the space entities from the model. There is no change to the flow diagram.

SOLUTION 5.5

(a) The first 12 activity times are: 18, 6, 20, 18, 2, 18, 6, 20, 18, 2, 18, 6; i.e., when the last entry in the timetable is used, we start at the beginning again.

(b)

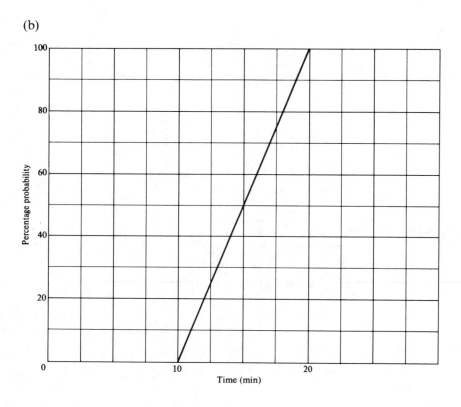

| Random number (Table 1) | Sample |
|---|---|
| 89 | 19 |
| 42 | 14 |
| 85 | 19 |
| 26 | 13 |
| 53 | 15 |
| 66 | 17 |

(c)

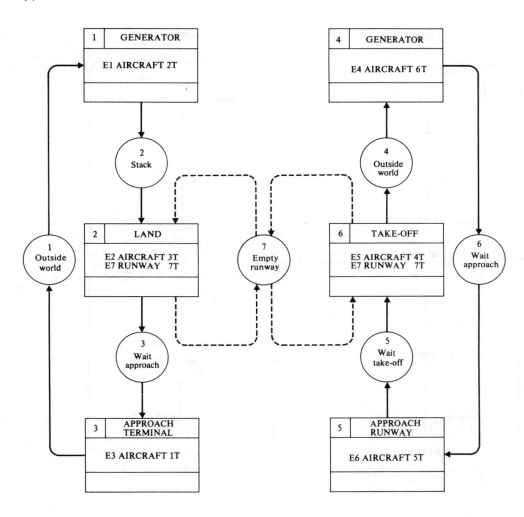

Because we are only modelling the runway, we are not interested in what happens to aircraft before joining the stack or at the terminal—hence the two generators. Note that the 'land' activity (A2) has priority over the take-off activity (A6).

(d) (i) We need two 'land', two 'take-off' activities, and two runways in queue 7.

    (ii) See diagram on page 100. Because the two runways are used for different purposes, we really have two models here.

Diagram for Solution 5.5 (d)

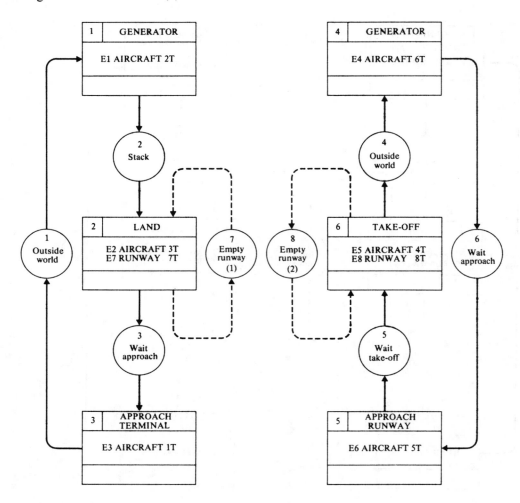

SOLUTION 5.6

(a) See diagram on page 101.
   The A-clock of Cust is switched on when he enters the shop and off when his haircut begins. The A-clock of Barber is switched on when he finishes a hair cut and off when he starts the next haircut.
(b) To measure the total time a customer spends in the barber's shop, switch the A-clock of Cust off at the end of the 'cut hair' activity instead of at the beginning.

## Diagram for Solution 5.6 (a)

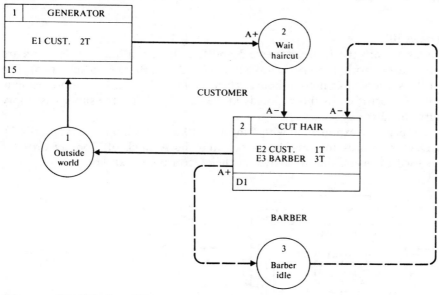

## Diagram for Solution 5.7

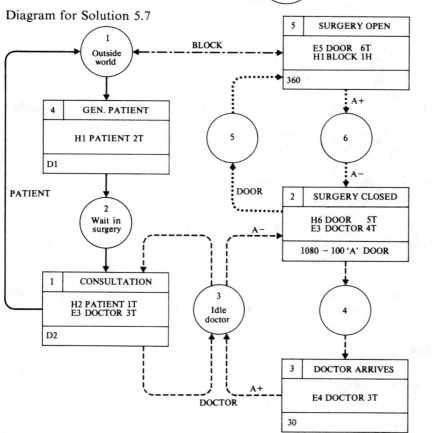

SOLUTION 5.7

See diagram on page 101.

The simulation starts with the Door in queue 5 and the Doctor in queue 4. Patients are generated from the outside world for a period of 3 hours (while the Block is in activity 5). The Doctor arrives at the surgery after half-an-hour. When the Door is closed, no more patients are generated, but the Doctor treats those already in the surgery. When the surgery is empty he leaves, to return the next day.

Distribution 1 is a negative exponential with a mean of 10 patients/hour (see Appendix 2). The A-clock of Doctor records the time he works, and the A-clock of Door records his overtime which is used to ensure that he arrives at the correct time next day.

SOLUTION 5.8

(a)

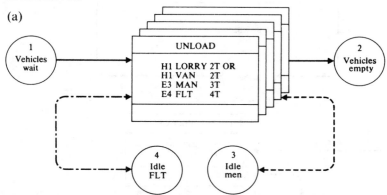

The 'unload' activity requires the Lorry or Van at the head of queue 1 together with a Man and a Fork lift truck.

(b)

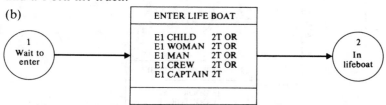

Because the source queue position is 'E', a Child will be put into the lifeboat before a Woman, irrespective of their positions in queue 1.

SOLUTION 5.9

To ensure that the cranes are never closer than the distance of two track elements, simply remove two elements from queue 4 at the beginning of the simulation.

SOLUTION 5.10

See diagram on page 103.

SOLUTION 5.11

See diagram on pages 104 and 105.

SOLUTION 5.12

See diagram on page 106.

Diagram for Solution 5.10

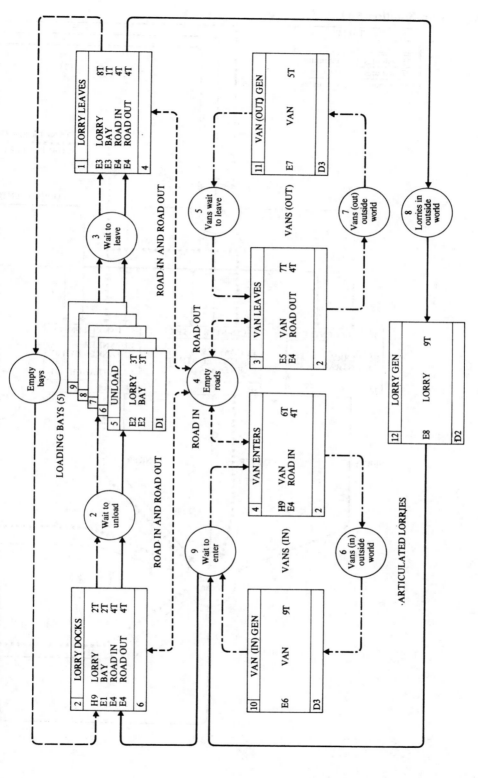

Diagram for Solution 5.11

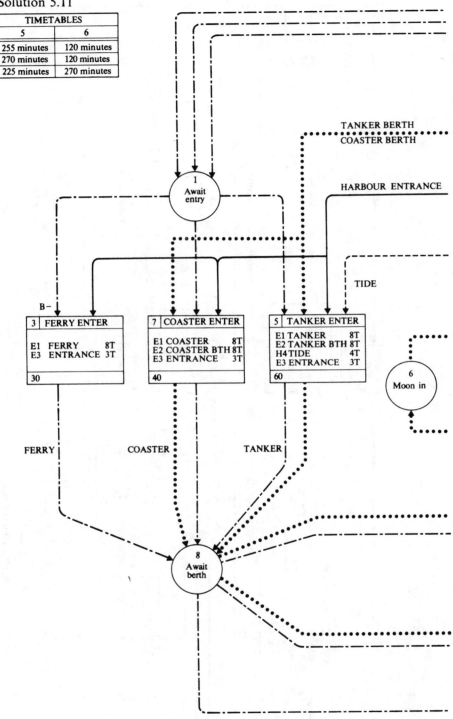

| TIMETABLES | |
|---|---|
| 5 | 6 |
| 255 minutes | 120 minutes |
| 270 minutes | 120 minutes |
| 225 minutes | 270 minutes |

TANKER BERTH

COASTER BERTH

HARBOUR ENTRANCE

1
Await
entry

TIDE

B−

| 3 | FERRY ENTER |
|---|---|
| E1 FERRY 8T | |
| E3 ENTRANCE 3T | |
| 30 | |

| 7 | COASTER ENTER |
|---|---|
| E1 COASTER 8T | |
| E2 COASTER BTH 8T | |
| E3 ENTRANCE 3T | |
| 40 | |

| 5 | TANKER ENTER |
|---|---|
| E1 TANKER 8T | |
| E2 TANKER BTH 8T | |
| H4 TIDE 4T | |
| E3 ENTRANCE 3T | |
| 60 | |

6
Moon in

FERRY

COASTER

TANKER

8
Await
berth

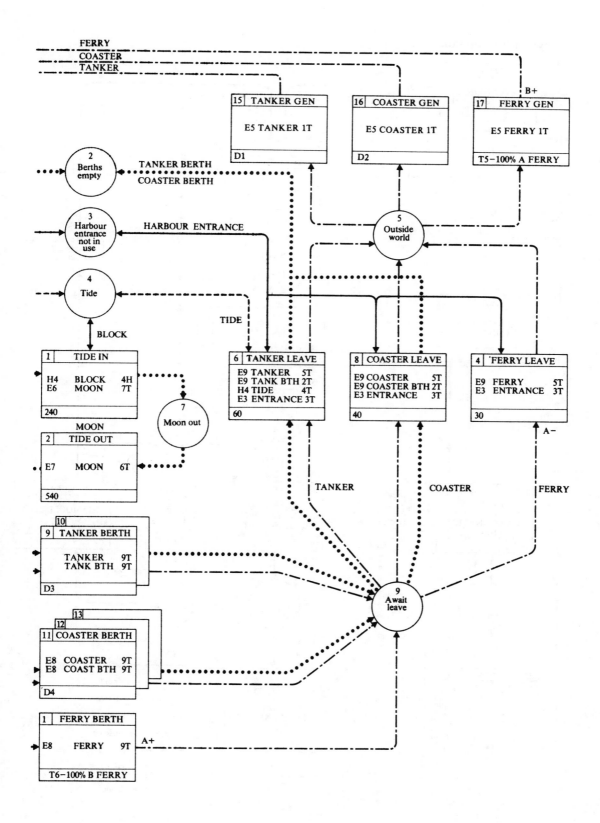

Diagram for Solution 5.12

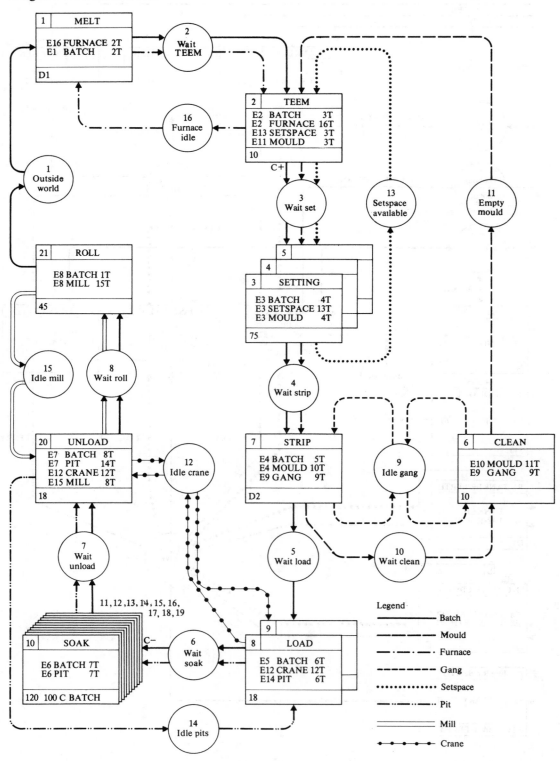

# 6.

## Hand simulating a formal model

We have seen in Chapters 3 and 4 how to hand simulate informal models. In this chapter we describe a similar approach for formal models, and illustrate the method using the machine maintenance model described in Fig. 5.4. We must first complete the flow diagram, however, by declaring the entities used and specifying the initial state of the model.

### Entity description

We define the entities on an Entity Description format by stating for each entity how many there are (number of members) and the number of clocks (attributes) used. Figure 6.1 shows one mechanic with one clock and three machines with one clock each.

| P-E ENTITY DESCRIPTION | | |
|---|---|---|
| ENTITY NAME | NUMBER OF MEMBERS | No OF ATTS |
| MECHANIC | 1 | 1 |
| MACHINE | 3 | 1 |
| | | |
| | | |
| | | |
| | | |
| | | |
| | | |
| | | |

**Figure 6.1**

### Initial conditions

We define the initial state of the model by specifying where the entities start. They must start in queues and these are entered on an Initial Conditions format as illustrated in Fig. 6.2. This shows the mechanic starting in queue 3, and the machines in queue 1.

| **P·E** INITIAL CONDITIONS | | | |
|---|---|---|---|
| ENTITY NAME | No OF MEMBERS ALLOCATED | QUEUE NUMBER | TRACE |
| M E C H A N I C | 1 | 3 | |
| M A C H I N E | 3 | 1 | |
| | | | |
| | | | |
| | | | |
| | | | |
| | | | |
| | | | |
| | | | |

**Figure 6.2**

Care should be taken to ensure that all entities are allocated. At the start of the simulation, they are put into the queues in the order given on the Initial Conditions format. Thus a queue of mixed entities can be produced by listing them in the required order. For example if, at the start of a traffic simulation, the queue of vehicles waiting at a set of traffic lights (queue 4) consists of three cars, a bus, a lorry, five cars and a bus, the Initial Conditions format is as shown in Fig. 6.3.

| **P·E** INITIAL CONDITIONS | | | |
|---|---|---|---|
| ENTITY NAME | No OF MEMBERS ALLOCATED | QUEUE NUMBER | TRACE |
| C A R | 3 | 4 | |
| B U S | 1 | 4 | |
| L O R R Y | 1 | 4 | |
| C A R | 5 | 4 | |
| B U S | 1 | 4 | |
| | | | |
| | | | |
| | | | |
| | | | |

**Figure 6.3**

The initial conditions must be logical. For example, if several different entities enter a queue together from an activity, one of each must be present as an initial condition, to ensure that subsequent activities can start. If, in a steel mill model, we wish to start with some steel in a mould, then we must place a steel entity and a mould entity together in the same queue.

# Hand simulation

In Chapter 3 we advanced an informal model through time using the three phases START—TIME—END. Here we use the same approach for a formal model and we show how to collect certain statistics about the model. The rules for hand simulation are described in the following steps:

*Step 1: Preparation*   Entities are represented by coloured counters or cards. The members of each entity type are numbered from 1 upwards, so that they can be recognized individually during the simulation.

*Step 2: Starting position*   We put the entities in their starting queues as specified on the initial conditions format, checking that they can logically exist there.

*Step 3: Record sheet*   We prepare a Simulation Record Sheet, as illustrated in Fig. 6.4. This sheet is used to record the progress of the simulation, and the switching of entity clocks. The clocks being used are entered as shown and the simulation starts with an initial clock time of zero.

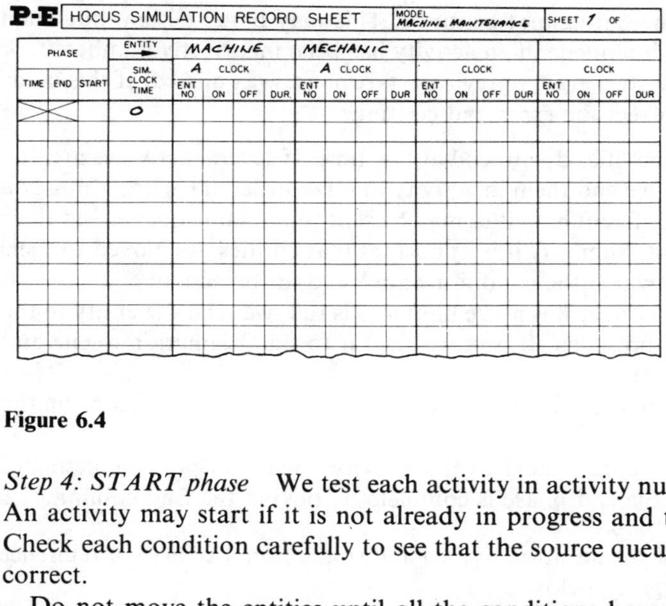

**Figure 6.4**

*Step 4: START phase*   We test each activity in activity number order to see which can start. An activity may start if it is not already in progress and the required entities are available. Check each condition carefully to see that the source queues and positions of the entities are correct.

Do not move the entities until all the conditions have been satisfied. It is easy to move visually an entity from a queue to an activity, but the initial purpose of hand simulation is to check the logic of the model. When an activity can start, move the entities into the activity format.

*Clock switches*   If any clocks are switched at the start of an activity we make an entry on the Simulation Record Sheet, and if appropriate, calculate any waiting time.

*Activity duration*   We calculate the duration of the activity just started from the time data specified at the base of the activity format. The duration is the sum of the three components:

- a constant;
- a value from a data field, which can be either a sample from a distribution or the next value from a timetable. The method of sampling from a distribution is described in Chapter 3. Any set of random number tables can be used but the ones given in Appendix 1 are those generated by the HOCUS program and should be used if we want the hand and computer simulations to produce identical results;
- a correlation term. This refers to the last duration time recorded on the Simulation Record Sheet for the specified entity member engaged in the activity (see Chapter 5).

*End time*    The time when the activity will end is the sum of the current clock time and the activity duration. We write this by the side of the activity format. When all possible activities have been started we tick the Start column of the Simulation Record Sheet to indicate that the start phase has been completed.

*Step 5: TIME phase*    We now look at the activities in progress and select the one (or ones) with the earliest end time. We advance the simulation clock to this time, by writing the time in the Sim Clock Time column and complete the time phase by ticking the Time column.

If no activities are in progress then the model has gone 'passive'. This means that the simulation has reached a stage where it cannot continue. This may be by design, but often happens when a source or destination queue in an activity has been incorrectly numbered, or when an activity which could have started in a previous start phase was missed. If this is the case we must retrace our steps, correct the error and continue.

*Step 6: END phase*    We end the activities due to end at this time. If several activities are due to end simultaneously at this time, we end them in activity number order. This order must be strictly observed, as entities from different activities may be sent to the same queue, and their relative positions may be important. Similarly it is important that entities are moved to their destination queues in the order in which the conditions are listed in the activity.

*Alternative queues*    If a destination queue has a size limit and is full, we send the entity to the alternative queue, if one has been provided. If not, we send it to the destination queue and note that the limit has been exceeded.

*Clock switches*    If any clocks are switched at the end of an activity we make an entry on the Simulation Record Sheet.

Finally we delete the end time recorded next to the activity. When all possible activities have been ended we indicate that the end phase is complete by ticking the End column.

SUMMARY    We repeat steps 4–6 for the duration of the hand simulation. For ease of reference a summary of the three phases is given below.

*Start phase*
Test activities in numerical order.
For each activity that can start:
- move entities into activity, checking source queue number and position;
- record any clock switches tripped on entry;
- calculate activity duration;
- write end time (clock time + activity duration) beside activity.
Tick Start column.

*Time phase*
Select activity with earliest end time.
Write this time in Sim Clock column.
Tick Time column.

*End phase*
End all activities with this end time.
For each activity that can end:
– check destination and alternative queues (note if queue size limit exceeded);
– move entities to destination queue;
– record any clock switches tripped on leaving;
– delete end time written beside activity.
Tick End column.

*Example—Machine maintenance*  We illustrate the formal approach to hand simulation using the machine maintenance model described in Fig. 5.4. The flow diagram is shown in Fig. 6.5, and we will follow the steps given earlier in this chapter, recording the idle time of the mechanic, and the time that machines wait for repair. The times for repair and running are given in Exercises 3.4 and 3.5, and are as follows:

*Distribution 1—Repair times*

| Percentage points: | | | | | | | | | | | | | |
|---|---|---|---|---|---|---|---|---|---|---|---|---|---|
| 1 | 1 | 4 | 12 | 24 | 40 | 52 | 71 | 79 | 85 | 92 | 97 | 100 | |
| Minutes: | | | | | | | | | | | | | |
| 10 | 20 | 30 | 40 | 50 | 60 | 70 | 80 | 90 | 100 | 110 | 120 | 130 | |

*Distribution 2—Running times*

| Percentage points: | | | | | | | | | | | | | | |
|---|---|---|---|---|---|---|---|---|---|---|---|---|---|---|
| 1 | 4 | 13 | 29 | 44 | 58 | 68 | 76 | 83 | 88 | 92 | 96 | 98 | 99 | 100 |
| Minutes: | | | | | | | | | | | | | | |
| 50 | 100 | 150 | 200 | 250 | 300 | 350 | 400 | 450 | 500 | 550 | 600 | 650 | 700 | 750 |

When a model includes distributions it is easier to take a number of samples before we begin hand simulation. The first 20 samples from each distribution are as follows (see Exercise 3.6):

| Distribution 1 | | Distribution 2 | |
|---|---|---|---|
| Random number (Table 1) | Repair time (minutes) | Random number (Table 2) | Running time (minutes) |
| 89 | 106 | 43 | 247 |
| 42 | 62 | 78 | 414 |
| 85 | 100 | 84 | 460 |
| 26 | 51 | 33 | 213 |
| 53 | 71 | 72 | 375 |
| 66 | 77 | 91 | 538 |
| 49 | 68 | 44 | 250 |
| 13 | 41 | 2 | 75 |
| 97 | 120 | 56 | 293 |
| 13 | 41 | 38 | 230 |
| 20 | 47 | 40 | 237 |
| 21 | 48 | 33 | 213 |
| 5 | 31 | 4 | 100 |
| 5 | 31 | 69 | 356 |
| 34 | 56 | 89 | 513 |
| 60 | 74 | 50 | 271 |
| 70 | 79 | 67 | 345 |
| 49 | 68 | 71 | 369 |
| 68 | 78 | 33 | 213 |
| 82 | 95 | 67 | 345 |
| 43 | 63 | 12 | 144 |
| 52 | 70 | 69 | 356 |
| 61 | 75 | 62 | 320 |
| 93 | 112 | 40 | 237 |
| 33 | 56 | 12 | 144 |

We can now proceed with the hand simulation:

*Step 1* Select coloured counters to represent the Mechanic and the three Machines. Number the Machines 1, 2 and 3.

*Step 2* Put the Mechanic in queue 3 and the three Machines in queue 1.

*Step 3* Prepare a Simulation Record Sheet (see Fig. 6.4). The completed Simulation Record Sheet is given in Fig. 6.6.

*Step 4* We now simulate using the three phases START—TIME—END.

*START phase* Test each activity in number order to see if it can start.

– Activity 1   Run (1).

        Is there a Machine in queue 1?—Yes (use Machine 1).

        All conditions satisfied so activity can start.

        Any clock switches at start of activity?—No.

        When will activity end—At time 0 + 247 = 247—write 247 by side of activty.

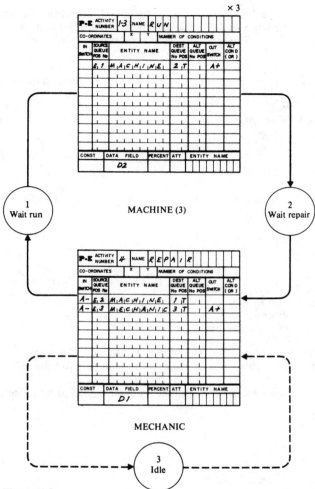

Figure 6.5

– Activity 2   Run (2).
              Is there a Machine in queue 1?—Yes (use Machine 2).
              All conditions satisfied so activity can start.
              Any clock switches at start of activity?—No.
              When will activity end?—At time 0 + 414 = 414—write 414 by side of activity.
– Activity 3   Run (3).
              Is there a Machine in queue 1?—Yes (use Machine 3).
              All conditions satisfied so activity can start.
              Any clock switches at start of activity?—No.
              When will activity end?—At time 0 + 460 = 460—write 460 by side of activity.
– Activity 4   Repair.
              Is there a Machine in queue 2?—No.
              Activity cannot start.
All activities have been tested and started where possible, so we tick the Start column next to time 0.

*TIME phase*   Nothing will change in the model until an activity comes to an end. Therefore, we can advance the clock to the earliest activity end time which is 247—that of activity 1|(Run 1). Enter 247 in the next row of the Sim Clock Time column. Tick the Time column in the same row to indicate that we have advanced the clock.

*END phase*   We end all activities which have time 247 and send the entities to their destination queues.
- Activity 1   Send Machine 1 to queue 2.
             Switch A-clock of Machine 1 On.
             Cross out the time by the side of activity.
- Activity 2   In progress until time 414.
- Activity 3   In progress until time 460.
- Activity 4   Not in progress.
All possible activities have been ended, so tick the End column.

*START phase*   We now return to the Start phase at time 247. Test each activity in number order.
- Activity 1   Run (1).
             Is there a Machine in queue 1?—No.
             Activity cannot start.
- Activity 2   In progress until time 414.
- Activity 3   In progress until time 460.
- Activity 4   Repair.
             Is there a Machine in queue 2?—Yes (use Machine 1).
             Is there a Mechanic in queue 3?—Yes.
             All conditions satisfied so activity can start.
             Switch A-clock of Machine 1 Off—Waiting time was 0 (247 − 247).
             Switch A-clock of Mechanic Off—Waiting time was 247 (247 − 0).
             When will activity end?—At time 247 + 106 = 353—Write 353 by side of activity.
All activities have been tested and started where possible, so tick the Start column next to time 247.

*TIME phase*   Earliest end time is 353 (activity 4). Advance clock time by entering 353 in Sim Clock Time column and tick the Time column.

*END phase*   End all activities with time 353.
- Activity 1   Not in progress.
- Activity 2   In progress until time 414.
- Activity 3   In progress until time 460.
- Activity 4   Send Machine 1 to queue 1 and Mechanic to queue 3.
             Switch A-clock of Mechanic On.
             Cross out time 353.
Tick the End column.

*START phase*   Start all activities possible at time 353.
- Activity 1   Is there a Machine in queue 1?—Yes (use Machine 1).
             All conditions satisfied so activity can start.
             When will activity end?—At time 353 + 213 = 566—Write 566 by side of activity (under crossed out 247).
- Activity 2   In progress until time 414.
- Activity 3   In progress until time 460.
- Activity 4   Is there a Machine in queue 2?—No.
             Activity cannot start.
Tick the Start column at time 353.

*TIME phase*   Activity 2 is earliest to finish with time 414 so advance clock to this time. Enter 414 in the Sim Clock Time column and tick the Time column.

*END phase*  End all activities possible.
- Activity 1  In progress until time 566.
- Activity 2  Send Machine 2 to queue 2.
             Switch A-clock of Machine 2 On.
             Cross out 414 by side of activity.
- Activity 3  In progress until time 460.
- Activity 4  Not in progress.
Tick the End column.

*START phase*  Start all activities possible at time 414.
- Activity 1  In progress until time 566.
- Activity 2  Is there a Machine in queue 1?—No.
             Activity cannot start.
- Activity 3  In progress until time 460.
- Activity 4  Is there a Machine in queue 2?—Yes (Machine 2).
             Is there a Mechanic in queue 3?—Yes.
             All conditions satisfied so activity can start.
             Switch A-clock of Machine 2 Off—Waiting time was 0 (414 − 414).
             Switch A-clock of Mechanic Off—Waiting time was 61 (414 − 353).
             When will activity end?—At time 414 + 62 = 476—Write 476 by side of activity (under
                crossed out 353).
Tick the Start column.

*TIME phase*  Activity 3 will end at time 460. We enter this in the Sim Clock Time column and tick the
Time column.

*END phase*  End all activities possible.
- Activity 1  In progress until time 566.
- Activity 2  Not in progress.
- Activity 3  Send Machine 3 to queue 2.
             Switch A-clock of Machine 3 On.
             Cross out 460 by side of activity.
- Activity 4  In progress until time 476.
Tick the End column.

*START phase*  Start all activities possible.
- Activity 1  In progress until time 566.
- Activity 2  Is there a Machine in queue 1?—No.
             Activity cannot start.
- Activity 3  Is there a Machine in queue 1?—No.
             Activity cannot start.
- Activity 4  In progress until time 476.
Although no activities can start, tick the Start column. It often happens that when an activity ends no
other activities can start until later activities come to an end so we just keep advancing the clock.

*TIME phase*  Advance clock to earliest end time of 476 and tick the Time column.

*END phase*
- Activity 1  In progress until time 566.
- Activity 2  Not in progress.
- Activity 3  Not in progress.
- Activity 4  Send Machine 2 and Mechanic to destination queues.
             Switch A-clock of Mechanic On.
Tick the End column.

*START phase*
- Activity 1  In progress until time 566.

– Activity 2   End time = 476 + 375 = 851.
– Activity 3   Cannot start.
– Activity 4   End time = 476 + 100 = 576.
                Switch A-clock of Machine 3 Off—Waiting time = 16 (476 − 460).
                Switch A-clock of Mechanic Off—Waiting time = 0 (476 − 476).
Tick the Start column.

*TIME phase*   Advance clock to earliest time (566) and tick the Time column.

*END phase*
– Activity 1   Send Machine 1 to queue 2.
                Switch A-clock of Machine 1 On.
– Activity 2   In progress until time 851.
– Activity 3   Not in progress.
– Activity 4   In progress until time 576.
Tick the End column.

*START phase*
– Activity 1   Cannot start.
– Activity 2   In progress.
– Activity 3   Cannot start.
– Activity 4   In progress.
Tick the Start column.

*TIME phase*   Advance clock to time 576 and tick the Time column.

*END phase*
– Activity 1   Not in progress.
– Activity 2   In progress until time 851.
– Activity 3   Not in progress.
– Activity 4   Send Machine 3 to queue 1 and Mechanic to queue 3.
                Switch A-clock of Mechanic On.
Tick the End column.

*START phase*
– Activity 1   End time = 576 + 538 = 1114.
– Activity 2   In progress until time 851.
– Activity 3   Cannot start.
– Activity 4   End time = 576 + 51 = 627.
                Switch A-clock of Machine 1 Off—Waiting time = 10 (576 − 566).
                Switch A-clock of Mechanic Off—Waiting time = 0 (576 − 576).
Tick the Start column.

*TIME phase*   Advance clock to time 627 and tick Time column.

*END phase*
– Activity 1   In progress until time 1114.
– Activity 2   In progress until time 851.
– Activity 3   Not in progress.
– Activity 4   Send Machine 1 to queue 1 and Mechanic to queue 3.
                Switch A-clock of Mechanic On.

*START phase*
– Activity 1   In progress until time 1114.
– Activity 2   In progress until time 851.
– Activity 3   End time = 627 + 250 = 877.
– Activity 4   Cannot start.
Tick the Start column.

*TIME phase*   Advance clock to time 851 and tick the Time column.

*END phase*
– Activity 1   In progress until time 1114.
– Activity 2   Send Machine 2 to queue 1.
             Switch A-clock of Machine 2 On.
– Activity 3   In progress until time 877.
– Activity 4   Not in progress.
Tick the End column.

*START phase*
– Activity 1   In progress until time 1114.
– Activity 2   Cannot start.
– Activity 3   In progress until time 877.
– Activity 4   End time = 851 + 71 = 922.
             Switch A-clock of Machine 2 Off—Waiting time = 0 (851 − 851).
             Switch A-clock of Mechanic Off—Waiting time = 224 (851 − 627).
Tick the Start column.

*TIME phase*   Advance the clock to time 877 and tick the Time column.

*END phase*
– Activity 1   In progress until time 1114.
– Activity 2   Not in progress.
– Activity 3   Send Machine 1 to queue 2.
             Switch A-clock of Machine 1 On.
– Activity 4   In progress until time 922.
Tick the End column.

*START phase*
– Activity 1   In progress until time 1114.
– Activity 2   Cannot start.
– Activity 3   Cannot start.
– Activity 4   In progress until time 922.
Tick the Start column.

*TIME phase*   Advance the clock to time 922 and tick the Time column.

*END phase*
– Activity 1   In progress until time 1114.
– Activity 2   Not in progress.
– Activity 3   Not in progress.
– Activity 4   Send Machine 2 to queue 1 and Mechanic to queue 3.
             Switch A-clock of Mechanic On.
Tick the End column.

*START phase*
– Activity 1   In progress until time 1114.
– Activity 2   End time = 922 + 75 = 997.
– Activity 3   Cannot start.
– Activity 4   End time = 922 + 77 = 999.
             Switch A-clock of Machine 1 Off—Waiting time = 45.
             Switch A-clock of Mechanic Off—Waiting time = 0.
Tick the Start column.

*TIME phase*   Advance clock to time 997 and tick Time column.

*END phase*
- Activity 1   In progress until time 1114.
- Activity 2   Send Machine 2 to queue 2.
             Switch A-clock of Machine 2 On.
- Activity 3   Not in progress.
- Activity 4   In progress until time 999.
Tick the End column.

*START phase*
- Activity 1   In progress until time 1114.
- Activity 2 . Cannot start.
- Activity 3   Cannot start.
- Activity 4   In progress until time 999.
Tick the Start column.

*TIME phase*   Advance clock to time 999 and tick Time column.

*END phase*
- Activity 1   In progress until time 1114.
- Activity 2   Not in progress.
- Activity 3   Not in progress.
- Activity 4   Send Machine 1 to queue 1 and Mechanic to queue 3.
             Switch A-clock of Mechanic On.
Tick the End column.

*START phase*
- Activity 1   In progress until time 1114.
- Activity 2   End time = 999 + 293 = 1292.
- Activity 3   Cannot start.
- Activity 4   End time = 999 + 68 = 1067.
             Switch A-clock of Machine 2 Off—Waiting time = 2.
             Switch A-clock of Mechanic Off—Waiting time = 0.
Tick the Start column.

*TIME phase*   Advance clock to 1067 and tick the Time column.

*END phase*
- Activity 1   In progress until time 1114.
- Activity 2   In progress until time 1292.
- Activity 3   Not in progress.
- Activity 4   Send Machine 2 to queue 1 and Mechanic to queue 3.
             Switch A-clock of Mechanic On.
Tick the End column.

EXERCISE 6.1
Continue simulating the machine maintenance model until the first event after time 2000, and compare your solution with Fig. 6.6.

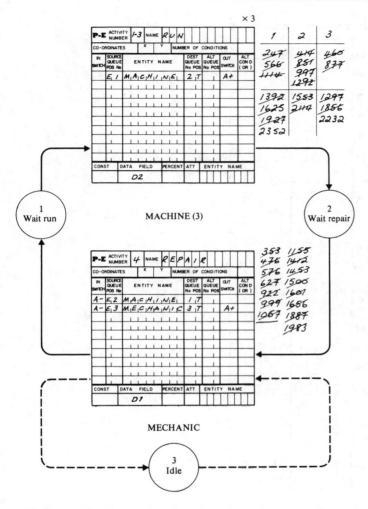

Figure 6.6 (continued overleaf)

# Results from hand simulation

Having hand simulated, we can now analyse the results from the model and the simulation record sheet.

## Histograms

From the record sheet we can produce histograms of the times measured with clocks. We select suitable ranges in which to slot the results, and place each observation in one of the slots to produce a histogram. We can also record the number of observations, the minimum and maximum values, and calculate the average waiting time.

| P·E | HOCUS SIMULATION RECORD SHEET | | MODEL | | | SHEET | OF | |

| PHASE | | | ENTITY SIM. CLOCK TIME | MACHINE A CLOCK | | | | MECHANIC A CLOCK | | | | CLOCK | | | | CLOCK | | | |
|---|---|---|---|---|---|---|---|---|---|---|---|---|---|---|---|---|---|---|---|
| TIME | END | START | | ENT NO | ON | OFF | DUR | ENT NO | ON | OFF | DUR | ENT NO | ON | OFF | DUR | ENT NO | ON | OFF | DUR |
| | | ✓ | 0 | | | | | | | | | | | | | | | | |
| ✓ | ✓ | ✓ | 247 | 1 | ✓ | ✓ | 0 | 1 | | ✓ | 247 | | | | | | | | |
| ✓ | ✓ | ✓ | 353 | | | | | 1 | ✓ | | | | | | | | | | |
| ✓ | ✓ | ✓ | 414 | 2 | ✓ | ✓ | 0 | 1 | | ✓ | 61 | | | | | | | | |
| ✓ | ✓ | ✓ | 460 | 3 | ✓ | | | | | | | | | | | | | | |
| ✓ | ✓ | ✓ | 476 | 3 | | ✓ | 16 | 1 | ✓ | ✓ | 0 | | | | | | | | |
| ✓ | ✓ | ✓ | 566 | 1 | ✓ | | | | | | | | | | | | | | |
| ✓ | ✓ | ✓ | 576 | 1 | | ✓ | 10 | 1 | ✓ | ✓ | 0 | | | | | | | | |
| ✓ | ✓ | ✓ | 627 | | | | | 1 | ✓ | | | | | | | | | | |
| ✓ | ✓ | ✓ | 851 | 2 | ✓ | ✓ | 0 | 1 | | ✓ | 224 | | | | | | | | |
| ✓ | ✓ | ✓ | 877 | 1 | ✓ | | | | | | | | | | | | | | |
| ✓ | ✓ | ✓ | 922 | 1 | | ✓ | 45 | 1 | ✓ | ✓ | 0 | | | | | | | | |
| ✓ | ✓ | ✓ | 997 | 2 | ✓ | | | | | | | | | | | | | | |
| ✓ | ✓ | ✓ | 999 | 2 | | ✓ | 2 | 1 | ✓ | ✓ | 0 | | | | | | | | |
| ✓ | ✓ | | 1067 | | | | | 1 | ✓ | | | | | | | | | | |
| | | | | | | | | | | | | | | | | | | | |
| | | ✓ | 1067 | | | | | | | | | | | | | | | | |
| ✓ | ✓ | ✓ | 1114 | 3 | ✓ | ✓ | 0 | 1 | | ✓ | 47 | | | | | | | | |
| ✓ | ✓ | ✓ | 1155 | | | | | 1 | ✓ | | | | | | | | | | |
| ✓ | ✓ | ✓ | 1292 | 1 | ✓ | ✓ | 0 | 1 | | ✓ | 137 | | | | | | | | |
| ✓ | ✓ | ✓ | 1297 | 2 | ✓ | | | | | | | | | | | | | | |
| ✓ | ✓ | ✓ | 1392 | 3 | ✓ | | | | | | | | | | | | | | |
| ✓ | ✓ | ✓ | 1412 | 2 | | ✓ | 115 | 1 | ✓ | ✓ | 0 | | | | | | | | |
| ✓ | ✓ | ✓ | 1453 | 3 | | ✓ | 61 | 1 | ✓ | ✓ | 0 | | | | | | | | |
| ✓ | ✓ | ✓ | 1500 | | | | | 1 | ✓ | | | | | | | | | | |
| ✓ | ✓ | ✓ | 1553 | 2 | ✓ | ✓ | 0 | 1 | | ✓ | 53 | | | | | | | | |
| ✓ | ✓ | ✓ | 1601 | | | | | 1 | ✓ | | | | | | | | | | |
| ✓ | ✓ | ✓ | 1625 | 1 | ✓ | ✓ | 0 | 1 | | ✓ | 24 | | | | | | | | |
| ✓ | ✓ | ✓ | 1656 | | | | | 1 | ✓ | | | | | | | | | | |
| ✓ | ✓ | ✓ | 1856 | 3 | ✓ | ✓ | 0 | 1 | | ✓ | 200 | | | | | | | | |
| ✓ | ✓ | ✓ | 1887 | | | | | 1 | ✓ | | | | | | | | | | |
| ✓ | ✓ | ✓ | 1927 | 1 | ✓ | ✓ | 0 | 1 | | ✓ | 40 | | | | | | | | |
| ✓ | ✓ | ✓ | 1983 | | | | | 1 | ✓ | | | | | | | | | | |
| ✓ | ✓ | | 2114 | 2 | ✓ | | | | | | | | | | | | | | |

**Figure 6.6 (continued)**

We plot each histogram to study its characteristics. Its shape can tell us a lot about the pattern of waiting time. Are the observations spread out evenly? Are there a few exceptionally large ones? Are they close together, or spread over a wide range? Are there several peaks in the observations? The shape can give us a deeper insight into the problem and we should be able to explain the behaviour causing the patterns before continuing with further experiments.

The histograms for the machine maintenance example are shown in Fig. 6.7. They summarize the results at the first events after time 1000 and time 2000 (see Exercise 6.1).

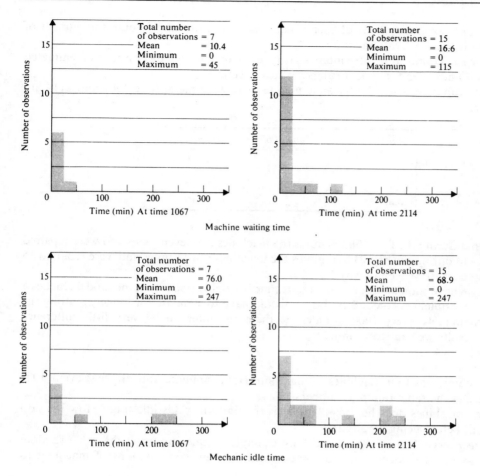

**Figure 6.7**

During the first 1067 minutes, seven machines waited for repair on average 10.4 minutes (times varying from 0 to 45), and the mechanic was idle for a total of 532 minutes (49.9 per cent of time).

During the first 2114 minutes, fifteen machines waited for repair on average 16.6 minutes (times varying from 0 to 115), and the mechanic was idle for a total of 1033 minutes (48.9 per cent of time).

## Activity run counts

When an activity is ended during hand simulation, we cross out the end time of the activity. Thus the number of end times crossed out by each activity gives the number of occasions each activity has taken place. This is known as the activity run count. Therefore if we want to know how many cars have entered a garage for petrol, or how many times a machine has broken down, or how many pints of beer a man has drunk, we simply count the number of times the appropriate activity has run.

Plotting the run counts at regular intervals (say at the end of each day or hour of simulated time), shows if and when the model reaches a steady state.

The activity run counts for the machine maintenance example at time 1067 and 2114 are shown below.

| Activity | Time 1067 | Time 2114 |
|---|---|---|
| 1 (run) | 2 | 6 |
| 2 (run) | 3 | 6 |
| 3 (run) | 2 | 4 |
| 4 (repair) | 7 | 15 |

They show that during the first 1067 minutes the machines ran seven times and were repaired seven times, and during the first 2114 minutes the machines ran 16 times and were repaired 15 times (machine 2 just broken down).

Although we have simulated for a very short time it would appear that the model reaches a steady state very quickly. To confirm this we would have to simulate for longer, plotting the results approximately every 1000 minutes. If there continues to be very little difference between the results we can stop simulating.

EXERCISE 6.2

The mechanic now has four machines to maintain. Hand simulate until the first event after time 2000, using the same random numbers.

How many machines does he repair? What is the pattern of his idle time? How long do machines wait before being repaired?

(*Note to teachers*   This is a good teaching example because by using the same random numbers, a group of students can experiment with different combinations of machines to mechanics.)

EXERCISE 6.3

To get practice at hand simulating a large model, select one of the models from Exercises 5.10, 5.11 or 5.12 (loading bay, tidal port or steel mill).

## Length of simulation

The purpose of hand simulation can be to:

– test the logic of the model;
– understand the problem better;
– collect results from the model.

We must continue hand simulating until we achieve our objective. If we are simply testing the logic of our model, the length of the simulation may be quite short. We stop when we have checked the life cycles of all the entities.

When simulating to gain a better understanding, we continue until we have explored the circumstances which are of interest to us. For example, we may be interested in how a chemical plant recovers from a major breakdown, or how a port copes with twice the planned number of ships. This may take a considerable time and will depend on the characteristics of the model and the initial conditions we choose.

Collecting resuls from a model by hand simulation takes a long time, and really is an ideal task for a computer. A formal model can be transferred very easily to a computer using a standard program, and we describe this procedure in Chapter 8. However, before concerning ourselves with the computer we see in Chapter 7 how to extend our models to include entities which have attributes.

## Solutions to exercises

SOLUTION 6.2

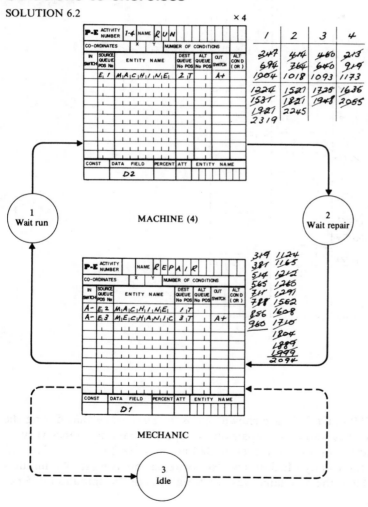

**P-E** HOCUS SIMULATION RECORD SHEET | MODEL | SHEET OF

| TIME | END | START | SIM. CLOCK TIME | MACHINE ENT NO | ON | OFF | DUR | MECHANIC ENT NO | ON | OFF | DUR | ENT NO | ON | OFF | DUR | ENT NO | ON | OFF | DUR |
|---|---|---|---|---|---|---|---|---|---|---|---|---|---|---|---|---|---|---|---|
|  |  | ✓ | 0 |  |  |  |  |  |  |  |  |  |  |  |  |  |  |  |  |
| ✓ | ✓ | ✓ | 213 | 4 | ✓ | ✓ | 0 | 1 |  | ✓ | 213 |  |  |  |  |  |  |  |  |
| ✓ | ✓ | ✓ | 247 | 1 | ✓ |  |  |  |  |  |  |  |  |  |  |  |  |  |  |
| ✓ | ✓ | ✓ | 319 | 1 |  | ✓ | 72 | 1 | ✓ | ✓ | 0 |  |  |  |  |  |  |  |  |
| ✓ | ✓ | ✓ | 381 |  |  |  |  | 1 | ✓ |  |  |  |  |  |  |  |  |  |  |
| ✓ | ✓ | ✓ | 414 | 2 | ✓ | ✓ | 0 | 1 |  | ✓ | 33 |  |  |  |  |  |  |  |  |
| ✓ | ✓ | ✓ | 460 | 3 | ✓ |  |  |  |  |  |  |  |  |  |  |  |  |  |  |
| ✓ | ✓ | ✓ | 514 | 3 |  | ✓ | 54 | 1 | ✓ | ✓ | 0 |  |  |  |  |  |  |  |  |
| ✓ | ✓ | ✓ | 565 |  |  |  |  | 1 | ✓ |  |  |  |  |  |  |  |  |  |  |
| ✓ | ✓ | ✓ | 640 | 3 | ✓ | ✓ | 0 | 1 |  | ✓ | 75 |  |  |  |  |  |  |  |  |
| ✓ | ✓ | ✓ | 694 | 4 | ✓ |  |  |  |  |  |  |  |  |  |  |  |  |  |  |
| ✓ | ✓ | ✓ | 711 | 4 |  | ✓ | 17 | 1 | ✓ | ✓ | 0 |  |  |  |  |  |  |  |  |
| ✓ | ✓ | ✓ | 764 | 2 | ✓ |  |  |  |  |  |  |  |  |  |  |  |  |  |  |
| ✓ | ✓ | ✓ | 788 | 2 |  | ✓ | 24 | 1 | ✓ | ✓ | 0 |  |  |  |  |  |  |  |  |
| ✓ | ✓ | ✓ | 856 |  |  |  |  | 1 | ✓ |  |  |  |  |  |  |  |  |  |  |
| ✓ | ✓ | ✓ | 919 | 1 | ✓ | ✓ | 0 | 1 |  | ✓ | 63 |  |  |  |  |  |  |  |  |
| ✓ | ✓ | ✓ | 960 |  |  |  |  | 1 | ✓ |  |  |  |  |  |  |  |  |  |  |
| ✓ | ✓ |  | 1004 | 3 | ✓ |  |  |  |  |  |  |  |  |  |  |  |  |  |  |
|  |  |  |  |  |  |  |  |  |  |  |  |  |  |  |  |  |  |  |  |
|  |  | ✓ | 1004 | 3 |  | ✓ | 0 | 1 |  | ✓ | 44 |  |  |  |  |  |  |  |  |
| ✓ | ✓ | ✓ | 1018 | 4 | ✓ |  |  |  |  |  |  |  |  |  |  |  |  |  |  |
| ✓ | ✓ | ✓ | 1093 | 2 | ✓ |  |  |  |  |  |  |  |  |  |  |  |  |  |  |
| ✓ | ✓ | ✓ | 1124 | 4 |  | ✓ | 106 | 1 | ✓ | ✓ | 0 |  |  |  |  |  |  |  |  |
| ✓ | ✓ | ✓ | 1165 | 2 |  | ✓ | 72 | 1 | ✓ | ✓ | 0 |  |  |  |  |  |  |  |  |
| ✓ | ✓ | ✓ | 1173 | 1 | ✓ |  |  |  |  |  |  |  |  |  |  |  |  |  |  |
| ✓ | ✓ | ✓ | 1212 | 1 |  | ✓ | 39 | 1 | ✓ | ✓ | 0 |  |  |  |  |  |  |  |  |
| ✓ | ✓ | ✓ | 1224 | 3 | ✓ |  |  |  |  |  |  |  |  |  |  |  |  |  |  |
| ✓ | ✓ | ✓ | 1260 | 3 |  | ✓ | 36 | 1 | ✓ | ✓ | 0 |  |  |  |  |  |  |  |  |
| ✓ | ✓ | ✓ | 1291 |  |  |  |  | 1 | ✓ |  |  |  |  |  |  |  |  |  |  |
| ✓ | ✓ | ✓ | 1521 | 4 | ✓ | ✓ | 0 | 1 |  | ✓ | 230 |  |  |  |  |  |  |  |  |
| ✓ | ✓ | ✓ | 1531 | 1 | ✓ |  |  |  |  |  |  |  |  |  |  |  |  |  |  |
| ✓ | ✓ | ✓ | 1552 | 1 |  | ✓ | 21 | 1 | ✓ | ✓ | 0 |  |  |  |  |  |  |  |  |
| ✓ | ✓ | ✓ | 1608 |  |  |  |  | 1 | ✓ |  |  |  |  |  |  |  |  |  |  |
| ✓ | ✓ | ✓ | 1636 | 3 | ✓ | ✓ | 0 | 1 |  | ✓ | 28 |  |  |  |  |  |  |  |  |
| ✓ | ✓ | ✓ | 1710 |  |  |  |  | 1 | ✓ |  |  |  |  |  |  |  |  |  |  |
| ✓ | ✓ | ✓ | 1725 | 2 | ✓ | ✓ | 0 | 1 |  | ✓ | 15 |  |  |  |  |  |  |  |  |
| ✓ | ✓ | ✓ | 1804 |  |  |  |  | 1 | ✓ |  |  |  |  |  |  |  |  |  |  |
| ✓ | ✓ | ✓ | 1821 | 1 | ✓ | ✓ | 0 | 1 |  | ✓ | 17 |  |  |  |  |  |  |  |  |
| ✓ | ✓ | ✓ | 1889 |  |  |  |  | 1 | ✓ |  |  |  |  |  |  |  |  |  |  |
| ✓ | ✓ | ✓ | 1921 | 4 | ✓ | ✓ | 0 | 1 |  | ✓ | 32 |  |  |  |  |  |  |  |  |
| ✓ | ✓ | ✓ | 1948 | 2 | ✓ |  |  |  |  |  |  |  |  |  |  |  |  |  |  |
| ✓ | ✓ | ✓ | 1999 | 2 |  | ✓ | 51 | 1 | ✓ | ✓ | 0 |  |  |  |  |  |  |  |  |
| ✓ | ✓ |  | 2055 | 3 | ✓ |  |  |  |  |  |  |  |  |  |  |  |  |  |  |

The histograms at times 1004 and 2055 are shown opposite. They show that during the first 1004 minutes, eight Machines waited for repair on average 20.9 minutes (times varying from 0 to 72) and the Mechanic was idle for a total of 384 minutes (38.2 per cent of time).

During the first 2055 minutes, twenty Machines waited for repair on average 24.6 minutes (times varying from 0 to 106) and the Mechanic was idle for a total of 750 minutes (36.5 per cent of time).

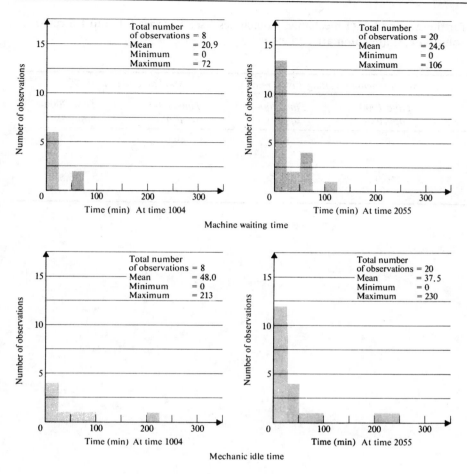

Machine waiting time

Mechanic idle time

The activity run counts at time 1004 and 2055 are shown below:

| Activity | Time 1004 | Time 2055 |
|---|---|---|
| 1 (run) | 3 | 6 |
| 2 (run) | 2 | 5 |
| 3 (run) | 2 | 5 |
| 4 (run) | 2 | 5 |
| 5 (repair) | 8 | 19 |

They show that during the first 1004 minutes the Machines ran 9 times and were repaired 8 times, and during the first 2055 minutes the Machines ran 21 times and were repaired 19 times.

The results for the two models (1 mechanic, 3 machines—see Exercise 6.1, and 1 mechanic, 4 machines—Solution 6.2) are summarized below:

| Model | Mean machine waiting time (min) | | Mechanic idle time (%) | |
|---|---|---|---|---|
| | *Time 1000 approx.* | *Time 2000 approx.* | *Time 1000 approx.* | *Time 2000 approx.* |
| 1 mechanic 3 machines | 10.4 | 16.6 | 49.9 | 48.9 |
| 1 mechanic 4 machines | 20.9 | 24.6 | 38.2 | 36.5 |

# 7.

## Building a formal model (with attributes)

We have seen in Chapter 5 how to build models involving entities which do not have attributes. While this is adequate for many problems, we must be able to handle attributes if we want to model more complex problems.

In this chapter we expand on the definition of attributes, and describe how to use them to model both discrete and continuous processes, under the following headings:

- manipulating attribute values—options;
- entity groups;
- continuous activities;
- ordered queues;
- hand simulation.

Many examples and exercises are given and, as before, the best way to check that you understand the examples is to complete the exercises and compare your solutions with those given at the end of the chapter. Let us first define what we mean by an attribute.

## What is an attribute?

An attribute of an entity is any property or characteristic of the entity which influences or measures its behaviour. For example, an attribute may be used to record the time an entity spends in some part of its life cycle. It may hold a quantity such as the load in a van or the number of passengers in an aeroplane. It may indicate the next machine on which a job is to be processed, show which batch a document belongs to, or be a measure of an order's priority. In fact, any property that can be expressed as a positive integer, can be defined as an attribute. Further examples are:

- the rate of flow along a pipe;
- the condition of a patient;
- the grade of a product;
- the driver of a lorry;
- the number of items a machine produces, before it has to be reset;
- the temperature of a chemical.

Each entity can have up to 20 attributes—referred to by the letters ABCDFGJKLM NPQRSUVWXY. (The reason for omitting EHTIO and Z is given later in this chapter—see Ordered queues). Thus, for example, in a model we can define ships with three attributes each:

– A-attribute, a clock to measure how long a ship waits before it is unloaded;
– B-attribute, the type of cargo carried;
– C-attribute, the size of cargo carried.

We can use the values held in the attributes to decide, for example, when to unload a ship (if the ship has been waiting for more than a certain time it is given priority), how to unload a ship (the type of cargo determines the method of unloading), and the duration of the unloading activity (the size of cargo determines the unloading time).

The precise method of modelling this, and other uses of attributes, are fully described in this chapter.

## Attribute maximum values

Any attribute, which is not used as a clock, can be given a maximum value. These maximum values are declared on an Attribute Maximum Value format. Figure 7.1 shows Ships with a capacity of 5000 units (maximum value on the C-attribute). Thus, nowhere in the model can the cargo on a Ship exceed 5000 units.

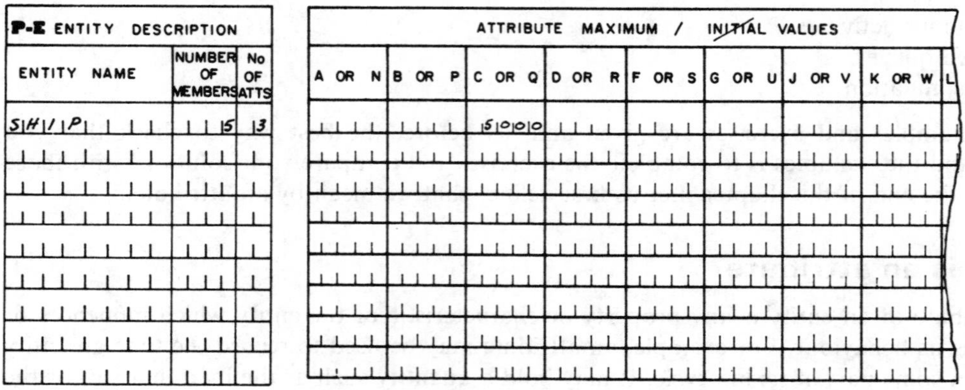

**Figure 7.1**

## Manipulating attribute values—options

If we build a model which includes attributes then we will want to manipulate the attributes in various ways. For example, we may want to:

– transfer the contents of a lorry into a bunker;
– route passengers through an airport terminal;
– match a customer order against product in stock;
– copy the details of a bus, which has broken down, to a relief bus;
– calculate the total stock in a number of silos;
– check the contents in a vessel;
– record values in a histogram.

We manipulate attributes using *options*. Each option performs a specific operation on an attribute and any number can be used in one activity. We describe their use, under the following headings:

- attribute transferring;
- attribute matching, comparing and copying;
- attribute alteration;
- data field manipulation;
- attribute checking;
- attribute arithmetic;
- attribute histograms;
- variable percentage;
- identical conditions;
- queue size testing and manipulation;
- extra correlation terms;
- output reports;
- clock switches and options;
- relating time to quantity moved (alpha);
- run termination;
- user-defined interfaces.

Within each heading we describe a number of options, and illustrate their use with examples and exercises. They are listed in order of importance, in the sense that the first option is likely to be used in more models than the last.

In order to accommodate attributes the activity format used in Chapter 5 is extended as shown in Fig. 7.2. The queue format is not altered.

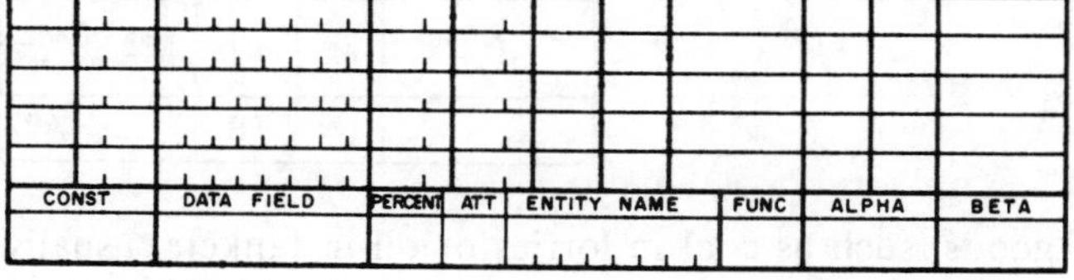

**Figure 7.2**

## Format details

Options

An activity with options usually has entries in the columns Att, Option and Percentage of att, or Percentage of quantity. The attribute letter is entered in Att. The option is a two-character code. The percentages must be numerical (or Var or Sup—see variable percentage options).

An option which takes the current value of an attribute, to set or control a quantity, uses the Percentage of att. An option which checks or alters the current value of an attribute by reference to some other quantity uses the Percentage of quantity. A few options use neither percentage, but no option uses both.

Each option description contains a table for quick reference indicating which percentage is used.

*Example*

The information shown is:

| | | |
|---|---|---|
| percentage of attribute— | $\checkmark$ | mandatory |
| | Op | optional |
| | | |
| attribute— | $\checkmark$ | mandatory |
| | Op | optional |
| | | |
| option— | | two character code |
| | | |
| percentage of quantity— | $\checkmark$ | mandatory |
| | Op | optional |

| PERCENTAGE OF ATT | ATT | OPTION | PERCENTAGE OF QUANTITY |
|---|---|---|---|
| | $\checkmark$ | TR | $\checkmark$ ($\neq 0$) |

Any restrictions on numerical values are indicated using conventional mathematical notation. This information is summarized for all options in Appendix 3.

Continuation lines may be used for a condition which has several options or clock switches.

## Attribute transferring

The first group of options we consider change the values of attributes. The TR, TH and TT options transfer a quantity into or out of attributes. The LQ, UQ, FQ, LL, UL, LE, and UE options impose constraints on the values transferred.

*TR—TRansfer*

| PERCENTAGE OF ATT | ATT | OPTION | PERCENTAGE OF QUANTITY |
|---|---|---|---|
| | $\checkmark$ | TR | $\checkmark$ ($\neq 0$) |

Models involving the movement of goods, such as coal in lorries or oil in tankers, usually include 'loading' and 'unloading' activities. Attributes have to be updated as the goods are transferred from one entity to another.

The TR option simply transfers a quantity between attributes. The quantity itself is the largest value that can be moved without any attribute exceeding its maximum or becoming negative.

*Example*  Coal is unloaded from lorries into a bunker. Each lorry carries a load and the bunker has a known capacity. The capacity of the bunker is set by a maximum value as described earlier in this chapter (attribute maximum values) and this restricts the loads that can be put into it. The activity of transferring coal from a lorry to the bunker is shown in Fig. 7.3.

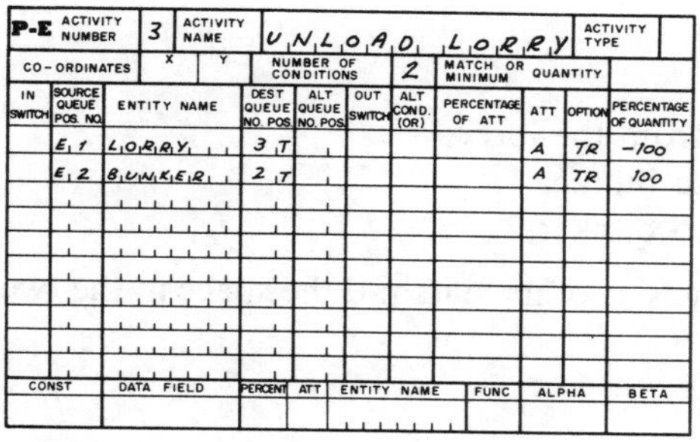

LORRY    A  Size of load
BUNKER  A  Amount in bunker
               (maximum = 200)

**Figure 7.3**

When the activity ends a quantity is TRansferred from the Lorry to the Bunker. The activity shows that 100 per cent of the quantity is transferred *from* the Lorry (percentage of quantity is negative) and 100 per cent of the quantity is transferred *into* the Bunker (percentage of quantity is positive). The amount which is actually moved depends on the load in the Lorry and the space in the Bunker. If there is sufficient space to take the entire load, then the Lorry is emptied, otherwise it is only partly unloaded.

If the Bunker has a capacity of 200 units and the Lorry currently being unloaded contains 50 units, there are three cases which we can consider:

- If the Bunker already holds 130 units then the entire load in the Lorry can be moved. At the end of the activity the Lorry will be empty and the Bunker will contain 180 units (130 + 50).
- If the Bunker already holds 180 units then only 20 units can be moved from the Lorry. The Lorry will still have a load of 30 units and the Bunker will be full (200 units).
- If the Bunker is already full (i.e., holds 200 units) the activity will still take place but the loads will remain unchanged.

In all three cases the Lorry will be put in queue 3 and the Bunker in queue 2. We can prevent the second and third cases from occurring if we wish, by using other options (see TT option and Minimum Quantity).

If instead of putting the contents of the Lorry into one Bunker, the load is divided into two—60 per cent going to one Bunker and 40 per cent to another—we modify the 'unload' activity as shown in Fig. 7.4.

| P-E | ACTIVITY NUMBER | 4 | ACTIVITY NAME | U N L O A D   L O R R Y | | ACTIVITY TYPE | | |
|---|---|---|---|---|---|---|---|---|
| CO - ORDINATES | | X | Y | NUMBER OF CONDITIONS | 3 | MATCH OR MINIMUM | QUANTITY | |
| IN SWITCH | SOURCE QUEUE POS. NO. | ENTITY NAME | | DEST QUEUE NO. POS. | ALT QUEUE NO. POS. | OUT SWITCH | ALT COND (OR) | PERCENTAGE OF ATT | ATT | OPTION | PERCENTAGE OF QUANTITY |
| | E, 1 | L O R R Y | | 3  T | | | | | A | TR | −100 |
| | E, 2 | B U N K E R 1 | | 2  T | | | | | A | TR | 60 |
| | E, 2 | B U N K E R 2 | | 2  T | | | | | A | TR | 40 |
| | | | | | | | | | | | |
| | | | | | | | | | | | |
| | | | | | | | | | | | |
| | | | | | | | | | | | |
| | | | | | | | | | | | |
| CONST | | DATA FIELD | | PERCENT | ATT | ENTITY NAME | | FUNC | ALPHA | BETA | |

LORRY    A  Size of load
BUNKER 1  A  Amount in bunker 1
              (maximum = capacity)
BUNKER 2  A  Amount in bunker 2
              (maximum = capacity)

**Figure 7.4**

This activity shows that:

100 per cent of the quantity transferred is taken from the lorry;
60 per cent of the quantity transferred is put into bunker 1;
40 per cent of the quantity transferred is put into bunker 2.

Whether the lorry is emptied or not depends on the size of its load and the space in the two bunkers.

EXERCISE 7.1
(a) Concrete is made in a mixer with 1 part cement, 3 parts sand, 1 part aggregate and water. After mixing, the concrete is used for the foundations of a building and another mix is made. Draw a flow diagram showing the 'mix' and 'empty' activities, defining the attributes you use.
(b) The furnace in a steel-making plant is loaded with 75 per cent scrap metal and 25 per cent liquid iron. Give details of the 'load furnace' activity.

### TH—Test and Hold

| PERCENTAGE OF ATT | ATT | OPTION | PERCENTAGE OF QUANTITY |
|---|---|---|---|
| | ✓ | TH | ✓ (≠0) |

The TH option is similar to TR except that the value of the attribute is not altered. The quantity to be transferred is calculated in the same way as with the TR option.

*Example*   A running total is kept of the number of items produced on a machine. When a batch arrives at the machine the number of items is added to the machine total but, of course, the number in the batch remains unaltered, and this is shown in Fig. 7.5.

The value in the A-attribute of Batch remains unaltered but is added to the A-attribute of Machine.

EXERCISE 7.2
A farmer wishes to fill his barn with feed ready for the winter, and sends an order to his supplier. Give details of the 'order feed' activity, which determines the quantity he orders.

| P-E | ACTIVITY NUMBER 5 | ACTIVITY NAME MACHINING | | | | | | ACTIVITY TYPE | |
|---|---|---|---|---|---|---|---|---|---|
| CO-ORDINATES | X | Y | NUMBER OF CONDITIONS 2 | | MATCH OR MINIMUM | QUANTITY | | | |
| IN SWITCH | SOURCE QUEUE POS. NO. | ENTITY NAME | DEST QUEUE NO. POS. | ALT QUEUE NO. POS. | OUT SWITCH | ALT COND (OR) | PERCENTAGE OF ATT | ATT | OPTION | PERCENTAGE OF QUANTITY |
| | E 1 | BATCH | 3 T | | | | | A | TH | -100 |
| | E 8 | MACHINE | 8 T | | | | | A | TR | 100 |

| CONST | DATA FIELD | PERCENT | ATT | ENTITY NAME | FUNC | ALPHA | BETA |
|---|---|---|---|---|---|---|---|

| BATCH | A | Number of items in batch |
|---|---|---|
| MACHINE | A | Total number of items produced on machine |

**Figure 7.5**

## TT—Total Transfer

| PERCENTAGE OF ATT | ATT | OPTION | PERCENTAGE OF QUANTITY |
|---|---|---|---|
| | ✓ | TT | ✓ ($\neq 0$) |

The TT option is used to empty or fill an attribute. If the attribute cannot be emptied or filled, the activity will not start.

*Example* Molten steel is poured from a furnace into a ladle, and as there are several ladles of different sizes we must select one large enough to take the total load. This is shown in Fig. 7.6.

| P-E | ACTIVITY NUMBER 6 | ACTIVITY NAME POUR | | | | | | ACTIVITY TYPE | |
|---|---|---|---|---|---|---|---|---|---|
| CO-ORDINATES | X | Y | NUMBER OF CONDITIONS 2 | | MATCH OR MINIMUM | QUANTITY | | | |
| IN SWITCH | SOURCE QUEUE POS. NO. | ENTITY NAME | DEST QUEUE NO. POS. | ALT QUEUE NO. POS. | OUT SWITCH | ALT COND (OR) | PERCENTAGE OF ATT | ATT | OPTION | PERCENTAGE OF QUANTITY |
| | E 1 | FURNACE | 4 T | | | | | A | TT | -100 |
| | E 3 | LADLE | 5 T | | | | | A | TR | 100 |

| CONST | DATA FIELD | PERCENT | ATT | ENTITY NAME | FUNC | ALPHA | BETA |
|---|---|---|---|---|---|---|---|

| FURNACE | A | Contents of furnace |
|---|---|---|
| LADLE | A | Contents of ladle (maximum = capacity) |

**Figure 7.6**

The activity will only start if there is a Ladle in queue 3 large enough to empty the Furnace. Note that the source queue position for the Ladle is 'E', which means we can search queue 3 for a suitable Ladle.

EXERCISE 7.3

A company producing rubber receives orders from its customers. Each order must be fully met before rubber from stock is loaded on a lorry. Give details of the 'load' activity.

### Minimum Quantity

Sometimes it is only worth while doing an activity if the quantity moved is greater than or equal to a minimum. If only a lesser quantity is possible, the activity will not start.

*Example* The final product of a chemical process is stored in silos and then delivered to customers by train. However, only silos which are at least a quarter full are emptied when a train arrives. If the silos have a capacity of 3600 tons, the 'empty silo' activity is as shown in Fig. 7.7.

SILO   A   Contents
TRAIN   A   Contents
               (maximum = capacity)

**Figure 7.7**

A minimum transfer quantity of 900 has been specified for the activity and only Silos with contents equalling or exceeding this value will be emptied.

---

**Format details**

Minimum quantity

Enter the minimum quantity for a transfer activity in the box marked Match or Minimum Quantity.

---

*Example* Routing by attribute value. One use of activities is to route entities to different destination queues according to the value held in an attribute. This is easily done using the TH option, which tests the attribute value without changing it, together with a minimum quantity.

Consider as an example a car entering a garage. It queues either for petrol (queue 4), air (queue 1), or car wash (queue 11) and this is shown in Fig. 7.8.

Each Car entering the garage has an A-attribute of 13 if it requires petrol, 2 if it requires air, and 1 if it requires car wash. If its A-attribute is at least 13 it goes to queue 4 (petrol), if it is at least 2 it goes to queue 1 (air) and if it is at least 1 it goes to queue 11 (car wash). Thus by testing for the largest value first, we achieve the desired routing.

Routing can also be achieved using the End Check options (see Attribute checking).

| P-E | ACTIVITY NUMBER | 8 | ACTIVITY NAME | ROUTE | | | | | ACTIVITY TYPE | |
|---|---|---|---|---|---|---|---|---|---|---|
| | CO-ORDINATES | X | Y | NUMBER OF CONDITIONS | 3 | MATCH OR MINIMUM | QUANTITY | 100 | | |

| IN SWITCH | SOURCE QUEUE POS NO | ENTITY NAME | DEST QUEUE NO POS | ALT QUEUE NO POS | OUT SWITCH | ALT COND (OR) | PERCENTAGE OF ATT | ATT | OPTION | PERCENTAGE OF QUANTITY |
|---|---|---|---|---|---|---|---|---|---|---|
| H, 2 | | CAR | 4 ,T | | | OR | | A | TH | – 13 |
| H, 2 | | CAR | 1 ,T | | | OR | | A | TH | – 2 |
| H, 2 | | CAR | 11 ,T | | | | | A | TH | – 1 |

| CONST | DATA FIELD | PERCENT ATT | ENTITY NAME | FUNC | ALPHA | BETA |
|---|---|---|---|---|---|---|

CAR  A  13 = petrol  
2 = air  
1 = car  wash

**Figure 7.8**

EXERCISE 7.4

(a) If the mixer in Exercise 7.1 has a capacity of 200 units, what modifications would you make to ensure that:
   (i) concrete is made only if the mixer is full;
   (ii) concrete is made only if the mixer is at least half full;
   (iii) the 'mix' activity takes place only when there is material available?
(b) Passengers arriving in a foreign country have to pass through Customs. They either go to the red channel (something to declare—queue 11) or the green channel (nothing to declare—queue 17). Passengers have an A-attribute of 1, if they are going to the red channel and 2 if they are going to the green channel. Give details of the 'routing' activity.

**LQ—Lower limit of Quantity**
**UQ—Upper limit of Quantity**
**FQ—Fixed Quantity**

| PERCENTAGE OF ATT | ATT | OPTION | PERCENTAGE OF QUANTITY |
|---|---|---|---|
| ✓ (>0) | ✓ | LQ | |
| ✓ (>0) | ✓ | UQ | |
| ✓ (>0) | ✓ | FQ | |

These options impose additional constraints on the quantity to be transferred. The LQ option sets a minimum quantity, UQ sets a maximum quantity and FQ fixes the quantity to a particular value.

*Example* (of LQ option)   One of the requirements for joining the police force is that men are at least 5 ft 8 in and women at least 5 ft 4 in. Part of the selection procedure is as shown in Fig. 7.9, where queue 2 consists of those selected and queue 4 of those rejected.

The minimum for the activity is 100 per cent of the B-attribute of Applicant. The Applicant's height is tested against the minimum (TH option). If it is greater than the minimum the first condition is satisfied and the Applicant is put into queue 2. Otherwise the alternative condition puts the Applicant into queue 4.

*Example* (of UQ option)   An oil company is temporarily short of oil for distribution, but attempts to satisfy up to 95 per cent of each customer's requirements, as shown in Fig. 7.10.

| P-E | ACTIVITY NUMBER | 9 | ACTIVITY NAME | S E L E C T | | | | | ACTIVITY TYPE | | |
|---|---|---|---|---|---|---|---|---|---|---|---|
| CO-ORDINATES | | X | Y | NUMBER OF CONDITIONS | 2 | MATCH OR MINIMUM | QUANTITY | | | | |
| IN SWITCH | SOURCE QUEUE POS. NO. | ENTITY NAME | DEST QUEUE NO. POS | ALT QUEUE NO. POS | OUT SWITCH | ALT COND. (OR) | PERCENTAGE OF ATT | ATT | OPTION | PERCENTAGE OF QUANTITY | |
| | H 1 | A P P L I C A N | 2 T | | | OR | 100 | B | LØ | | |
| | | | | | | | | A | TH | −100 | |
| | H 1 | A P P L I C A N | 4 T | | | | | | | | |
| | | | | | | | | | | | |
| | | | | | | | | | | | |
| | | | | | | | | | | | |
| | | | | | | | | | | | |
| CONST | | DATA FIELD | PERCENT | ATT | ENTITY NAME | | FUNC | ALPHA | BETA | | |

APPLICAN (T)  A  Height
B  Minimum height,
68in. if man,
64in. if woman

**Figure 7.9**

| P-E | ACTIVITY NUMBER | 10 | ACTIVITY NAME | D I S T R I B U T E | | | | | ACTIVITY TYPE | | |
|---|---|---|---|---|---|---|---|---|---|---|---|
| CO-ORDINATES | | X | Y | NUMBER OF CONDITIONS | 3 | MATCH OR MINIMUM | QUANTITY | | | | |
| IN SWITCH | SOURCE QUEUE POS. NO. | ENTITY NAME | DEST QUEUE NO. POS | ALT QUEUE NO. POS | OUT SWITCH | ALT COND. (OR) | PERCENTAGE OF ATT | ATT | OPTION | PERCENTAGE OF QUANTITY | |
| | E 1 | O R D E R | 2 T | | | | 95 | A | UØ | | |
| | E 3 | T A N K E R | 4 T | | | | | A | TR | 100 | |
| | E 5 | S T O C K | 5 T | | | | | A | TR | −100 | |
| | | | | | | | | | | | |
| | | | | | | | | | | | |
| | | | | | | | | | | | |
| CONST | | DATA FIELD | PERCENT | ATT | ENTITY NAME | | FUNC | ALPHA | BETA | | |

ORDER  A  Size of order
TANKER  A  Size of load for delivery
(maximum = capacity)
STOCK  A  Amount of oil in stock

**Figure 7.10**

The quantity put into the Tanker from Stock must be less than or equal to 95 per cent of the Order size.

*Example* (of FQ option)   Lorries arrive at a dispatch bay and are loaded with heavy plant by a crane, as shown in Fig. 7.11.

The weight of the Plant fixes the quantity to be moved. This is added to the load on the Lorry by a Crane. Note that the FQ option is similar to the TT (Total Transfer) option, except that the attribute value is not altered.

| P-E | ACTIVITY NUMBER | 11 | ACTIVITY NAME | L O A D   L O R R Y | | | | | ACTIVITY TYPE | | |
|---|---|---|---|---|---|---|---|---|---|---|---|
| CO-ORDINATES | | X | Y | NUMBER OF CONDITIONS | 3 | MATCH OR MINIMUM | QUANTITY | | | | |
| IN SWITCH | SOURCE QUEUE POS. NO. | ENTITY NAME | DEST QUEUE NO. POS | ALT QUEUE NO. POS | OUT SWITCH | ALT COND. (OR) | PERCENTAGE OF ATT | ATT | OPTION | PERCENTAGE OF QUANTITY | |
| | E 1 | C R A N E | 1 T | | | | | | | | |
| | E 2 | P L A N T | 4 T | | | | 100 | A | FØ | | |
| | E 3 | L O R R Y | 4 T | | | | | A | TR | 100 | |
| | | | | | | | | | | | |
| | | | | | | | | | | | |
| | | | | | | | | | | | |
| | | | | | | | | | | | |
| | | | | | | | | | | | |
| CONST | | DATA FIELD | PERCENT | ATT | ENTITY NAME | | FUNC | ALPHA | BETA | | |

CRANE  −
PLANT  A  Weight of plant
LORRY  A  Load on lorry
(maximum = capacity)

**Figure 7.11**

EXERCISE 7.5

(a) A coach tour operator runs a sightseeing tour only if the coach is at least a quarter full. Give details of the 'tour' activity, defining the attributes you use.

(b) Repeat Exercise 7.4 (a) using the LQ option.

**LL**—*Lower Limit of attribute*
**UL**—*Upper Limit of attribute*
**LE**—*Lower Extent of attribute*
**UE**—*Upper Extent of attribute*

| PERCENTAGE OF ATT | ATT | OPTION | PERCENTAGE OF QUANTITY |
|---|---|---|---|
| ✓ (>0) | ✓ | LL | |
| ✓ (>0) | ✓ | UL | |
| ✓ (>0) | ✓ | LE | |
| ✓ (>0) | ✓ | UE | |

With these options we can impose further restrictions on the quantity to be transferred, by specifying that the values remaining in those attributes affected by a negative transfer do not fall below a lower limit, and those attributes affected by a positive transfer do not exceed an upper limit.

The distinction between the two sets is that whereas LL and UL operate on all transfer options, LE and UE only apply to the condition in which they are specified, and only to subsequent transfer options.

*Example* Aeroplanes have a major overhaul after a given number of flying hours, which varies with the type of plane. No journey can be started which causes a plane to exceed this time. This is shown in Fig. 7.12.

| P-E | ACTIVITY NUMBER 12 | ACTIVITY NAME | F L Y | | | | | ACTIVITY TYPE | |
|---|---|---|---|---|---|---|---|---|---|
| CO-ORDINATES | X | Y | NUMBER OF CONDITIONS 2 | MATCH OR MINIMUM | QUANTITY | | | | |
| IN SWITCH | SOURCE QUEUE POS. NO. | ENTITY NAME | DEST QUEUE NO. POS | ALT QUEUE NO. POS | OUT SWITCH | ALT COND (OR) | PERCENTAGE OF ATT | ATT | OPTION | PERCENTAGE OF QUANTITY |
| E,1 | PLANE | 2,T | | | | | 100 | A | UL | |
| | | | | | | | | B | TR | 100 |
| E,8 | JOURNEY | 8,T | | | | | | A | TT | -100 |
| CONST | DATA FIELD | PERCENT | ATT | ENTITY NAME | FUNC | ALPHA | BETA | | | |
| | | 100 | A | JOURNEY | | | | | | |

PLANE   A   Time between overhauls
         B   Flying hours since last overhaul
JOURNEY   A   Length of journey in flying hours

**Figure 7.12**

The time between overhauls sets the upper limit on the final values in the other attributes affected by a positive transfer. Thus the B-attribute of the Plane cannot exceed this upper limit, when a total journey time is added to it.

EXERCISE 7.6

Credit card holders have credit limits (A-attribute) which must not be exceeded. Give details of an activity involving the purchase of goods which ensures that the credit limit of an individual is not exceeded.

## Attribute matching, comparing and copying

Options under this heading enable us to select entities with attributes which match values or ranges of values, and also to update attributes.

The MQ, MX, M1...M9, G1...G9, L1...L9, X1...X9 options match or compare attribute values and the I1...I9 and J1...J9 options copy values from one attribute to another.

*MQ—Match with match Quantity*
*MX—Must not match*

| MATCH OR MINIMUM | QUANTITY | ✓ (>0) | |
|---|---|---|---|
| PERCENTAGE OF ATT | ATT | OPTION | PERCENTAGE OF QUANTITY |
| ✓ (>0) | ✓ | MQ | |
| ✓ (>0) | ✓ | MX | |

The MQ option is used to match an attribute value against a fixed value. The value is entered in the Match Quantity box on the activity format and is used in all subsequent MQ options.

The MX option requires an attribute value which does not match with any of the matching masters set by MQ or M1...M9 options.

*Example*   Some patients, arriving at a hospital casualty department, require an X-ray (3 in their A-attribute). The 'X-ray' activity is shown in Fig. 7.13.

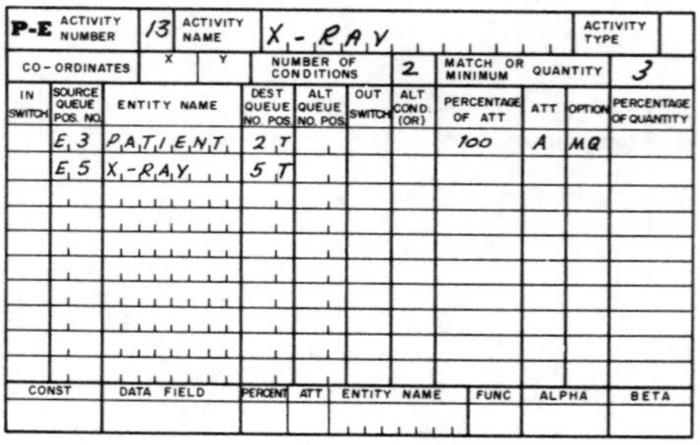

PATIENT A   Treatment required
1 = Blood test
2 =
3 = X-ray
4 =

X-RAY        –

**Figure 7.13**

The following Patients are waiting in queue 3.

|  | *A-attribute* |
|---|---|
| Patient (8) | 2 |
| Patient (2) | 3 |
| Patient (7) | 1 |
| Patient (4) | 3 |
| Patient (1) | 4 |
| Patient (6) | 3 |

Only Patients with an A-attribute of 3 are X-rayed and assuming no additional patients arrive they are dealt with in the order Patient (2), Patient (4) and Patient (6).

EXERCISE 7.7
Repeat the routing example (Fig. 7.8) using the MQ option.

### M1 to M9—Match

| PERCENTAGE OF ATT | ATT | OPTION | PERCENTAGE OF QUANTITY |
|---|---|---|---|
| ✓ (>0) | ✓ | M1 | |

Rather than matching against a fixed value (MQ option) we may want to match attribute values with one another. We do this using the M1...M9 options which enable us to have up to nine independent matchings in one activity.

The first condition using an M option becomes the matching master and all subsequent conditions with the same M option are followers.

If a match is not possible with the current matching master, and the source queue position is E or I, or there is an alternative condition, other entities are tried to establish a new matching master. If no acceptable match is possible, the activity does not start.

*Example* A production unit makes motors and frames to customer specifications. Each motor and its associated frame is given an order number at the beginning of production. They are produced on separate lines and when complete, are assembled and dispatched to the customer. Obviously each motor must be fitted to the correct frame, and the 'assemble' activity shown in Fig. 7.14 ensures a correct match.

MOTOR A Order number
FRAME A Order number

**Figure 7.14**

The following Motors are waiting in queue 1 and the following Frames in queue 2:

| | A-attribute | | A-attribute |
|---|---|---|---|
| Motor (9) | 1 | Frame (1) | 3 |
| Motor (2) | 2 | Frame (7) | 18 |
| Motor (8) | 7 | Frame (9) | 13 |
| Motor (4) | 3 | Frame (4) | 2 |

As the source queue position for Motor is 'E', each Motor is taken in turn and its corresponding Frame searched for. The first match is with Motor (2) and Frame (4) and the second match is with Motor (4) and Frame (1).

*Example* Lorries are loaded for dispatch to one of five areas with orders for one of four types of material, which are stored in silos. The activity shown in Fig. 7.15 ensures that complete orders are loaded on lorries going to the correct destination and that the material is taken from the correct silos.

| | | | | | | | | | | |
|---|---|---|---|---|---|---|---|---|---|---|

ORDER A Destination (1–5)
B Size of order
C Product type (1–4)

LORRY A Destination (1–5)
B Size of load
C Product type (1–4)

SILO A –
B Amount in stock
C Product type (1–4)

**Figure 7.15**

The following entities are available:

| | | A-attribute | B-attribute | C-attribute |
|---|---|---|---|---|
| Queue 2 | Order (9) | 4 | 120 | 1 |
| | Order (2) | 3 | 150 | 1 |
| | Order (3) | 1 | 90 | 4 |
| | | | (maximum = 300) | |
| Queue 1 | Lorry (1) | 3 | 50 | 1 |
| | Lorry (8) | 4 | 40 | 4 |
| | | | (maximum = 800) | |
| Queue 4 | Silo (1) | | 210 | 1 |
| | Silo (4) | | 70 | 4 |
| | Silo (3) | | 540 | 3 |
| | Silo (2) | | 240 | 2 |

The total Order must be satisfied (TT option). The destinations of the Order and Lorry are matched (M1 option). The grades of the Order, Lorry and Silo are matched (M2 option). The material is loaded from the Silo to the Lorry (TR option). Thus the activity starts with Order (2), Lorry (1) and Silo (1) and moves a quantity of 150.

EXERCISE 7.8
(a) A company has a number of salesmen who have to make a given number of sales visits in a day, the number depending on each salesman's area and capability. When a salesman has reached his target he may go home. Give the details of an activity entitled 'go home'.

(b) Jobs arrive at a repair shop and are broken down into four parts—A, B, C and D. Each part has to be examined and repaired. All four parts of a job have previously been given an order number (A-attribute).

The repair times for the different parts vary, and there are two lines for repairing part A, two lines for repairing part B, three lines for repairing part C and one line for repairing part D. The parts are then reassembled and tested. Draw a flow diagram showing this.

**G1 to G9—compare Greater than or equal to**
**L1 to L9—compare Less than or equal to**
**X1 to X9—compare not equal to**

| PERCENTAGE OF ATT | ATT | OPTION | PERCENTAGE OF QUANTITY |
|---|---|---|---|
| ✓ (>0) | ✓ | G1 | |
| ✓ (>0) | ✓ | L1 | |
| ✓ (>0) | ✓ | X1 | |

These options allow the current value of an attribute, multiplied by a percentage, to be compared with the value set up by a matching master option (M1...M9).

*Example*  A number of steel ingots are tested for quality control purposes. To be accepted, the tensile strength of a steel ingot must be at least equal to a standard value and its hardness must not exceed a standard value, as shown in Fig. 7.16.

| TENSILE | A | Standard Strength |
|---|---|---|
| HARDNESS | A | Standard Hardness |
| STEEL | D | Tensile Strength |
| | F | Hardness |

**Figure 7.16**

If the Steel fails either of the requirements, it is rejected and passed to queue 15.

**I1 to I9—Insert**
**J1 to J9—Join**

| PERCENTAGE OF ATT | ATT | OPTION | PERCENTAGE OF QUANTITY |
|---|---|---|---|
| | ✓ | I1 | ✓ (>0) |
| | ✓ | J1 | ✓ (≠0) |

These options enable us to copy values from one attribute to another. They are used with the corresponding M1...M9 options, which set a matching master. The I1...I9 options copy a percentage of this value into an attribute replacing the value already there, and the J1...J9 options join the value to the existing attribute.

*Example* Steel plates are rolled, side trimmed and then divided into two. The original plates have as attributes, a thickness, a width, and a length. The activity in Fig. 7.17 shows how an original plate is divided into two (using a new plate from the outside world—queue 90).

| P·E ACTIVITY NUMBER | 19 | ACTIVITY NAME | DIVIDE PLATE | ACTIVITY TYPE | |
|---|---|---|---|---|---|
| CO-ORDINATES | X | Y | NUMBER OF CONDITIONS | 2 | MATCH OR MINIMUM QUANTITY |

| IN SWITCH | SOURCE QUEUE POS NO | ENTITY NAME | DEST QUEUE NO POS | ALT QUEUE NC POS | OUT SWITCH | ALT COND | PERCENTAGE OF ATT | ATT | OPTION | PERCENTAGE OF QUANTITY |
|---|---|---|---|---|---|---|---|---|---|---|
| | E 7 | PLATE | 5 T | | | | 100 | A | M1 | |
| | | | | | | | 100 | B | M2 | |
| | | | | | | | 100 | C | M3 | |
| | | | | | | | | C | J3 | -50 |
| | E 90 | PLATE | 5 T | | | | | A | I1 | 100 |
| | | | | | | | | B | I2 | 100 |
| | | | | | | | | C | I3 | 50 |
| | | | | | | | | | | |
| | | | | | | | | | | |
| | | | | | | | | | | |

| CONST | DATA FIELD | PERCENT | ATT | ENTITY NAME | FUNC | ALPHA | BETA |
|---|---|---|---|---|---|---|---|
| | | | | | | | |

Figure 7.17

PLATE A Thickness
B Width
C Length

The thickness of the original Plate is inserted into the A-attribute of the new Plate (M1 and I1 options). The width of the original Plate is inserted into the B-attribute of the new Plate (M2 and I2 options). The length of the original Plate is halved and half the original length is inserted into the new Plate (M3, J3 and I3 options).

## Attribute alteration

The options under this heading change the values of attributes. The XR and XS options reset an attribute to a value between zero and its maximum. The UR option changes an attribute value by a constant amount. The PI and PJ options give access to the simulation clock time.

***XR—eXtra Reset***
***XS—eXtra Set***

| PERCENTAGE OF ATT | ATT | OPTION | PERCENTAGE OF QUANTITY |
|---|---|---|---|
| | ✓ | XR | ✓ (0–100) |
| | ✓ | XS | ✓ (0–100) |

The XR and XS options reset the value in an attribute to a percentage of its maximum. These options are independent of all other options. The XS option takes effect when the activity starts, the XR option sets values at the end of the activity.

*Example* After emptying its load, a lorry is cleaned and refuelled as shown in Fig. 7.18.

The A-attribute of the Lorry is set at zero and the B-attribute is set to its maximum, irrespective of the starting values of the attributes. Thus if the Lorry was originally carrying sand (type of load = 4) and had only 32 units of fuel left, it would finish up in queue 2, clean (zero in A-attribute) and with a full tank (maximum in B-attribute).

| CONST | DATA FIELD | PERCENT | ATT | ENTITY NAME | FUNC | ALPHA | BETA |

LORRY A Type of load
(maximum = 100)
B Amount of fuel
(maximum = 150)

**Figure 7.18**

## UR—Unit Rate

| PERCENTAGE OF ATT | ATT | OPTION | PERCENTAGE OF QUANTITY |
|---|---|---|---|
| | ✓ | UR | ✓ (≠0) |

The UR option changes an attribute value by a constant amount (1 multiplied by a percentage). This option is independent of all other options.

*Example* A lorry is used to deliver orders from a warehouse and is serviced after every 50 journeys. The 'delivery' activity is shown in Fig. 7.19.

ORDER A Size of order (1–4)
LORRY A Size of load
B Number of journeys
since last service

**Figure 7.19**

Every time the activity takes place, the B-attribute of Lorry is increased by 1 (100 per cent of 1), and when the value becomes 50, the Lorry goes into a higher priority activity for servicing (not shown—but see MQ options).

## PI—Present time Insert
## PJ—Present time Join

| PERCENTAGE OF ATT | ATT | OPTION | PERCENTAGE OF QUANTITY |
|---|---|---|---|
| | ✓ | PI | ✓ (>0) |
| | ✓ | PJ | ✓ (≠0) |

These options give access to the current simulation clock time. They operate when an activity ends, and therefore use the *END* time of an activity.

The PI option inserts the present simulation time, multiplied by a percentage, into the attribute replacing the value already there. The PJ option joins the present simulation time, multiplied by a percentage, to the value already in the attribute.

*Example* A manufacturer stamps each batch of yogurt with a 'sell by' date which is five days after manufacture, as shown in Fig. 7.20.

| P·E ACTIVITY NUMBER | 25 | ACTIVITY NAME | SELL BY DATE | ACTIVITY TYPE | |
|---|---|---|---|---|---|
| CO-ORDINATES | X | Y | NUMBER OF CONDITIONS | 1 | MATCH OR MINIMUM QUANTITY |

| IN SWITCH | SOURCE QUEUE POS. NO | ENTITY NAME | DEST QUEUE NO. POS. | ALT QUEUE NC POS. | OUT SWITCH | ALT COND. | PERCENTAGE OF ATT | ATT | OPTION | PERCENTAGE OF QUANTITY |
|---|---|---|---|---|---|---|---|---|---|---|
| | E 11 | YOGURT | 20 T | | | | | A | PI | 100 |
| | | | | | | | | A | UR | 500 |
| | | | | | | | | | | |
| | | | | | | | | | | |
| | | | | | | | | | | |
| | | | | | | | | | | |
| | | | | | | | | | | |
| | | | | | | | | | | |
| | | | | | | | | | | |

| CONST | DATA FIELD | PERCENT | ATT | ENTITY NAME | FUNC | ALPHA | BETA |
|---|---|---|---|---|---|---|---|
| | | | | | | | |

YOGURT A 'Sell by' date

**Figure 7.20**

If the time units in the model are days, the PI option inserts the current time in the A-attribute, and the UR option adds five to it.

## Data field manipulation

Data fields can be used in three different ways. They can contribute to the duration of activities, as has been seen frequently in earlier chapters. They can also be used to set values in attributes—for example a product code or the next process in a production sequence. The third use is to hold data which is used throughout the model and is not specific to a particular entity. In some models stock levels are best held in this way.

There are numerous options available to manipulate and access data fields but they have a logical coding structure. Families of options have the same initial letter, and the second letter defines the function performed.

The first family of options is used to obtain random samples from a distribution or the next entry from a timetable. All these options begin with the letter 'G', denoting a 'get' from a data field.

***GD—Get Data***
***GI—(Get) Insert data***
***GJ—(Get) Join data***

| PERCENTAGE OF ATT | ATT | OPTION | PERCENTAGE OF QUANTITY |
|---|---|---|---|
| | ✓ | GD | |
| 1 – N* | | GD | |
| | ✓ | GI | ✓ (>0) |
| | ✓ | GJ | ✓ (≠0) |

*N = Number of data fields

The GD option 'samples' from a data field and sets up a value for subsequent GI or GJ options to use. The data field number can be a constant or a value held in an attribute. The GI option inserts the sample (multiplied by a percentage) in the attribute, replacing the value already there. The GJ option joins the sample (multiplied by a percentage) to the value already in the attribute.

Any number of GD options may be used within an activity, but each must be followed by at least one GI or GJ option.

*Example*  Orders for a product are received for any of four grades, with varying quantities and delivery dates, as shown in Fig. 7.21.

ORDER  A  Type of order (1–4)
B  Size of order
C  Delivery date

**Figure 7.21**

The grade of material to be supplied is sampled from data field 6, and inserted in the A-attribute. There are four grades, and the Order sizes are different for each grade. These sizes are stored in distributions 1–4. The grade determines which of these distributions is sampled, and the Order size is inserted into the B-attribute. The delivery period is sampled from distribution 7, and added to the C-attribute, which already holds the current date, to give the actual delivery date.

EXERCISE 7.9

(a) In the above example 20 per cent of orders are for grade 1, 25 per cent for grade 2, 5 per cent for grade 3 and 50 per cent for grade 4. Give the coordinates and plot the distribution (data field 6) used to generate the grade of an order.

(b) A company has two gear-cutting machines. Both take between 22 and 25 minutes (distribution 2) to cut a pair of gears but one machine is older and breaks down more frequently. The older machine produces between 97 and 123 pairs of gears (distribution 3) before it breaks down while the other machine produces between 275 and 350 pairs of gears (distribution 11) before it breaks down. It takes between 70 and 120 minutes (distribution 5) to repair either machine. Draw a flow diagram of this, using the distribution numbers given. List the entities and their attributes.

The next family of options select from a data field in a directed rather than a random manner. They all begin with the letter 'D', denoting a 'direct' access.

***DD—Direct Data***
***DE—Direct Entry***
***DI—Data Insert***
***DJ—Data Join***

| PERCENTAGE OF ATT | ATT | OPTION | PERCENTAGE OF QUANTITY |
|---|---|---|---|
| | ✓ | DD | |
| 1–N* | | DD | |
| ✓(>0) | | DE | |
| Op(>0) | ✓ | DE | |
| | ✓ | DI | ✓ (>0) |
| | ✓ | DJ | ✓ (≠0) |

* N = Number of data fields

The DD option specifies which distribution is to be accessed. The DE option defines which point in the data field is to be selected. The order in which these two options are specified does not matter, but they must both be specified before the corresponding DI or DJ options, which perform similar functions to the GI or GJ options. After at least one use of DI or DJ, one or both of the DD and DE options may be respecified.

*Example* A part undergoes a number of different processes depending upon the part type. Figure 22 shows an activity to set the next process required. Timetables 1 to 10 hold lists of processes for Part types 1 to 10.

| P·E ACTIVITY NUMBER | | ACTIVITY NAME | SET PROCESS | ACTIVITY TYPE | |
|---|---|---|---|---|---|
| CO-ORDINATES | X | Y | NUMBER OF CONDITIONS | | MATCH OR MINIMUM QUANTITY |

| IN SWITCH | SOURCE QUEUE POS NO | ENTITY NAME | DEST QUEUE NO POS | ALT QUEUE NC POS | OUT SWITCH | ALT COND | PERCENTAGE OF ATT | ATT | OPTION | PERCENTAGE OF QUANTITY |
|---|---|---|---|---|---|---|---|---|---|---|
| | H B | PART | 14 T | | | | | A | DD | |
| | | | | | | | | B | UR | 100 |
| | | | | | | | | B | DE | |
| | | | | | | | | C | DI | 100 |
| | | | | | | | | | | |
| | | | | | | | | | | |
| | | | | | | | | | | |
| | | | | | | | | | | |
| | | | | | | | | | | |
| | | | | | | | | | | |

| CONST | DATA FIELD | PERCENT | ATT | ENTITY NAME | FUNC | ALPHA | BETA |
|---|---|---|---|---|---|---|---|
| | | | | | | | |

Figure 7.22

PART A Part number (1–10)
B Number of processes completed
C Next process code

The family of options, starting with 'S' for 'search' is used to find (and use) the locations of values in data fields and therefore in a sense perform the reverse of options DD, DE, DI and DJ.

***SD—Search Data***
***SE—Search Entry***
***SI—Search Insert***
***SJ—Search Join***

| PERCENTAGE OF ATT | ATT | OPTION | PERCENTAGE OF QUANTITY |
|---|---|---|---|
| | ✓ | SD | |
| ✓(>0) | | SE | |
| Op(>0) | ✓ | SE | |
| 1–N* | | SD | |
| | ✓ | SI | ✓ (>0) |
| | ✓ | SJ | ✓ (≠0) |

* N = Number of data fields

To show the distinction, consider a timetable with the five entries:

| 11 | 13 | 8 | 30 | 26 |

If the DE option is given a value of 4 (fourth entry in timetable) it will return the value 30.
If the SE option is given a value of 13, it will return the value 2 (second entry in timetable).
The SI and SJ options perform similar functions for SD as the DI and DJ options do for DD.

The next family of options allow the updating of data fields. They all begin with the letter 'R' for 'revision'.

*RD—Revise Data field*
*RE—Revise Entry point*
*RI—Revise Insert*
*RJ—Revise Join*

| PERCENTAGE OF ATT | ATT | OPTION | PERCENTAGE OF QUANTITY |
|---|---|---|---|
| | ✓ | RD | |
| 1–N* | | RD | |
| ✓ (>0) | | RE | |
| Op(>0) | ✓ | RE | |
| ✓ (>0) | ✓ | RI | |
| ✓ (≠0) | ✓ | RJ | |

\* N = Number of data fields

The RD option specifies the data field number to be used.
The RE option, when used with a timetable, specifies which entry is to be revised (counting from the first). When used with a distribution it specifies the pair of entries for which the 'time' coordinate is to be revised.
The RI and RJ options take the current value of an attribute, multiplied by a percentage, and either insert the result in place of, or join it to, the value in the specified data field.

*TD—Timetable Data*
*TE—Timetable Entry*
*TI—Timetable Insert*
*TJ—Timetable Join*

| PERCENTAGE OF ATT | ATT | OPTION | PERCENTAGE OF QUANTITY |
|---|---|---|---|
| | ✓ | TD | |
| 1–N* | | TD | |
| ✓ (>0) | | TE | |
| Op(>0) | ✓ | TE | |
| ✓ (>0) | ✓ | TI | |
| ✓ (≠0) | ✓ | TJ | |

\* N = Number of data fields

The options TD, TE, TI, TJ together perform a similar function to the RD, RE, RI, RJ options except that the T options update the value in the data field in the start phase while the R options perform updating in the end phase. They can therefore be used to control whether an activity starts.

The TD and TE options are also used to specify timetable entries for the I-options (start phase timetable checking—see below) The TD option specifies the data field and the TE option specifies the point in the data field which is to be modified. The order in which these two options are specified does not matter, but they must both be specified before the corresponding TI, TJ or I-option.

The TI option inserts an attribute value into a timetable, whereas the TJ adds (joins) the attribute value.

*Example* The activity in Fig. 7.23 shows how timetable 3 (which records the usage of track sections by automated guided vehicles—AGVs) is updated by inserting the AGV number into the appropriate timetable location.

AGV A AGV number
    B Track element required

**Figure 7.23**

This process is only of real value if the track element is currently free—this leads to the closely allied concept of start phase timetable checking.

The final main family of data field options perform precisely this task. The appropriate I options must be used in conjunction with TD and TE options (which select the data field value) to perform the check.

*IE—Initial Empty*
*IC—Initial Contents*
*IL—Initial Less than or equal to*
*IM—Initial More than or equal to*
*IX—Initial not equal to*

| PERCENTAGE OF ATT | ATT | OPTION | PERCENTAGE OF QUANTITY |
|---|---|---|---|
| | | IE | |
| ✓ (>0) | Op | IC | |
| ✓ (>0) | Op | IL | |
| ✓ (>0) | Op | IM | |
| ✓ (>0) | Op | IX | |

The IE option checks if the data field value is zero. No percentage is required.

The IC option checks if the data field value is either equal to a stated percentage of a given attribute, or equal to the specified numeric value if no attribute letter is given.

The IL option checks if the data field value is either less than or equal to a stated percentage of a given attribute, or less than or equal to a specified numeric value if no attribute is given.

The IM option checks if the data field value is either more than or equal to a stated percentage of a given attribute, or more than or equal to a specified numeric value if no attribute is given.

The IX option checks if the data field value is either not equal to a stated percentage of a given attribute, or not equal to a specified numeric value if no attribute is given.

*Example*   Figure 7.24 shows how to modify the activity shown in Fig. 7.23 to ensure that the required section of track is clear before using it.

| P-E ACTIVITY NUMBER | | ACTIVITY NAME | R E S E R V E   T R | | | ACTIVITY TYPE | |
|---|---|---|---|---|---|---|---|
| CO-ORDINATES | | X | Y | NUMBER OF CONDITIONS | | MATCH OR MINIMUM | QUANTITY |
| IN SWITCH | SOURCE QUEUE POS. NO. | ENTITY NAME | DEST QUEUE NO POS | ALT QUEUE NO POS | OUT SWITCH | ALT COND | PERCENTAGE OF ATT | ATT | OPTION | PERCENTAGE OR QUANTITY |

AGV   A   AGV number
      B   Track element required

**Figure 7.24**

EXERCISE 7.10

(a) When completed, a production batch goes into stock. The product type and quantity vary for each batch. Give details of the 'complete' activity which updates the stock level for a completed batch.

(b) There are several pans, one for each type of object. An object is added into its pan, if the total weight of objects in the pan would not exceed 100 kg. The current pan weights are held in a timetable. The time required to add an object is proportional to its weight, and a 1 kg object takes five seconds to be added. Give details of an activity which adds an object to a pan.

## Attribute checking

This group of options enables us to test the values of attributes and then take a variety of courses of action. The options do not change the attribute values and operate independently of other options used in the activity.

The first set of options in this group are CE, CC, CL, CM and CX.

*CE—Check Empty*
*CC—Check Contents*
*CL—Check Less than or equal to*
*CM—Check More than or equal to*
*CX—Check not equal to*

| PERCENTAGE OF ATT | ATT | OPTION | PERCENTAGE OF QUANTITY |
|---|---|---|---|
| | ✓ | CE | |
| | ✓ | CC | Op(0–100) |
| | ✓ | CL | ✓(1–100) |
| | ✓ | CM | ✓(1–100) |
| | ✓ | CX | ✓(0–100) |

The CE option checks if the attribute value is zero. No percentage is required.

The CC option checks if the attribute value equals a specified percentage of the attribute maximum. If no percentage is specified 100 per cent is presumed.

The CL option checks if the attribute value is less than or equal to a specified percentage of the attribute maximum.

The CM option checks if the attribute value is greater than or equal to a specified percentage of the attribute maximum.

The CX option checks if the attribute value is not equal to a specified percentage of the attribute maximum.

*Example*　An engineer is eligible for promotion from grade 2 to grade 1 if he

- is 35 or over;
- is less than 50;
- has had 3 years' experience in his present grade;
- has had 6 years combined experience in his present and previous grade.

The activity in Fig. 7.25 selects an engineer for promotion. The activity will start if the A-attribute of Engineer is greater than or equal to 35 (CM option) and less than 50 (CL and CX options), the B-attribute is greater than or equal to 3 and the C-attribute is greater than or equal to 6.

ENGINEER　A　Age (maximum = 100)
B　Years in present grade (maximum) = 100)
C　Years in present and previous grade (maximum = 100)

**Figure 7.25**

The 'C' series of options described above is used to control the starting of activities. A second set of options, the 'E' series, checks the values of attributes at the end of an activity. They allow entities to be routed to alternative destination queues depending upon their final attribute values.

*EE—End check contents—Empty*
*EC—End check Contents equal*
*EL—End check contents Less than or equal*
*EM—End check contents More than or equal*
*EX—End check contents not equal*
*EA—End check—Always satisfied*

| PERCENTAGE OF ATT | ATT | OPTION | PERCENTAGE OF QUANTITY |
|---|---|---|---|
| | ✓ | EE | |
| | ✓ | EC | ✓ (0–100) |
| | ✓ | EL | ✓ (1–100) |
| | ✓ | EM | ✓ (1–100) |
| | ✓ | EX | ✓ (0–100) |
| | | EA | |

To use these options the alternative queue number and position must be entered on a continuation line with the appropriate End Check option that will control the move to the alternative queue. When the activity ends the current value of each attribute is checked against the specified percentage of its maximum value. If the result is satisfactory the entity will be moved to the alternative queue specified in the same line as the option. Any number of routed alternative queues may be specified in the same condition and the entity is moved to the first one whose associated End Check option is satisfied. If the checks fail, the entity will go to the normal destination queue.

A further extension of the End Check facilities allows an attribute letter to be entered in the alternative queue number space so that the alternative queue required is given by the current value of that attribute.

If all entities are to be routed by an attribute value the EA option together with the selected attribute letter is used instead of a queue number for the alternative queue. If the attribute value is zero the EA option fails.

One or more of the routed alternative queues may be the same as the destination queue if the logic of the model requires it.

If a destination clock switch is entered on the same continuation line as the End Check option, this switch will operate only when that option is satisfied and used.

*Example* Maintenance and repair work at a factory is carried out by a team of fitters, each doing one job at a time. Fitters are of different grades, from grade 1 (apprentice) to grade 5 (working chargehand). This is modelled in Fig. 7.26.

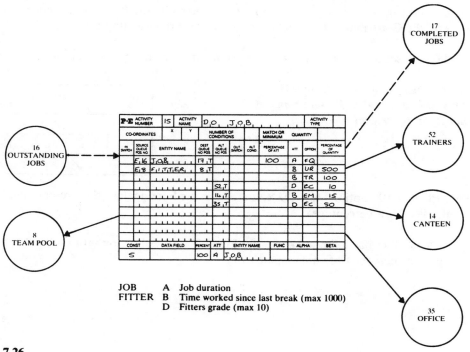

| JOB | A | Job duration |
| FITTER | B | Time worked since last break (max 1000) |
| | D | Fitters grade (max 10) |

**Figure 7.26**

The D attribute of Fitter holds the grade and has a maximum value of 10. The duration of each Job is stored in its A attribute, a further five minutes is spent collecting the Job docket and walking to the Job. The total time a Fitter has worked since his last break is recorded in his B attribute (maximum value 1000); each Fitter is entitled to a break after 150 minutes' work.

Most Fitters go straight from one job to the next. This is simulated by making queue 8 both the source queue and the destination queue for the Fitter. An apprentice always reports to the training supervisor on finishing a Job, even if his break is due. All other Fitters, including the chargehand, will take their break (if it is due) as soon as they finish their current Job. The chargehand always calls at the office before another Job.

The example above illustrates that the value of an attribute used by an End Check option may be altered by previous options. Options are processed in order, and the value used in the End Check option is the value of the attribute when the option is processed.

A further extension of the End Check facilities allows an attribute letter to be entered in the alternative queue number space so that the alternative queue required is given by the current value of the attribute.

EXERCISE 7.11

(a) An oven is lit only if a hopper containing coke (B-attribute equals 3) or coal (B-attribute equals 6) is available and is more than one-third full. Give details of an activity which selects a suitable hopper.

(b) A part is picked up by a labourer if it has been painted (A-attribute equals 1) and is carried to the next process (process input queue given by the B-attribute, and travel time given by the C-attribute). Give details of an activity representing this task.

The following set of options allows comparison with the current simulation time.

**PM—More than or equal to Present time**
**PL—Less than or equal to Present time**
**PX—not equal to Present time**

| PERCENTAGE OF ATT | ATT | OPTION | PERCENTAGE OF QUANTITY |
|---|---|---|---|
| | ✓ | PM | ✓ (>0) |
| | ✓ | PL | ✓ (>0) |
| | ✓ | PX | ✓ (>0) |

The PM, PL and PX options test the value of an attribute against the present simulation time (multiplied by a percentage).

*Example* A product has a limited shelf life; Fig. 7.27 shows how only those batches which have not passed their shelf life are dispatched.

| P-E ACTIVITY NUMBER | 3 | ACTIVITY NAME | SHIP BATCH | ACTIVITY TYPE | |
|---|---|---|---|---|---|
| CO-ORDINATES | X | Y | NUMBER OF CONDITIONS | 1 | MATCH OR MINIMUM QUANTITY |

| IN SWITCH | SOURCE QUEUE POS NO | ENTITY NAME | DEST QUEUE NO POS | ALT QUEUE NO POS | OUT SWITCH | ALT COND | PERCENTAGE OF ATT | ATT | OPTION | PERCENTAGE OF QUANTITY |
|---|---|---|---|---|---|---|---|---|---|---|
| | E43 | BATCH | 58T | | | | | A | PM | 100 |
| | | | | | | | | | | |
| | | | | | | | | | | |
| | | | | | | | | | | |
| | | | | | | | | | | |
| | | | | | | | | | | |
| | | | | | | | | | | |
| | | | | | | | | | | |
| | | | | | | | | | | |

| CONST | DATA FIELD | PERCENT | ATT | ENTITY NAME | FUNC | ALPHA | BETA |
|---|---|---|---|---|---|---|---|
| | | | | | | | |

**Figure 7.27**

| | | |
|---|---|---|
| BATCH | A | Time by which batch must be shipped |

If the current simulation time exceeds the value in the A-attribute, the Batch will not be sent out.

If the attribute value is required to be exactly equal to the present time then both the PL and PM options are used.

## Attribute arithmetic

This group of options enables us to add, substract, multiply and divide attribute values. The results of the calculations are held in an accumulator which has a maximum value and this must not be exceeded during any stage of the calculations. The final result can be used to update attributes.

The AC option defines the maximum on the accumulator. The AA, AP, BA and BP options are used for addition and subtraction. The BM and BD options are used for multiplication and division. The AI, AJ and AS options take the result of the calculations to update attributes. The AR option resets the accumulator.

### *AC—Arithmetic Calculation*

| PERCENTAGE OF ATT | ATT | OPTION | PERCENTAGE OF QUANTITY |
|---|---|---|---|
| ✓ (>0) | ✓ | AC | |

This option sets the maximum for the accumulator and if used must be the first of any of the attribute arithmetic options in an activity. The maximum is the current attribute value of the entity (multiplied by a percentage). If it is not used the maximum will be set to the largest number possible.

### *AA—Add All*
### *AP—Add Part*

| PERCENTAGE OF ATT | ATT | OPTION | PERCENTAGE OF QUANTITY |
|---|---|---|---|
| ✓ (≠0) | ✓ | AA | |
| ✓ (≠0) | ✓ | AP | |

The AA option adds the value of an attribute (multiplied by a percentage) to the accumulator, and reduces the attribute by the same amount.

The AP option adds as much of the value of an attribute (multiplied by a percentage) as possible to the accumulator, and reduces the attribute by the same amount. If this amount is zero the entity is rejected.

*Example*  Two types of passengers are waiting for a flight—full-fare and standby. The full-fare passengers embark first, and the details are given in Fig. 7.28.

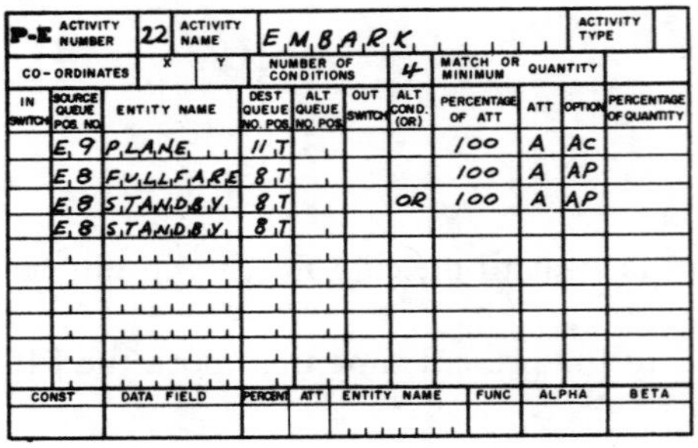

| PLANE | A | Number of seats |
|---|---|---|
| FULL-FARE | A | Number of full-fare passengers |
| STANDBY | A | Number of standby passengers |

**Figure 7.28**

The following entities are available:

| | | *A-attribute* |
|---|---|---|
| Queue 9 | Plane | 180 |
| Queue 8 | Full-fare | 164 |
| | Standby | 26 |

The accumulator maximum is set to 180 (A-attribute of Plane), and the Plane is loaded with 164 Full-fare and 16 Standby passengers (i.e. 10 Standby passengers are left behind).

If, instead, the Standby passengers form a party which must go on the same flight, the option for Standby becomes 'AA'. The Plane is then loaded with 164 Full-fare and no Standby passengers, leaving 16 empty seats.

**BA—Book All**
**BP—Book Part**

| PERCENTAGE OF ATT | ATT | OPTION | PERCENTAGE OF QUANTITY |
|---|---|---|---|
| ✓ (≠0) | Op | BA | |
| ✓ (≠0) | Op | BP | |

These options are similar to the AA and AP options, except that the attribute values themselves remain unchanged and that constants may be used instead of attribute values.

**BM—Multiply**
**BD—Divide**

| PERCENTAGE OF ATT | ATT | OPTION | PERCENTAGE OF QUANTITY |
|---|---|---|---|
| ✓ (≠0) | Op | BM | |
| ✓ (≠0) | Op | BD | |

These options multiply or divide the total in the accumulator by an attribute value (multiplied by the percentage) or a constant so long as the accumulator does not exceed its maximum. The attribute value remains unchanged when the activity ends. If a BD option is used and the attribute value is zero, the entity is rejected.

*AI—Arithmetic Insert*
*AJ—Arithmetic Join*
*AS—Arithmetic Shortfall*
*AR—Arithmetic Reset*

| PERCENTAGE OF ATT | ATT | OPTION | PERCENTAGE OF QUANTITY |
|---|---|---|---|
| | ✓ | AI | ✓ ($\neq$0) |
| | ✓ | AJ | ✓ ($\neq$0) |
| | ✓ | AS | ✓ ($\neq$0) |
| | | AR | ✓ (0–100) |

At any stage after the calculations have started, the accumulator total, or the difference between the total and the accumulator maximum (the shortfall) can be used to modify attribute values. The accumulator total can be reset at any stage.

The AI option inserts the accumulator total, multiplied by a percentage, into an attribute, replacing the value already there.

The AJ option adds the accumulator total, multiplied by a percentage, to the value already in the attribute.

The AS option adds the shortfall (multiplied by a percentage) to the value already in the attribute.

The AR option resets the total in the accumulator to the specified percentage of the accumulator maximum set by the AC option.

*Example*  Batches of work arrive at a machine shop. Each batch consists of a number of similar items and there are standard times for each type of item. Figure 7.29 shows how the total time for a batch is calculated.

JOBLIST  A  Type of job
         B  Standard time to produce one item
BATCH    A  Type of job
         B  Number in batch
         C  Time to produce batch

**Figure 7.29**

The Batch is matched against a Joblist (M1 option). The standard time to produce one item is added to the accumulator (BA option) and multiplied by the number in the batch (BM option). This value is then inserted into the C-attribute of Batch (AI option).

EXERCISE 7.12
Material is held in three stock areas. When the total stock falls below a minimum quantity, an order for sufficient material to fill the stock areas, is generated. Give details of the 'order' activity.

## Attribute histograms

There are two options under this heading which enable us to record information in histograms. The HS option records quantities moved in or out of attributes and the HE option records the current values of attributes. These histograms are in addition to those which record clock times, described in Chapter 6.

### HS—HiStogram

| PERCENTAGE OF ATT | ATT | OPTION | PERCENTAGE OF QUANTITY |
|---|---|---|---|
| Op($\neq 0$) | Op | HS | |

The HS option records the values moved into or out of an attribute and must immediately follow the attribute concerned. If required the values can be multiplied by a percentage before being entered into the histogram.

*Example*  When a lorry is unloaded into a bunker, the load moved is recorded in a histogram, as shown in Fig. 7.30.

LORRY    A Size of load
BUNKER   A Contents

**Figure 7.30**

Because the quantity is taken *from* the Lorry, the entry in the histogram will be negative. We can make the entry positive by specifying the percentage of attribute as $-100$.

In Fig. 7.30 the values are recorded in the histogram on the A-attribute of Lorry. If this histogram is used for some other purpose (for example, recording the amount being loaded *into* the Lorry in another activity), we can use another histogram (say on the B-attribute) to record the amount unloaded, as shown in Fig. 7.31.

The quantity taken from the A-attribute of the Lorry will be stored as a positive value in the histogram on the B-attribute of Lorry.

| P-E | ACTIVITY NUMBER | 25 | ACTIVITY NAME | U N L O A D | | | | | ACTIVITY TYPE | |
|---|---|---|---|---|---|---|---|---|---|---|
| CO-ORDINATES | | X | Y | NUMBER OF CONDITIONS | | 2 | MATCH OR MINIMUM | QUANTITY | | |
| IN SWITCH | SOURCE QUEUE POS. NO. | ENTITY NAME | DEST QUEUE NO. POS | ALT QUEUE NO. POS | OUT SWITCH | ALT COND. (OR) | PERCENTAGE OF ATT | ATT | OPTION | PERCENTAGE OF QUANTITY |
| | E.1 | L O R R Y | 2 T | | | | | A | TR | -100 |
| | | | | | | | -100 | B | HS | |
| | E.4 | B U N K E R | 4 T | | | | | A | TR | 100 |
| CONST | | DATA FIELD | PERCENT | ATT | ENTITY NAME | | FUNC | ALPHA | | BETA |

LORRY    A   Size of load
         B   For recording quantities unloaded
BUNKER   A   Contents

**Figure 7.31**

## HE—Histogram of Existing values

| PERCENTAGE OF ATT | ATT | OPTION | PERCENTAGE OF QUANTITY |
|---|---|---|---|
| Op(>0) | Op | HE | |

This option records the existing value of any attribute of an entity (not just those explicitly listed in the activity).

*Example*   Ships deliver various grades of chemical to a home port from ports around the world. They unload into storage tanks. Figure 7.32 shows how histograms are collected of the grades and quantities moved, together with a histogram of the ports from which the ships have come.

| P-E | ACTIVITY NUMBER | 26 | ACTIVITY NAME | U N L O A D | | | | | ACTIVITY TYPE | |
|---|---|---|---|---|---|---|---|---|---|---|
| CO-ORDINATES | | X | Y | NUMBER OF CONDITIONS | | 2 | MATCH OR MINIMUM | QUANTITY | | |
| IN SWITCH | SOURCE QUEUE POS. NO. | ENTITY NAME | DEST QUEUE NO. POS | ALT QUEUE NO. POS | OUT SWITCH | ALT COND. (OR) | PERCENTAGE OF ATT | ATT | OPTION | PERCENTAGE OF QUANTITY |
| | E.7 | S H I P | 7 T | | | | 100 | A | M1 | |
| | | | | | | | 100 | A | HE | |
| | | | | | | | | B | TR | -100 |
| | | | | | | | -100 | B | HS | |
| | | | | | | | 100 | C | HE | |
| | E.9 | T A N K | 9 T | | | | 100 | A | M1 | |
| | | | | | | | | B | TR | 100 |
| CONST | | DATA FIELD | PERCENT | ATT | ENTITY NAME | | FUNC | ALPHA | | BETA |

SHIP   A   Grade of chemical
       B   Size of load
       C   Originating port
TANK   A   Grade of chemical
       B   Size of contents
           (maximum = capacity)

**Figure 7.32**

The grade of chemical on a Ship is matched against a Tank (M1 option) and recorded in a histogram (HE option). The chemical is transferred from the Ship to the Tank (TR option) and the quantity recorded in a histogram (HS option). The port from which the Ship has come is also recorded in a histogram (HE option).

## Variable percentage

In the options we have described so far all percentages have been specified as constants. However, there are occasions when a percentage cannot be fixed in advance and needs to be calculated each time the activity runs. The calculated percentage is stored in a variable called Var. The supplementary percentage (100 minus Var) is stored in the variable Sup. Var and Sup are then used instead of constant percentages.

The options in this group used to calculate Var and Sup are VV, NV, and DV.

### VV—Variable Value

| PERCENTAGE OF ATT | ATT | OPTION | PERCENTAGE OF QUANTITY |
|---|---|---|---|
| ✓ (>0) | ✓ | VV | |

With the VV option, Var is the ratio of an attribute value to its maximum (multiplied by the percentage).

*Example*  In making chipboard, batches of chipped wood are dried prior to mixing with resin. The weight of a batch of dried wood depends on its original moisture content. The drying process, in which the weight of wood is reduced, is shown in Fig. 7.33.

BATCH       A Percentage of water (maximum = 100)
            B Weight of batch
DRIER       —

**Figure 7.33**

If a Batch consists of 20 per cent water (Batch A-attribute = 20), the VV option gives the values of Var and Sup as:

$$\text{Var} = \frac{\text{attribute value}}{\text{attribute maximum}} \times \text{percentage} = \frac{20}{100} \times 100\% = 20\%$$

$$\text{Sup} = 100 - \text{Var} = 80\%$$

Var per cent of the original weight of the Batch is subtracted from the original weight (FQ and TR options) to give the weight of dried wood. If the original weight was 250 units, the final weight is 200 units (250 − 20% of 250).

*NV—Numerator Value*
*DV—Denominator Value*

| PERCENTAGE OF ATT | ATT | OPTION | PERCENTAGE OF QUANTITY |
|---|---|---|---|
| ✓ (>0) | ✓ | NV | |
| ✓ (>0) | ✓ | DV | |

These options jointly determine the value of Var and Sup. The value of NV or DV is the ratio of an attribute value to its attribute maximum (multiplied by the percentage). The value of Var is then NV divided by DV, expressed as a percentage.

*Example* ¡Virgin polymer and Reclaim polymer are mixed in an extruder in such proportions that all the available Reclaim polymer is divided evenly between all batches ordered. This is shown in Fig. 7.34.

If the total order is for 20 000 units (Totbatch A-attribute) and originally there are 5000 units of Reclaim (A-attribute) then:

$$NV = \frac{\text{attribute value}}{\text{attribute maximum}} \times \text{percentage} = \frac{5000}{\text{maximum}} \times 100\%$$

$$DV = \frac{\text{attribute value}}{\text{attribute maximum}} \times \text{percentage} = \frac{20\,000}{\text{maximum}} \times 100\%$$

$$\text{Var} = \frac{NV}{DV} \times 100\% \text{ because both maxima are the same} = 25\%$$

$$\text{Sup} = 100 - \text{Var} = 75\%$$

| BATCH | A Batch size |
|---|---|
| TOTBATCH | A Total amount of polymer to be made* |
| RECLAIM | A Original amount of reclaimed polymer |
| | B Current amount of reclaimed polymer* |
| VIRGIN | A Current amount of virgin polymer |

*Both attributes have some maximum value

**Figure 7.34**

Thus each Batch consists of 25 per cent Reclaim polymer and 75 per cent Virgin polymer.

EXERCISE 7.13
The furnace in a steel-making plant is loaded with scrap metal and liquid iron. The percentage of scrap depends on the quality specified on an order. Give details of the 'load furnace' activity.

## Identical conditions

A common requirement in a simulation model is that several similar entities are required simultaneously in the same activity. For example, a number of men come on shift, or take a break together; all dirty containers are collected and cleaned; at the end of the day all trucks are parked.

This can be represented by activities with several identical conditions. (See Fig. 7.35.)

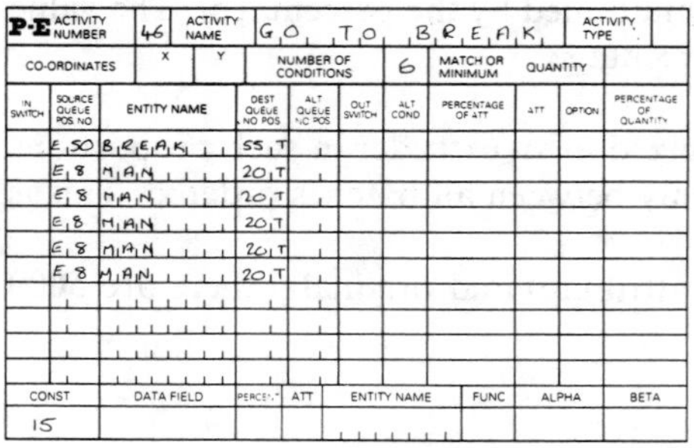

**Figure 7.35**

If the number of men concerned is variable then the activity is as shown as Fig. 7.36.

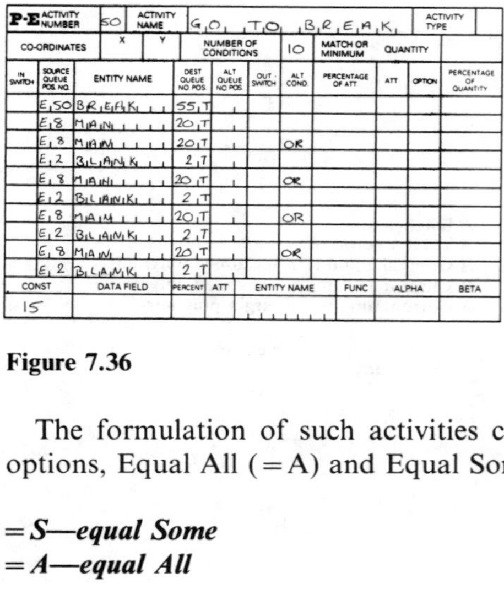

**Figure 7.36**

The formulation of such activities can be simplified by use of the Identical Condition options, Equal All ($=A$) and Equal Some or all ($=S$).

$=S$—*equal Some*
$=A$—*equal All*

| PERCENTAGE OF ATT | ATT | OPTION | PERCENTAGE OF QUANTITY |
|---|---|---|---|
| ✓ (>1) | | =S | |
| ✓ (>1) | | =A | |

The Equal All ($=A$) option requires that a specified number of entities must be present for the activity to commence. The number is specified in the 'Percentage of Attribute' space.

Figure 7.37 shows how the activity in Fig. 7.35 can be simplified by use of the $=A$ option.

| P-E ACTIVITY NUMBER | 46 | ACTIVITY NAME | G O   T O   B R E A K | | ACTIVITY TYPE | |
|---|---|---|---|---|---|---|
| CO-ORDINATES | X | Y | NUMBER OF CONDITIONS | 2 | MATCH OR MINIMUM | QUANTITY |
| IN SWITCH | SOURCE QUEUE POS NO | ENTITY NAME | DEST QUEUE NO POS | ALT QUEUE NO POS | OUT SWITCH | ALT COND | PERCENTAGE OF ATT | ATT | OPTION | PERCENTAGE OF QUANTITY |

E 50 BREAK — SS T
E 8 MAN — 20 T — PERCENTAGE OF ATT 5 — OPTION =A

| CONST | DATA FIELD | PERCENT | ATT | ENTITY NAME | FUNC | ALPHA | BETA |
|---|---|---|---|---|---|---|---|

**Figure 7.37**

The Equal Some or all ( = S) option requires that up to the specified number of entities may be present, but with a minimum of one.

Figure 7.38 shows how the activity in Fig 7.36 can be simplified.

| P-E ACTIVITY NUMBER | 50 | ACTIVITY NAME | G O   T O   B R E A K | | ACTIVITY TYPE | |
|---|---|---|---|---|---|---|
| CO-ORDINATES | X | Y | NUMBER OF CONDITIONS | 2 | MATCH OR MINIMUM | QUANTITY |
| IN SWITCH | SOURCE QUEUE POS NO | ENTITY NAME | DEST QUEUE NO POS | ALT QUEUE NO POS | OUT SWITCH | ALT COND | PERCENTAGE OF ATT | ATT | OPTION | PERCENTAGE OF QUANTITY |

E 50 BREAK — SS T
E 8 MAN — 20 T — PERCENTAGE OF ATT 5 — OPTION = S

| CONST | DATA FIELD | PERCENT | ATT | ENTITY NAME | FUNC | ALPHA | BETA |
|---|---|---|---|---|---|---|---|
| 15 | | | | | | | |

**Figure 7.38**

## Queue size testing and manipulation

These options give access to the current queue sizes. The referenced queue must have a queue size limit greater than zero specified by the user.

The QE, QC, QL, QM and QX options check the current queue size against its limit. The QI and QJ options alter the value of an attribute using the current queue size.

*Specifying the queue*

The queue number must be specified before a queue size option is used. Any number of queues may be specified within the same activity, provided that each is used by at least one option before another queue is specified.

The queue number is entered on a continuation line in the source queue or destination queue columns, according to the particular queue option which is being used, as shown in Fig. 7.39.

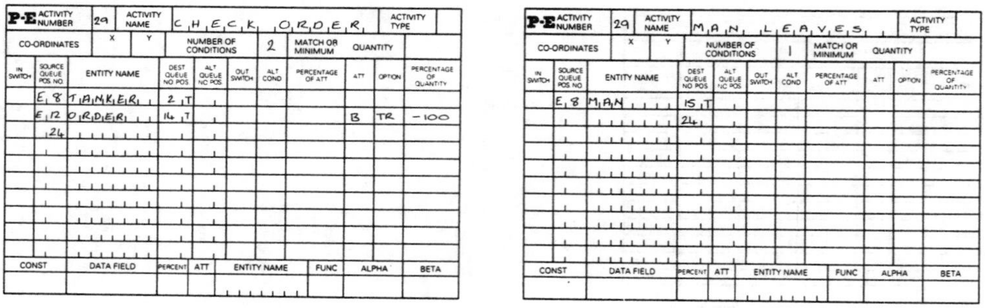

**Figure 7.39**

Both examples find the current size of queue 24. In the first case, using the source queue column, the size is found when the activity starts and in the second case, using the destination queue column, the size is found when the activity ends.

The size of the actual source or destination queue in the condition can be used. In this case, the queue size allows for the movement of the entity concerned.

*QE—Queue Empty*
*QC—Queue Contents*
*QL—Queue size Less than or equal to*
*QM—Queue size More than or equal to*
*QX—Queue size not equal to*

| PERCENTAGE OF ATT | ATT | OPTION | PERCENTAGE OF QUANTITY |
|---|---|---|---|
| | | QE | |
| | | QC | ✓ (>0) |
| | | QL | ✓ (>0) |
| | | QM | ✓ (>0) |
| | | QX | ✓ (≥0) |

These options check the queue size against its limit and are used to test whether an activity can start. Therefore the queue number must be entered in the source queue column.

The QE option checks if the queue size is zero. No percentage is required.

The QC option checks if the queue size equals the specified percentage of the limit.

The QL option checks if the queue size is less than or equal to the specified percentage of the limit.

The QM option checks if the queue size is more than or equal to the specified percentage of the limit.

The QX option checks if the queue size is not equal to the specified percentage of the limit.

*Example* A clerk has two types of document to process. Documents of type 1 wait in queue 11 and documents of type 2 in queue 12. The clerk continues processing one type of document until there are more than 20 documents of the other type waiting. If the two queues of documents each has a size limit of 20, the activity of moving from document type 1 to document type 2 is shown in Fig. 7.40.

The clerk moves from queue 21 (processing document type 1) to queue 22 (processing document type 2) when queue 12 has 20 or more documents in it.

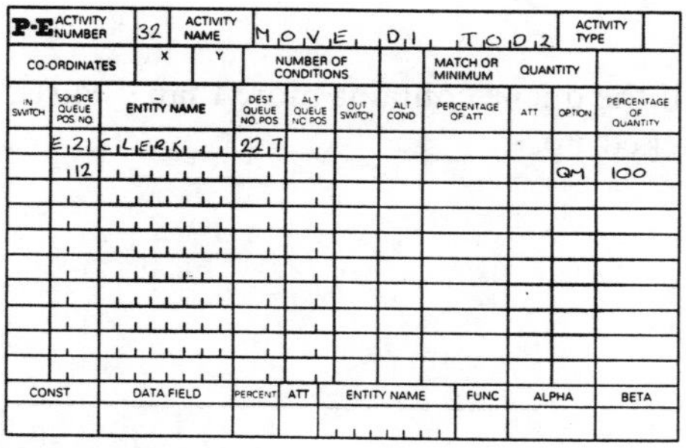

**Figure 7.40**

*QI—Queue size Insert*
*QJ—Queue size Join*

| PERCENTAGE OF ATT | ATT | OPTION | PERCENTAGE OF QUANTITY |
|---|---|---|---|
|  | ✓ | QI | ✓ (>0) |
|  | ✓ | QJ | ✓ (≠0) |

These options alter the value of an attribute using the current size of a queue. They take effect when an activity ends, and therefore the queue number must be entered in the destination queue column.

The QI option inserts the queue size, multiplied by a percentage, into an attribute, replacing the value already there.

The QJ option adds the queue size, multiplied by a percentage, to the value already in the attribute.

*Example* At the end of each shift in a production unit the total number of unfinished jobs is recorded in a histogram. The unfinished jobs are in five queues (queues 6–10 say). These are recorded in a histogram as shown in Fig. 7.41.

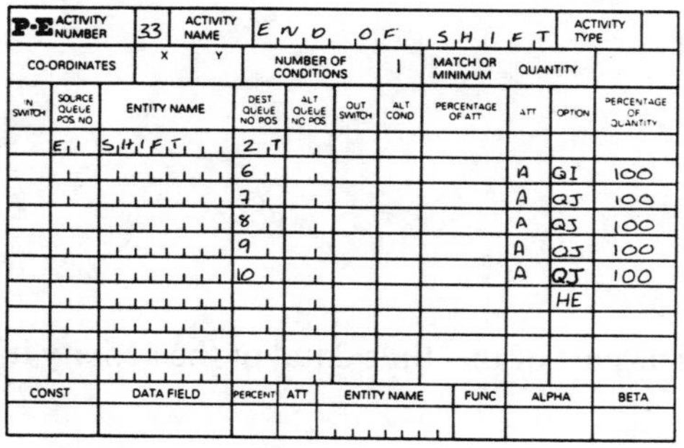

SHIFT  A  Number of unfinished jobs

**Figure 7.41**

The size of queue 6 is inserted into the A-attribute of Shift and then the sizes of queues 7–10 are added. The final value of the A-attribute is then recorded in a histogram using the HE option.

EXERCISE 7.14
Describe an activity which picks a Part from a queue if the queue contains more than 4 Parts, and records the queue size after the Part has been picked up.

## Extra correlation term

### *XC—eXtra Correlation*

| PERCENTAGE OF ATT | ATT | OPTION | PERCENTAGE OF QUANTITY |
|---|---|---|---|
| ✓ (≠0) | ✓ | XC | |

The correlation term (see Chapter 5) allows the duration of a discrete activity to be modified by adding (or subtracting) a percentage of the value of an attribute of only one of the entities involved in the activity.

The extra correlation (XC) option enables the duration of a discrete activity to be modified by adding (or subtracting) percentages of attribute values of any number of entities in the activity. This facility is additional to the correlation term facility.

*Example* Passengers on a one man operated bus pay their fares as they board. The duration of the pick up activity will therefore depend upon the number of passengers who board at a particular bus stop. The times taken to pay fares are held in the C-attribute of Passengers (see Fig. 7.42).

| P·E ACTIVITY NUMBER | 15 | ACTIVITY NAME | PICK UP | | | | | | ACTIVITY TYPE | |
|---|---|---|---|---|---|---|---|---|---|---|
| CO-ORDINATES | X | Y | NUMBER OF CONDITIONS | 3 | MATCH OR MINIMUM | QUANTITY | | | | |
| IN SWITCH | SOURCE QUEUE POS. NO. | ENTITY NAME | DEST QUEUE NO POS | ALT QUEUE NC POS | OUT SWITCH | ALT COND | PERCENTAGE OF ATT | ATT | OPTION | PERCENTAGE OF QUANTITY |
| | E 22 | BUS | 22 T | | | | | | | |
| | E 22 | DRIVER | 22 T | | | | | | | |
| | E 8 | PASSENGER | 22 T | | | | 100 | C | XC | |
| | | | | | | | 12 | | =5 | |
| | | | | | | | | | | |
| | | | | | | | | | | |
| | | | | | | | | | | |
| | | | | | | | | | | |
| | | | | | | | | | | |
| | | | | | | | | | | |
| CONST | DATA FIELD | PERCENT | ATT | ENTITY NAME | FUNC | ALPHA | BETA | | | |
| 1 | | | | | | | | | | |

PASSENGER C Time to pay fare

**Figure 7.42**

Note that if a correlation term were to be specified as part of the 'time data' of the activity it would be defined by the first Passenger selected.

## Output reports

As will be seen in Chapter 9, there are 23 standard output reports available to the user. These provide information on the history and current state of a simulation.

The usual way of accessing reports is to take a 'snapshot' view at a particular time, or to produce reports which monitor the model over a period of time. In some circumstances, however, it may be desirable to obtain a report when a particular activity starts or ends, rather than at a specific time. This is made possible by the output report options 01–22.

### 01 to 22—output report

| PERCENTAGE OF ATT | ATT | OPTION | PERCENTAGE OF QUANTITY |
|---|---|---|---|
|  |  | 01 |  |

*Example*  An entity location (level two) report and a histogram report are to be printed whenever a machine has been repaired. Figure 7.43 shows an activity to perform this operation.

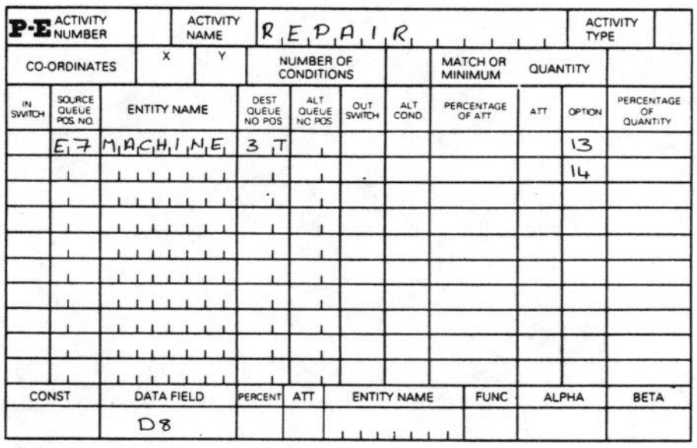

**Figure 7.43**

The entity location (level two) report is report 13, and histograms are obtained from report 14 (see Chapter 9).

In addition to the standard report, it is possible to construct up to nine user-defined reports (see Chapter 9) which can access and present any information contained in a model. These reports can be accessed at the start or end of an activity by the user-defined report options U1 to U9.

### U1 to U9—User-defined report

| PERCENTAGE OF ATT | ATT | OPTION | PERCENTAGE OF QUANTITY |
|---|---|---|---|
|  |  | U1 |  |

Options U1 to U9 display user-defined reports 1 to 9 on both screen and printer. They operate at the start *or* end of the activity, or at the start *and* end depending on the report definition.

## Clock switches and options

When a clock is switched on and then off, the duration is held in the attribute as a positive value, and this value may be manipulated by other options. A clock is not switched at the beginning of an activity until the activity actually starts.

However the clock time that an attribute will hold, if the activity does start, can be used in the options of that activity.

*Example*  Orders which have waited more than 168 hours have their priority increased, as shown in Fig. 7.44.

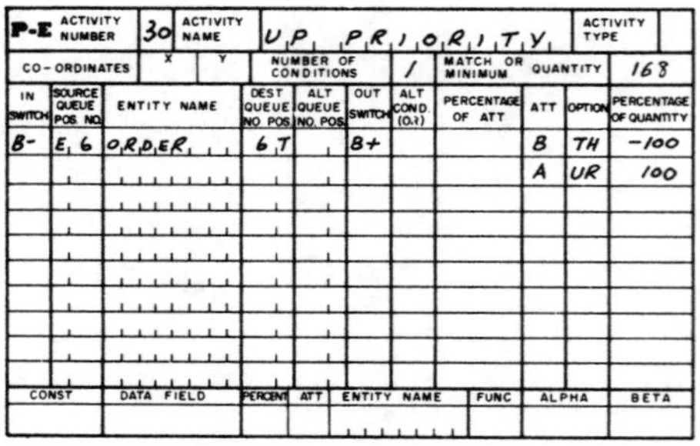

ORDER  A Priority
       B Clock, measuring
         waiting time

**Figure 7.44**

An Order which has been waiting for more than 168 hours is taken from queue 6, its priority increased by one, and put back into queue 6. The B clock is switched on, and if an Order is still waiting after a further 168 hours, its priority is increased again.

## Relating time to quantity moved—Alpha

In some activities in which attribute values are transferred (TR, TH or TT options) the duration of the activity depends on the quantity moved.

*Example*  The containers on a ship are unloaded using a crane. The duration of the 'unload' activity depends on the number of containers on the ship. If the crane first opens the hatch which takes ten minutes, and then takes two minutes to unload each container, the 'unload' activity is as shown in Fig. 7.45.

The rate of transfer is specified as a percentage (in the box marked Alpha). The duration of the activity is this percentage of the quantity moved, plus any other 'time data' (constant, data field, correlation term—see Chapter 5). Thus the duration of the 'unload' activity is $10 + 200$ per cent of the quantity moved. So if there are 18 containers to move, the activity lasts 46 minutes $(10 + 36)$.

| P-E | ACTIVITY NUMBER | 31 | ACTIVITY NAME | U,N,L,O,A,D, | | | | | | ACTIVITY TYPE | | |
|---|---|---|---|---|---|---|---|---|---|---|---|---|
| CO-ORDINATES | | X | Y | NUMBER OF CONDITIONS | | 2 | MATCH OR MINIMUM | | QUANTITY | | | |
| IN SWITCH | SOURCE QUEUE POS. NO. | ENTITY NAME | | DEST QUEUE NO. POS | ALT QUEUE NO. POS | OUT SWITCH | ALT COND. (OR) | PERCENTAGE OF ATT | ATT | OPTION | PERCENTAGE OF QUANTITY | |
| | E,3 | S,H,I,P, | | 5,T | | | | | A | TR | -100 | |
| | E,2 | C,R,A,N,E, | | 2,T | | | | | | | | |
| | | | | | | | | | | | | |
| | | | | | | | | | | | | |
| | | | | | | | | | | | | |
| | | | | | | | | | | | | |
| | | | | | | | | | | | | |
| | | | | | | | | | | | | |
| CONST | | DATA FIELD | | PERCENT | ATT | ENTITY NAME | | FUNC | ALPHA | | BETA | |
| 10 | | | | | | | | | 200 | | | |

SHIP   A  Number of containers to be unloaded

CRANE  –

**Figure 7.45**

---

### Format details

Activity duration—Alpha

If, in an activity involving a TR, TH or TT option, the duration is related linearly to the quantity moved, the percentage which relates quantity to time is entered in the box marked Alpha.

---

## Run termination

It is sometimes desirable to stop the computer run when a particular set of circumstances occurs, rather than at a specified simulation time. The R9 and UC options can be used to achieve this.

*R9—Run stop*
*UC—User Control*

| PERCENTAGE OF ATT | ATT | OPTION | PERCENTAGE OF QUANTITY |
|---|---|---|---|
| | | R9 | |
| | | UC | |

The R9 option may be used in any condition of any discrete activity, and will take effect when the activity ends with that condition having been satisfied. Thus the simulation is ended and the reports normally associated with Run Switch 9 are printed (see chapter 9—menu 1, option C). If the model is being used interactively, the UC option, which returns control to the user, may be preferable.

*Example* In Fig. 7.46 control is returned to the user if a Part with an A-attribute of 35 has been processed.

| P-E | ACTIVITY NUMBER | 4 | ACTIVITY NAME | PROCESS | | | ACTIVITY TYPE | |
|---|---|---|---|---|---|---|---|---|
| CO-ORDINATES | | X | Y | NUMBER OF CONDITIONS | 2 | MATCH OR MINIMUM | QUANTITY | |

| IN SWITCH | SOURCE QUEUE POS NO | ENTITY NAME | DEST QUEUE NO POS | ALT QUEUE NO POS | OUT SWITCH | ALT COND | PERCENTAGE OF ATT | ATT | OPTION | PERCENTAGE OF QUANTITY |
|---|---|---|---|---|---|---|---|---|---|---|
| E | 8 | PART | 9 T | | | OR | | A | CX | 35 |
| E | 8 | PART | 9 T | | | | | | UC | |

| CONST | DATA FIELD | PERCENT | ATT | ENTITY NAME | FUNC | ALPHA | BETA |
|---|---|---|---|---|---|---|---|
| | | 100 | B | PART | | | |

PART  A   Part number
(maximum = 100)

**Figure 7.46**

## User-defined interfaces

Although the standard HOCUS environment provides a highly sophisticated modelling regime, there are circumstances where it may be more desirable to model a certain piece of logic or perform a particular calculation from within the HOCUS mechanism. An example of an application where this has occurred was in designing a production scheduling algorithm. The algorithm was written in Fortran and interfaced to HOCUS so that its performance could be tested under a wide variety of situations. The end result was a piece of Fortran which could be used for scheduling on a microcomputer.

Although the need for these features occurs rarely (the authors can recall no more than a handful of occasions) two interface mechanisms are provided to permit the calling of Fortran subroutines which have access to all the model data and variables.

The first interface is via the box marked 'FUNC' on the activity format card. If a function number is entered in this box, the appropriate user-written function is called when the duration of the activity is calculated, and the result of this function is added to all the other components of the activity duration which may have been defined (such as constant or correlation term).

The second interface is the special subroutine options.

### *S1 to S9—Special subroutine*

| PERCENTAGE OF ATT | ATT | OPTION | PERCENTAGE OF QUANTITY |
|---|---|---|---|
| | Op | S1 | |

Use of these options permits an attribute value to be carried across into a Fortran subroutine which has access to the whole model. This can access or even revise any part of the model. The use of these options requires care, since the sophisticated logic checking normally performed by HOCUS is bypassed when applying these options.

## Entity groups

If a model contains several entity types which are similar in nature, these can be linked together to form an *entity group*. Thus, in a traffic simulation involving cars, lorries, buses and vans, we can form a group of vehicles and when appropriate use the group name instead of listing 'car or lorry or bus or van'.

Any entities which have common characters in their name can form a group. The group name consists of the common characters with asterisks (or blanks) replacing the other characters. Thus the entities, Man and Lad can form a group which may be coded as *A* (or *A or *A******). At least one character of the group name must be an asterisk.

Entity names may have to be modified in order to form a group that includes only the types required. In the traffic example, the entities can be given the names Vcar, Vlorry, Vbus and Van forming an entity group V*. The two activities in Fig. 7.47 are equivalent.

A group name can be used anywhere in a model, wherever an entity name can be used.

If the entities in a group have different numbers of attributes, the group itself takes the smallest number of attributes. If Vcar has 3 attributes, Vlorry has 4 attributes, Vbus has 11 attributes and Van has 6 attributes, V* will have 3 attributes. Thus when V* is used, only the A-, B- or C-attributes can be used. There would obviously be difficulties if we specified a D-attribute and selected a Vcar.

| P-E | ACTIVITY NUMBER 41 | ACTIVITY NAME A D M I T V E H I C L E | | | | ACTIVITY TYPE | |
|---|---|---|---|---|---|---|---|
| CO – ORDINATES | X Y | NUMBER OF CONDITIONS 4 | MATCH OR MINIMUM | QUANTITY | | | |
| IN SWITCH | SOURCE QUEUE POS. NO. | ENTITY NAME | DEST QUEUE NO. POS | ALT QUEUE NO. POS | OUT SWITCH | ALT COND (OR) | PERCENTAGE OF ATT | ATT | OPTION | PERCENTAGE OF QUANTITY |
| | H, 17 | V C A R | 9 T | | | OR | | | | |
| | H, 17 | V L O R R Y | 9 T | | | OR | | | | |
| | H, 17 | V B U S | 9 T | | | OR | | | | |
| | H, 17 | V A N | 9 T | | | | | | | |
| CONST | | DATA FIELD | PERCENT | ATT | ENTITY NAME | FUNC | ALPHA | BETA | | |

| P-E | ACTIVITY NUMBER 41 | ACTIVITY NAME A D M I T V E H I C L E | | | | ACTIVITY TYPE | |
|---|---|---|---|---|---|---|---|
| CO – ORDINATES | X Y | NUMBER OF CONDITIONS 1 | MATCH OR MINIMUM | QUANTITY | | | |
| IN SWITCH | SOURCE QUEUE POS. NO. | ENTITY NAME | DEST QUEUE NO. POS | ALT QUEUE NO. POS | OUT SWITCH | ALT COND (OR) | PERCENTAGE OF ATT | ATT | OPTION | PERCENTAGE OF QUANTITY |
| | H, 17 | V * | 9 T | | | | | | | |
| CONST | | DATA FIELD | PERCENT | ATT | ENTITY NAME | FUNC | ALPHA | BETA | | |

**Figure 7.47**

A group can be a subset of another group. For example, LorryA1 and LorryA2 can form an entity group LorryA*, which together with Lorry B can form a group Lorry*. Thus LorryA* is a subset of Lorry*.

Histograms of group attributes are collected in the normal way using the HS and HE options.

---

### Format details

Entity groups

Entity groups are coded on the Entity Description format after all the entity types have been entered (see this chapter—Hand simulation). If one group is a subset of another, the smaller group should be defined first.

## Continuous activities

In the examples we have considered so far, once an activity starts and its end time is calculated, it runs for that time without interruption. In reality many activities are not like this but may, by a combination of circumstances, be interrupted. For example in a port simulation, oil is pumped from a tanker to a storage tank until either the tanker is empty, the storage tank is full or the pump breaks down.

We model such a situation by introducing the concept of a *continuous activity*. This is an activity which, when started, processes material at a specified *rate*. The activity ends when either the material runs out, there is nowhere to put the material, or the activity is interrupted by another activity of higher priority (lower activity number).

If the tanker originally nas 10 000 units of oil and is emptied at the rate of 50 units per minute, the activity can last for up to 200 minutes. If the pump breaks down after 30 minutes the pump must be repaired before the remaining 8500 units of oil can be moved.

---

### Format details

Continuous activities

(a) A continuous activity has 'C' coded in Activity type.
(b) The source queue position can only be E or I.
(c) The destination queue number and position must be identical to those of the source queue.
(d) Func and Alpha are not used.

---

### Interrupting continuous activities

If an activity of higher priority (lower activity number) requires an entity currently in a continuous activity, the continuous activity is 'examined'. The attributes of the entities are adjusted to the values they would take if the continuous activity were to stop. If the interrupting activity can start with one of the entities, the continuous activity stops and its entities released. If it cannot start, the continuous activity runs to its originally calculated end time (unless it is interrupted before).

Consider the following activities:

| Activity number | Name |
| --- | --- |
| 10 | Breakdown |
| 11 (continuous) | Priority run |
| 12 (continuous) | Normal run |
| 13 | Lubricate |

Breakdown can interrupt either Priority run or Normal run but Lubricate must wait until they have finished. Priority run can interrupt Normal run.

## Options with continuous activities

An essential property of a continuous activity is that it involves the transferring of attribute values. Therefore, a TR option, a UR option or the FC and FR options described below, must be specified in the activity. Constraints can be imposed on the starting of continuous activities, by using the KA, KS and KP options, and in addition some of the options already described for discrete activities can also be used.

### TR—TRansfer

| PERCENTAGE OF ATT | ATT | OPTION | PERCENTAGE OF QUANTITY |
|---|---|---|---|
| | ✓ | TR | ✓ ($\neq 0$) |

The TR option transfers attribute values at the *rate* specified by the 'time data' (constant, data field and correlation term).

*Example* Beer is pumped from a fermenting vessel through a chiller into a conditioning tank. The rate of transfer depends on the temperature of the beer (the cooler the beer, the faster the chilling rate), as shown in Fig. 7.48.

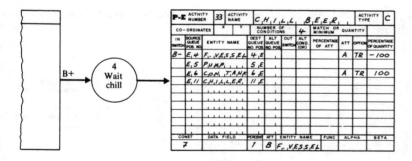

**Figure 7.48**

The time units in the model are tenths of an hour, and the B-attribute of F.Vessel measures the time the fermenting vessel waits to chill the beer. The chilling rate is seven barrels per time unit plus 1 per cent of the waiting time. Thus if F.Vessel waits 100 time units before chilling, the rate is eight (7 + 1 per cent of 100) barrels per time unit. If the F.Vessel holds 240 barrels of beer and the Con.Tank can also hold 240 barrels, the activity will run for 30 time units, unless it is interrupted by an activity such as 'pump failure', which has a lower activity number, as shown in Fig. 7.49.

When the Break enters queue 2 the 'chill beer' activity (A33) is interrupted by the 'pump failure' activity (A2) which takes the Pump for a time sampled from distribution 2 (not shown).

| P-E | ACTIVITY NUMBER | 2 | ACTIVITY NAME | P U M P   F A I L U R E | | ACTIVITY TYPE | |
|---|---|---|---|---|---|---|---|
| CO-ORDINATES | | X | Y | NUMBER OF CONDITIONS | 2 | MATCH OR MINIMUM | QUANTITY |

| IN SWITCH | SOURCE QUEUE POS. NO. | ENTITY NAME | DEST QUEUE NO. POS. | ALT QUEUE NO. POS. | OUT SWITCH | ALT COND | PERCENTAGE OF ATT | ATT | OPTION | PERCENTAGE OF QUANTITY |
|---|---|---|---|---|---|---|---|---|---|---|
| | E 2 | 3 R E B K | 7 T | | | | | | | |
| | E 5 | P U M P | 5 T | | | | | | | |
| | | | | | | | | | | |

| CONST | DATA FIELD | PERCENT | ATT | ENTITY NAME | FUNC | ALPHA | BETA |
|---|---|---|---|---|---|---|---|
| | D2 | | | | | | |

**Figure 7.49**

## UR—Unit Rate

| PERCENTAGE OF ATT | ATT | OPTION | PERCENTAGE OF QUANTITY |
|---|---|---|---|
| | ✓ | UR | ✓ (≠0) |

The UR option changes an attribute value at a constant *rate* of 1 multiplied by a percentage for each unit of time the activity runs. This option is independent of all other options.

*Example* The chiller in the previous example (Fig. 7.48) must be inspected every 80 hours of running. The activity is modified as shown in Fig. 7.50.

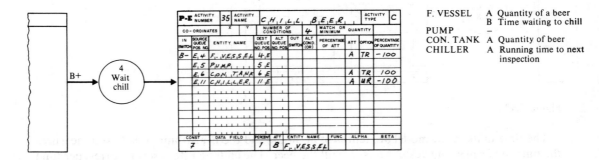

| P-E | ACTIVITY NUMBER | 35 | ACTIVITY NAME | C H I L L   B E E R | | ACTIVITY TYPE | C |
|---|---|---|---|---|---|---|---|
| CO-ORDINATES | | X | Y | NUMBER OF CONDITIONS | 4 | MATCH OR MINIMUM | QUANTITY |

| IN SWITCH | SOURCE QUEUE POS. NO. | ENTITY NAME | DEST QUEUE NO. POS. | ALT QUEUE NO. POS. | OUT SWITCH | ALT COND (OR) | PERCENTAGE OF ATT | ATT | OPTION | PERCENTAGE OF QUANTITY |
|---|---|---|---|---|---|---|---|---|---|---|
| B- | E 4 | F VESSEL | 4 E | | | | | A | TR | -100 |
| | E 5 | PUMP | 5 E | | | | | | | |
| | E 6 | CON TANK | 6 E | | | | | A | TR | 100 |
| | E 11 | CHILLER | 11 E | | | | | A | UR | -100 |
| | | | | | | | | | | |

| CONST | DATA FIELD | PERCENT | ATT | ENTITY NAME | FUNC | ALPHA | BETA |
|---|---|---|---|---|---|---|---|
| 7 | | 1 | B | F VESSEL | | | |

F. VESSEL   A Quantity of a beer
            B Time waiting to chill
PUMP   –
CON. TANK   A Quantity of beer
CHILLER   A Running time to next
            inspection

**Figure 7.50**

The time units in the model are tenths of an hour. The A-attribute of Chiller (initially set to 800) is reduced by 1 for every unit of time the 'chill beer' activity runs. The activity stops when it reaches zero. The 'inspect' activity then takes place (not shown) and resets the A-attribute of Chiller to 800.

**FC—Flow Control**
**FR—Flow Rate**

| PERCENTAGE OF ATT | ATT | OPTION | PERCENTAGE OF QUANTITY |
|---|---|---|---|
| ✓ (≠0) | ✓ | FC | |
| | ✓ | FR | ✓ (≠0) |

The FC option enables an attribute value to contribute to the rate of transfer for the activity and therefore has a similar effect as the correlation term in the 'time data'. However, any number of FC options can be used in an activity and the overall rate, used in the TR option, is the sum of the FC options plus the 'time data' contribution.

The FR option changes an attribute using the rate set by the FC option in the same condition.

*Example* A chemical is pumped continuously from Tank 1 to 2, and then into one of two driers (see Fig. 7.51). Drier 2 is old and used only as a standby, as its rate of drying is much less than Drier 1.

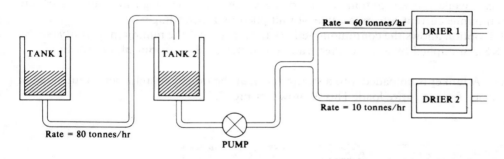

**Figure 7.51**

Pumping and drying is modelled in the continuous activity shown in Fig. 7.52.

| P-E ACTIVITY NUMBER | 37 | ACTIVITY NAME | PUMP AND DRY | | ACTIVITY TYPE | C |

| CO-ORDINATES | X | Y | | NUMBER OF CONDITIONS | MATCH OR MINIMUM | QUANTITY |

| IN SWITCH | SOURCE QUEUE POS NO | ENTITY NAME | DEST QUEUE NO POS | ALT QUEUE NO POS | OUT SWITCH | ALT COND | PERCENTAGE OF ATT | ATT | OPTION | PERCENTAGE OF QUANTITY |
|---|---|---|---|---|---|---|---|---|---|---|
| | E,3 | DRIER1 | 3 E | | | OR | −100 | A | FC | |
| | E,3 | DRIER2 | 3 E | | | | −100 | A | FC | |
| | E,2 | TANK | 2 E | | | | 100 | B | FC | |
| | | | | | | | | A | FR | −100 |
| | E,2 | TANK | 2 E | | | | | A | TR | 100 |
| | E,5 | PUMP | 5 E | | | | | | | |

| CONST | DATA FIELD | PERCENT | ATT | ENTITY NAME | FUNC | ALPHA | BETA |

| DRIER 1 | A | Rate of drying (60) |
| DRIER 2 | A | Rate of drying (10) |
| TANK 1 | A | Contents |
| | B | Rate of flow out of tank (80) |
| TANK 2 | A | Contents |
| PUMP | | |

**Figure 7.52**

The rate of flow into Tank 2 is the sum of the Flow Controls (FC options). It is 20 (80 − 60) when Drier 1 is used and 70 (80 − 10) when Drier 2 is used. Tank 1 is emptied at a Flow Rate (FR option) equal to its Flow Control, i.e. 80.

**KA—Key Amount**
**KS—Key Space**
**KP—Key Pass**

| PERCENTAGE OF ATT | ATT | OPTION | PERCENTAGE OF QUANTITY |
|---|---|---|---|
| ✓ (>0) | ✓ | KA | |
| ✓ (>0) | ✓ | KS | |
| | ✓ | KP | ✓ (≠0) |

These key options control the starting of continuous activities. Usually, a continuous activity will start even if it can only move one unit of quantity. With these options, starting can be prevented until some key (minimum) quantity can be moved; for example, until an attribute can be completely filled or a substantial quantity moved.

Both the KA and KS options specify the key (minimum) quantity that must be transferred. The KA option sets the minimum to the current value of an attribute (multiplied by a percentage), while the KS option sets it to the space available in an attribute—attribute maximum minus current attribute value—(multiplied by a percentage).

The KP option allows the continuous activity to start only if the minimum quantity (set by KA or KS), multiplied by a percentage, can be transferred into, or out of, an attribute.

*Example*   A tanker is unloaded into a storage area, at the rate of 80 units per minute, only if there is space for the entire load. This is shown in Fig. 7.53.

TANKER   A   Size of load
STORAGE   A   Amount in stock

**Figure 7.53**

The key (minimum) quantity is set to the size of the load (KA option) and the Storage area must be able to take the quantity, before the activity will start (KP option).

*Example*   A vessel is charged with a chemical and diluent in the ratio of one to three. Charging takes place at a rate of 15 units of chemical per minute, but will not start until there is sufficient chemical and diluent to fill the vessel. This is shown in Fig. 7.54.

| P-E | ACTIVITY NUMBER 39 | ACTIVITY NAME | F I L L   V E S S E L | ACTIVITY TYPE | C |
|---|---|---|---|---|---|

| CO-ORDINATES | X | Y | NUMBER OF CONDITIONS 3 | MATCH OR MINIMUM | QUANTITY |
|---|---|---|---|---|---|

| IN SWITCH | SOURCE QUEUE POS. NO. | ENTITY NAME | DEST QUEUE NO. POS. | ALT QUEUE NO. POS. | OUT SWITCH | ALT COND. (OR) | PERCENTAGE OF ATT | ATT | OPTION | PERCENTAGE OF QUANTITY |
|---|---|---|---|---|---|---|---|---|---|---|
| | E,6 | VESSEL | 6,E | | | | 100 | A | KS | |
| | | | | | | | | A | TR | 400 |
| | E,20 | CHEMICAL | 20,E | | | | | A | KP | -25 |
| | | | | | | | | A | TR | -100 |
| | E,21 | DILUENT | 21,E | | | | | A | KP | -75 |
| | | | | | | | | A | TR | -300 |

| CONST 15 | DATA FIELD | PERCENT | ATT | ENTITY NAME | FUNC | ALPHA | BETA |
|---|---|---|---|---|---|---|---|

| VESSEL | A | Contents (maximum = capacity) |
|---|---|---|
| CHEMICAL | A | Amount of stock |
| DILUENT | A | Amount of stock |

**Figure 7.54**

The minimum quantity is set to the space available in the Vessel (KS option). The minimum quantity of Chemical is 25 per cent of this space (KP option), and the minimum quantity of Diluent is 75 per cent of this space (KP option). If there is sufficient Chemical and Diluent available, the transfer rate is 15 units per minute: 60 units per minute ($15 \times 400$ per cent) is put into the Vessel; 15 units per minute ($15 \times 100$ per cent) is Chemical and 45 units per minute ($15 \times 300$ per cent) is Diluent.

EXERCISE 7.15

Grain is transferred from a silo to a lorry through an auger. This operation is continued until:

(a) the lorry is full and departs;
(b) the silo is emptied and awaits refilling;
(c) the auger breaks down and awaits repair.

The entities and their attributes are:

AUGER:  A—Transfer rate
        C—Running time to next breakdown
LORRY:  B—Contents (maximum = capacity)
SILO:   B—Contents
Give details of the activity.

In addition to the TR, UR, FC, FR, KA, KS and KP options, many of the options described earlier in the chapter can be used in continuous activities. These are:

LL, UL, LE, UE—Limits on attributes involved in a transfer
MQ—Match with match Quantity
MX—Must not match
M1 to M9—Match
G1 to G9—compare Greater than or equal to
L1 to L9—compare Less than or equal to
X1 to X9—compare not equal to
I1 to I9—Insert
J1 to J9—Join

XR, XS—attribute reset
PI, PJ—Present time
DD, DE, DI, DJ—Direct entry
SD, SE, SI, SJ—Search entry
RD, RE, RI, RJ—Revise entry
CE, CC, CL, CM, CX—Check attribute values
PM, PL, PX—Present time testing
HS, HE—Histogram entry
VV, NV, DV—Variable percentages
=A, =S—Identical conditions
QE, QC, QL, QM, QX—Queue size checking
R9, UC—Run termination
S1 to S9—Special subroutines
U1 to U9—User-defined reports

*Example*   A ship is loaded with oil from a tank at a fast rate (10 units per minute) until it is 95 per cent full and then at a slow rate (5 units per minute). There are a number of tanks storing different grades of oil, and the ship requires a specific grade, as shown in Fig. 7.55.

| P-E | ACTIVITY NUMBER 40 | ACTIVITY NAME | L O A D   S H I P | ACTIVITY TYPE | C |
|---|---|---|---|---|---|
| CO-ORDINATES | X | Y | NUMBER OF CONDITIONS 3 | MATCH OR MINIMUM 3 | QUANTITY |

| IN SWITCH | SOURCE QUEUE POS. NO. | ENTITY NAME | DEST QUEUE NO. POS. | ALT QUEUE NO. POS | OUT SWITCH | ALT COND (OR) | PERCENTAGE OF ATT | ATT | OPTION | PERCENTAGE OF QUANTITY |
|---|---|---|---|---|---|---|---|---|---|---|
| | E,3 | S H I P | 3 E | | | OR | 95 | B | UL | |
| | | | | | | | 10 | D | FC | |
| | | | | | | | | C | TR | 100 |
| | | | | | | | 100 | A | MI | |
| | E,3 | S H I P | 3 E | | | | 5 | D | FC | |
| | | | | | | | | C | TR | 100 |
| | | | | | | | 100 | A | MI | |
| | E,8 | T A N K | 8 E | | | | 100 | A | M1 | |
| | | | | | | | 100 | B | TR | -100 |

| CONST | DATA FIELD | PERCENT | ATT | ENTITY NAME | FUNC | ALPHA | BETA |
|---|---|---|---|---|---|---|---|

SHIP   A   Grade of oil
      B   Capacity of ship
      C   Contents
         (maximum = capacity)
      D   Constant value 100
TANK   A   Grade of oil
      B   Contents

**Figure 7.55**

The grade of oil required by the Ship is matched against a Tank (M1 option) and the oil is transferred at a rate of 10 units per minute (FC option) until the Ship is 95 per cent full (UL option). The activity will then stop and restart with the alternative Ship condition (the first condition will not be satisfied because the Ship is now 95 per cent full) transferring at a rate of 5 units per minute (FC option).

## Alternative destination queues in continuous activities

The destination queue number and position for a continuous activity must be identical to that of the source queue. When a continuous activity ends, it may be necessary to move one or more of its entities to alternative queues. The alternative queue facility permits an entity involved in a continuous activity to move to an alternative queue once its part in the activity has been completed, that is, when the value of a relevant attribute of the entity reaches a permitted limit.

An attribute letter may be entered in the alternative queue number space so that the alternative queue required is given by the current value of the attribute.

If a destination clock switch is entered on the same continuation line as an alternative queue, this switch will operate only when the entity member moves to that alternative queue.

*Example*   In Fig. 7.56 a lorry is used to make some deliveries. The expected time for this task is held in the B-attribute of the Lorry. The amount of fuel in the fuel tank and the rate of use of fuel, are represented by the values of attributes A and D respectively. After a certain number of running hours, the lorry must undergo routine maintenance, the limit for this being held as the maximum value of the C-attribute.

LORRY   A   Fuel in tank
B   Delivery time
C   Running hours since
last maintenance
(maximum = maintenance period)
D   Fuel consumption rate

**Figure 7.56**

The activity 'Run Lorry' will continue until one of four events occurs:

(a) A higher priority activity interrupts the activity, and the Lorry returns to queue 6.
(b) The fuel runs out, and the Lorry will go to queue 7 for refuelling.
(c) The deliveries are completed and the Lorry goes to queue 8.
(d) Routine maintenance becomes due and the Lorry joins queue 9 to await service.

## Split entities

Normally, an entity can only be in one queue or one activity at any point in time. However, in the real world, a single object—such as a storage tank—may be used in several activities simultaneously. A typical situation is in a mixing plant, shown in Fig. 7.57.

Three mixers, any of which may be running or shut down, feed into one tank. From the tank, fluid is drawn off as required to a drier, which in turn discharges into a silo.

The behaviour of the mixers and the drier can be simulated by four continuous activities, but the inter-connecting resource, the tank, may be involved in all four activities simultaneously. To model such a situation, we introduce the concept of a *split entity*.

A split entity is defined by an oblique stroke (/) as the first character of its name. In general it behaves as an ordinary entity—except that it cannot form a group with ordinary entities. A group of split entities must itself have an oblique stroke as the first character of its name.

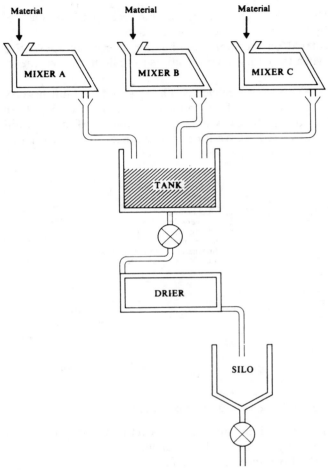

**Figure 7.57**

A split entity can take part in more than one continuous activity at the same time—provided all the continuous activities take the split entity from the same queue. The rate of transfer in each continuous activity is set by the activity but the rates are combined to make a net alteration to the attributes concerned.

In the mixing plant example, the four continuous activities may be formulated as shown in Fig. 7.58.

Suppose all four activities start at the same time, and that rates for Mixer A, Mixer B, Mixer C and the Drier are 12, 12, 16 and 32 units per minute respectively.

The total rate of flow into the /Tank is 40 units per minute $(12 + 12 + 16)$ and the rate of flow out is 32 units per minute. So with all four activities running the value of the A-attribute of /Tank increases at a net rate of 8 units per minute. If later Mixer B shuts down, the net rate for the /Tank becomes $-4$ units per minute $(12 + 16 - 32)$ and the value of the A-attribute decreases at that rate.

MATERIAL A Amount in stock
MIXER A –
MIXER B –
MIXER C –
/TANK A Contents
DRIER –
SILO A Contents

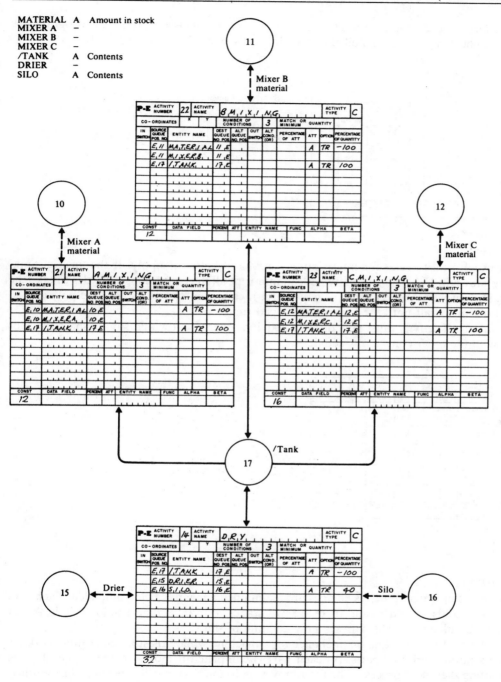

**Figure 7.58**

If the Drier is to start only when the /Tank is more than 20 per cent full the CM option (see Attribute checking) can be included in the 'dry' activity as shown in Fig. 7.59.

| P-E | ACTIVITY NUMBER | 14 | ACTIVITY NAME | D R Y | | | | | | | | ACTIVITY TYPE | C |
|---|---|---|---|---|---|---|---|---|---|---|---|---|---|
| CO-ORDINATES | | X | Y | | NUMBER OF CONDITIONS | | | MATCH OR MINIMUM | QUANTITY | | | | |
| IN SWITCH | SOURCE QUEUE POS. NO. | ENTITY NAME | DEST QUEUE NO. POS | ALT QUEUE NO. POS | OUT SWITCH | ALT COND. (OR) | PERCENTAGE OF ATT | ATT | OPTION | PERCENTAGE OF QUANTITY | | | |
| | E,17 | /,T,A,N,K | 17,E | | | | | A | CM | 20 | | | |
| | | | | | | | | A | TR | -100 | | | |
| | E,15 | D,R,I,E,R | 15,E | | | | | | | | | | |
| | E,16 | S,I,L,O | 16,E | | | | | A | TR | 40 | | | |
| | | | | | | | | | | | | | |
| | | | | | | | | | | | | | |
| | | | | | | | | | | | | | |
| | | | | | | | | | | | | | |
| CONST | | DATA FIELD | PERCENT | ATT | ENTITY NAME | | FUNC | ALPHA | | BETA | | | |
| 32 | | | | | | | | | | | | | |

/TANK  A Contents
DRIER  –
SILO   A Contents

**Figure 7.59**

The usual priority rules for interrupting continuous activities apply. If the 'inspect tank' activity shown in Fig. 7.60 is activity 8 it can interrupt all the continuous activities to take the /Tank. If, however, 'inspect tank' is activity 18, it cannot interrupt the 'dry' activity and so inspection must wait until the Drier has stopped running.

The interrupt activity must be a discrete activity, otherwise it would simply share the split entity with the other continuous activities.

| P-E | ACTIVITY NUMBER | 8 | ACTIVITY NAME | I N S P E C T   T A N K | | | | | | | | ACTIVITY TYPE | |
|---|---|---|---|---|---|---|---|---|---|---|---|---|---|
| CO-ORDINATES | | X | Y | | NUMBER OF CONDITIONS | 2 | | MATCH OR MINIMUM | QUANTITY | | | | |
| IN SWITCH | SOURCE QUEUE POS. NO. | ENTITY NAME | DEST QUEUE NO. POS | ALT QUEUE NO. POS | OUT SWITCH | ALT COND. (OR) | PERCENTAGE OF ATT | ATT | OPTION | PERCENTAGE OF QUANTITY | | | |
| | E,4 | S,H,I,F,T,M,A,N | 21,T | | | | | | | | | | |
| | E,17 | /,T,A,N,K | 17,T | | | | | | | | | | |
| | | | | | | | | | | | | | |
| | | | | | | | | | | | | | |
| | | | | | | | | | | | | | |
| | | | | | | | | | | | | | |
| | | | | | | | | | | | | | |
| | | | | | | | | | | | | | |
| CONST | | DATA FIELD | PERCENT | ATT | ENTITY NAME | | FUNC | ALPHA | | BETA | | | |
| 5 | | | | | | | | | | | | | |

**Figure 7.60**

EXERCISE 7.16
(a) When a ship enters port, its engines are maintained while it is being unloaded. Each ship has two holds, A and B, and there are two cranes, 1 and 2. Crane 1 unloads hold A and Crane 2 unloads hold B. Draw a flow diagram of this.
(b) A fitter performs routine maintenance on a machine while it is still performing work on two separate series of parts. As each part is completed it moves to the queue of parts awaiting their next process. The fitter moves on to the next machine when he has finished his maintenance. A major breakdown can interrupt all normal activities. Draw a flow diagram of this.

## Inhibiting interruption

*NI—No Interruption*

| PERCENTAGE OF ATT | ATT | OPTION | PERCENTAGE OF QUANTITY |
|---|---|---|---|
| | | NI | |

A continuous activity will normally be interrupted by any other activity of higher priority (lower activity number) that requires one or more of its entities.

In certain circumstances this may be unrealistic, particularly as the starting activity will take the first entity member it finds, and so may interrupt a continuous activity even though another suitable entity member is idle further down the source queue.

The No Interruption (NI) option prevents any entity member already engaged in a continuous activity from satisfying the condition concerned.

*Example*   A salesman in a department store serves one customer at a time. This is represented by a continuous activity (not shown), as he is liable to interruption by external telephone calls or a tea break. When his break is due, he will take it before accepting a new customer, but will not abandon a customer he is already serving. The activity of taking a break is shown in Fig. 7.61.

| P·E ACTIVITY NUMBER | 8 | ACTIVITY NAME | TAKE BREAK | | ACTIVITY TYPE | | |
|---|---|---|---|---|---|---|---|

BREAK        C   Salesman number
SALESMAN   A   Number

Figure 7.61

The NI condition option prevents the Salesman from being taken from the continuous activity in progress, in order to start the 'take break' activity.

# Ordered queues

Instead of putting entities to the head or tail of a queue, we may want to put them in a position which depends on the value of their attributes. A queue of such entities is called an *ordered queue,* and consists of entities held in ascending order of the attribute value. An ordered queue is set up by simply specifying the attribute as the destination queue position of the entity, in the activities which feed the queue.

*Example* Jobs are processed on a machine in due date order. Each Job has its due date stored as an A-attribute. Jobs are put into the queue for machining in due date order by specifying 'A' as the destination queue position in the 'job arrival' activity, as shown in Fig. 7.62. As the Jobs are in ascending order (smallest value at the head) the 'machining' activity takes the Job from the head of the queue.

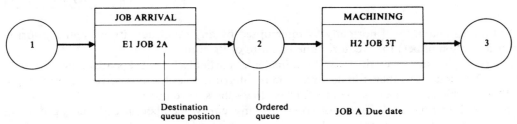

**Figure 7.62**

If different entity types are put into an ordered queue, either from the same or different activities, care must be taken to ensure that the same attribute is used in all the destination queue positions. If in our model a Batch is also put into queue 2, the destination queue position of the Batch must also be 'A'.

Entities must not be put to the head or tail of an ordered queue using the 'H' or 'T' notation, as this will destroy the order of the attribute values.

It is because of ordered queues that the letters E, H, T, I and Z are not used as attributes. If T were an attribute it would be impossible to know whether an entity is to be put to the tail of a queue or ordered according to the T-attribute. The letter O is also omitted because it often gets confused with 0, which is important when we input data to the computer (see Chapter 8).

EXERCISE 7.17

(a) Patients arrive at a casualty department of a hospital and an initial diagnosis is made at reception. They are then treated by a doctor in the order of the severity of their ailment.

Draw a flow diagram of this, assuming that the ailment of a patient is stored as an A-attribute, and that the scale of severity is 1–5 (1 = emergency, 5 = minor).

(b) To maximize money in a company account, cheques arriving into a large accounting system are processed in cash value order. Draw a flow diagram showing cheque arrival, sorting and banking.

## Further exercises

We have now seen how, by defining and using attributes, we are able to model very complex problems involving both discrete and continuous processes. Although a number of exercises have been given in this chapter, you may like further practice in model building. The first of the following exercises requires details of single activities and related queues. In some cases there are several alternative solutions. The remaining two exercises are variations of the tidal port and steel mill exercises given at the end of Chapter 5, and require some of the facilities described in this chapter to produce a solution.

After the exercises we describe how to hand simulate a model involving attributes.

EXERCISE 7.18

List the attributes you require and give the activity and queue details for each of the following:

(a) Unload a ship putting 38 per cent of the contents into warehouse 1, and 60 per cent into warehouse 2. The rest is spilt.
(b) Fill a lorry, which could already be partially full, to its capacity.
(c) Send a lorry to queue 1 if it contains sand (product 3),
    to queue 2 if it contains cement (product 5),
    or to queue 4 if it contains aggregate (product 12).
(d) The A-attribute of a delivery van is used to measure the time taken to travel from one customer to the next. Produce an activity which accumulates these times in another attribute of the van. (This represents the total time for the outward journey and so can be used in an activity for the return journey.)
(e) Take half the contents out of a tanker.
(f) In any model where we use attributes except as clocks, we must 'zeroize' the attributes before the entities are recycled. Produce an activity which will clear all the attributes of an entity.
(g) A depot distributes four grades of oil to customers in seven districts. It has twenty tankers of its own and can hire more. Each tanker can only carry one grade of oil at a time, and can only make one round trip to any one district each day. Part deliveries are not allowed. Priority orders must be delivered the same day even if extra transport has to be hired. Once an extra tanker has been hired it will be loaded up like an owned tanker with suitable orders.

EXERCISE 7.19

*Tidal port*　This exercise can be used either on its own or as an extension to Exercise 5.11.

Tankers carry their load in two holds which may contain the same or different product types. There are four product types and care must be taken that they do not mix.

The port has two berths and when a tanker arrives, it waits to enter until there is a berth available. At the berth the tanker is unloaded into storage tanks. A hold is connected to a storage tank as follows:

- if possible an empty tank which previously held the same product is chosen;
- if not then the least full tank (if there is one) of the same product is chosen;
- if an empty tank which previously held a different product must be used, it has to be cleaned first.

The two holds of a tanker may be connected simultaneously to different storage tanks.

The storage tanks are emptied by a trunk pipe line which is connected to the tanks in turn. The next tank to be emptied is chosen as follows:

- the tank must be at least half full;
- the tank must not be connected to a ship;
- the fullest tank with the same product as the pipe previously carried is chosen first;
- if a tank with a different product is chosen the fullest tank is used, but the pipe must first be cleaned.

The capacities of the two holds of a tanker are 1500 and 1000 units. Tankers arrive with both holds full but product types held are distributed independently with the following probabilities:

Product type:    1      2      3      4
Probability:   0.30   0.27   0.13   0.30

A hold is emptied at a rate of 60 units per hour and each connection and each disconnection takes 45 minutes.

The storage tanks are emptied by the trunk pipe line at a rate of 180 units per hour, and each connection and each disconnection takes 45 minutes.

Cleaning takes 3 hours for a storage tank, 45 minutes for the trunk pipe line. There are eight storage tanks each with a capacity of 2500 units.

A tanker takes two hours to dock at a berth and one hour to leave the port.

*Ship inter-arrival times*

| Percentage points: | | 1 | 5 | 25 | 50 | 75 | 90 | 96 | 100 |
|---|---|---|---|---|---|---|---|---|---|
| Hours: | | 3 | 6 | 8 | 12 | 16 | 20 | 24 | 28 |

*Problem*   It is important that the time tankers spend in the port is kept to a minimum. Draw a flow diagram which can be used (see Exercise 9.2) to examine the utilization of resources and ways of reducing the turnround time of the tankers. Take 20 samples from distributions 1–4 using random numbers 1–4 in Appendix 1.

EXERCISE 7.20
*Steel mill*   This exercise is an extension to Exercise 5.12.
A steel slab production plant has the following processes:

*Furnace preparation*   The furnace is cleaned of any residue of steel and is prepared for a new load of steel.

*Furnace loading and melting*   A load of steel is put into the furnace and melted. The quantity varies from one load to the next.

*Teeming*   Steel is poured from the furnace into a ladle which in turn pours the steel into a batch of moulds. As the load in the furnace is greater than the capacity of the ladle several pourings will be made. Each batch is given a due date and order number (from 1 upwards). The date is the time when the batch is required for delivery. The time between pouring and delivery (in days) is given as a distribution which must be sampled and added to the pouring date to give due date.

*Setting*   The steel is allowed to set in the moulds to form ingots which remain together as a batch.

*Stripping and mould cleaning*   After the batch has set, the moulds are stripped away by a gang and the ingots are transported to the soaking pit area. The moulds are later cleaned by the gang.

*Loading or putting outside*  On arrival at the soaking pits the batch joins the end of the queue (if any) of batches awaiting loading and eventually is loaded into the pits. However, if its arrival creates a queue of four batches the batch from among the four with the latest due date is moved outside the area to a back-up queue.

*Re-entry from back-up queue*  If there are three or more pits not in use, then one batch is brought from the back-up queue, the one with the earliest due date first. Alternatively, any batch which is within one day of its due date is brought back and is given first priority for loading into the pits.

*Soaking*  After loading into the soaking pit a batch is allowed to soak for a time of two hours after it has reached operating temperature. The time needed to bring it to operating temperature is equal to the time for which it has been cooling since pouring, unless this is over 2 hours in which case 2 hours is sufficient to bring it to the operating temperature.

*Unloading and rolling*  When it has finished reheating the batch waits in the pit until it can be unloaded and rolled.

The following resources are available:

- one furnace;
- seven sets of moulds;
- three setting locations (room for three batches of ingots to form);
- one gang of men (who do both stripping and mould cleaning);
- two cranes (which can both do loading or unloading);
- ten soaking pits;
- one rolling mill.

The performance of the resources cannot be improved, but their numbers can be changed to increase throughput. It is possible to change the number of moulds, setting locations, gangs of men and cranes. Draw a flow diagram which can be used (see Exercise 9.3) to examine the utilization of resources and ways of overcoming bottlenecks. Take 20 samples from distributions 1–4 using random number Tables 1–4 in Appendix 1.

*Times*

| | |
|---|---|
| Furnace preparation: | —120 minutes |
| Melting: | —45–85 minutes (distribution 1) |
| Filling ladle: | —10 minutes |
| Teeming: | —10 minutes |
| Setting: | —75 minutes |
| Stripping: | —6–19 minutes (distribution 2) |
| Mould cleaning: | —10 minutes |
| Loading: | —18 minutes |
| Moving outside: | —10 minutes |
| Moving inside: | —10 minutes |
| Soaking: | —120 minutes + cooling time, where cooling time is the time taken by the batch of ingots from teeming to be ready to soak (maximum soaking time is 240 minutes) |

| | |
|---|---|
| Unloading: | —18 minutes |
| Rolling: | —45 minutes (can start after first six minutes of unloading) |

*Quantities*

| | |
|---|---|
| Contents of furnace: | —110–300 tons (distribution 3) |
| Capacity of ladle: | —25 tons |
| Contents of batch of ingots: | —25 tons |

*Due dates*

| | |
|---|---|
| Time between pouring and required delivery: | —5–18 days (distribution 4) |

| Percentage points | | 1 | 5 | 10 | 20 | 40 | 60 | 80 | 90 | 95 | 100 |
|---|---|---|---|---|---|---|---|---|---|---|---|
| Dist. 1, | minutes: | 45 | 48 | 53 | 58 | 63 | 67 | 73 | 79 | 83 | 85 |
| Dist. 2, | minutes: | 6 | 8 | 9 | 10 | 11 | 12 | 13 | 15 | 16 | 19 |
| Dist. 3, | tons: | 110 | 120 | 170 | 180 | 200 | 220 | 240 | 260 | 280 | 300 |
| Dist. 4, | days: | 5 | 6 | 7 | 8 | 10 | 13 | 15 | 16 | 17 | 18 |

## Hand simulation

The steps involved in hand simulating a model with attributes are similar to those described in Chapter 6 and are listed below. However, we must first complete the flow diagram by declaring the entities used, together with their attributes and maximum values, defining any entity groups, and specifying the initial state of the model.

### Entity and entity group description

We define the entities on an Entity Description format and an Attribute Maximum Value format, by stating for each entity the number of members, the number of attributes and any attribute maximum values. Figure 7.63 shows ten cars with 3 attributes, twenty lorries with 4 attributes, thirty buses with 11 attributes and five vans with 6 attributes. On all vehicle types, the A-attributes store the number of people being carried, and so the carrying capacities have been specified as maximum values. If an entity has more than ten attributes, the next line should be reserved for maximum values on attributes N to Y.

At the end of the entity types, we list the entity groups. At least one character in each group name must be an asterisk. If one group is a subset of another, the smaller group should be defined first.

**P-E ENTITY DESCRIPTION**

| ENTITY NAME | NUMBER OF MEMBERS | No OF ATTS |
|---|---|---|
| V C A R | 1/0 | 3 |
| V L O R R Y | 20 | 4 |
| V B U S | 30/1/1 | |
| | | |
| V A N | 5 | 6 |
| V * | | |
| | | |
| | | |
| | | |

**ATTRIBUTE MAXIMUM / INITIAL VALUES**

| A OR N | B OR P | C OR Q | D OR R | F OR S | G OR U | J OR V | K OR |
|---|---|---|---|---|---|---|---|
| 4 | | | | | | | |
| 2 | | | | | | | |
| 76 | | | | | | | |
| | | | | | | | |
| 2 | | | | | | | |
| | | | | | | | |
| | | | | | | | |
| | | | | | | | |
| | | | | | | | |

**Figure 7.63**

## Initial conditions

We define the initial state of the model by specifying where the entities start and the initial values of the attributes on an Initial Conditions format and an Attribute Initial Value format.

Entities must start in queues. The initial conditions shown in Fig. 7.64 refer to the entity descriptions in Fig. 7.63 and show that all the vehicles, except buses, start in queue 4. The first three buses start in queue 1, and the remaining buses in queue 2. The three buses in queue 1 each start with two people on board.

If an entity has more than ten attributes then the next line is reserved for initial values of attributes N to Y.

**P-E INITIAL CONDITIONS**

| ENTITY NAME | No OF MEMBERS ALLOCATED | QUEUE NUMBER | TRACE |
|---|---|---|---|
| V C A R | 1/0 | 4 | |
| V L O R R Y | 20 | 4 | |
| V B U S | 3 | 1 | |
| | | | |
| V B U S | 2 7 | 2 | |
| | | | |
| V A N | 5 | 4 | |
| | | | |
| | | | |

**ATTRIBUTE MAXIMUM / INITIAL VALUES**

| A OR N | B OR P | C OR Q | D OR R | F OR S | G OR U | J OR V | K OR |
|---|---|---|---|---|---|---|---|
| | | | | | | | |
| | | | | | | | |
| 2 | | | | | | | |
| | | | | | | | |
| | | | | | | | |
| | | | | | | | |
| | | | | | | | |
| | | | | | | | |
| | | | | | | | |

**Figure 7.64**

## Steps in hand simulation

We hand simulate using the three phases START—TIME—END, as previously described in Chapters 3 and 6. The rules for hand simulating a model involving attributes are as follows:

*Step 1: Preparation*  Entities are represented by coloured counters or cards. Entities with attributes are best represented by cards, as the attributes can be listed and updated as the entities move around the diagram. The members of each entity type are numbered from 1 upwards, so that they can be recognized individually during the simulation.

*Step 2: Starting position*  We put the entities in their starting queues as specified on the initial conditions format, checking that they can logically exist there. Take particular care with ordered queues. Copy any initial values on to the cards representing the entities.

Select markers of a separate colour, to mark entities involved in continuous activities, and place these on the activity formats. There should be one marker for each entity listed in the activity and the markers should all bear the activity number.

*Step 3: Record sheet*  The Simulation Record Sheet is illustrated in Fig. 7.65. The sheet is used to record the progress of the simulation, the switching of entity clocks and histogram values.

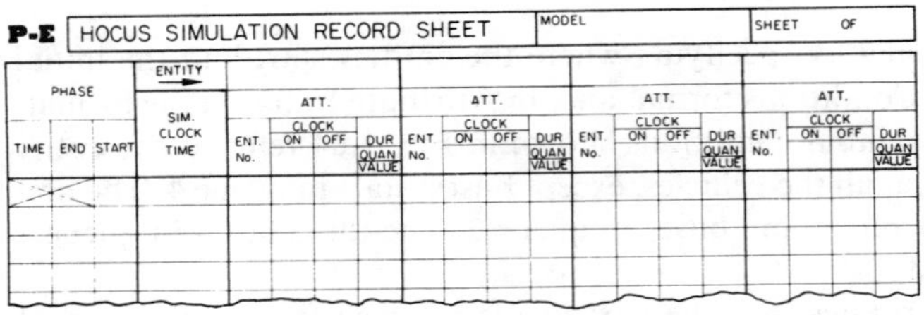

**Figure 7.65**

When a histogram is required of either changes in an attribute value (HS option), or existing attribute values (HE option) the values are recorded in the Quan or Value columns. The value is determined in the end phase because a continuous activity may be interrupted.

The simulation starts with an initial clock time of zero.

*Step 4: Start phase*  We test each activity in activity number order to see which can start. An activity may start if it is not already in progress and the required entities with acceptable attributes are available.

Check each condition in turn ensuring that the entity is available in the designated source queue and position. If the entity is involved in a continuous activity, the activity being tested must be of higher priority than the continuous activity if it is to be interrupted. If the entity is a split entity it can be used simultaneously in any number of continuous activities.

For each condition check all the options in turn for a suitable entity. If the entity being checked is involved in a continuous activity, calculate the attribute values as if the continuous activity was to end now.

If any continuous activities have to be interrupted, end them by moving the activity markers back to the activity formats. Check any clock switches and histogram options (see below) and make an entry on the Simulation Record Sheet. Cross out the activity end time.

For discrete activities move the entities to the activity format. For continuous activities move the markers from the activity format and cover the entities used. The entities used in a continuous activity maintain their position in the source queue. Any options which modify attributes or data fields in the start phase should be actioned.

*Clock switches*   If there are any clock switches in the In Switch column we make an entry on the Simulation Record Sheet.

*End time*   Calculate the duration for discrete activities and the maximum duration for continuous activities. Add this to the simulation clock time (from record sheet) and enter the end time next to the activity format.

For a continuous activity, note also the start time and transfer rate in case the continuous activity is interrupted before the maximum end time is reached.

When all the activities have been checked, tick the Start column on the Simulation Record Sheet.

*Step 5: Time phase*   We now look at the activities in progress and select the one or ones with the earliest end time. We advance the simulation clock to this time, by writing the time in the Sim Clock Time column and complete the time phase by ticking the Time column.

*Step 6: End phase*   If several activities are due to end simultaneously at this time, we end them in activity number order. This order must be strictly observed, as entities from different activities may be sent to the same queue, and their relative positions may be important. Similarly it is important that entities are moved to their destination queues in the order in which the conditions are listed in the activity.

*Attribute value*   Calculate the new attribute values. Enter them on the entity cards and if there are any histogram options, make entries on the Simulation Record Sheet.

*Clock switches*   If there are any clock switches in the Out Switch column of the activity make an entry on the Simulation Record Sheet.

For discrete activities, move the entities to their destination queue. Check for queue size limits, alternative queues and ordered queues.

For continuous activities, move the activity markers back to the activity.

Finally, delete the end time recorded next to the activity. When all possible activities have been ended indicate that the end phase is complete by ticking the End column.

*Summary*   Repeat steps 4–6 for the duration of the hand simulation.

## Solutions to exercises

SOLUTION 7.1
(a) The quantity transferred into the mixer consists of 20 per cent cement, 60 per cent sand, and 20 per cent aggregate. The mixer is then emptied in activity 2. Note that the contents in the mixer *do not* have to be transferred into another entity.

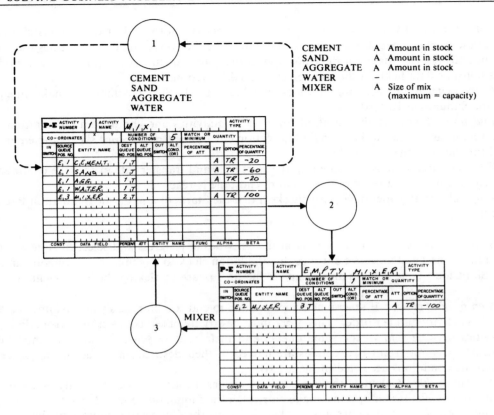

CEMENT       A   Amount in stock
SAND         A   Amount in stock
AGGREGATE    A   Amount in stock
WATER        –
MIXER        A   Size of mix
                 (maximum = capacity)

(b) The quantity transferred into the furnace consists of 75 per cent scrap and 25 per cent iron.

FURNACE   A   Size of load
              (maximum = capacity)
SCRAP     A   Amount of scrap
              available
IRON      A   Amount of iron
              available

## SOLUTION 7.2

| P-E | ACTIVITY NUMBER | ACTIVITY NAME | | | | ACTIVITY TYPE |
|---|---|---|---|---|---|---|
| | 2 | ORDER FEED | | | | |
| CO-ORDINATES | X | Y | NUMBER OF CONDITIONS | MATCH OR MINIMUM | QUANTITY | |
| | | | 2 | | | |

| IN SWITCH | SOURCE QUEUE POS.NO | ENTITY NAME | DEST QUEUE NO.POS | ALT QUEUE NO.POS | OUT SWITCH | ALT COND (OR) | PERCENTAGE OF ATT | ATT | OPTION | PERCENTAGE OF QUANTITY |
|---|---|---|---|---|---|---|---|---|---|---|
| | E,3 | BARN | 3,T | | | | | A | TH | 100 |
| | E,9 | ORDER | 10,T | | | | | A | TR | 100 |

| CONST | DATA FIELD | PERCENT | ATT | ENTITY NAME | FUNC | ALPHA | BETA |
|---|---|---|---|---|---|---|---|

BARN  A  Amount of feed currently in barn (maximum = capacity)

ORDER  A  Size of order

The quantity transferred to the order is that required to fill the barn, but in this activity the barn itself is *not* filled.

## SOLUTION 7.3

| P-E | ACTIVITY NUMBER | ACTIVITY NAME | | | | ACTIVITY TYPE |
|---|---|---|---|---|---|---|
| | 7 | LOAD | | | | |
| CO-ORDINATES | X | Y | NUMBER OF CONDITIONS | MATCH OR MINIMUM | QUANTITY | |
| | | | 3 | | | |

| IN SWITCH | SOURCE QUEUE POS.NO | ENTITY NAME | DEST QUEUE NO.POS | ALT QUEUE NO.POS | OUT SWITCH | ALT COND (OR) | PERCENTAGE OF ATT | ATT | OPTION | PERCENTAGE OF QUANTITY |
|---|---|---|---|---|---|---|---|---|---|---|
| | E,3 | ORDER | 2,T | | | | | A | TT | -100 |
| | E,9 | STOCK | 9,T | | | | | A | TR | -100 |
| | E,8 | LORRY | 8,T | | | | | A | TR | 100 |

| CONST | DATA FIELD | PERCENT | ATT | ENTITY NAME | FUNC | ALPHA | BETA |
|---|---|---|---|---|---|---|---|

ORDER  A  Size of order

STOCK  A  Amount in stock

LORRY  A  Size of load

The quantity loaded from stock to the lorry must be exactly the total order size.

## SOLUTION 7.4

### (a) (i)

| P-E | ACTIVITY NUMBER | ACTIVITY NAME | | | | ACTIVITY TYPE | |
|---|---|---|---|---|---|---|---|
| | 1 | MIX | | | | | |
| CO-ORDINATES | X | Y | NUMBER OF CONDITIONS | MATCH OR MINIMUM | QUANTITY | 200 | |
| | | | 5 | | | | |

| IN SWITCH | SOURCE QUEUE POS.NO | ENTITY NAME | DEST QUEUE NO.POS | ALT QUEUE NO.POS | OUT SWITCH | ALT COND (OR) | PERCENTAGE OF ATT | ATT | OPTION | PERCENTAGE OF QUANTITY |
|---|---|---|---|---|---|---|---|---|---|---|
| | E,1 | CEMENT | 1,T | | | | | A | TR | -20 |
| | E,1 | SAND | 1,T | | | | | A | TR | -60 |
| | E,1 | AGG. | 1,T | | | | | A | TR | -20 |
| | E,3 | MIXER | 2,T | | | | | A | TR | 100 |
| | E,1 | WATER | 1,T | | | | | A | | |

| CONST | DATA FIELD | PERCENT | ATT | ENTITY NAME | FUNC | ALPHA | BETA |
|---|---|---|---|---|---|---|---|

A maximum quantity of 200 units ensures that concrete is made only when the mixer is full.

(ii)

| P-E | ACTIVITY NUMBER | 1 | ACTIVITY NAME | M I X | | | | | ACTIVITY TYPE | | |
|---|---|---|---|---|---|---|---|---|---|---|---|
| CO-ORDINATES | | X | Y | NUMBER OF CONDITIONS | 5 | MATCH OR MINIMUM | QUANTITY | 100 | | | |
| IN SWITCH | SOURCE QUEUE POS. NO. | ENTITY NAME | DEST QUEUE NO. POS. | ALT QUEUE NO. POS. | OUT SWITCH | ALT COND. (OR) | PERCENTAGE OF ATT | ATT | OPTION | PERCENTAGE OF QUANTITY |
| | E 1 | C E M E N T | 1 T | | | | | A | TR | -20 |
| | E 1 | S A N D | 1 T | | | | | A | TR | -60 |
| | E 1 | A G G | 1 T | | | | | A | TR | -20 |
| | E 3 | M I X E R | 2 T | | | | | A | TR | 100 |
| | E 1 | W A T E R | 1 T | | | | | | | |
| | | | | | | | | | | |
| | | | | | | | | | | |
| | | | | | | | | | | |
| | | | | | | | | | | |
| | | | | | | | | | | |
| CONST | | DATA FIELD | PERCENT | ATT | ENTITY NAME | | FUNC | ALPHA | | BETA |

A minimum quantity of 100 units ensures that the mixer is at least half full.

(iii)

| P-E | ACTIVITY NUMBER | 1 | ACTIVITY NAME | M I X | | | | | ACTIVITY TYPE | | |
|---|---|---|---|---|---|---|---|---|---|---|---|
| CO-ORDINATES | | X | Y | NUMBER OF CONDITIONS | 5 | MATCH OR MINIMUM | QUANTITY | 1 | | | |
| IN SWITCH | SOURCE QUEUE POS. NO. | ENTITY NAME | DEST QUEUE NO. POS. | ALT QUEUE NO. POS. | OUT SWITCH | ALT COND. (OR) | PERCENTAGE OF ATT | ATT | OPTION | PERCENTAGE OF QUANTITY |
| | E 1 | C E M E N T | 1 T | | | | | A | TR | -20 |
| | E 1 | S A N D | 1 T | | | | | A | TR | -60 |
| | E 1 | A G G | 1 T | | | | | A | TR | -20 |
| | E 3 | M I X E R | 2 T | | | | | A | TR | 100 |
| | E 1 | W A T E R | 1 T | | | | | | | |
| | | | | | | | | | | |
| | | | | | | | | | | |
| | | | | | | | | | | |
| | | | | | | | | | | |
| CONST | | DATA FIELD | PERCENT | ATT | ENTITY NAME | | FUNC | ALPHA | | BETA |

A minimum quantity of 1 unit stops the activity taking place when there is no material available.

(b)

| P-E | ACTIVITY NUMBER | 8 | ACTIVITY NAME | R O U T E | | | | | ACTIVITY TYPE | | |
|---|---|---|---|---|---|---|---|---|---|---|---|
| CO-ORDINATES | | X | Y | NUMBER OF CONDITIONS | 2 | MATCH OR MINIMUM | QUANTITY | 100 | | | |
| IN SWITCH | SOURCE QUEUE POS. NO. | ENTITY NAME | DEST QUEUE NO. POS. | ALT QUEUE NO. POS. | OUT SWITCH | ALT COND. (OR) | PERCENTAGE OF ATT | ATT | OPTION | PERCENTAGE OF QUANTITY |
| | H 1 | P A S S | 17 T | | | OR | | A | TH | -2 |
| | H 1 | P A S S | 11 T | | | | | A | TH | -1 |
| | | | | | | | | | | |
| | | | | | | | | | | |
| | | | | | | | | | | |
| | | | | | | | | | | |
| | | | | | | | | | | |
| | | | | | | | | | | |
| | | | | | | | | | | |
| CONST | | DATA FIELD | PERCENT | ATT | ENTITY NAME | | FUNC | ALPHA | | BETA |

PASS  A  2 if nothing to declare
         1 if something to declare

Passengers are put into queue 17 if their A-attribute is at least 2 and into queue 11 if their A-attribute is at least 1. Note the order of the alternative conditions.

SOLUTION 7.5

(a)

| P-E | ACTIVITY NUMBER | ACTIVITY NAME | | | | ACTIVITY TYPE | |
|---|---|---|---|---|---|---|---|
| | 9 | T O U R | | | | | |
| CO-ORDINATES | X | Y | NUMBER OF CONDITIONS | | MATCH OR MINIMUM | QUANTITY | |
| | | | | 1 | | | |
| IN SWITCH | SOURCE QUEUE POS. NO. | ENTITY NAME | DEST QUEUE NO. POS | ALT QUEUE NO. POS | OUT SWITCH | ALT COND. (OR) | PERCENTAGE OF ATT | ATT | OPTION | PERCENTAGE OF QUANTITY |
| E 1 | COACH | 2 T | | | | 25 | A | LQ | |
| | | | | | | | B | TH | -100 |

COACH  A  Capacity of coach
       B  Number of passengers

| CONST | DATA FIELD | PERCENT | ATT | ENTITY NAME | FUNC | ALPHA | BETA |
|---|---|---|---|---|---|---|---|

The tour will take place when the B-attribute of coach is at least 25 per cent of the A-attribute of coach.

(b)

| P-E | ACTIVITY NUMBER | ACTIVITY NAME | | | | ACTIVITY TYPE | |
|---|---|---|---|---|---|---|---|
| | 4 | M I X | | | | | |
| CO-ORDINATES | X | Y | NUMBER OF CONDITIONS | | MATCH OR MINIMUM | QUANTITY | |
| | | | | 5 | | | |
| IN SWITCH | SOURCE QUEUE POS. NO. | ENTITY NAME | DEST QUEUE NO. POS | ALT QUEUE NO. POS | OUT SWITCH | ALT COND. (OR) | PERCENTAGE OF ATT | ATT | OPTION | PERCENTAGE OF QUANTITY |
| E 1 | CEMENT | 1 T | | | | | A | TR | -20 |
| E 1 | SAND | 1 T | | | | | A | TR | -60 |
| E 1 | AGG | 1 T | | | | | A | TR | -20 |
| E 3 | MIXER | 2 T | | | | 100 | B | LQ | |
| | | | | | | | A | TR | 100 |
| E 1 | WATER | 1 T | | | | | | | |

CEMENT     A  Amount in stock
SAND         A  Amount in stock
AGGREGATE  A  Amount in stock
MIXER       A  Size of mix
            B  Mixer capacity (200)
WATER       –

| CONST | DATA FIELD | PERCENT | ATT | ENTITY NAME | FUNC | ALPHA | BETA |
|---|---|---|---|---|---|---|---|

(i) The lower quantity is set by the mixer capacity.
(ii) As (i) but the percentage on the LQ option for Mixer is 50.
(iii) As (i) but the percentage on the LQ option for Mixer is 1.

SOLUTION 7.6

No quantity can be added to the debt of the card holder (B-attribute) which increases it above the credit limit (A-attribute).

| P-E | ACTIVITY NUMBER | ACTIVITY NAME | | | | ACTIVITY TYPE | |
|---|---|---|---|---|---|---|---|
| | 7 | P U R C H A S E | | | | | |
| CO-ORDINATES | X | Y | NUMBER OF CONDITIONS | | MATCH OR MINIMUM | QUANTITY | |
| | | | | 2 | | | |
| IN SWITCH | SOURCE QUEUE POS. NO. | ENTITY NAME | DEST QUEUE NO. POS | ALT QUEUE NO. POS | OUT SWITCH | ALT COND. (OR) | PERCENTAGE OF ATT | ATT | OPTION | PERCENTAGE OF QUANTITY |
| E 1 | CARDHOLD | 2 T | | | | 100 | A | UL | |
| | | | | | | | B | TR | 100 |
| E 3 | GOODS | 4 T | | | | 100 | A | FQ | |

CARD HOLD  A  Credit limit
            B  Debt
GOODS       A  Cost of goods

| CONST | DATA FIELD | PERCENT | ATT | ENTITY NAME | FUNC | ALPHA | BETA |
|---|---|---|---|---|---|---|---|

SOLUTION 7.7

The Match Quantity is 26. A Car is sent to queue 2 (petrol) if 200 per cent of its A-attribute equals 26 (i.e., A-attribute equals 13), queue 1 (air) if 1300 per cent of its A-attribute equals 26 (i.e. A-attribute equals 2), or queue 11 (car wash) if 2600 per cent of its A-attribute equals 26 (i.e. A-attribute equals 1).

| P-E | ACTIVITY NUMBER | | ACTIVITY NAME | ROUTE | | | | ACTIVITY TYPE | | |
|---|---|---|---|---|---|---|---|---|---|---|
| CO-ORDINATES | | X | Y | NUMBER OF CONDITIONS | | | | MATCH OR MINIMUM | QUANTITY | 26 |
| IN SWITCH | SOURCE QUEUE POS. NO. | ENTITY NAME | | DEST QUEUE NO. POS. | ALT QUEUE NO. POS | OUT SWITCH | ALT COND (OR) | PERCENTAGE OF ATT | ATT | OPTION | PERCENTAGE OF QUANTITY |
| | H, 2 | CAR | | 4 ,T | | | OR | 200 | A | MØ | |
| | H, 2 | CAR | | 1 ,T | | | OR | 1300 | A | MØ | |
| | H, 2 | CAR | | 11 ,T | | | | 2600 | A | MØ | |
| CONST | | DATA FIELD | PERCENT | ATT | ENTITY NAME | | FUNC | ALPHA | BETA | |

CAR   A   13 = Petrol
          2 = Air
          1 = Car wash

SOLUTION 7.8

(a)

| P-E | ACTIVITY NUMBER | 3 | ACTIVITY NAME | GO HOME | | | | ACTIVITY TYPE | L | |
|---|---|---|---|---|---|---|---|---|---|---|
| CO-ORDINATES | | X | Y | NUMBER OF CONDITIONS | | | | MATCH OR MINIMUM | QUANTITY | |
| IN SWITCH | SOURCE QUEUE POS. NO | ENTITY NAME | | DEST QUEUE NO. POS | ALT QUEUE NO. POS | OUT SWITCH | ALT COND (OR) | PERCENTAGE OF ATT | ATT | OPTION | PERCENTAGE OF QUANTITY |
| | E, 1 | SALESMAN | | 3 ,T | | | | 100 | A | MI | |
| | | | | | | | | 100 | B | MI | |
| CONST | | DATA FIELD | PERCENT | ATT | ENTITY NAME | | FUNC | ALPHA | BETA | |

SALESMAN   A   Number of visits
                  to date
           B   Target

The salesman can go home when his A-attribute matches his B-attribute.

(b)

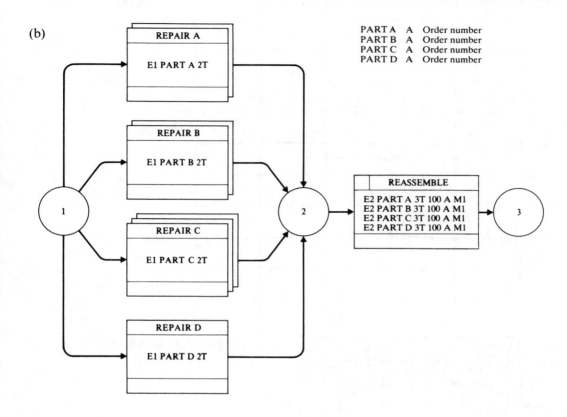

| PART A | A | Order number |
|--------|---|--------------|
| PART B | A | Order number |
| PART C | A | Order number |
| PART D | A | Order number |

The parts are put into queue 2 after repair. Parts with the same order number are then reassembled (M1 option).

SOLUTION 7.9

(a) See diagram on page 196

(b) See diagram on page 196

If there is a positive value in the B-attribute, activities 1 and 2 can take place and the B-attribute is reduced by 1 (UR option). Otherwise activities 3 and 4 take place and a new sample is taken from distribution 3 or 11 (GD option) and put into the B-attribute (GI option). Note that the 'cut gears' activity has priority over the 'repair' activity.

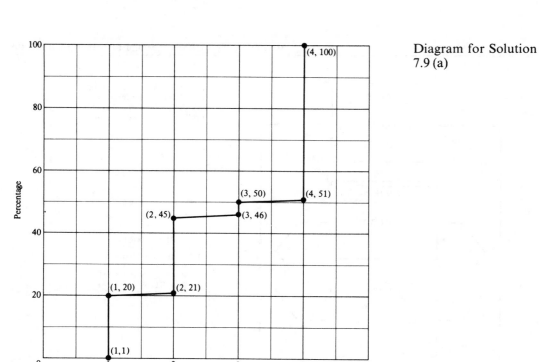

Diagram for Solution
7.9 (a)

Diagram for Solution 7.9 (b)

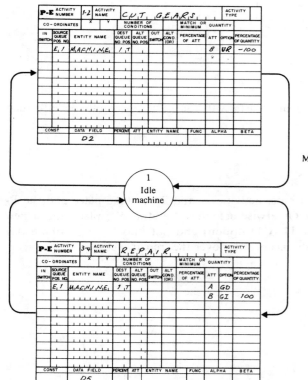

MACHINE  A  Distribution number
                  3 if old machine
                  11 if new machine
         B  Number of pairs of
                  gears to next breakdown

SOLUTION 7.10

(a)

| P-E | ACTIVITY NUMBER | | ACTIVITY NAME | C O M P L E T E | | | | ACTIVITY TYPE | |
|---|---|---|---|---|---|---|---|---|---|
| CO-ORDINATES | | X | Y | NUMBER OF CONDITIONS | | MATCH OR MINIMUM | QUANTITY | | |
| IN SWITCH | SOURCE QUEUE POS NO | ENTITY NAME | DEST QUEUE NO POS | ALT QUEUE NO POS | OUT SWITCH | ALT COND | PERCENTAGE OF ATT | ATT | OPTION | PERCENTAGE OF QUANTITY |
| E1 | | BATCH | 2 T | | | | 1 | | RD |
| | | | | | | | 100 | A | RE |
| | | | | | | | | B | RJ | 100 |
| | | | | | | | | | |
| | | | | | | | | | |
| | | | | | | | | | |
| | | | | | | | | | |
| | | | | | | | | | |
| CONST | DATA FIELD | | PERCENT | ATT | ENTITY NAME | FUNC | ALPHA | BETA | |

BATCH  A  Type
       B  Quantity

Timetable 1 holds the stock levels for each product type.

(b)

| P-E | ACTIVITY NUMBER | | ACTIVITY NAME | A D D   O B J E C T | | | | ACTIVITY TYPE | |
|---|---|---|---|---|---|---|---|---|---|
| CO-ORDINATES | | X | Y | NUMBER OF CONDITIONS | | MATCH OR MINIMUM | QUANTITY | | |
| IN SWITCH | SOURCE QUEUE POS NO | ENTITY NAME | DEST QUEUE NO POS | ALT QUEUE NO POS | OUT SWITCH | ALT COND | PERCENTAGE OF ATT | ATT | OPTION | PERCENTAGE OF QUANTITY |
| E1 | | OBJECT | 1 T | | | | | B | TE |
| | | | | | | | 1 | | TD |
| | | | | | | | 100 | A | TJ |
| | | | | | | | 100 | | IL |
| | | | | | | | | | |
| | | | | | | | | | |
| | | | | | | | | | |
| | | | | | | | | | |
| CONST | DATA FIELD | | PERCENT | ATT | ENTITY NAME | FUNC | ALPHA | BETA | |
| | | | 500 | A | OBJECT | | | | |

OBJECT  A  Weight in kg
        B  Pan number

Timetable 1 holds the weights in each of the pans.

SOLUTION 7.11

(a)

| P-E | ACTIVITY NUMBER | 6 | ACTIVITY NAME | L I G H T   O V E N | | | | ACTIVITY TYPE | |
|---|---|---|---|---|---|---|---|---|---|
| CO-ORDINATES | | X | Y | NUMBER OF CONDITIONS | 3 | MATCH OR MINIMUM | QUANTITY | | |
| IN SWITCH | SOURCE QUEUE POS NO | ENTITY NAME | DEST QUEUE NO POS | ALT QUEUE NO POS | OUT SWITCH | ALT COND (OR) | PERCENTAGE OF ATT | ATT | OPTION | PERCENTAGE OF QUANTITY |
| E1 | | OVEN | 2 T | | | | | | |
| E3 | | HOPPER | 2 T | | | OR | | B | CC | 3 |
| | | | | | | | | A | CM | 33 |
| E3 | | HOPPER | 2 T | | | | | B | CC | 6 |
| | | | | | | | | A | CM | 33 |
| | | | | | | | | | |
| | | | | | | | | | |
| | | | | | | | | | |
| CONST | DATA FIELD | | PERCENT | ATT | ENTITY NAME | FUNC | ALPHA | BETA | |

OVEN     –
HOPPER   A  Size of load
            (maximum = capacity)
         B  Type of fuel
            (maximum = 100)

The B-attribute of Hopper is given a maximum of 100. The Oven is lit when there is a Hopper with a B-attribute of 3 or 6 and an A-attribute more than 33 per cent full.

**(b)**

| P-E | ACTIVITY NUMBER | | ACTIVITY NAME | T R A N S F E R | | ACTIVITY TYPE | |
|---|---|---|---|---|---|---|---|
| CO-ORDINATES | | X | Y | NUMBER OF CONDITIONS | | MATCH OR MINIMUM | QUANTITY |
| IN SWITCH | SOURCE QUEUE POS NO | ENTITY NAME | DEST QUEUE NO.POS | ALT QUEUE NO.POS | OUT SWITCH | ALT COND | PERCENTAGE OF ATT | ATT | OPTION | PERCENTAGE OF QUANTITY |
| E 1 | P A R T | 1 T | | | | | A | CC | 1 |
| | | B T | | | | | | EA | |
| H 5 | L A B O U R E R S | T | | | | | | | |
| | | | | | | | | | |
| | | | | | | | | | |
| | | | | | | | | | |
| | | | | | | | | | |
| | | | | | | | | | |
| CONST | DATA FIELD | PERCENT | ATT | ENTITY NAME | FUNC | ALPHA | BETA |
| | | 100 | C | P A R T | | | |

PART    A   State
              (maximum = 100)
            B   Next process
            C   Travel time
LABOURER

The B-attribute of Part does not need a maximum value.

## SOLUTION 7.12

| P-E | ACTIVITY NUMBER | 5 | ACTIVITY NAME | O R D E R   S T O C K | | ACTIVITY TYPE | |
|---|---|---|---|---|---|---|---|
| CO-ORDINATES | | X | Y | NUMBER OF CONDITIONS | 5 | MATCH OR MINIMUM | QUANTITY |
| IN SWITCH | SOURCE QUEUE POS NO | ENTITY NAME | DEST QUEUE NO. POS | ALT QUEUE NO. POS | OUT SWITCH | ALT COND (OR) | PERCENTAGE OF ATT | ATT | OPTION | PERCENTAGE OF QUANTITY |
| E 1 | A R E A 1 | 1 T | | | | | 100 | B | AC | |
| | | | | | | | 100 | A | BA | |
| E 1 | A R E A 2 | 1 T | | | | | 100 | A | BA | |
| E 1 | A R E A 3 | 1 T | | | | | 100 | A | BA | |
| E 3 | O R D E R | 3 T | | | OR | | | A | AS | 100 |
| E 3 | O R D E R | 4 T | | | | | | B | AS | 100 |
| | | | | | | | | | | |
| | | | | | | | | | | |
| CONST | DATA FIELD | PERCENT | ATT | ENTITY NAME | FUNC | ALPHA | BETA |
| | | | | | | | |

AREA 1   A   Amount in stock 1
          B   Total capacity of the
             three areas
AREA 2   A   Amount in stock 2
AREA 3   A   Amount in stock 3
ORDER   A   (maximum = minimum
             order size)
          B   Size of order

The maximum on the accumulator is set to the total capacity of the three storage areas. The current contents are added into the accumulator. The difference between the total capacity and the total stock is either added to the A-attribute of Order if it is less than the minimum order size, or otherwise added to the B-attribute of Order. If it is added to the A-attribute the order is returned to queue 3, otherwise it is sent to queue 4 for dispatch.

## SOLUTION 7.13

| P-E | ACTIVITY NUMBER | 6 | ACTIVITY NAME | L O A D   F U R N A C E | | ACTIVITY TYPE | |
|---|---|---|---|---|---|---|---|
| CO-ORDINATES | | X | Y | NUMBER OF CONDITIONS | 4 | MATCH OR MINIMUM | QUANTITY |
| IN SWITCH | SOURCE QUEUE POS NO | ENTITY NAME | DEST QUEUE NO.POS | ALT QUEUE NO.POS | OUT SWITCH | ALT COND (OR) | PERCENTAGE OF ATT | ATT | OPTION | PERCENTAGE OF QUANTITY |
| E 1 | O R D E R | 2 T | | | | | 100 | A | VV | |
| E 3 | S C R A P | 3 T | | | | | | A | TR | -VAR |
| E 4 | I R O N | 4 T | | | | | | A | TR | -SUP |
| E 5 | F U R N A C E | 6 T | | | | | | A | TR | 100 |
| | | | | | | | | | | |
| | | | | | | | | | | |
| | | | | | | | | | | |
| CONST | DATA FIELD | PERCENT | ATT | ENTITY NAME | FUNC | ALPHA | BETA |
| | | | | | | | |

ORDER    A   Percentage of scrap
SCRAP    A   Scrap available
IRON      A   Iron available
FURNACE A   Size of load
               (maximum. = capacity)

The A-attribute of Order determines the value of Var. Thus the furnace is filled with Var per cent of Scrap and 100-Var per cent (Sup) of Iron.

## SOLUTION 7.14

| P-E | ACTIVITY NUMBER | | ACTIVITY NAME | P I C K | | | ACTIVITY TYPE | |
|---|---|---|---|---|---|---|---|---|

| CO-ORDINATES | | X | Y | | NUMBER OF CONDITIONS | | MATCH OR MINIMUM | QUANTITY | |

| IN SWITCH | SOURCE QUEUE POS NO | ENTITY NAME | DEST QUEUE NO POS | ALT QUEUE NO POS | OUT SWITCH | ALT COND | PERCENTAGE OF ATT | ATT | OPTION | PERCENTAGE OF QUANTITY |
|---|---|---|---|---|---|---|---|---|---|---|
| H | 1 | PART | 2 | T | | | | | | |
| | 1 | | | | | | | | QM | 4 |
| | 1 | | | | | | | | QI | 100 |
| | | | | | F | | | | HE | |
| | | | | | | | | | | |
| | | | | | | | | | | |
| | | | | | | | | | | |
| | | | | | | | | | | |
| | | | | | | | | | | |

| CONST | DATA FIELD | PERCENT | ATT | ENTITY NAME | FUNC | ALPHA | BETA |
|---|---|---|---|---|---|---|---|

PART  F   Working attribute

The maximum size limit for queue 1 should be set to 100.

## SOLUTION 7.15

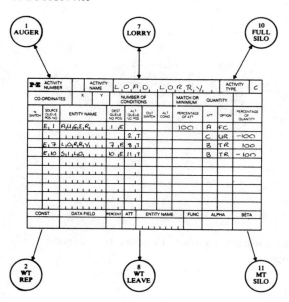

SOLUTION 7.16

(a)

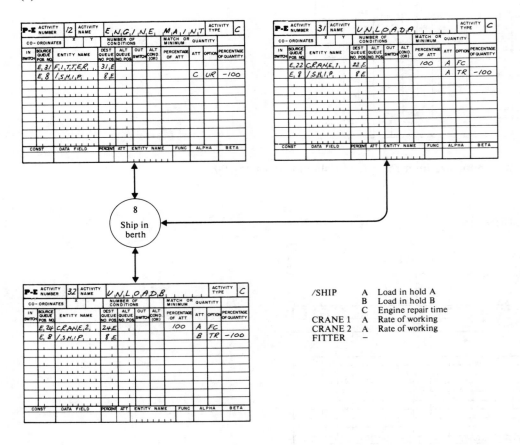

The engine maintenance activity must be a continuous activity in order to share the /Ship. The time for the activity is set by the UR option.

(b)

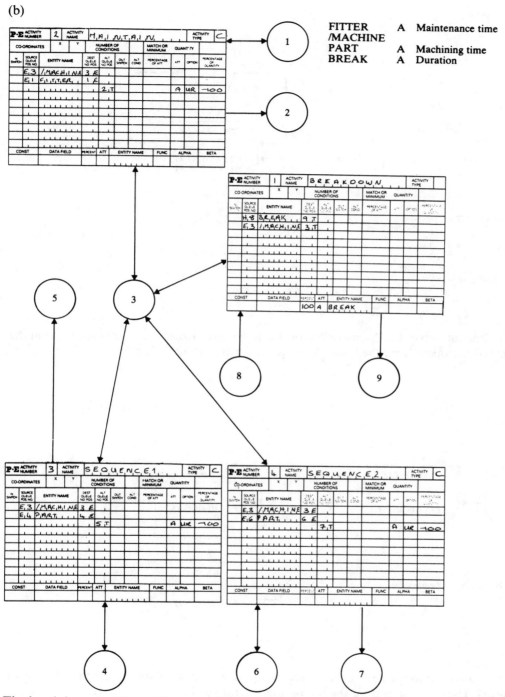

FITTER      A  Maintenance time
/MACHINE
PART        A  Machining time
BREAK       A  Duration

The breakdown activity is discrete and has the highest priority. Note the moves of the Fitter and the Parts are controlled by alternative destinations.

SOLUTION 7.17

(a)

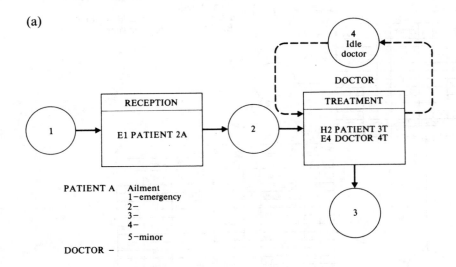

PATIENT A   Ailment
             1–emergency
             2–
             3–
             4–
             5–minor

DOCTOR –

Patients are put into queue 2, ordered according to their A-attribute (i.e., smallest value at the head), and are taken from the head of the queue for treatment.

(b)

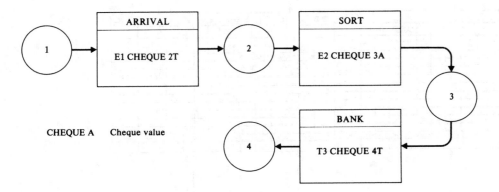

CHEQUE A   Cheque value

Cheques are put into queue 3, ordered according to their A-attribute (i.e., smallest value at the head). They are taken from the *tail* of queue 3 for banking.

SOLUTION 7.18

(a)

| SHIP | A | Size of load |
|------|---|--------------|
| WARE 1 | A | Contents |
| WARE 2 | A | Contents |

38 per cent of the quantity moved from the Ship is put in Warehouse 1 and 60 per cent in Warehouse 2. The rest disappears!

(b) Solution 1

LORRY A Size of load

Whatever quantity is needed to fill the Lorry is transferred into the A-attribute.

(b) Solution 2

LORRY A Size of load
(maximum = capacity)

## (c) Solution 1

| P-E | ACTIVITY NUMBER | 5 | ACTIVITY NAME | R O U T E | | | | ACTIVITY TYPE | | |
|---|---|---|---|---|---|---|---|---|---|---|
| CO-ORDINATES | | X | Y | NUMBER OF CONDITIONS | | 3 | MATCH OR MINIMUM | QUANTITY | 100 | |
| IN SWITCH | SOURCE QUEUE POS. NO | ENTITY NAME | DEST QUEUE NO POS | ALT QUEUE NO POS | OUT SWITCH | ALT COND (OR) | PERCENTAGE OF ATT | ATT | OPTION | PERCENTAGE OF QUANTITY |
| | E 9 | L O R R Y | 4 T | | | OR | | A | TH | – 12 |
| | E 9 | L O R R Y | 2 T | | | OR | | A | TH | – 5 |
| | E 9 | L O R R Y | 1 T | | | | | A | TH | – 3 |
| | | | | | | | | | | |
| | | | | | | | | | | |
| | | | | | | | | | | |
| | | | | | | | | | | |
| | | | | | | | | | | |
| CONST | | DATA FIELD | | PERCENT | ATT | ENTITY NAME | | FUNC | ALPHA | BETA |

LORRY  A  12 if aggregate
     5 if cement
     3 if sand

If the A-attribute of Lorry is at least 12 it is sent to queue 4, if it is at least 5 it is sent to queue 2, and if it is at least 3 it is sent to queue 1. Note that the biggest attribute value is tested first.

## (c) Solution 2

| P-E | ACTIVITY NUMBER | | ACTIVITY NAME | R O U T E | | | MATCH OR MINIMUM | QUANTITY | ACTIVITY TYPE | |
|---|---|---|---|---|---|---|---|---|---|---|
| CO-ORDINATES | | X | Y | NUMBER OF CONDITIONS | | | | | | |
| IN SWITCH | SOURCE QUEUE POS NO | ENTITY NAME | DEST QUEUE NO POS | ALT QUEUE NO POS | OUT SWITCH | ALT COND | PERCENTAGE OF ATT | ATT | OPTION | PERCENTAGE OF QUANTITY |
| | E 9 | L O R R Y | 4 T | | | OR | | A | CC | 12 |
| | E 9 | L O R R Y | 2 T | | | OR | | A | CC | 5 |
| | E 9 | L O R R Y | 1 T | | | | | A | CC | 3 |
| | | | | | | | | | | |
| | | | | | | | | | | |
| | | | | | | | | | | |
| | | | | | | | | | | |
| | | | | | | | | | | |
| CONST | | DATA FIELD | | PERCENT | ATT | ENTITY NAME | | FUNC | ALPHA | BETA |

LORRY  A  12 if aggregate
     5 if cement
     3 if sand
     (maximum = 100)

Note that the A-attribute of Lorry has the same definition as for solution 1, but has a maximum of 100 in this case.

## (c) Solution 3

| P-E | ACTIVITY NUMBER | | ACTIVITY NAME | R O U T E | | | MATCH OR MINIMUM | QUANTITY | ACTIVITY TYPE | |
|---|---|---|---|---|---|---|---|---|---|---|
| CO-ORDINATES | | X | Y | NUMBER OF CONDITIONS | | | | | | |
| IN SWITCH | SOURCE QUEUE POS NO | ENTITY NAME | DEST QUEUE NO POS | ALT QUEUE NO POS | OUT SWITCH | ALT COND | PERCENTAGE OF ATT | ATT | OPTION | PERCENTAGE OF QUANTITY |
| | E 9 | L O R R Y | 9 T | | | | | | | |
| | | | | 4 T | | | | A | EC | 12 |
| | | | | 2 T | | | | A | EC | 5 |
| | | | | 1 T | | | | A | EC | 3 |
| | | | | | | | | | | |
| | | | | | | | | | | |
| | | | | | | | | | | |
| | | | | | | | | | | |
| CONST | | DATA FIELD | | PERCENT | ATT | ENTITY NAME | | FUNC | ALPHA | BETA |

LORRY  A  12 if aggregate
     5 if cement
     3 if sand
     (maximum = 100)

The A-attribute of Lorry should again have a maximum of 100. In this case incorrectly coded Lorries are routed back to the tail of queue 9.

## (d) Solution 1

| P-E | ACTIVITY NUMBER | 4 | ACTIVITY NAME | JOURNEY | | | ACTIVITY TYPE | |
|---|---|---|---|---|---|---|---|---|
| CO-ORDINATES | | X | Y | NUMBER OF CONDITIONS | 1 | MATCH OR MINIMUM | QUANTITY | |
| IN SWITCH | SOURCE QUEUE POS. NO. | ENTITY NAME | DEST QUEUE NO. POS. | ALT QUEUE NO. POS | OUT SWITCH | ALT COND. (OR) | PERCENTAGE OF ATT | ATT | OPTION | PERCENTAGE OF QUANTITY |
| | E.1 | VAN | 3 T | | | | | A | TH | -100 |
| | | | | | | | | B | TR | 100 |

| CONST | DATA FIELD | PERCENT | ATT | ENTITY NAME | FUNC | ALPHA | BETA |
|---|---|---|---|---|---|---|---|
| | | 100 | A | VAN | | | |

VAN A Journey time
B Accumulated journey time

The value in the A-attribute is added to the B-attribute (without changing the A-attribute), and this value is used as the time for the activity.

## (d) Solution 2

| P-E | ACTIVITY NUMBER | | ACTIVITY NAME | JOURNEY | | | ACTIVITY TYPE | |
|---|---|---|---|---|---|---|---|---|
| CO-ORDINATES | | X | Y | NUMBER OF CONDITIONS | | MATCH OR MINIMUM | QUANTITY | |
| IN SWITCH | SOURCE QUEUE POS. NO. | ENTITY NAME | DEST QUEUE NO POS | ALT QUEUE NC POS | OUT SWITCH | ALT COND | PERCENTAGE OF ATT | ATT | OPTION | PERCENTAGE OF QUANTITY |
| | E.1 | VAN | 3 T | | | | 100 | A | XC | |
| | | | | | | | 100 | A | BA | |
| | | | | | | | | B | AJ | 100 |

| CONST | DATA FIELD | PERCENT | ATT | ENTITY NAME | FUNC | ALPHA | BETA |
|---|---|---|---|---|---|---|---|

VAN A Journey time
B Accumulated journey time

Note the use of the XC option replacing the correlation term.

## (e) Solution 1

| P-E | ACTIVITY NUMBER | 2 | ACTIVITY NAME | UNLOAD | | | ACTIVITY TYPE | |
|---|---|---|---|---|---|---|---|---|
| CO-ORDINATES | | X | Y | NUMBER OF CONDITIONS | 1 | MATCH OR MINIMUM | QUANTITY | |
| IN SWITCH | SOURCE QUEUE POS. NO. | ENTITY NAME | DEST QUEUE NO. POS. | ALT QUEUE NC POS | OUT SWITCH | ALT COND (OR) | PERCENTAGE OF ATT | ATT | OPTION | PERCENTAGE OF QUANTITY |
| | E.1 | TANKER | 2 T | | | | 50 | A | FQ | |
| | | | | | | | | A | TR | -100 |

| CONST | DATA FIELD | PERCENT | ATT | ENTITY NAME | FUNC | ALPHA | BETA |
|---|---|---|---|---|---|---|---|

TANKER A Size of load

50 per cent of the A-attribute fixes the quantity (FQ option) and this value is transferred out of the A-attribute.

## (e) Solution 2

| P-E ACTIVITY NUMBER | | ACTIVITY NAME | U N L O A D | | | ACTIVITY TYPE | |
|---|---|---|---|---|---|---|---|
| CO-ORDINATES | X | Y | NUMBER OF CONDITIONS | | MATCH OR MINIMUM | QUANTITY | |
| IN SWITCH | SOURCE QUEUE POS. NO. | ENTITY NAME | DEST QUEUE NO POS | ALT QUEUE NO POS | OUT SWITCH | ALT COND | PERCENTAGE OF ATT | ATT | OPTION | PERCENTAGE OF QUANTITY |

| IN SWITCH | SOURCE QUEUE POS. NO. | ENTITY NAME | DEST QUEUE NO POS | ALT QUEUE NO POS | OUT SWITCH | ALT COND | PERCENTAGE OF ATT | ATT | OPTION | PERCENTAGE OF QUANTITY |
|---|---|---|---|---|---|---|---|---|---|---|
| E | 1 | TANKER | 2 T | | | | 50 | A | BA | |
| | | | | | | | | A | AI | 100 |
| | | | | | | | | | | |
| CONST | DATA FIELD | PERCENT | ATT | ENTITY NAME | | FUNC | ALPHA | BETA | | |

TANKER  A  Size of load

The accumulator is set to half the load and this is returned to the attribute.

## (f)

| P-E ACTIVITY NUMBER | 8 | ACTIVITY NAME | Z E R O I S E | | | ACTIVITY TYPE | |
|---|---|---|---|---|---|---|---|
| CO-ORDINATES | X | Y | NUMBER OF CONDITIONS | 1 | MATCH OR MINIMUM | QUANTITY | |

| IN SWITCH | SOURCE QUEUE POS. NO. | ENTITY NAME | DEST QUEUE NO. POS. | ALT QUEUE NO. POS. | OUT SWITCH | ALT COND. (OR) | PERCENTAGE OF ATT | ATT | OPTION | PERCENTAGE OF QUANTITY |
|---|---|---|---|---|---|---|---|---|---|---|
| H | 1 | PATIENT | 1 T | | | | | A | XR | 0 |
| | | | | | | | | B | XR | 0 |
| | | | | | | | | C | XR | 0 |
| | | | | | | | | D | XR | 0 |
| | | | | | | | | F | XR | 0 |
| | | | | | | | | | | |
| CONST | DATA FIELD | PERCENT | ATT | ENTITY NAME | | FUNC | ALPHA | BETA | | |

PATIENT  A  
B  
C  } Attributes to be cleared  
D  
F

Each attribute is set to 0 per cent of its maximum

(g)

| P-E NUMBER | ACTIVITY NUMBER 9 | ACTIVITY NAME A L L O C A T E | | ACTIVITY TYPE | |
|---|---|---|---|---|---|
| CO-ORDINATES | X | Y | NUMBER OF CONDITIONS 6 | MATCH OR MINIMUM | QUANTITY |

| IN SWITCH | SOURCE QUEUE POS. NO. | ENTITY NAME | DEST QUEUE NO. POS. | ALT QUEUE NO. POS | OUT SWITCH | ALT COND. (OR) | PERCENTAGE OF ATT | ATT | OPTION | PERCENTAGE OF QUANTITY |
|---|---|---|---|---|---|---|---|---|---|---|
| | E,10 | O,R,D,E,R | 11,T | | | OR | | D | CC | 100 |
| | | | | | | | 100 | D | M1 | |
| | | | | | | | 100 | B | M2 | |
| | | | | | | | 100 | C | M3 | |
| | | | | | | | 100 | A | FQ | |
| | E,10 | O,R,D,E,R | 11,T | | | | 100 | D | M1 | |
| | | | | | | | 100 | B | M2 | |
| | | | | | | | 100 | C | M3 | |
| | | | | | | | 100 | A | FQ | |
| | E,4 | O,W,N,T,A,N,K,R | 4,T | | OR | | 100 | B | M2 | |
| | | | | | | | 100 | C | M3 | |
| | | | | | | | | A | TR | 100 |
| | E,4 | H,I,R,E,D,T,K,R | 4,T | | OR | | 100 | B | M2 | |
| | | | | | | | 100 | C | M3 | |
| | | | | | | | | A | TR | 100 |
| | E,4 | O,W,N,T,A,N,K,R | 4,T | | OR | | | B | CE | |
| | | | | | | | | C | CE | |
| | | | | | | | | B | I2 | 100 |
| | | | | | | | | C | I3 | 100 |
| | | | | | | | | A | TR | 100 |
| | E,15 | H,I,R,E,D,T,K,R | 4,T | | | | 100 | D | M1 | |
| | | | | | | | | B | I2 | 100 |
| | | | | | | | | C | I3 | 100 |
| | | | | | | | | A | TR | 100 |
| CONST | DATA FIELD | PERCENT ATT | ENTITY NAME | FUNC | ALPHA | BETA | | | | |

ORDER
A  Order size
B  Grade (1–4)
C  District (1–7)
D  Priority:
  1 = non-priority
  2 = priority
  (maximum = 2)

OWN TANKER
A  Size of load
  (maximum = 20000)
B  Grade (1–4), 0 if clean
C  District (1–7), 0 if clean

HIRED TANKER
A  Size of load
  (maximum = 15000)
B  Grade (1–4), 0 if clean
C  District (1–7), 0 if clean
D  Constant value 2

QUEUE  4 –  Tanker queue
  10 –  Orders to be allocated
  11 –  Orders allocated
  15 –  Tankers for hire

A priority order is selected in preference to a non-priority order. (D-attribute equal to 2—CC option.) An own or hired tanker which is partly full is selected in preference to an own or hired tanker which is empty. The grade and district are matched against the tanker (M2 and M3 options). If an empty tanker is used (B- and C-attributes of own tanker empty—or hired tanker in queue 15) the grade and district of the current order are copied to the tanker (I2 and I3 options). Note that a hired tanker from queue 15 is selected only if the order is priority 2 (M1 option). The order size fixes the quantity to be transferred (FQ option) which ensures that only complete orders are delivered.

SOLUTION 7.19
Contents of attributes

| Entity | Attribute | Contents | Maximum |
|---|---|---|---|
| Tanker A | A | load in first hold | 1000 |
| | B | product type | |
| | C | tanker number | |
| Tanker B | A | load in second hold | 600 |
| | B | product type | |
| | C | tanker number | |
| Pipe | A | not used | |
| | B | product type | |
| Tank | A | load in tank | 1600 |
| | B | product type | |
| Number | A | tanker number | |

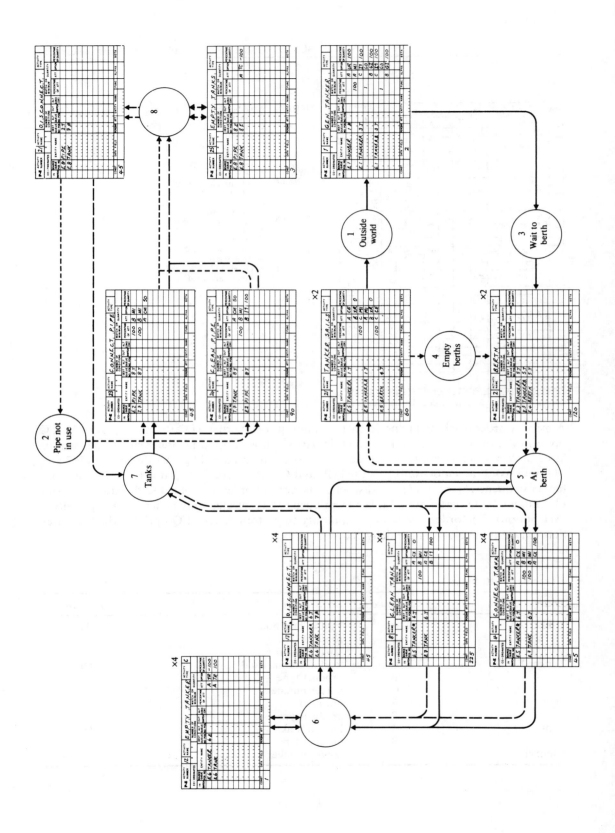

SOLUTION 7.20

Contents of attributes

| Entity | Attribute | Contents | Maximum |
|--------|-----------|----------|---------|
| Batch | A | order number | |
| | B | due date in days–1 | |
| | C | cooling time in minutes | |
| Day | A | day number | |
| Furnace | A | load in tons | |
| Ladle | A | load in tons | 25 |
| Order | A | order number | |
| Pit | A | set to 120 minutes | |

(*Solution continued overleaf.*)

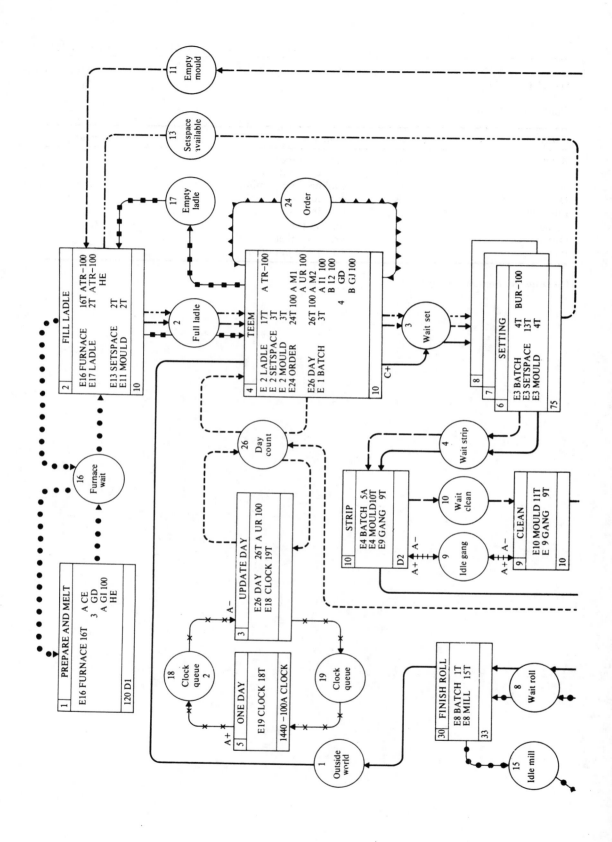

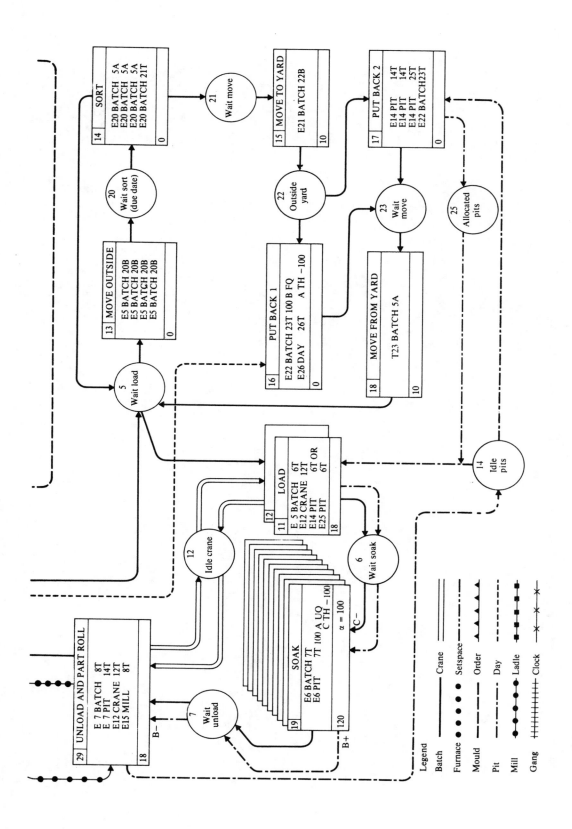

# Part Three

## Computer simulation

# 8.

## Preparing for the computer

Simulation is an ideal task for a computer because, as we have already seen with hand simulation, the rules for operating a model are repetitive yet very simple in concept. A great many programming languages have been developed, mainly in the UK and USA, for computer simulation. They each have particular advantages, and every simulator has his own preference.

In this chapter we discuss some criteria for selecting a simulation language, and give as an example the approach adopted by one major international corporation. We then describe features of the HOCUS suite of programs—the simulation system featured in this book. It has facilities which any simulator should look for when either selecting a system or writing his own. Finally, we illustrate how to transfer a hand simulation model into a computer simulation model. In Chapter 9 we describe how to run the simulation model on the computer and how to obtain results. In both chapters examples have been drawn mainly from the steel mill model described in Exercise 7.20. Chapter 10 discusses the value of colour graphics and describes how to obtain colour displays from HOCUS models.

### Selecting a simulation system

When selecting a simulation system we need to ask a number of questions:

- How easy is it to build a simulation model which we can demonstrate to management as being accurate? How long will it take to build?
- How easy will it be to modify and experiment with? How long will it take to verify the changes?
- Can we use the system ourselves or do we need to use an expert? Is there an expert available? What training is available and how long does it take? What ongoing support is provided by the supplier?
- Is the language free from errors? If it is used widely, fewer errors are likely.
- What costs are associated with using the package and what benefits are likely to be obtained?

We need to consider the features required to make it fit the business needs of the organization, but be careful over who is 'defining' the business needs. The 'requirements' specified by operational research specialists will be very different from the requirements of production engineers.

It is our experience that the most effective methods of assessment and selection are based on comparing prospective systems against a list of required features and criteria. This list should be sufficiently detailed to allow a sensible level of discrimination without being so

215

extensive that the key issues become confused. A list might contain some or all of the following:

*Model building*
Design aids
Ease of understanding
Activity life cycle diagrams
Ease of translation from design to computer model

*Model features*
Sufficient complexity possible
Database manipulation
Reporting (user defined)
Continuous activities
Complicated arithmetic
Access to external data or calculations

*Graphics*
Ease of specification
Resolution of screens

*Hardware*
Processor options—mainframe/mini/micro versions
Graphics terminal options

*Costs*
Processor
Software
Graphics
Installation
Maintenance

*General*
Level of support
Training
Documentation

A matrix should be drawn with columns (say) for the required features and criteria, and rows for the available packages. By the end of the evaluation every cell in the matrix should contain sufficient information to allow a satisfactory assessment. Products, for which evaluation information cannot be obtained, should be eliminated. Having said this, it is the authors' experience that considerable tenacity is often required during an evaluation exercise to ensure the answer received is interpreted correctly.

A number of the criteria suggested, such as costs and hardware requirements, can normally be established rapidly. Other aspects will be harder to determine accurately. Obviously demonstrations of the products are essential. To get an indication of the ease of use of the product, ask to see details of demonstration models; try to get a feel for the time required to set up the models. Look for responsive pre-sales support—if the company offers poor support before you purchase it is unlikely to be any better after you have parted with your cash. Find out how many existing users there are—avoid being an unwitting guinea-pig. Ask to talk to current users to find out their views of the product. Ask what developments are being planned and what life is seen for the product; check how often new versions of the products are released.

In addition to the capabilities of the package it is essential to establish the credentials of the company from which you intend to purchase—the best product in the world is of little use if its authors go into liquidation the day after you get it.

The next step in the evaluation is to discard all products which are clearly inadequate in some key area. This is likely to be a continuous process to some degree throughout the evaluation. Then discard criteria which are satisfied by all the remaining products. This will leave a core area for assessment. There is a growing trend towards using weighted average techniques at this stage of the analysis (or even earlier); each criterion is given a weight and each product is given a score for each criterion. In this way each product can be given a single score. It is the authors' view that this approach can be dangerous if not used with extreme care (particularly with regard to the sensitivity to changes in weights and individual scores). If the assessor wishes to use such an approach it should be applied as a prompt—does the product it recommends agree with the assessor's 'feeling' or instinct, and if not, why not?

Simulation, when properly applied, has the potential for saving organizations significant sums of money. Effort expended in ensuring the acquisition of the simulation tool best suited to the business needs of an organization will repay itself many times over.

The selection approach described above is illustrated by the following extracts based on an evaluation exercise carried out by a major multinational corporation (Figs 8.1(a), (b)). The identity of the corporation and the competitive simulation products cannot be revealed.

---

**Memo**

**Subject: Meeting on Shop Floor Simulation Software Packages**

A meeting was held on 4 June to review the results of the simulation software evaluation and trials. The centre presented the consolidated results of the joint reviews, trials and verifications which were carried out by the subsidiaries.

There was full concensus with respect to the applied evaluation criteria and their individual importance.

The study evidenced that HOCUS is the superior package, particularly due to its:

- superior modelling technique;
- ease of model building;
- user friendliness;
- superior features (i.e., continuous activities and flexibility).

This was supported by presentations from the subsidiaries on their specific trial projects.

The summary of the results is attached . . .

A description of the trial projects is attached . . .

The participating companies highlighted the need for HOCUS installations in their own system houses to enable full-time availability of the system for multi-task applications . . .

The commercial figures are attached.

The procurement of a simulation package is the responsibility of the system houses.

The centre will arrange HOCUS training courses upon demand from the subsidiaries.

We would appreciate your comments on the study and would like to encourage you to think about shop floor simulation in your company.

Regards

---

**Figure 8.1 (a)**

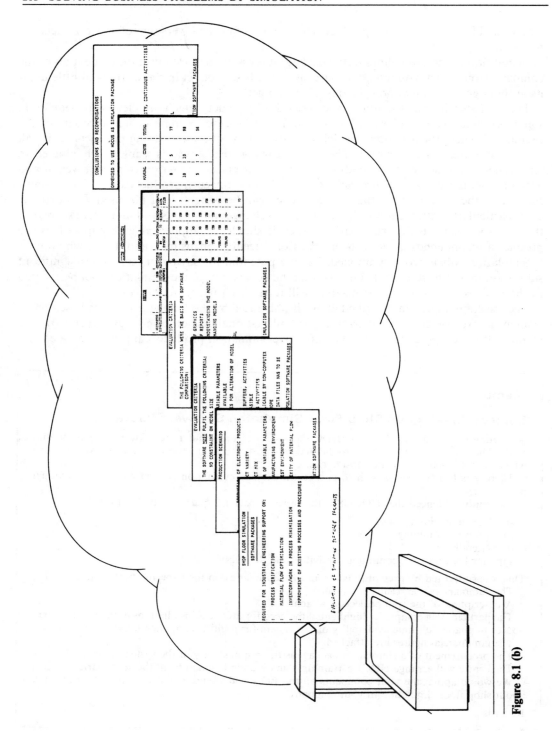

**Figure 8.1 (b)**

# The HOCUS suite of programs

Our approach to running models on a computer has been to develop a suite of three standard programs which replace the need for one-off user-written programs. This is possible because the basic structure of a model is always the same—entities, with or without attributes, have life cycles consisting of queues and activities. Only the details of a model make it unique.

To run models on a computer using this suite of standard programs requires no further creativity on the part of the model builder. The procedures are simple and mainly clerical. We have concentrated our effort into building an accurate, acceptable model quickly. All we want the computer to do is to repeat rapidly what we do by hand and show us the consequences of the changes we make to the model.

The first program in the suite is the 'Input' program. This is a screen-based data entry program which allows the user to enter and modify details of a model. The program generates a text file which has a format based on the design of the model on paper. Details of the input required are given in subsequent sections of this chapter.

Once the text file has been created it is run through a program called the 'Verifier'. This performs detailed checking for errors and inconsistencies in the model. It can produce model listings if required and provides a list of errors found (if any). Errors are classed as fatal (F-error) or cautionary (C-error). F-type errors are such that the model as specified is not valid. C-type errors are such that minor parts of the model do not conform to usual practice, or defaults have been used where information has not been supplied. A full list of error messages is given in Appendix 4.

When a model has no F-errors the user is given the option of storing a compacted version of the model on file – a save file – although the presence of C-errors implies that the model may still be incorrect. The save file contains all of the logic specified in the model text, but stores it in a form which allows for efficient running of the model.

The third and final program in the suite, the 'Interactive' program, allows the user to access the save files and perform simulations under user control. The various features of this program are described in Chapter 9.

The operation of the HOCUS suite is shown diagrammatically in Fig. 8.2.

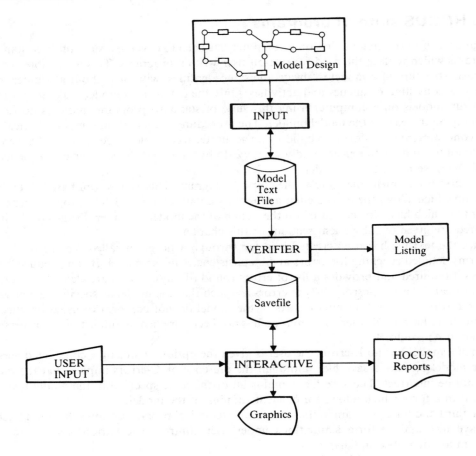

**Figure 8.2**

## Header data

Before the model data can be processed by the verifier, preliminary data and control switches must be set.

*Run header switches* Control of the verifier and interactive programs can be executed through run switches. These switches are discussed in more detail in Chapter 9, but those allowed on the run header are:

1   Read new data (this switch is supplied automatically by the input program).
5   Reset to zero any activity duration that is calculated to be negative, without stopping the simulation.
10   Store the initial state of the model.
16   Sample from distributions using antithetic numbers. For a random number, N, in the range 1 to 100, its antithesis is $101 - N$.

17 Suppress printing of P-type errors (see Chapter 9) during a simulation run. Any errors which occur are counted and the total number is printed at the end of each simulation run or when run switch R7 is used (see Chapter 9).

20 Override the rule that no report (except 1, 2, 10, 11, 15, 16, 17, 19, 20, 21, 23 and 24) is printed more than three times while advancing the simulation.

22 Override fatal error F746 if there are more than 500 alternative routes through the conditions of an activity (and so checking of all routes through an activity is not performed).

25 and over   New base value for random streams. The default base value is 1100.

*Model name header*   Contains the name of the model and the date specified as day, month, year.

*Model size header*   Specifies the number of entity types, entity groups, queues, data fields, activities, histograms, queue logs and graphics-related definitions (see Chapter 10) in the model. These values are supplied by the input program.

*Monitor header*   This line, identified by 'M', controls the printing of the model data during verification as follows:

*Switch*
1   entity list;
2   queue list;
3   data field list;
4   activity list;
5   histograms and queue logs;
6   initial conditions;
7   entity, data field, histogram, queue log and initial condition formats;
8   queue formats;
9   activity formats;
10   attribute description format;
11   reserved;
12   reserved;
13   join list (graphics related);
14   feature list (graphics related).

The number of iterations permitted at any one simulation clock time is normally set to 1000. It can, however, be reset to any value greater than 14 by an entry on the Monitor header line.

## Model data

The input program allows free format input of fields. When creating the data file, the program left-justifies names and right-justifies numbers. Any fields which are not used are left blank.

The general form of an input screen is a numbered listing of a section of the data file and a section at the top of the screen which is used to hold an expanded version of the current entry (being added or modified). The bottom of the screen normally contains a help display showing the options available and a field for data entry. The user can issue commands to change, delete, insert, add, move or repeat blocks of data. Comments can be inserted at any point in the model. When entering an item of data, special commands can be input instead.

The commands are Z to make a field blank, J to jump to the next entry, X to exit the current level, or (return) to leave the item unchanged.

The following sections describe the basic simulation records necessary. Chapter 10 describes the specification of graphics.

## Entity description

These lines describe the entities used in the model. They are entered directly from Entity Description and Attribute Maximum Value format cards. They are stored with an identifier 'E' in column one. Figure 8.3 shows an entity input screen.

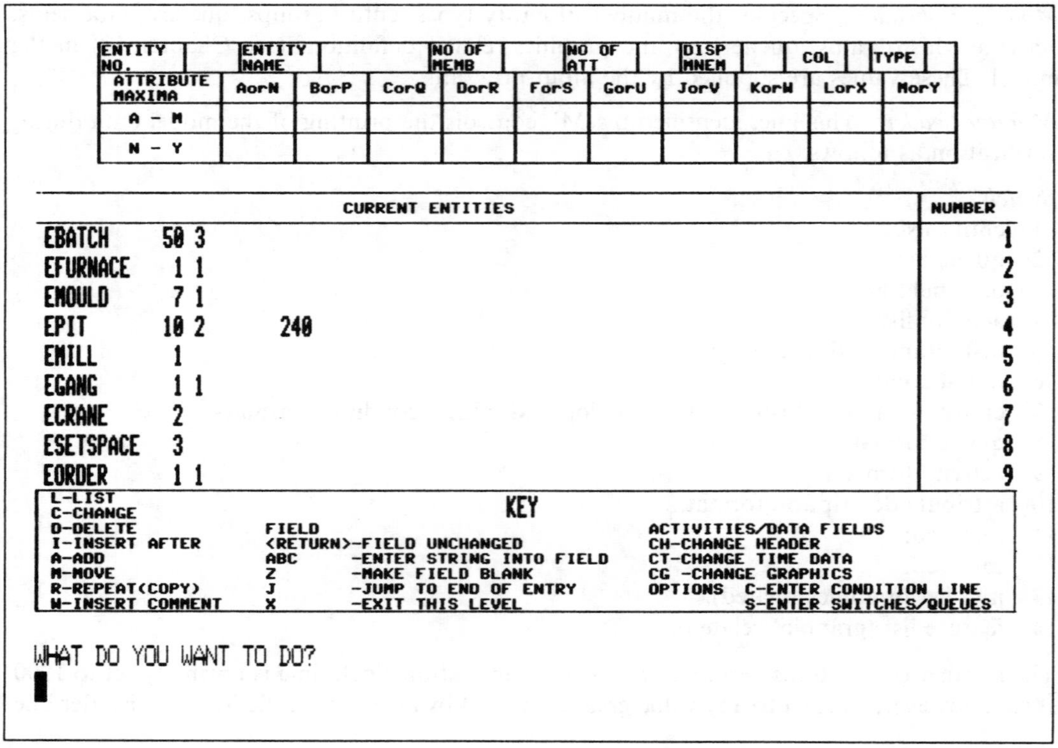

Figure 8.3

## Entity group description

These lines show the entity groups in the model, and the details come from the Entity Description format cards. The identifier in column one is 'G' as shown in Fig. 8.4.

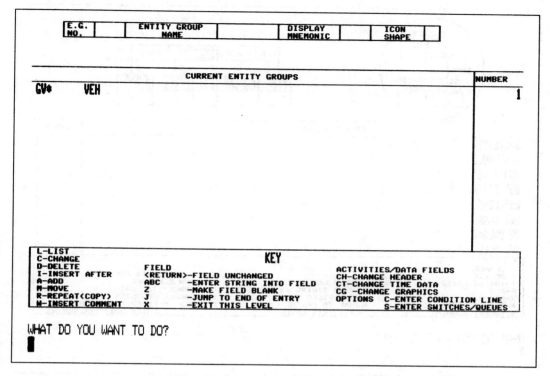

**Figure 8.4**

If an entity group is a subset of another group (see Chapter 7—entity groups) then the smaller group must be listed first.

## Queue description

The queues in the model are listed in numerical order. Most details come from the queue format cards. The identifier in column one is 'Q' (see Fig. 8.5). Note that queue numbers are not explicitly given to queues.

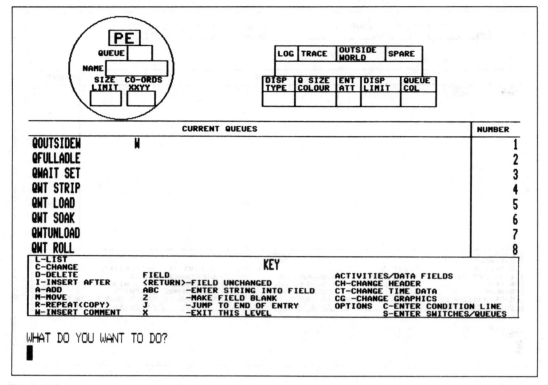

**Figure 8.5**

In addition to the data supplied on format cards a number of additional items may be specified:

- Queue Log (L): monitoring a queue to give a detailed report of variations in queue length occurring during a simulation.
- Queue Trace (T): up to 20 queues can be traced. This enables a report to be produced whenever a traced queue is disturbed.
- Outside World (W): if one or more queues represent the outside world a flag may be set which will cause the simulation to halt if such a queue becomes empty. This prevents the results of simulation becoming distorted when an activity requiring an entity from the outside world cannot start because the appropriate queue is empty.
- Spare Queue (S): Certain queues may not be part of the simulation, but may function as a depository for entities not currently required (such as extra men or machines). Designating such queues as spare excludes entities in them from histogram utilization calculations.

## Data field description

The data fields must be listed in numerical order. A data field may be either a distribution or a timetable.

Distributions are identified by 'D' in column one. This is followed by the number of pairs of coordinates which make up the distribution. The coordinates are entered in sequence in (value, probability) pairs. The first probability in a distribution must be 1 and the last must be 100.

In addition to user-defined distributions the following standard distributions can be accessed:

| Distribution | Code | Parameter one | Parameter two |
|---|---|---|---|
| Poisson | P | mean, $\lambda$ | |
| Normal | N | mean, $\mu$ | standard deviation, $\sigma$ |
| Binomial | B | mean, $\mu$ | sample size, n |
| Negative exponential | E | mean, $\lambda$ | |
| Weibull | W | scale parameter, b | shape parameter, $\gamma$ |
| Log Normal | L | median, $\mu$ | standard deviation of underlying normal distribution, $\sigma$ |

For a timetable 'T' is entered in column one, followed by the number of values which make up the timetable. The actual entries are then input in sequence. Abbreviated forms of input are allowed; for example 30 thousand can be entered as 30K, four entries of 2 can be entered as 4*2, and 'R' can be used to denote the remaining entries of a timetable (so R*0 would set remaining entries to zero). Figure 8.6 shows the top level and low level input screens for data fields.

| | | | CURRENT DATA FIELDS |
|---|---|---|---|
| **NUMBER** | **TYPE** | **NO OF ENTRIES** | **COMMENT** |
| 1 | D | 10 | MELTING TIME |
| 2 | D | 10 | STRIPPING TIME |
| 3 | D | 10 | CONTENTS OF FURNACE |
| 4 | D | 10 | TIME BETWEEN POURING AND REQUIRED DELIVERY |

```
                                     KEY
L-LIST
C-CHANGE
D-DELETE              FIELD                            ACTIVITIES/DATA FIELDS
I-INSERT AFTER       <RETURN>-FIELD UNCHANGED          CH-CHANGE HEADER
A-ADD                ABC      -ENTER STRING INTO FIELD  CT-CHANGE TIME DATA
M-MOVE               Z        -MAKE FIELD BLANK         CG -CHANGE GRAPHICS
R-REPEAT(COPY)       J        -JUMP TO END OF ENTRY    OPTIONS  C-ENTER CONDITION LINE
W-INSERT COMMENT     X        -EXIT THIS LEVEL                  S-ENTER SWITCHES/QUEUES
```

WHAT DO YOU WANT TO DO?

▉

| DATA FIELD | NUMBER | 1 | TYPE | D | NUMBER OF ENTRIES | 10 | | | | |
|---|---|---|---|---|---|---|---|---|---|---|

| TIME | TIME/ PROB | TIME | TIME/ PROB | TIME | TIME/ PROB | TIME | TIME/ PROB | TIME | TIME/ PROB | LOCATION RANGE |
|---|---|---|---|---|---|---|---|---|---|---|
| W MELTING TIME | | | | | | | | | | |
| 45 | 1 | 48 | 5 | 53 | 10 | 58 | 20 | 63 | 40 | 1- 10 |
| 67 | 60 | 73 | 80 | 79 | 90 | 83 | 95 | 85 | 100 | 11- 20 |
| | | | | | | | | | | |
| | | | | | | | | | | |
| | | | | | | | | | | |
| | | | | | | | | | | |
| | | | | | | | | | | |
| | | | | | | | | | | |
| | | | | | | | | | | |
| | | | | | | | | | | |

```
                                     KEY
L-LIST
C-CHANGE
D-DELETE              FIELD                            ACTIVITIES/DATA FIELDS
I-INSERT AFTER       <RETURN>-FIELD UNCHANGED          CH-CHANGE HEADER
A-ADD                ABC      -ENTER STRING INTO FIELD  CT-CHANGE TIME DATA
M-MOVE               Z        -MAKE FIELD BLANK         CG -CHANGE GRAPHICS
R-REPEAT(COPY)       J        -JUMP TO END OF ENTRY    OPTIONS  C-ENTER CONDITION LINE
W-INSERT COMMENT     X        -EXIT THIS LEVEL                  S-ENTER SWITCHES/QUEUES
```

WHAT DO YOU WANT TO DO?

▉

**Figure 8.6**

| CURRENT ACTIVITIES | | | | | |
|---|---|---|---|---|---|
| NUMBER(S) | NAME | NUMBER(S) | NAME | NUMBER(S) | NAME |
| 1 | PREPARE/MELT | 13 | MOVE OUTSIDE | | |
| 2 | FILL LADLE | 14 | SORT | | |
| 3 | UPDATE DAY | 15 | MOVE TO YARD | | |
| 4 | TEEM | 16 | PUT BACK 1 | | |
| 5 | ONE DAY | 17 | PUT BACK 2 | | |
| 6- 8 | SETTING | 18 | MOVE FROM YD | | |
| 9 | CLEAN | 19- 28 | SOAK | | |
| 10 | STRIP | 29 | UNLOAD/PT RL | | |
| 11- 12 | LOAD | 30 | FINISH ROLL | | |

```
                                          KEY
L-LIST
C-CHANGE
D-DELETE          FIELD                           ACTIVITIES/DATA FIELDS
I-INSERT AFTER    <RETURN>-FIELD UNCHANGED        CH-CHANGE HEADER
A-ADD             ABC      -ENTER STRING INTO FIELD CT-CHANGE TIME DATA
M-MOVE            Z        -MAKE FIELD BLANK       CG -CHANGE GRAPHICS
R-REPEAT(COPY)    J        -JUMP TO END OF ENTRY   OPTIONS  C-ENTER CONDITION LINE
M-INSERT COMMENT  X        -EXIT THIS LEVEL                 S-ENTER SWITCHES/QUEUES
```

WHAT DO YOU WANT TO DO?
█

| PE | ACTIVITY NUMBER | 19 | | ACTIVITY NAME | SOAK | | ACTIVITY TYPE | A | NUMBER OF IDENTICALS | 10 | | HEADER |
|---|---|---|---|---|---|---|---|---|---|---|---|---|
| CO-ORDINATES XXYY | | | | NUMBER OF CONDITIONS | | 2 | MATCH OR MINIMUM | | QUANTITY | | | HEADER |
| IN SWITCH | SOURCE Q POS NO | ENTITY NAME | DEST Q NO POS | ALT Q NO POS | | OUT SWITCH | ALT COND | % OF ATT | ATT OPT | % OF QTY | NO DISP | NUMBER |
| C- | E   6 | BATCH | 7   T | | | | | | | | | 1 |
| | E   6 | PIT | 7   T | | | B+ | | | A  TR | 100 | | 2 |
| | | | | | | | | | A  XR | 0 | | 3 |
| | | | | | | | | | | | | |
| | | | | | | | | | | | | |
| | | | | | | | | | | | | |
| | | | | | | | | | | | | |
| | | | | | | | | | | | | |

| CONSTANT | DATA FIELD | PERCENT | ATT | ENTITY NAME | FUNCTION | ALPHA | BETA | |
|---|---|---|---|---|---|---|---|---|
| 120 | | 100CBATCH | | | | 100 | 100 | TIME |
| GRAPHICS TYPE | BOX COLOUR | TEXT COLOUR | ICON COLOUR | TIME COLOUR | HEIGHT | ENTITY LIST | OFFSET | |
| | | | | | | | | GRAPHICS |

```
                                          KEY
L-LIST
C-CHANGE
D-DELETE          FIELD                           ACTIVITIES/DATA FIELDS
I-INSERT AFTER    <RETURN>-FIELD UNCHANGED        CH-CHANGE HEADER
A-ADD             ABC      -ENTER STRING INTO FIELD CT-CHANGE TIME DATA
M-MOVE            Z        -MAKE FIELD BLANK       CG -CHANGE GRAPHICS
R-REPEAT(COPY)    J        -JUMP TO END OF ENTRY   OPTIONS  C-ENTER CONDITION LINE
M-INSERT COMMENT  X        -EXIT THIS LEVEL                 S-ENTER SWITCHES/QUEUES
```

WHAT DO YOU WANT TO DO?
█

Figure 8.7

## Activity description

Activity descriptions normally form the bulk of a model. Activities are transcribed directly from the format cards except that the lower part of the card (specifying activity duration) is moved to the header line.

The header line has an identifier in column one which is 'A' for discrete and 'B' for continuous activities. The 'number of conditions' entry should contain the number of entity name entries in the activity (including alternative and non-compulsory conditions, but counting each condition using =S or =A options as one).

If the activity is the first of a series of identical activities the total number in the set must be specified. The activities must be identical in all respects and they must be numbered consecutively from the first in the series.

Conditions are copied directly from the format cards. Figure 8.7 shows the activity list and the main input screen for one activity.

## Histogram description

These entries are required only if histograms of clock times, quantities moved or attribute values are required. The identifier in column one is 'H'.

A histogram is defined by specifying the entity name, attribute (clock), lower boundary, interval width, number of intervals and histogram title. In addition to the specified ranges

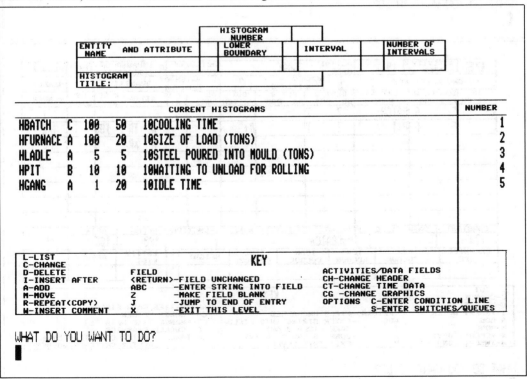

**Figure 8.8**

each histogram has two cells, one containing recorded values less than the lower boundary, the other contains values larger than the upper boundary (implicitly) specified.

The entry screen for histograms is shown in Fig. 8.8.

## Queue log description

Every queue for which a queue log is required must have a queue log entry. The identifier in column one is 'L'.

A queue log is defined by specifying the queue number, lower boundary, interval width, number of intervals and queue log title. In addition to the specified ranges (of equal width), there are lower and upper cells which record all queue sizes outside the specified ranges.

The entry screen for queue logs is shown in Fig. 8.9.

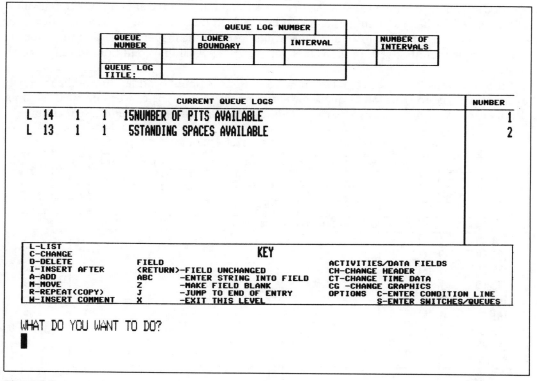

**Figure 8.9**

## Initial conditions description

These entries define the starting positions of all the entities in the model (with their initial attribute values). The data are transferred directly from the Attribute Initial Values format cards. The identifier in column one is 'I'.

A line is used for each allocation of a particular entity type to a single queue. Entities are allocated to the tail of the specified queue. If entities of more than one type are to be allocated to a given queue they must be listed in the desired order. If entities are allocated to an ordered queue, the order in which they are specified is immaterial—they are ordered by the appropriate attribute value.

The life cycles of up to 12 entities can be checked in considerable detail against the hand simulation. In this way we can verify that the model has been transferred to the computer correctly. Traced entities are denoted by 'T' in the appropriate column. In addition to entity traces, an individual attribute value from each of up to 15 entities can be traced; an attribute trace is denoted by placing the attribute letter in the 'trace' cell.

Attributes having non-zero starting values should be entered. The letter 'K' may be used to denote a multiple of 1000. The letter 'M' denotes the attribute maximum value (if one was specified in the entry description) or the largest integer allowed in the simulation (normally 200 000 000).

A number of shorthand ways of specifying attribute values for more than one entity exists. The code 'S' in an attribute value will enter the serial number of the entity as the initial value. Initial values for blocks of entities can also be specified by the '+' or '−' specification. For example, the entry '10 + 5' in an attribute would result in the first entity getting the value 10, and subsequent entities getting the values 15, 20, 25 . . . An initial conditions screen is shown in Fig. 8.10.

All entities must be allocated in the initial conditions. After allocating some of the members of an entity type to their initial queues, the remainder of the type can be allocated, without defining the exact number, by entering 'R' in the 'number of members allocated' column.

| CONDITION NUMBER | ENTITY NAME | | | NUMB ALLOC | | QUEUE NUMBER + TRACE | | | 1ST MOD | NO DISP |
|---|---|---|---|---|---|---|---|---|---|---|
| INITIAL ATTRIBUTES | AorN | BorP | CorQ | DorR | ForS | GorU | JorV | KorW | LorX | MorY |
| A − M | | | | | | | | | | |
| N − Y | | | | | | | | | | |

| CURRENT INITIAL CONDITIONS | NUMBER |
|---|---|
| IBATCH      1   1T | 1 |
| IBATCH     49   1 | 2 |
| IFURNACE    1  16T | 3 |
| IMOULD      7  11 | 4 |
| IPIT       10  14 | 5 |
| IMILL       1  15T | 6 |
| IGANG       1   9 | 7 |
| ICRANE      2  12 | 8 |
| ISETSPACE   3  13 | 9 |

```
                                              KEY
L-LIST
C-CHANGE
D-DELETE         FIELD                              ACTIVITIES/DATA FIELDS
I-INSERT AFTER   <RETURN>-FIELD UNCHANGED           CH-CHANGE HEADER
A-ADD            ABC      -ENTER STRING INTO FIELD   CT-CHANGE TIME DATA
M-MOVE           Z        -MAKE FIELD BLANK          CG -CHANGE GRAPHICS
R-REPEAT(COPY)   J        -JUMP TO END OF ENTRY      OPTIONS  C-ENTER CONDITION LINE
W-INSERT COMMENT X        -EXIT THIS LEVEL                    S-ENTER SWITCHES/QUEUES
```

WHAT DO YOU WANT TO DO?

**Figure 8.10**

# 9.

## Interactive simulation

For many years simulation was an arcane art practised by management services and operational research specialists. As described in Chapter 1 the difficulties of the 'communications chain' between the manager with the problem and the computer were sufficient to cast doubt on the ability of simulation to provide accurate, acceptable and rapid answers. The use of the formal model approach described in earlier chapters goes a long way towards addressing these issues.

### Interactive control

The recent explosion in computing technology and sophisticated computing techniques enables users to experiment with their computer models interactively and hence perform numerous experiments quickly. This reinforces the overall highly participative approach to problem solving and leads to successful projects.

This chapter describes the use of interactive simulation, which allows the model builder and his client to sit in front of a computer terminal, and either one of them can control the course of the simulation. They can:

- advance the simulation, checking logic interactively;
- examine parts of the model at any stage;
- stop the model when particular events or combinations of events occur;
- change details of the model before continuing the simulation.

The HOCUS interactive program described in this chapter takes the 'save file' generated from the verifier program described in Chapter 8 and offers the user a set of menus by which the progress of the simulation can be controlled. Once familiar with the basic operations available a wide range of free format 'expert' commands can be used to speed up interaction. These expert commands are of four basic types:

| | | |
|---|---|---|
| F | forward command | —advance the simulation. |
| S | snapshot command | —examine model details or results. |
| R | run switch | —simulation control commands. |
| V | vary command | —change model details. |

In the following sections a syntactical notation is used to describe expert commands:

| | |
|---|---|
| &lt;item&gt; | defines a single item. |
| (optional) | defines an optional item or text. |
| /repeat/ | defines a section which can be repeated. |

While going through the menu structures a user might make an input error or decide not to continue with the command currently being defined. For this reason an abandon character (defaulting to 'X') is defined. Entering this at any stage abandons the current command and returns to the main menu from which the command was initiated.

This chapter has four main sections—the first three are based on the three main HOCUS menus, and the fourth describes the menu to generate user-defined outputs from the simulation.

## Menu 1—Main menu

This is the standard menu accessed whenever a newly verified save file is picked up for interaction. The options are:

A—ADVANCE THE SIMULATION
B—PRINT REPORT
C—END THE RUN
D—CHANGE MODEL DETAILS (MENU 3)
E—SAVE THE MODEL AT CURRENT SIMULATION CLOCK TIME
F—USER-DEFINED MENU (MENU 4)
G—CONTINUE WITH GRAPHICS
Y—SWITCH THIS MENU DISPLAY OFF
Z—MOVE TO MINOR ITEMS MENU (MENU 2)

### Option A—Advance the simulation

This option allows the user to continue the simulation with a selection of reports being printed. There are 23 standard HOCUS reports, and the user-defined report generator. Some of these reports are available as 'monitor' reports—printing as a simulation progresses. Others are 'snapshot' reports—allowing access to details of the model at a particular time. Of the 24 reports some can be used both as monitor and snapshot reports. The full list of reports is given below, showing which reports are snapshot (S) and which are monitor (M).

| Report | Type | Details |
|---|---|---|
| 1 | M | Activities started. Printed whenever an activity starts, this report gives:<br>– the number of the activity;<br>– the time the activity is due to end;<br>– the rate of transfer for a continuous activity. |
| 2 | M | Activities ended<br>(a) Printed whenever an activity ends, this report gives:<br>– the number of the activity;<br>– the transfer quantity for a discrete activity, if appropriate.<br>(b) Printed whenever a continuous activity is examined or ends, this report gives:<br>– the number and name of the activity;<br>– the time since the activity started or was last examined, and cumulative time;<br>– the time the activity is due to end (if examined). |

| Report | Type | Details |
|--------|------|---------|

*Report*   *Type*   *Details*

(c) Printed whenever the end time of a continuous activity using a split entity is revised, this report gives:
- the number of the activity;
- the original end time;
- the revised end time.

3   S   Activity run count. Printed after the end phase, this report gives:
(a) For discrete activities
- the number of times each activity has ended;
- the cumulative and mean quantity transferred;
- the last (or due) end time for active and passive activities.

(b) For continuous activities
- the cumulative time for which each activity has been active;
- the cumulative quantity and the mean rate;
- the last (or due) end time for active and passive activities.

4   S   Activity detail (level one). Printed after the end phase, this report gives for each active activity:
- the activity number and name;
- the time it is due to end.

5   S   Activity detail (level two). Printed after the end phase, this report gives for each active activity:
- the activity number and name;
- the time it is due to end;
- the entities used in the activity.

6   S   Activity detail (level three). Printed after the end phase, this report gives for each active activity:
- the activity number and name;
- the time it is due to end;
- the entities used in the activity together with their attribute values.

7   S   Queue detail (level one). Printed after the start phase, this report gives for every queue:
- the queue number and name;
- the number of entities in the queue.

8   S   Queue detail (level two). Printed after the start phase, this report gives for queues which are not empty:
- the queue number and name;
- the queue size;
- the entities in the queue;

9   S   Queue detail (level three). Printed after the start phase, this report gives for queues which are not empty:
- the queue number and name;
- the queue size;
- the entities in the queue together with their attribute values.

10   MS   Entity trace (level one). Printed whenever one of the traced entities changes state, this report gives:
- the activity number or queue number holding the entity.

| Report | Type | Details |
|--------|------|---------|
| 11 | MS | Entity trace (level two). Printed whenever one of the traced entities changes state, this report gives:<br>– the activity number or queue number holding the entity;<br>– the attribute values of the entity. |
| 12 | S | Entity location (level one). Printed after both the start and end phases this report gives for each entity type:<br>– the entity name;<br>– the activity number or queue number holding each entity. |
| 13 | S | Entity location (level two). Printed after both the start and end phases, this report gives for each entity type:<br>– the entity name;<br>– the activity number or queue number holding each entity;<br>– the attribute values for each entity. |
| 14 | S | Histograms. Printed after the end phase, this report gives for each histogram:<br>– the histogram title;<br>– the entity name and attribute on which data is being collected;<br>– the number of observations in each of the ranges and a pictorial display;<br>– the total number of observations, the mean, the variance, the minimum and the maximum values;<br>– utilization figures, if the histogram records clock times. |
| 15 | MS | Graphics. Chapter 10 describes this report in more detail. |
| 16 | MS | Attribute trace. Printed whenever one of the traced attributes changes value, this report gives:<br>– the current attribute value. |
| 17 | M | Attribute trace. Printed whenever one of the traced attributes changes value, output report option 17 is set in an activity and monitor switch 17 is set, this report gives:<br>– the current attribute value. |
| 18 | S | Queue logs. Printed after the end phase, this report gives for each queue log:<br>– the queue log title;<br>– the queue number, name, size limit and current size;<br>– for each size range; the number of incidents (changes in queue size), the average size, the cumulative percentage of time spent (in increasing and decreasing order), the time spent and a pictorial display;<br>– the total time, the total number of incidents, average time between incidents, minimum size, maximum size and average queue size throughout the simulation period. |
| 19 | M | Queue trace (level one). Printed whenever one of the traced queues is disturbed, this report gives:<br>– the queue number and name;<br>– the queue size. |

| Report | Type | Details |
|--------|------|---------|
| 20 | M | Queue trace (level two). Printed whenever one of the traced queues is disturbed, this report gives:<br>– the queue number and name;<br>– the queue size;<br>– the entities in the queue. |
| 21 | M | Queue trace (level three). Printed whenever one of the traced queues is disturbed, this report gives:<br>– the queue number and name;<br>– the queue size;<br>– the entities in the queue together with their attribute values. |
| 22 | S | Data fields. Printed after the end phase this report gives details of all the data fields and is particularly useful if data fields are changed during the simulation. |
| 23 | M | Activities failing to start. Printed after the start phase this report gives a list of activities for which an unsuccessful attempt has been made to start. For each activity the report gives:<br>– the activity number;<br>– the failure condition number;<br>– the queue size;<br>– the preceding condition from whence recycling has occurred (where relevant). |
| 24 | MS | User defined reports. Any data available in standard reports can be accessed. Construction of these reports is described later in this chapter. |

When option A is selected the user is prompted for a list of monitor reports. For each report the user can select whether it is sent to the screen and printer or to the printer alone. For some of the more extensive reports an 'editing list' can be defined; for example an activity editing list would restrict the number of activities for which a report would be printed.

During the course of a simulation events may occur which would not be expected from a simulation adhering strictly to the implied rules. Examples of such events are an attribute exceeding its maximum or an outside world queue becoming empty. Errors such as these generate P-errors as the simulation progresses. A list of these errors and the recovery actions taken (when appropriate) is given in Appendix 4.

---

**Expert command**

Advance the simulation:

   F <time> <report><options> <report><options> . . .

where <time>        is the time to which the simulation is to be advanced
      <report>      is a monitor report number
      <options>     no entry—full report to screen and printer
                    P—report to printer only
                    L—use editing list
                    PL or LP—edited report to printer only
                    list—implicit definition of an editing list

Valid expert commands would be:
   F 1000
   F 600 1 2
   F 800 1P 2P 23
   F 900 11(1, 2, 5–8)

---

## Option B—Print report

This option prompts the user for a list of 'snapshot' reports.

---

**Expert command**

   S <report><options> <report><options>. . .

where <report>     is a snapshot report number
      <options>    are as for expert command F described above

Valid expert commands would be:
   S 12 11P
   S 3 (1, 2, 5–8)

---

## Option C—End the run

When the user has finished with a model, this option is used to terminate the run. The user can have a small set of snapshot reports (numbers 3, 14 and 18), or sufficient to allow every entity and attribute value in the model to be placed (numbers 3, 6, 9, 12, 14 and 18), or no reports at all.

---

**Expert command**

| | |
|---|---|
| R2 | run switch 2—end run with no reports |
| R9 ⟨option⟩ | run switch 9—end run with full set of reports |
| R19 ⟨option⟩ | run switch 19—end run with reduced set of reports |
| | |
| where ⟨option⟩ | is blank, for reports to screen and printer |
| | P, for reports to printer only |

---

After ending the run the user is presented with three sub-options:

A—STOP
B—RESTORE A SAVED MODEL
C—RETURN TO INITIAL STATE OF MODEL JUST RUN

Sub-option B allows the user to access one of the other verified 'save files'. Sub-option C reloads the initial conditions of the current model. The user is offered the following menu:

A—RESET NEGATIVE DURATIONS TO ZERO
B—USE NEW RANDOM NUMBERS
C—USE ANTITHETIC RANDOM NUMBERS
D—SUPPRESS P ERROR PRINTING
E—SPECIFY NEW RANDOM NUMBER SEED

### Option D—Change model details (Menu 3)

This option moves the user to menu 3 as described below.

### Option E—Save the model at current simulation clock time

The present state of the model can be saved on one of the 'save files'.

---

**Expert command**

R6(n) where n is the appropriate file number

---

### Option F—User-defined menu (Menu 4)

This menu presents a number of 'command files' which can be executed by inexpert users. The files are created via option G on Menu 2.

### Option G—Continue with graphics

The sequence of prompts is identical to option A—continue the simulation. The difference between the two options is that the graphics report (15) is automatically included in the report list when option G is selected.

### Option Y—Switch this menu display off

This turns off the menu printing for this menu. It can be turned back on again by responding 'Y' when asked to select an option from Menu 1 at a later stage.

### Option Z—Move to minor items menu (Menu 2)

The program will now move to Menu 2 as described below.

## Menu 2—Minor items menu

This menu contains a number of technical adjustments and system resetting options.

A—RESET ACTIVITY RUN COUNT/HISTOGRAMS/QUEUE LOGS
B—PRINT LIST OF SAVED MODELS
C—PRINT ACTIVITY PICTURE
D—CHANGE MODEL NAME
E—SET UP EDITING LIST
F—RESET SIMULATION TIME TO ZERO
G—COMMAND FILE OPTIONS
H—WRITE COMMENT ON PRINTOUT
I—CHANGE ABANDON CHARACTER
J—USER DEFINED REPORTS
K—GRAPHICS FILE CONTROL (ON/OFF)
L—CHANGE GRAPHICS DISPLAY ORIGIN
M—CHANGE GRAPHICS ANIMATION SPEED
Y—SWITCH THIS MENU DISPLAY OFF
Z—RETURN TO MENU 1

### Option A—Reset activity run count/histograms/queue logs

When a model is built, initial conditions rarely reflect the normal state of affairs. It is usually necessary to 'run in' the model to achieve an equilibrium or steady state. Data collected in activity run counts, queue logs and histograms during the run-in period are often misleading. This option allows the observations to be selectively zeroed.

### Expert command

R7 <selection><destination>

where <selection>    A—run counts
                        H—histograms
                        L—queue logs
                        or any combination.
                        If <selection> is blank all are reset
      <destination>    N—no output
                        P—printer only
                        If <destination> is blank output is sent to screen and printer

Valid expert commands would be:
R7 AH
R7 LN

## Option B—Print list of saved models

Presents a list of the names and current simulation times of the models held as save files.

### Expert command

VLIB(RARY)

## Option C—Print activity picture

While checking the logic it is often valuable to view the details of an activity. This option prints a picture of a specified activity in a format which mimics the activity cards.

### Expert command

VPIC(TURE) <activity>

where <activity> is an activity name or number

Valid expert commands would be:
VPIC UNLOAD
VPIC 6

## Option D—Change model name

Allows the name of the model (as printed in libraries, printed outputs and graphical displays) to be changed.

---

### Expert command

N <name> <date>

---

## Option E—Set up editing list

Sets up a selection list for use with the standard HOCUS reports described above.

---

### Expert command

U <code><list> <code><list>...

where <code>   defines the type of list to be set up. It is a single letter with
        meaning:
        A—Activities
        D—Data fields
        E—Entities
        H—Histograms
        L—Queue logs
        Q—Queues

  <list>     is a list of numbers in parentheses, separated by commas. It is
         possible to use the minus sign to indicate a range of numbers
         the letter C indicating a previously defined list is to be cancelled

Valid expert commands would be:
 U A(1–4) E(5, 7, 9)
 U H C A(1–10)

---

## Option F—Reset simulation time to zero

This command can be used in conjunction with Option A to remove traces of a 'run-in' period. Care should be taken with any clocks which are on when this option is used, to avoid misleading results.

---

**Expert command**

R8

---

## Option G—Command file options

HOCUS allows a user-defined menu to be created and accessed (via Option F on Menu 1). Each option in the special menu accesses a different command file created through the present option. These command files comprise a number of command lines which are executed in sequence when the appropriate user-defined menu option is selected. The function of the command line is determined by the first characters on the line as follows:

| *Initial character(s)* | *Function of line* |
|---|---|
| QUERY %n% | Waits for user to input a Value. This value is stored in one of nine accumulators as specified by %n%, where n is a digit between 1 and 9. The value input may be checked to be within a certain range—if the value is out of range it is rejected and has to be re-entered by the user. For example QUERY %3% >19<101 allows the user to input a number between 20 and 100 and store it in accumulator 3. |
| ! | Comment in command file—not displayed to screen but written to file. |
| : | Text written to screen. Any reference to an accumulator, e.g., (%n%) is replaced by the current value of that accumulator. |
| MESSAGE | Signal to switch normal output to screen/printer on and off as follows: |

MESSAGE POFF—printer off
MESSAGE PON—printer on
MESSAGE SOFF—screen off
MESSAGE SON—screen on

Any error messages will still be printed, both to the screen and the print file.

F
N
R
S  } Any HOCUS expert commands. They may use accumulator values previously input using QUERY %n%.
U     Example: VACT MACHINE CON TO %1% changes the duration of the activity MACHINE constant value to the value input in a preceding QUERY line.
V
W

*  Indicates the end of the command file and normally returns user to the user-defined menu.

Z  By using the Z option immediately preceding the final *, the user is returned to Menu 1 instead of the user-defined menu.

*Note* If the user is to be exited from HOCUS then the final * must be preceded by an 'ending' command such as R19P.

A simple example of a command file to simulate and present reports is given below:

RUN FOR 1 MONTH AND PRINT REPORTS
! The above line is the command file description
! All lines that start with an exclamation
! mark are not shown on the screen or printed
: Enter number of machines (1–3)
QUERY %1% >0 <4
VMOV %1% MACHINE FROM Q1 TO Q2
F 1000
: Simulation finished
S 24
R 2
*

On selecting option G the user is given a list of the currently defined command files and is presented with the sub-options:

A—Create Command File
B—Delete Command File
C—List Command File Descriptions
D—Exit
F—Save Model with User Menu default

Sub-option F is of interest since it allows an environment to be set up in which an inexpert user can access a pre-constructed model and perform experiments created previously and stored as command files. It locks a user out of the conventional HOCUS menus, but if used correctly can provide the facility to perform a wide range of tasks. A typical menu set up in this environment might look as follows:

A—Add AGVs
B—Modify transit time
C—Change scheduling logic
D—Adjust machining times
E—Use different work schedule
F—Run model for 1 month
G—Run model with graphics
H—Print reports
I—End HOCUS run

where each of these functions is handled by a HOCUS command file.

## Option H—Write comment on printout

Allows the user to place text in the middle of a HOCUS print file.

---

**Expert command**

W <text>

---

## Option I—Change abandon character

The user can enter any special character or one of M, O, R, S, U, V, W and X to act as the character used to abandon a command sequence.

## Option J—User defined reports

This option is the entry point for the user-defined report generator menu, which is described in a later section of this chapter.

## Option K—Graphics file control (on/off)

This acts as a toggle on the printing of graphics commands to a data file for subsequent replay.

---

**Expert command**

VFIL(E)

---

## Option L—Change graphics display origin

This allows the user to change the portion of the graphics map shown on the screen (see Chapter 10 for details of this process).

---

**Expert command**

VGOR <X coordinate> <Y coordinate>

---

### Option M—Change graphics animation speed

This option can be used to modify the rate at which animation occurs on a graphics display. Chapter 10 describes this process in more detail.

---

**Expert command**

VSPE(ED) ⟨speed⟩

where ⟨speed⟩ is an integer between 1 and 3

---

### Option Y—Switch this menu display off

This turns off the menu printing for this menu. It can be turned back on again by responding 'Y' when asked to select an option from Menu 2 at a later stage.

### Option Z—Return to Menu 1

The program returns to Menu 1.

## Menu 3—Change model details menu

This menu allows the user to modify interactively the state of the model. It is the key to the power of interactive simulation as can be seen even from a listing of the options available.

A—CHANGE CURRENT ATTRIBUTE VALUE(S)
B—MOVE ENTITY FROM ONE QUEUE TO ANOTHER
C—CHANGE ACTIVITY END TIME
D—CHANGE ATTRIBUTE MAXIMUM VALUE(S)
E—CHANGE ACTIVITY DURATION DATA
F—CHANGE DATA FIELD VALUE(S)
G—SWITCH CLOCK ON OR OFF
H—CHANGE TRACED ENTITIES
I—CHANGE TRACED ATTRIBUTES
J—UPDATE ATTRIBUTES IN RUNNING CONTINUOUS ACTIVITY
K—CHANGE NO OF CYCLES BEFORE CONTROL RETURNED TO USER
L—CHANGE MAX NO OF ITERATIONS AT SAME SIMULATION TIME
Y—SWITCH THIS MENU DISPLAY OFF
Z—RETURN TO MENU 1

## Option A—Change current attribute value(s)

The user is led through a series of prompts which allow two ways of specifying which attributes are to be changed. Entities in a particular queue can be changed, or alternatively entities can be specified by entity member number.

---

### Expert command

VATT(RIBUTE) <specifier><name> (ATT) <attribute> (IN) Q<queue>
    <direction><change>

where <specifier>    is either a number of members, a range (e.g. 2–4 meaning at
                        least 2 but not more than 4) or ALL
    <name>        is an entity name
    <attribute>    is a valid attribute for the entity type
    <queue>        is a queue name or number
    <direction>    is either blank meaning supply suitable entities by searching
                        from the head or T meaning search from the tail
    <change>        is either an integer by which the attribute is to be incremented
                        or the following construct
                    TO <integer>
                    which replaces the present attribute by <integer>


The alternative syntax is:
    VATT(RIBUTE) <name><list> (ATT)/<attribute><change>/

where <list>        is a list of entity members
  and <name>,
    <attribute> and
    <change>        are as defined above

valid expert commands would be:

    VATT ALL MACHINE ATT A IN Q4 TO 26
    VATT 1 LORRY B Q3 T5
    VATT MILL 3–6 B TO 7 C TO 8

---

## Option B—Move entity from one queue to another

This option is frequently used to change the number of entities in the system by moving them to and from spare queues. The user is led through a sequence which builds up a command in one of two ways.

---

### Expert command

VMOV(E) <specifier><name> FROM Q<queue> TO Q<queue><location>

| where <specifier> | is either a number of members, a range (e.g., 2–4 meaning at least 2 but not more than 4) or ALL |
| <name> | is an entity or entity group name |
| <queue> | is a queue name or number |
| <location> | is either blank which means place at the tail of the queue or H if the entities are to be placed at the head of the queue |

The alternative is:

VMOV <name><specifier> FROM Q<queue> TO Q<queue><location>

| where <name> | is an entity name |
| <specifier> | is a member number, or a range or list of member numbers |
| <queue> and | |
| <location> | are as defined above |

Valid expert commands would be:

VMOV 1 BAY FROM Q10 TO Q1
VMOV LORRY 2–4 FROM Q3 TO Q7

---

## Option C—Change activity end time

This option allows the end time of any activities which are currently running to be varied.

---

### Expert command

VEND/<activity><time>/

| where <activity> | is an activity name or number |
| <time> | is either an end time greater than the present time or NOW |

Valid expert commands would be:

VEND 4 NOW UNLOAD 1000

## Option D—Change attribute maximum value(s)

If capacities of entities such as tanks and bunkers are held as attribute maximum values, this option allows the value to be changed interactively.

---

### Expert command

VMAX(IMUM) <name> ATT <attribute><change>

| where <name> | is an entity name |
|---|---|
| <attribute> | is a valid attribute for the entity type |
| <change> | is either an integer by which the maximum is to be incremented or the following construct |
| | TO <integer> |
| | which sets the maximum to <integer> |

Valid expert commands would be:

VMAX BAY ATT A 100
VMAX LORRY ATT B TO 1000

---

## Option E—Change activity duration data

Any of the values specifying the duration of an activity (including the Match or Minimum Quantity) can be modified interactively.

---

### Expert command

VACT(IVITY) <activity><change code><change>

| where <activity> | is an activity name or number |
|---|---|
| <change code> | is one of: |
| | MQ Match or minimum quantity |
| | CON Constant |
| | DATA Data field number |
| | PERC Correlation term percentage |
| | ATT Correlation term attribute |
| | ENT Correlation term entity name |
| | FUNC Function number |
| | ALPHA Alpha percentage |
| <change> | is an integer by which the value is to be incremented or the following construct |
| | TO <integer> |
| | signifying replacement by <integer> |

Valid expert commands would be:

VACT UNLOAD CON TO 10
VACT 6 PERC – 20

## Option F—Change data field value(s)

This option allows values in timetables and distributions to be modified interactively.

---

**Expert command**

For a timetable:
  VDAT(A) <data field>/<entry><change>/

where   <data field>     is a timetable number
      <entry>         is a number, a list or ALL
      <change>       is an integer increment or the following construct
                           TO|<integer>
                           signifying replacement by <integer>

For a distribution:
  VDAT(A) <data field>/<coordinate number> TO<value> <percentage>/

where   <data field>     is a distribution number
      <coordinate>    is the number of the coordinate to be changed
      <value>         is the new value to be inserted
      <percentage>    is the cumulative percentage at which the new value occurs

Valid expert commands would be:
  VDAT 2 1 TO 4 2 TO 17 3 TO 30  (if data field 2 is a timetable)
  VDAT 4 6 TO 7000 50  (if data field 4 is a distribution, and the cumulative frequency curve is
                            not made to dip by this change)

---

## Option G—Switch clock on or off

This option allows access to clocks in the system. It is particularly valuable when resetting of simulation time or histograms has occurred, since it can be used to avoid unrepresentative values being entered in histograms.

---

**Expert command**

Two structures are allowed:

VCLO(CK) <number><name><clock> (IN) Q<queue><on/off><histogram><time>

or

VCLO(CK) <name><list>/<clock><on/off><histogram><time>/

where   <number>      is a number of entities, a range of numbers (e.g., 2–4 meaning at least 2 but not exceeding 4), or **ALL**
     <name>      is a valid entity name
     <list>      is a list of entity numbers
     <clock>      is a clock letter valid for the specified entity
     <queue>      is a queue number
     <on/off>      is either **ON** or **OFF** depending upon which way the clock is to be switched
     <histogram>      is a blank if a histogram entry is to be recorded or **NOHIS** if the entry is to be suppressed
     <time>      is either a valid clock time or **NOW**

Valid expert commands would be:
VCLO ALL ORDER A Q2 OFF NOHIS NOW
VCLO LORRY 1,2,5 A ON 2000

---

## Option H—Change traced entities

The user can add to, remove from or list the entities marked for tracing. These are the entities shown when standard reports 10 or 11 are requested.

---

**Expert command**

VTRA(CE) <name><list>
VUNT(RACE) <name><list>

where   <name>      is an entity name
     <list>      is a list of entity numbers

Valid expert commands would be:
VTRA LORRY 7–15
VUNT LORRY 9

## Option I—Change traced attributes

This is similar to option H but affects the attribute trace reports 16 and 17.

---

**Expert command**

   VMON(ITOR) <name> (ATT) <attribute><number>

   VUNM(ONITOR) <name> (ATT) <attribute><number>

where  <name>         is an entity name
       <attribute>      is an attribute letter
       <number>       is a list of entity member numbers

Valid expert commands would be:
   VMON LORRY A 7–15
   VUNM LORRY C 9, 10

---

## Option J—Update attributes in running continuous activity

Continuous activities which are active do not normally have their attribute values updated until they are ended. It is possible that a user would be interested in the value an attribute would take if the activity were interrupted, and stopped at the current clock time. This option allows the user to examine these values.

---

**Expert command**

   VEXA(M) <activities>

where <activities>     is an activity name, a list of activity numbers or ALL denoting all active
                   continuous activities.

---

## Option K—Change number of cycles

This changes the number of start—time—end phases which the model undergoes before control is returned to the user.

---

**Expert command**

   VCYC(LE) <number>

## Option L—Change maximum number of iterations

This changes the maximum number of zero time advances which the model can undergo at any one clock time.

---

**Expert command**

VITE(RS) <number>

---

## Option Y—Switch this menu display off

This turns off the menu printing for this menu. It can be turned back on again by responding 'Y' when asked to select an option from Menu 3 at a later stage.

## Option Z—Return to Menu 1

The program returns to Menu 1.

# The report generator

The standard HOCUS reports allow access to every piece of information in a model. In some circumstances, however, the presentation of the data may not be tailored to a user's particular needs. If reports are to be supplied to senior management, for example, it may be desirable to extract key data from the model and present it with text interpreting it in a way relevant to the manager. For this reason a sophisticated report generator exists for HOCUS. This allows a number of user-defined report formats to be created and stored on file. The user has access to all the information available in standard reports, but can manipulate data by means of the ten 'accumulators' and present and print data in a format selected to suit his presentation needs.

When defining a report it is built up a line at a time using a menu-driven system. Before entering this menu a number of preliminaries are established.

*Report type*

Major—allocated a whole page and printed a maximum of three times as a result of a monitor request.

Minor—other output is allowed on the same page, and the report is printed as many times as appropriate following a monitor request.

Trace—the standard report heading is printed once only, the first time the report is printed.

Line—no headings are printed with a line report.

*Phase*

Reports can be printed during the start phase, end phase or both.

*Report width*
Reports which are screen-based should be restricted to 80 characters, but printer reports can be up to 120 characters.

*Default field length*
Every time a number is printed the user is prompted for the format. The entry allows a default format to be specified.

Whenever a user requests that a number be printed, a standard 'print' menu is presented. This offers four options:

A—PRINT THE NUMBER
B—STORE IT IN AN ACCUMULATOR
C—MANIPULATE AN ACCUMULATOR WITH IT
D—UPDATE A DATA FIELD VALUE WITH IT

Option A lets a value be scaled before presenting it in one of two ways. It can either be placed with a specified format in a specified position on the current line in the report or it can be placed in a specified location on the graphics screen. In the latter case the location and colour of the numbers can be given as constant values or can be specified by the accumulator values. Option B enters the number into one of the data accumulators, whereas option C allows the present value of an accumulator to be added to, subtracted from, multiplied or divided by the number, and the result can be placed back in any one of the accumulators. Option D allows the number to be added to or to replace a timetable value. The timetable number and entry point can be given by a constant or an accumulator.

The functions offered by the main report generator menu are:

A—MOVE TO NEXT LINE
B—SKIP LINE(S)
C—MOVE TO NEXT PAGE
D—FETCH ENTITY INFORMATION
E—FETCH QUEUE INFORMATION
F—FETCH DATA FIELD INFORMATION
G—FETCH ACTIVITY INFORMATION
H—FETCH HISTOGRAM INFORMATION
I—FETCH QUEUE LOG INFORMATION
J—TEXT
K—FETCH OR MANIPULATE ACCUMULATOR VALUE
L—FETCH CURRENT SIMULATION TIME
M—END REPORT
N—GRAPHICAL FEATURES
Y—SWITCH OFF MENU DISPLAY
Z—EXIT FROM SKIP MODE

### Option A—Move to next line

Terminates the build-up of information on the present line and increments the line counter by one.

## Option B—Skip line(s)

Leaves a user-defined number of lines blank on the report.

## Option C—Move to next page

Increments the page counter by one.

## Option D—Fetch entity information

The user is asked for an entity type and is offered the following sub-options:

A—Maximum for a given attribute.
B—Current value of a given attribute of a particular entity.
C—Information based on entity location if entity is in:
  – any queue;
  – a particular queue;
  – any activity;
  – a particular activity;
  – in either a queue or activity.
  The information can be the activity or queue name or number, or a piece of text.
D—Text dependent on attribute value—printed if the attribute value is zero, equal to the maximum, equal to a given value or in a specific range.

## Option E—Fetch queue information

The user is asked for a queue number and then offered the following sub-options:

A—Current queue size.
B—Maximum queue size.
C—Name or attribute value of entity at the head or tail or a given location in the queue.

## Option F—Fetch data field information

The user can access a timetable whose number can be given by a constant or an accumulator and pick up an entry whose number can also be given by a constant or an accumulator.

## Option G—Fetch activity information

Once the user has defined the activity (or identical activities) from which the data is to be extracted the following menu is offered:

A—Current state of activities: either the number of activities running or text dependent upon whether the activity is active or passive.
B—Activity run count for discrete activities or cumulative duration for continuous activities.
C—Cumulative transfer quantity.
D—Average transfer quantity for discrete activities or average rate for continuous activities.

E—Current/last end time if the activity is running, or passive, or regardless of state.
F—Current/last end time for discrete activities or current rate for continuous activities.
G—Start time for continuous activities.

## Option H—Fetch histogram information

Histograms can be specified by number or entity and attribute. Then the user can select from:

A—Number of observations.
B—Minimum.
C—Maximum.
D—Mean.
E—Standard deviation.
F—On time per member.
G—On time as per cent of total.
H—Number of observations in an interval or range of intervals. This can be expressed as a percentage of the total number of observations if required.

## Option I—Fetch queue log information

After specifying which queue log, any one of the following can be chosen:

A—Number of incidents.
B—Minimum size.
C—Maximum size.
D—Total time (since last reset).
E—Average time between incidents.
F—Average size.
G—Number of incidents in an interval or range of intervals.
H—Time for which a queue is the size given in an interval or range of intervals.

## Option J—Text

A piece of text can be placed anywhere on the report, or placed anywhere on the graphics screen using given size and constant or accumulator values to specify the location and display colours.

## Option K—Fetch or manipulate accumulator value

This option offers considerable flexibility in terms of arithmetic and 'conditional' execution. The major sub-options are:

A—Print accumulator value.
B—Manipulate an accumulator using a constant (Addition, Subtraction, Multiplication and Division are allowed).
C—Manipulate an accumulator using another accumulator (Arithmetic as for sub-option B is allowed).

D—Update a timetable entry: the accumulator value can be used to replace or add to a value whose timetable number and entry number can be given by constant or accumulator.

E—Reset an accumulator to zero.

F—Skip mode test: the present value of an accumulator is tested. If it passes the test all subsequent commands are ignored until 'skip mode' is terminated. The accumulator can undergo one of the following tests:

  – equal to a constant;
  – not equal to a constant;
  – less than a constant;
  – less than or equal to a constant;
  – greater than a constant;
  – greater than or equal to a constant;
  – in a given range;
  – not in a given range.

## Option L—Fetch current simulation time

Offers the print menu selection for the current clock time.

## Option M—End report

Terminates the commands defining the report.

## Option N—Graphical features

Allows the user to create graphical features such as lines, circles, boxes, arcs and seed fills. Accumulator values can be used as parameters to give a considerable degree of flexibility. This option allows the production of animated histograms and displays imitating filling or emptying bunkers for example.

## Option Y—Switch off menu display

This turns the menu printing for this menu off. It can be turned back on again by responding 'Y' when asked to select an option from this menu at a later stage.

## Option Z—Exit from skip mode

This option is only available when the user is in 'skip mode'. It marks the end of the section of the report to be skipped if the accumulator value satisfies the test.

The scope of the report generator is such that simple summary reports (see Fig. 9.1) can be built in minutes.

```
            SUMMARY PERFORMANCE REPORT
            ==========================
            ROBOT MOVE TIME 10 SECONDS

    MACHINE 1 SPEED      100 % OF NOMINAL VALUE
    MACHINE 2 SPEED      100 % OF NOMINAL VALUE

THROUGHPUT:        8 TYPE A          4 TYPE B
TIME SPENT IN SYSTEM:      /52.50 MEAN            1040 MAXIMUM

UTILISATIONS
ROBOT:     12.85 %      MACHINE 1:     97.83 %     MACHINE 2:     71.74

QUEUE SIZES                  MINIMUM          MEAN          MAXIMUM
WAITING FOR MACHINE 1           0             0.09             1
WAITING FOR MACHINE 2           0             0.29             2
```

**Figure 9.1**

Even more complex reports such as the trace report shown in Fig. 9.2 can be built up quickly. This report shows which machines in a production facility are active and which batch number they are working on. It gives an immediate indication of which machines are most often running in parallel. This report was used by an organization as the basis for the preparation of a staff skills matrix, and showed how they could significantly increase the flexibility of the workforce.

```
------------------------------------------------------------------------------
    500 SOP 16              COP 11
    525                     COP 16                    CLD 11
    550          STM  9     COP 16     LCB  9         CLD 11
    575          STM  9     COP 13     LCB  9         CLD 11
    600          STM  9     COP 13     LCB  9         CLD 11
    625          STM  9     COP 13                    CLD 11
    650                     COP 13                    CLD 11
    675                     COP 12                    CLD 11
    700                     COP 12     LCB 13         CLD 11
    725                     COP 12     LCB 13         CLD 11
    750                     COP 12                    CLD 11
    775                     COP 12                    CLD 11
    800                     COP 12                    CLD 11
    825                     COP 16                    CLD 11        LCD  8
    850                     COP 16                    CLD 11        LCD  8
    875                     COP 16                    CLD 11        LCD  8
    900                     COP 16                    CLD 11            BOX  8
    925                     COP 16                    CLD 11            BOX  8
    950                                               CLD 11            BOX  8
    975                                               CLD 11
------------------------------------------------------------------------------
```

```
1000                                      CLD 11
1025                                      CLD 11              LCD  8
1050                                      CLD 11                      3OX  8
1066  OPERATION       8 COMPLETED
1075 SOP 14                COP 14         CLD 11
1100 SOP 14      STM 12    COP 14  LCB 12 CLD 11
1125 SOP 15      STM 12    COP 14  LCB 12 CLD 11
1150             STM 12    COP 14  LCB 12 CLD 11              LCD  9
1175             STM 12    COP 14         CLD 11              LCD  9
1200                       COP 14         CLD 11              LCD  9
1225                       COP 14         CLD 11                      BOX  9
1250                       COP 15                                     BOX  9
1275                       COP 15                                     BOX  9
1300                       COP 15                             LCD  9
1325                       COP 15                             LCD  9
1350                       COP 18                                     BOX  9
1351  OPERATION       9 COMPLETED
1375                       COP 18  LCB 11         T/F 11      LCD 13
1400                       COP 18  LCB 11         T/F 11      LCD 13
1425                       COP 18  LCB 11         T/F 11      LCD 13
1450                                                                 BOX 13
1475                                                                 BOX 13
1495  OPERATION      13 COMPLETED
------------------------------------------------------------------------
1500 SOP 19                COP 19
1525 SOP 19      STM 11    COP 19
1550             STM 11    COP 19  LCB 16  CLD 16
1575             STM 11    COP 19         CLD 16
1600             STM 11    COP 19         CLD 16
1625             STM 11    COP 19  LCB 14  CLD 16
1650             STM 11    COP 19  LCB 14  CLD 16
1675             STM 14            LCB 14  CLD 16
1700             STM 14                    CLD 16              LCD 12
1725             STM 14                    CLD 16              LCD 12
1750             STM 14                    CLD 16              LCD 12
1775                                       CLD 16                     3OX 12
1800                                       CLD 16                     3OX 12
1825                                       CLD 16                     3OX 12
1850                                       CLD 16              LCD 12
1875                                       CLD 16                     3OX 12
1894  OPERATION      12 COMPLETED
1900 SOP 20                COP 20          CLD 16
1925 SOP 20                COP 20  LCB 18  CLD 16
1950                       COP 20  LCB 18  CLD 16
1975                       COP 20          CLD 16
------------------------------------------------------------------------
```

**Figure 9.2**

*Example*  As an example of the use of the program we have run the steel mill model (see Exercise 7.20). The model was run for 7200 minutes (5 days) and summary statistics collected from time 5760 (day 4). Two of the reports—activity run counts and histograms—are shown in Fig. 9.3. The activity run count report shows that in the fifth day:

- 3 loads of steel were melted (A1);
- the ladle was filled 31 times (and is currently being filled) (A3);
- 30 batches have set (and two are currently setting) (A6, 7, 8);
- 29 sets of moulds were cleaned (A9);
- 29 sets of moulds were stripped (and one is currently being stripped) (A10);

– 28 batches have been loaded into soaking pits (and one is currently being loaded) (A11, 12);
– no batches have been put into the outside yard or brought back (A13, 18);
– 29 batches have been reheated in the soaking pits (and four are currently being reheated) (A19–28);
– 28 batches have been rolled (and one is currently being rolled) (A30).

The histograms show:

– the cooling time for the 28 batches was between 104 and 252 minutes (average 164.0 minutes) (H1);
– the amount of steel in the furnace varied between 200 and 224 tons (average 209.0 tons) (H2);
– the amount of steel in the ladle varied between 3 and 25 tons (average 24.0 tons) (H3);
– the time batches wait to be unloaded from the soaking pits varies between 213 and 249 minutes (average 234.4 minutes) (H4);
– the gang was idle for 82.7 per cent of the time (H5).

```
TIME    7200   ACTIVITY RUN COUNT AND QUANTITY RECORD   RE-SET AT TIME 5760.
               ***********************************
```

| NO. | NAME | RUN COUNT | | END TIME | CUM. QUANTITY | MEAN QUANTITY |
|---|---|---|---|---|---|---|
| 1 | PREPARE/MELT | 3 | | 6987 | 0. | 0.0 |
| 2 | FILL LADLE | 31 | R | 7207 | 745. | 24.0 |
| 3 | UPDATE DAY | 1 | | 5768 | 0. | 0.0 |
| 4 | TEEM | 32 | | 7197 | 770. | 24.1 |
| 5 | ONE DAY | 1 | | 7200 | 0. | 0.0 |
| 6 | SETTING | 11 | R | 7272 | 0. | 0.0 |
| 7 | SETTING | 11 | | 7197 | 0. | 0.0 |
| 8 | SETTING | 8 | R | 7217 | 0. | 0.0 |
| 9 | CLEAN | 29 | | 7198 | 0. | 0.0 |
| 10 | STRIP | 29 | R | 7210 | 0. | 0.0 |
| 11 | LOAD | 28 | R | 7212 | 0. | 0.0 |
| 12 | LOAD | 0 | | 529 | 0. | 0.0 |
| 13 | MOVE OUTSIDE | 0 | | 5391 | 0. | 0.0 |
| 14 | SORT | 0 | | 5391 | 0. | 0.0 |
| 15 | MOVE TO YARD | 0 | | 5401 | 0. | 0.0 |
| 16 | PUT BACK 1 | 0 | | 0 | 0. | 0.0 |
| 17 | PUT BACK 2 | 0 | | 0 | 0. | 0.0 |
| 18 | MOVE FROM YD | 0 | | 0 | 0. | 0.0 |
| 19 | SOAK | 6 | R | 7401 | 1424. | 237.3 |
| 20 | SOAK | 5 | R | 7248 | 1184. | 236.8 |
| 21 | SOAK | 6 | R | 7299 | 1425. | 237.5 |
| 22 | SOAK | 6 | | 7197 | 1426. | 237.7 |
| 23 | SOAK | 5 | R | 7337 | 1171. | 234.2 |
| 24 | SOAK | 1 | | 6330 | 240. | 240.0 |
| 25 | SOAK | 0 | | 2557 | 0. | 0.0 |
| 26 | SOAK | 0 | | 2151 | 0. | 0.0 |
| 27 | SOAK | 0 | | 0 | 0. | 0.0 |
| 28 | SOAK | 0 | | 0 | 0. | 0.0 |
| 29 | UNLOAD/PT RL | 29 | | 7194 | 0. | 0.0 |
| 30 | FINISH ROLL | 28 | R | 7227 | 0. | 0.0 |

TIME  7200  HISTOGRAM CONTENTS - AFTER END PHASE                                    REPORT 14
              ******************************************

```
HISTOGRAM   1     COOLING TIME                          ( BATCH   C - ATT )  RE-SET AT TIME  5760.

RANGE                   FREQUENCY     PERCENT      DISPLAY
            -      99        0          0.0       +
          100-    149       12         42.9       +************
          150-    199       10         35.7       +**********
          200-    249        4         14.3       +****
          250-    299        2          7.1       +**
          300-    349        0          0.0       +
          350-    399        0          0.0       +
          400-    449        0          0.0       +
          450-    499        0          0.0       +
          500-    549        0          0.0       +
          550-    599        0          0.0       +
          600-             0          0.0       +
                                                  +---------+---------+
                                                  0         10        20

    TOTAL NO. OF OBSERVATIONS        28
    MINIMUM                          104
    MEAN                             164.0
    MAXIMUM                          252
    STANDARD DEVIATION               46.9
    'ON' TIME PER MEMBER             91.8
    'ON' AS PERCENT OF TOTAL          6.4


HISTOGRAM   2     SIZE OF LOAD (TONS)                   ( FURNACE A - ATT )  RE-SET AT TIME  5760.

RANGE                   FREQUENCY     PERCENT      DISPLAY
            -      99        0          0.0       +
          100-    119        0          0.0       +
          120-    139        0          0.0       +
          140-    159        0          0.0       +
          160-    179        0          0.0       +
          180-    199        0          0.0       +
          200-    219        2         66.7       +**
          220-    239        1         33.3       +*
          240-    259        0          0.0       +
          260-    279        0          0.0       +
          280-    299        0          0.0       +
          300-             0          0.0       +
                                                  +---------+---------+
                                                  0         10        20

    TOTAL NO. OF OBSERVATIONS         3
    MINIMUM                          200
    MEAN                             209.0
    MAXIMUM                          224
    STANDARD DEVIATION               13.1


HISTOGRAM   3     STEEL POURED INTO MOULD (TONS) ( LADLE   A - ATT )  RE-SET AT TIME  5760.

RANGE                   FREQUENCY     PERCENT      DISPLAY
            -       4        1          3.2       +.
            5-      9        0          0.0       +
           10-     14        0          0.0       +
           15-     19        1          3.2       +.
           20-     24        0          0.0       +
           25-     29       29         93.5       +*************
           30-     34        0          0.0       +
           35-     39        0          0.0       +
           40-     44        0          0.0       +
           45-     49        0          0.0       +
           50-     54        0          0.0       +
           55-              0          0.0       +
                                                  +---------+---------+
                                                  0         20        40

    TOTAL NO. OF OBSERVATIONS        31
    MINIMUM                           3
    MEAN                             24.0
    MAXIMUM                          25
    STANDARD DEVIATION                4.2
```

```
HISTOGRAM    4      WAITING TO UNLOAD FOR ROLLING  ( PIT         B - ATT )     RE-SET AT TIME     5760.
RANGE                        FREQUENCY    PERCENT    DISPLAY
              -            9        0        0.0     +
            10-           19        0        0.0     +
            20-           29        0        0.0     +
            30-           39        0        0.0     +
            40-           49        0        0.0     +
            50-           59        0        0.0     +
            60-           69        0        0.0     +
            70-           79        0        0.0     +
            80-           89        0        0.0     +
            90-           99        0        0.0     +
           100-          109        0        0.0     +
           110-                    28      100.0     +**************
                                                    +---------+---------+
                                                    0        20        40

TOTAL NO. OF OBSERVATIONS             28
MINIMUM                              213
MEAN                               234.4
MAXIMUM                             249
STANDARD DEVIATION                   6.9
'ON' TIME PER MEMBER               656.4
'ON' AS PERCENT OF TOTAL            45.6

HISTOGRAM    5      IDLE TIME                       ( GANG      A - ATT )     RE-SET AT TIME     5760.
RANGE                        FREQUENCY    PERCENT    DISPLAY
              -            0        0        0.0     +
             1-           20       19       63.3     +********************
            21-           40        1        3.3     +*
            41-           60        6       20.0     +******
            61-           80        0        0.0     +
            81-          100        0        0.0     +
           101-          120        0        0.0     +
           121-          140        0        0.0     +
           141-          160        0        0.0     +
           161-          180        3       10.0     +***
           181-          200        1        3.3     +*
           201-                     0        0.0     +
                                                    +---------+---------+
                                                    0        10        20

TOTAL NO. OF OBSERVATIONS             30
MINIMUM                              10
MEAN                               39.7
MAXIMUM                            181
STANDARD DEVIATION                  56.1
'ON' TIME PER MEMBER              1191.0
'ON' AS PERCENT OF TOTAL           82.7
```

**Figure 9.3**

EXERCISE 9.1

*Warehouse unloading bays* (see Exercise 5.10)   Use the model to determine the best course of action for management. For each experiment determine:

– the time lorries wait to enter;
– the time lorries spend at an unloading bay;
– the time lorries wait to leave;
– the time vans wait to enter;
– the time vans wait to leave.

EXERCISE 9.2

*Tidal port* (see Exercises 5.11 and 7.19)   Use the model to determine:

– how long each type of ship waits to enter and leave the port;
– the effect of changing the priority rules for entering and leaving the port;
– the effect of reducing the tanker unloading times by 20 per cent.

EXERCISE 9.3

*Steel mill* (see Exercises 5.12 and 7.20) The performance of the resources cannot be improved, but the numbers can be changed in order to increase throughput. It is possible to change the number of moulds, setting locations, gangs of men and cranes. Use the model to examine the utilization of resources and consider ways of overcoming bottlenecks.

# 10.

## Simulation with colour graphics

### Why use colour graphics?

Simulation is becoming increasingly valuable in many areas of endeavour, where the complexity of problems encountered is such that theoretical or intuitive approaches do not provide credible or accurate solutions. The increasing demand for simulation and the increasing recognition of its potential have led to pressure upon simulation practitioners to make their work more immediately available to management.

Interactive simulation has become the norm over the last five years. The trend towards increasing approachability has also picked up threads from the explosion in consumer electronics. Many children (whatever their age) now have computers of their own; most of these computers are capable of generating colour graphics displays which have a sophistication and immediacy previously confined to the most 'high tech' environments. The expectations raised by such products have carried over into the business environment—business graphics have become an indispensable method of presenting the outputs of 'decision support systems'.

The training simulator market has been using graphics to astounding effect for many years now. Indeed flight simulator companies are among the forerunners in the application of graphics technology; the real-time flight simulators in use today provide images to the trainee of startling realism. This quality of image helps produce a feeling of involvement and identification with the environment. In a similar way the use of graphics in presenting the results of a simulation can help in convincing managers of the accuracy of a simulation model and in explaining the implications of management decisions.

Our experience of the use of colour graphical displays with simulation models convinces us that there are several areas where such a presentation provides a valuable alternative to text reports. The most obvious area is in presenting ideas to senior management. In most organizations such people have come to expect the immediacy of presentation available from business graphics. Well-composed colour graphical displays of a simulation are not only attention-demanding, but can present ideas and results quickly and convincingly. In such an environment animated displays provide a focus for discussion and involvement in a way that text never can.

At a working level this ability of graphics to focus attention is also invaluable. It allows the model-builder to present his detailed assumptions to staff with working knowledge of the environment being modelled and is excellent for generating the degree of interest and contribution necessary for successful simulation.

The initial reaction of 'serious' simulation practitioners is often to dismiss graphics as either a gimmick or selling aid. Although it can often be either, our experience is that graphics displays are also of intrinsic value to a model-builder. Colour graphical displays allow the user to present the current state of a whole model and follow its progress as the simulation is advanced. This often uncovers flaws in a model logic which would be difficult to recognize by conventional means. These displays allow valuable insights into mechanisms within the system being modelled which are often unanticipated, such as contention.

Although colour graphics displays are undoubtedly of immense value in simulation their very power of communication makes them dangerous. Their capacity for unwitting deception is great—it is always tempting to believe a picture—but, whatever means have been used to produce and sell the results of simulation, its accuracy must be of paramount importance.

This warning apart, we feel that in most simulation exercises there is a valuable role to be played by colour graphics, and the remainder of this chapter describes the way in which HOCUS simulations can be presented graphically.

## What do you want to see?

The aim of HOCUS graphics is to provide a means of presenting a simulation model in such a way that the addition of graphics leaves the fundamental logic intact, and the presentation reflects the logic as faithfully as possible. The philosophy is to maintain the prime importance of model logic but make it as easy as possible for users to present a model graphically.

From Chapter 2 onwards three elements of a simulation model have been encountered again and again—entities, activities and queues. Any graphical representation of a simulation must allow these building blocks to be displayed.

As will be seen later in this chapter HOCUS allows two types of display for activities and queues—a faithful representation of the standard flow chart (type 1) and nothing! (type 0). The latter type allows entities to be placed anywhere on the display with no HOCUS-related surroundings. The context of such displays is left entirely to the user's imagination and can lead to some remarkably complex and evocative images.

When a simulation is actually in progress entities move to and from activities and queues. The way HOCUS displays this movement is by allowing the definition of 'joins' along which entities can move from queue to activity and on to the next queue. In addition to this fundamental data the user can supply background features to set activities, queues and entities in context. It is also possible to display or use any data which can be accessed from the user-defined report generator described in the previous chapter. This allows a great degree of flexibility in the production of graphical displays.

## Fundamentals of the display

Data can be placed anywhere on a 1000 by 1000 pixel graphics map. The graphics display provides a window on to this map. The size of this window depends upon the graphics terminal in use, but 640 by 480 pixels is a typical size.

Two basic types of data are displayed. The first is information such as joins, activity boxes, queue circles and features. These are all drawn at the start of a simulation and form a fixed background. The progress of the simulation is recorded by the movement of entity 'icons', changing activity end times and data displayed by user-defined reports. Information such as this is the second type of data to be displayed—animation data.

A standard palette of 16 colours is provided for each graphics data type. These default palettes are given in Fig. 10.1. The colours comprising these palettes can be set to any one of 4096 colours.

| Fixed colours | Animation colours |
|---|---|
| 0 – Black | 0 – Clear |
| 1 – Red | 1 – Red |
| 2 – Green | 2 – Green |
| 3 – Blue | 3 – Blue |
| 4 – Yellow | 4 – Yellow |
| 5 – Magenta | 5 – Magenta |
| 6 – Cyan | 6 – Cyan |
| 7 – Grey | 7 – Grey |
| 8 – White | 8 – White |
| 9 – Pink | 9 – Pink |
| A – Light Green | A – Light Green |
| B – Orange | B – Orange |
| C – Air Force Blue | C – Air Force Blue |
| D – Salmon | D – Salmon |
| E – Brown | E – Brown |
| F – Slate | F – Slate |

**Figure 10.1**

## Entity displays

Every entity type which is to be displayed must have a graphics 'icon' defined. This icon can be either a small block (icon type 'A') or a mnemonic up to three characters in length.

Often the ability to change the colour of the icon during the simulation is useful, for example, colour coding lorries according to whether they are empty or full, denoting changes in entity state or the current value of an attribute. HOCUS provides a mechanism for this by allowing a letter 'C' to be placed in one of the 'Attribute Maximum' definition columns (see Fig. 8.3 for an example of an entity definition input screen). The attribute denoted in this way is automatically given a maximum of 100, and whenever one of the entities is displayed its colour depends upon the current value of that attribute. Attribute values less than 10 correspond exactly with the colour value. The colours A to F are represented by the attribute values 10 to 15 respectively. In this way any of the many ways of changing attribute values can be used to modify the colour in which icons are displayed.

## Queue displays

As described earlier, two types of display are provided. For type 0 displays the entities are listed away from the point specified as the queue location. The entities can be listed up, down, left or right from the specified location (see Fig. 10.2). The maximum number of entities displayed can be restricted independently of the queue maximum. This is achieved by defining

Beer drinking - 1

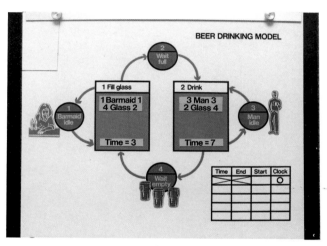

Beer drinking - 2

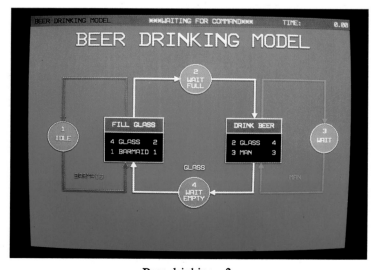

Beer drinking - 3

**Plate 1**

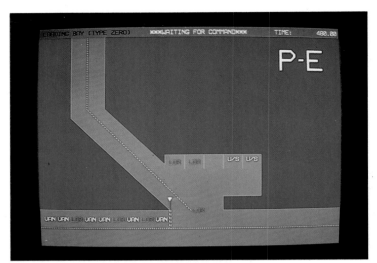

Loading bay - 1

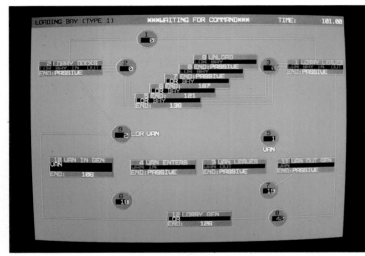

Loading bay - 2

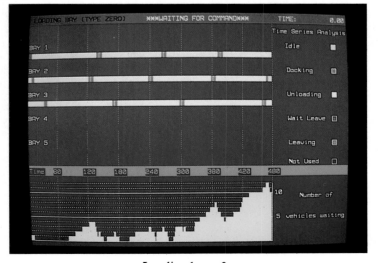

Loading bay - 3

**Plate 2**

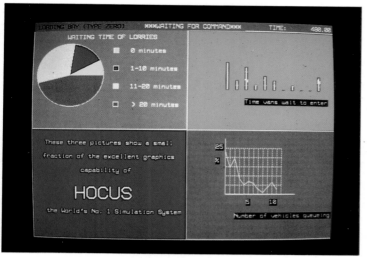

Loading bay - 4

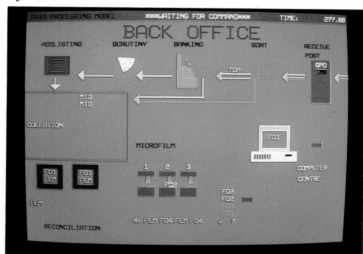

Stockbroking back office

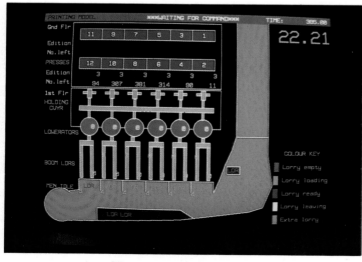

Newspaper printing plant

**Plate 3**

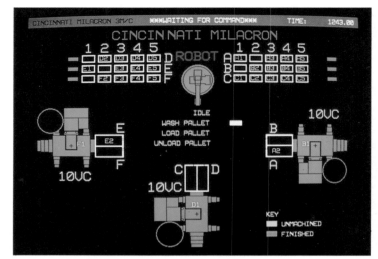

Computer integrated manufacturing - 1

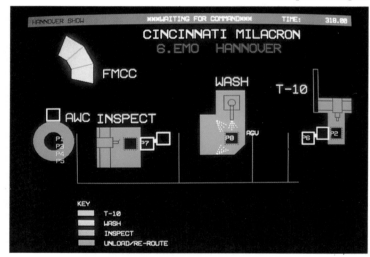

Computer integrated manufacturing - 2

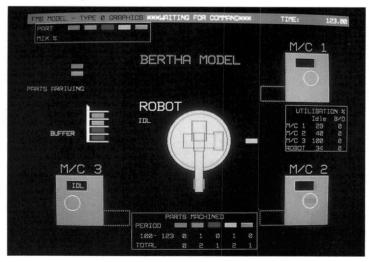

Computer integrated manufacturing - 3

**Plate 4**

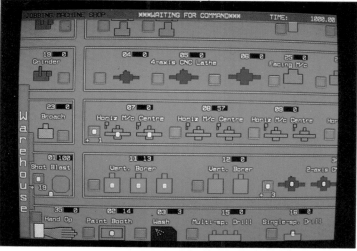

Jobbing shop

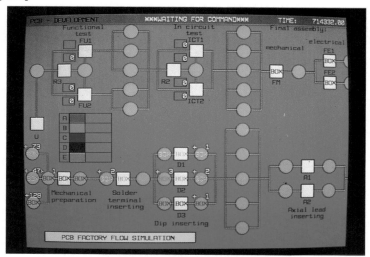

Printed circuit board manufacture

Engine production

**Plate 5**

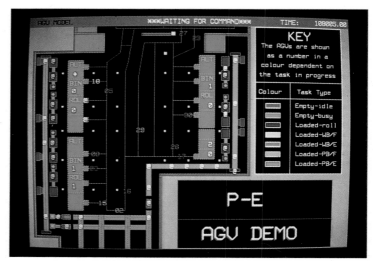

Automated guided vehicles - 1

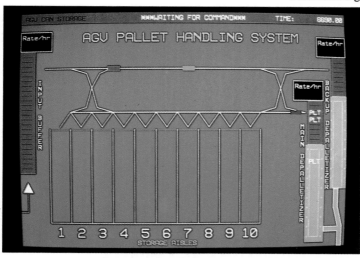

Automated guided vehicles - 2

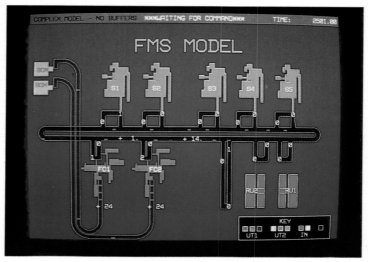

Flexible manufacturing system

**Plate 6**

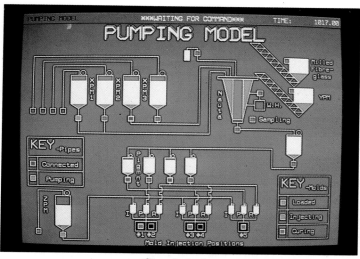

Chemical plant

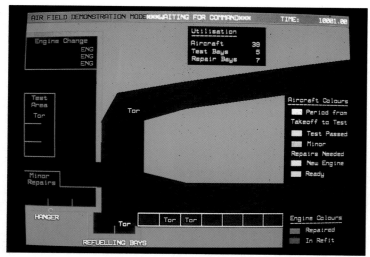

Airfield

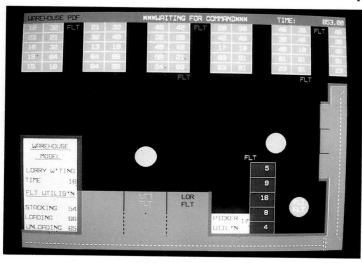

Warehouse

**Plate 7**

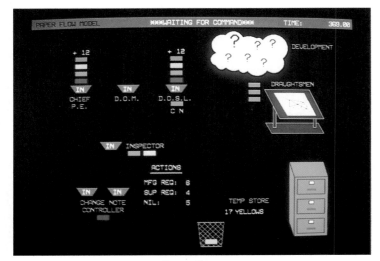

Paper flow

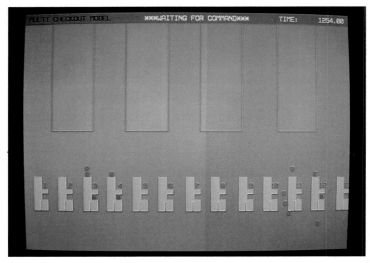

Supermarket

**Plate 8**

a display maximum. If the display maximum is exceeded the number of entities not displayed is quoted at the end of those displayed in a colour defined as the queue size colour. This feature allows an abbreviated version of large queues to be displayed.

**Figure 10.2**

Type 1 queues are a simplified version of the queue cards. A filled circle of a user-definable colour is centred on the specified location. The queue number and queue size are displayed inside this circle. Examples of type 1 queues are shown in Fig. 10.3.

**Figure 10.3**

The input screen shown in Fig. 8.5 shows the data required to specify graphics for queues:

Display type (0 or 1)
Queue size colour
Listing direction (U, D, L or R for up, down, left or right)
Display size limit

and the queue colour for type 1 queues.

## Activity displays

Activity locations are specified by the usual X and Y coordinates. For type 0 activities, entities are drawn when the activities are active. The icons are listed away from the specified location either down or to the right (see Fig. 10.4). When a type 0 activity is passive nothing appears on the display. Identical activities are represented by placing activities next to each other with a constant separation between them.

M/C \_/ SA2 SA3      M/C      M/C      M/C
                     \_/      \_/      \_/
                     SA2      SA2      SA2
M/C \_/ SA2 SA3      SA3      SA3      SA3


M/C \_/ SA2 SA3

**Figure 10.4**


Type 1 activities are simplified versions of the activity cards. The top band has the activity number and name. Continuous activities are denoted by a 'C' preceding the activity number. The main body of the activity rectangle has a listing of icons representing the conditions in the activity. Some of the activity logic is also represented, viz.:

– Non-compulsory conditions and condition sets are enclosed in parentheses.
– Alternative conditions are separated by a solidus (/).
– The start and end of a condition set are denoted by a vertical stroke.
– A condition with an = S or = A option will be shown with an appropriate coding, e.g.,

| VAN | 4 = A | shown as | VAN = 4 |
| VAN | 4 = S | shown as | VAN < 5 |

The activity duration data is not shown explicitly, but the bottom of an activity rectangle contains an area which shows the end time for active activities, 'PASSIVE' if the activity is passive or 'INTERRUPT' if it is a continuous activity in the process of being interrupted.

Identical type 0 activities are placed next to each other in the same way as type 0 queues, but identical type 1 activities are 'stacked', just as the cards are in hand simulation. Figure 10.5 shows some type 1 activities.

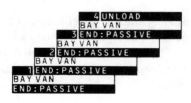

**Figure 10.5**

The input screen shown in Fig. 8.7 shows the data required to specify graphics for activities:

| *Type 0* | *Type 1* |
|---|---|
| Listing direction (R or D for right or down) | Box colour |
| Separation (for identical activities) | Text colour |
| | Passive icon colour |
| | Time colour |
| | Box size |

## Graphical joins

Entity icons move along 'joins' from activities to queues and vice versa. To specify a join the activity and queue to be 'joined' must be defined (by name or number). The join comprises up to eight connected straight lines from the specified activity location (denoted by A) to the specified queue location (denoted by Q) via up to seven map coordinates. The join can take any colour and be of one of six types, as shown in Fig. 10.6.

Solid

Short dash

Long dash

Dash dot

Centre line

Dotted line

**Figure 10.6**

If the activity or queue is not displayed, the first or last coordinate must be specified, and must be on the edge of the graphics map.

The input screen for joins is shown in Fig. 10.7. When icons move along joins the bottom left-hand corner of the icon traces along the join. Icons can move at three speeds. Speed two is the default, speed one is a third of this speed, and at speed three icons jump from activity to queue or vice versa without following the join.

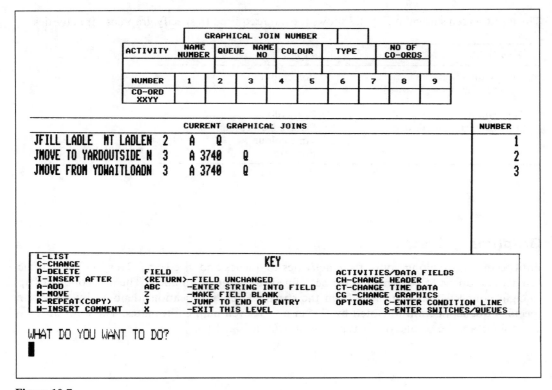

**Figure 10.7**

## Graphical features

The background drawn for type 1 activities and queues is very closely defined. To obtain graphics displays which are more evocative of the environment being modelled HOCUS allows the user access to a number of standard features which can be used to modify the display. These features are:

– *Lines* (of any type allowed for joins);
– *Circles* (or disks);
– *Boxes* (specified by diagonally opposite vertices);
– *Arcs* (or sectors);
– *Text* (chosen from nine sizes and four orientations);
– *Fills* (to flood an area with a specified colour);
– *Colours* (each index can be associated independently with a particular colour by specifying red, green and blue intensities)

An input screen for features is shown is shown in Fig. 10.8

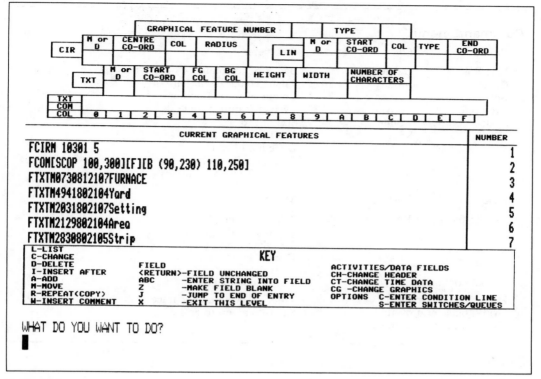

**Figure 10.8**

## Sketchpad

This utility is part of the input program, and allows all the graphics elements described in the previous section to be combined interactively on a design screen. It helps the user in three ways:

- it simplifies the process of laying out model elements (activities, queues and joins);
- it permits graphical features to be created and displayed as they will appear in the simulation;
- it allows the user to see immediately the interaction between the model elements and the graphical features.

The sketchpad uses a simple menu system for control, and displays a portion of the full display map for design purposes. At any stage, context-sensitive help can be requested and a grid can be imposed to help the layout process.

The basic menu structure is shown in Fig. 10.9, and examples of the design screen can be seen in the colour plates.

**Command menu**

| Create | Edit | Parameter |
|--------|------|-----------|
| Line/Polyline | Delete | Background colour |
| Circle | Modify | Palette colour definitions |
| Box | Translate | Colour of feature outlines |
| Arc/Sector | Copy | Type of feature outline |
| Text | Rotate | Size of text |
| Fill | Scale | Justification of text |
| | | Direction of text |
| | | Origin of view port |
| | | Relative to map or display |

| Save | Restore | Model |
|------|---------|-------|
| Save to file | Restore from file | Add model graphics |
| | | Remove model graphics |
| | | Translate model graphics |
| | | Display listed items |

| Global commands | Cursor commands |
|-----------------|-----------------|
| Help – toggle help menu | Trace – toggle numeric trace |
| Grid – toggle grid overlay | Snap – snap on to grid |
| eXit – quit current command | |

**Figure 10.9**

The majority of the main menu commands deal with the manipulation of graphical features. 'Create' allows the interactive definition of entries for any of the features referred to above (lines, circles, boxes, arcs, text or fills). 'Edit' allows features to be deleted, modified, translated (i.e., moved without changing orientation), copied, rotated and scaled. The edit can be applied to a single feature, or to a group of features picked by the user. The 'Parameter' sub-menu allows modification of the current parameter applied to a newly defined feature (colours, line type and text size, justification and direction as appropriate). The origin of the viewpoint given on the map and whether features are to be placed relative to map or display can also be changed via this sub-menu. 'Save' and 'Restore' allow the user to place a set of feature definitions (for example a company logo) in a file for use in another model.

The final sub-menu allows the user to manipulate model graphics. It is possible to 'Add' or 'Remove' queues, activities and joins. The coordinates of queues, activities or individual nodes on a join can be 'Translated', i.e., moved. Finally, it is possible to control how much of the model-related graphics is shown on the sketchpad viewport; this means that the screen need not become cluttered with information which would not appear on the final display, but can be made available 'on demand', for fine placing of features, for example.

## User-defined reports (on graphic displays)

As explained in Chapter 9, any data held in a model can be presented on the graphics screen by specifying a user-defined report. It is also possible to insert model data as a parameter into any graphics report sent to the terminal.

User-defined reports are generally used to complement the animated display.

The simplest way to incorporate user-defined graphics into a model is to define a report which is sent to the display every start or end phase (or both). This is achieved by running the simulation forward with report 24 (user-defined) in the report list.

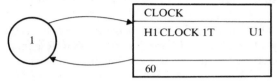

**Figure 10.10**

The most powerful application of user-defined reports with graphics is in combination with the set of options U1–U9. These allow reports to be executed at the start or end of an activity. A simple example of the use of these options is to give the display a more sophisticated clock than the standard. This is achieved by having a single 'clock' entity moving in a single activity—queue life cycle (see Fig. 10.10). The first user-defined report, called by the U1 option in the activity, accesses the current clock time and manipulates the value using accumulator arithmetic to obtain the number of days, hours and minutes. These numbers are then printed on the screen—every minute if the time units in the model are seconds.

A more sophisticated example of user-defined reports with graphics is the production of varying 'bunker' displays. In such a display the current level of a bunker is shown continually varying as product is moved in and out by means of a number of activities. The bunker could, of course, be replaced by a stock-level, a tank or even a utilization. The HOCUS activity, queue and entity to obtain such a display are the same as the previous example (see Fig. 10.10), but the activity duration should be adjusted to obtain the best effect. The user-defined report in this case accesses the varying attribute or the other data element, and draws two shapes. Figure 10.11 shows the example of a rectangular bunker with a maximum capacity of 100 units. Using accumulator arithmetic the coordinates of the top and bottom rectangles can be calculated. These are used simply to draw the bottom rectangle in the 'full' colour and the top rectangle in the 'empty' colour.

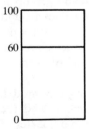

**Figure 10.11**

## Controlling the graphics

Although details of the control of graphics are spread throughout Chapter 9, it is worth reviewing that information in a single section. The two basic operations which can be performed are:

- take a snapshot of the present situation (via Option B on Menu 1 or Expert command S15);
- follow the progress of the simulation (via Option G on Menu 1 or Expert command F<time>15).

Depending on the type of user-defined graphics reports in use, report 24 may also be necessary.

The window presented by the (typically) 640 by 480 graphics screen on the 1000 by 1000 display map can be altered. This is done by Option L on Menu 2 (or the VGOR expert command), which allows the bottom left-hand corner of the screen to be located anywhere on the graphics map.

As an animation progresses the speed of motion of the icons can be controlled by Option M on Menu 2 (or the VSPEED command). This allows two smooth rates of progress or makes icons jump.

## Display sophistication

The simplest graphics display can be created in a few minutes by using all the graphics defaults available. On the other hand it is possible to spend more time creating a highly sophisticated graphics display. In the authors' experience the most effective way is to think carefully about the layout required. This can be used to good effect before diving into the 'sketchpad', which is fun to use, but benefits from having a draft layout before putting finger to cursor key!

The user will build up his own repertoire of techniques for producing evocative displays, but the judicious use of colour in backgrounds, the careful superposition of type 0 activities and queues and imaginative use of user-defined reports to display text and numbers can lead to presentations which really sell the results of a simulation exercise.

Although it is difficult to convey the effects of animated colour graphics, this chapter concludes with a description of some displays which are based on one of the simplest HOCUS models, the loading bay model developed in earlier chapters.

The top of Plate 2 shows a type 0 representation of the loading bay problem. The queue of vans outside the gate can be seen, as can the bays having lorries unloading. This is achieved by the appropriate use of type 0 activities and queues imposed on a background composed of features. The basic layout of activities and queues is built up first, with joins defined to give the movements required as the simulation is run forward in time. Once the model 'skeleton' has been defined, the sketchpad can be used to build up a picture of as much complexity or accuracy as is desired.

The centre of Plate 2 shows the basic HOCUS flowchart behind the loading bay model. This display shows an interim stage between the hand-drawn HOCUS flowchart and the fidelity of the type 0 graphics. Type 1 displays like this can be constructed within a quarter of an hour by using all the default options provided.

Two other displays are based on the same simple model. Plate 2 (bottom) contains two time series displays that can be built up as the simulation progresses. The background to the display was created using the sketchpad. A simple clock activity like that shown in Fig. 10.10 is added to the model. The 'U1' option is put into the Clock entity to call a graphics user-defined report. Each time the activity ends, this report checks the current status of the bays—whether a lorry is docking, unloading, waiting to leave or leaving, or whether the bay is idle or unused. Then, using accumulator arithmetic, it calculates the position to draw a small rectangle showing the current status of the bays. In this way a coloured status chart is built up for each of them; this is a very simple artifice to provide an effective record of the history of the bay's utilization. At the same time as the report draws this upper chart it accesses the current size of the queue of vehicles waiting to enter the warehouse. It then draws a bar in the bottom half of the display to create a growing display of the queue size.

The display at the bottom of Plate 2 is an 'animated' display, in that it is built up continually as a simulation progresses. The complexity in the display comes from the gradual build-up of simple elements.

The display at the top of Plate 3 is a 'snapshot' display. Once the simulation has been run to a convenient point, this type of display summarizes the progress of the model to date. The display has been split into quarters to provide a number of views of the model. The top left quarter uses accumulator arithmetic to access the histogram entries for a clock measuring the time that lorries wait to enter the warehouse. It converts these histogram values into the angles necessary to construct a pie chart, and then creates that pie chart. The top right quarter of the display shows a more conventional means of presenting a histogram. In this case the histogram entries for a clock measuring the van waiting time are used. Again, each bar is built up from the histogram entries and attribute arithmetic. The bottom left quarter of the display is used to house explanatory text in this instance. The bottom right quarter of the display shows a summary of the size of the queue of vehicles waiting to enter. The basic data is drawn from a queue log, and successive values are simply joined by straight lines.

Each of these loading bay displays is impressive on its own. When the graphics capabilities are integrated into a tailored simulation system, by using the power of the user-defined menu facilities, it is possible to produce an extremely effective configuration that can really sell the results of a simulation in a way that was not possible five years ago.

The remaining plates in the book give examples of type 0 displays for practical simulation models. Some use histogram and queue log information, as described above, and some make careful use of type 0 queues with display length of zero (to give a simple numerical value for the queue length at any time). All the displays show how the thoughtful use of background drawings (aided and abetted by the sketchpad facility) can bring a simulation model to life.

The use of colour graphics for presenting simulations is a relatively new area at the time of writing, and the number of applications to which it is being put to good effect is increasing phenomenally. As we said at the beginning of this chapter, we think that the users' requirements are bound to grow in this area; rising to meet their expectations is one of the most demanding tasks facing simulation software developers in the short term.

# Part Four

Experimentation, implementation
and project management

# 11.

## Some thoughts on experimentation

We have built a simulation model to solve a problem. It does not matter whether it is a hand or computer model so long as we can use it to produce a solution quickly. In this chapter we discuss various aspects of experimentation. We do not attempt to describe the statistical design of experiments, because in our experience it has very little practical application. (There are many books on the subject and some are listed in the Bibliography.) Instead we indicate in general terms how a model is used to produce answers.

### Gaining understanding

Throughout the book we have stressed that the first stage in any simulation project is to gain understanding of the problem. This can only come from a model which is understood by both manager and modeller. Working together, both contribute and provide each other with insights into the problem. Often the manager and modeller see the problem and possible solutions in different ways. The manager is likely to see solutions and difficulties in physical terms, because this is the environment in which he works, while the modeller might see them in terms of his model. He is obviously influenced by his basic training. If he has a scientific background he may think of solutions in terms of (say) scheduling rules or decision trees. Both points of view are important and together they spark off inspiration and ideas in each other. This is the real benefit of the visual approach described in this book—hand simulation, interactive computer simulation and colour graphics displays. The computer is simply a calculating machine. Most original thoughts and possible solutions come while referring to the hand model or computer graphics.

It is worth remembering also that simulation is a question and answer technique. We build a model and ask a question. We observe the answer and as a result understand the problem better. This leads to another question and corresponding answer and so the process continues until a satisfactory solution is found. The better the questions we ask, the better the answers we get.

We stop asking questions when we find a good or satisfactory solution to the problem. It is most unlikely that our solution is the optimum one, because simulation does not give optimum solutions. We do not even know how close we are to the optimum.

### What questions to ask

Having built our model, either we have solved the problem because the solution is now obvious (and this has been known to happen), or we want to ask a number of 'what if' questions. For example, questions like—What if . . .

– another crane is added?
– the loading time is reduced by 20 per cent?
– a crane is taken out?
– shift working is introduced?
– a different scheduling rule is used?
– a flow rate is increased?
– the frequency or duration of breakdowns is reduced?
– we introduce a high capacity filtration unit?
– we introduce automated guided vehicles (AGVs)?
– we introduce more robot-controlled processes?
– we move towards Just-In-Time (JIT) manufacture?

Such questions are typical, but naturally the precise questions will depend on the problem. The more general questions (like 'moving towards JIT manufacture') need to be made more specific and broken down into more detailed questions. We must list the questions and rank them in the order likely to give greatest benefit and always ask those with the biggest potential first.

Do not be deterred by getting fairly obvious answers. We will almost certainly produce a lot of additional information which was not obvious, and this may generate additional questions to ask.

## Base run

The first run should always be a base run against which all improvements are measured. If the model is of an existing system, the run should replicate the system and produce results similar to those actually achieved. For example, it should give similar throughputs and machine utilizations. Any differences are caused either by inaccuracies in the logic of the model or in the data used. These discrepancies must be corrected or at least recognized before experimenting with the model.

The simulation approach described in this book ensures that the model-builder has an in-depth understanding of the system being modelled. This enables him, firstly, to take a heuristic approach to validation—i.e., do the model and the results *feel* right? Secondly, however, the model will produce a significant amount of detail which should be analysed and compared to the real-world results—detail such as queue lengths, occurrence of bottlenecks, rates of output at all significant stages, manning levels, breakdown patterns. Thirdly, the model should be tested under limiting conditions, such as deterministic arrivals, zero processing times and zero breakdowns. Thus at the end of this process the model-builder can be confident of having a valid base case.

If the model is of a system not yet in operation then the base run should reflect the latest plans against which relative improvements can be measured. While there will not be the same amount of real-world data to compare with, the approach described above can be adopted to a limited extent to ensure a valid base case.

# Initial conditions

We must give careful thought to how we start our model to ensure that it simulates the circumstances we are interested in. In general there are three cases.

The first is when we build a model to examine a particular transient state. This means that the problem has characteristics which are not permanent, and so we build a model of the extreme case. An example is a hospital during a major disaster. On this occasion we are not interested in how the hospital performs under normal circumstances. We want to know what facilities are needed to cope with the hopefully rare event. Therefore the initial conditions must represent the major disaster—for example a large number of patients arriving simultaneously from the outside world.

Another example is the build-up and run-down of a major civil engineering project. The construction of a motorway builds up to a peak as equipment is brought in and then runs down as the equipment is taken out. The timing of this is critical and the purpose of a model may be to look at the consequences of alternative equipment leasing strategies. Both the model and the initial conditions must reflect this build-up and run-down.

The second and third cases concern the steady state of a system. We want to know, for example, how the hospital performs under normal circumstances, and what the typical demand is on the operating theatre equipment. We run the model for a short period, say over one month, and predict what will happen over a year. We have a choice as to what initial conditions to specify. We can either start our model from 'cold' or guess what the steady state will be.

In starting the model from cold, we simply say that nothing is working. The model starts with no patients in the hospital and builds up a steady state.

We can learn a lot about the system from the way this build-up occurs. It may reach a steady state quickly or slowly, smoothly or erratically, and seeing how our model behaves can give us a better insight into the dynamics and stability of the problem under study.

However, if we are not interested in how the system builds up to a steady state, we will be wasting effort, because the early results are of no value to us. We can avoid this by guessing at the steady state and using this as the initial condition. This is not always easy because it prejudges, to some extent, the solution. However, if the initial conditions are realistic the model will reach the steady state much quicker, and we will have useful results that much sooner.

# Length of simulation run

Having specified the initial conditions we now run the model until we achieve our objectives—until the model either completes the required transient state or reaches a steady state (or possibly terminates with an error!). It is obvious when a model has completed a transient state and hence when to stop the run—all the emergency patients have been treated or the motorway is finished.

However, deciding when a model has reached a steady state is not so obvious. If, during the run, we periodically (say every day, week or month, depending on the time units) ask for output which summarizes the run, like histograms and activity run counts, we can compare the results between periods and conclude that a steady state has been reached when there is little or no change. Plotting the results can be most enlightening. We take each parameter in turn—say machine down time recorded in a histogram, or number of steel bars produced as recorded in the activity run count—and for each period plot the change in values over that period. Figure 11.1 shows two curves which may be produced.

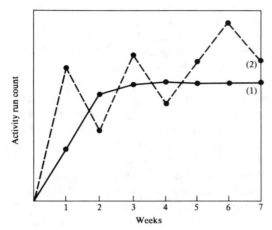

**Figure 11.1**

Curve (1) shows a model which takes around three weeks to settle down. By this time it has reached a steady state and the results are now meaningful. There is no need to continue for much longer than say seven weeks, unless we suspect that something unusual will happen.

Curve (2) shows a model which has not yet reached a stable state. This could mean either that it needs more time to reach stability or that we have an inherently unstable system (which of course would be a very good argument for its redesign). There is another faint possibility and that is that our model is wrong! However, it is essential that we determine the cause of the instability. Our hand model and computer graphics will help.

We must be careful not to plot the parameters at too frequent intervals, as this may give exaggerated importance to minor fluctuations.

## Effects of random numbers

When examining results we should give some thought to the subject of random numbers. In our opinion, far too much emphasis is usually put on this aspect of simulation, but it is a subject which needs a brief mention.

Random numbers can be generated both mechanically and electronically. Examples of mechanical methods are tossing a coin, throwing dice, shuffling a pack of cards, turning a roulette wheel. Electronic methods make use of small variations in the emissions from electronic components or radioactive sources.

These methods generate sequences of numbers which cannot be repeated. This is a considerable disadvantage because we cannot repeat an experiment with the same numbers (unless, of course, we record all the numbers as a list in the first place and simply repeat the experiment using the list—but this poses a serious storage problem).

Therefore, in practice, methods are used which generate sequences of random numbers which can be repeated. These are known as psuedo-random numbers, and have properties similar to truly random sequences. They are generated by various mathematical procedures, and various statistical tests can be used to check that the numbers are random (see Bibliography—Tocher).

One such mathematical procedure is to take any number between 0 and 1 which has a large number of significant digits and multiply by a prime number. Take the decimal part of this and multiply by the same prime number.

For example, if the starting number is 0.645 329 and the prime is 317, then:

$$0.645\,329 \times 317 = 204.569, \quad \text{random no.} = 0.569$$
$$0.569 \quad\;\; \times 317 = 180.373, \quad \text{random no.} = 0.373$$
$$0.373 \quad\;\; \times 317 = 118.241, \quad \text{random no.} = 0.241$$
$$0.241 \quad\;\; \times 317 = \;\;76.397, \quad \text{random no.} = 0.397$$
$$0.397 \quad\;\; \times 317 = 125.849, \quad \text{random no.} = 0.849$$

If we require integer random numbers between 0 and 100, we multiply each random number by 100 and round up or down.

If we require random numbers between 0 and 25, we use the same sequence but ignore every number over 25.

In simulation we use random numbers every time a sample is taken from a distribution. It is important that we take sufficient samples in order to duplicate reality. If, in sampling from a distribution, we generate four random numbers between 1 and 100 and by chance obtain 8, 2, 7 and 11, we would not produce representative times. If we generate 20 numbers and obtain similar values, we would suspect that there was something wrong with our random number generator. However, if our generator is a good one, our results will not be adversely affected if we sample each distribution about 20 times as a minimum.

We can always check that we have sampled adequately, by monitoring the distribution with a clock and collecting a histogram of the samples. Plotting the histogram and distribution together will show how accurate the sampling is. If we wish, we can apply statistical tests (chi-squared goodness of fit, see Bibliography—Moore) to see if the two are significantly different.

There may be a distribution in our model which is not used very often, say to generate rare but catastrophic breakdowns. It would be expensive in time and probably money to run until it has sampled about 20 times, as we may have to simulate many years! In such circumstances it may be better to remove the catastrophic breakdown from the general model and feed it as the initial conditions for a separate run.

In any simulation, it is important that every distribution has its own sequence of random numbers and that each run should start at the same point in the sequence. In this way any differences in results between runs will be caused by the modifications made to the model and not by variations in the random numbers.

## Antithetic random numbers

In generating a sequence of random numbers, we may find that there is a slight bias towards, say, the high numbers. If the numbers are used to generate arrivals into a system, they will produce slightly longer inter-arrival times, and this will give biased results.

One way of overcoming this is to simulate for a longer period, generate more random numbers and thus remove the bias. Another way is to carry out a second run of the same duration, and instead of using the random numbers themselves, subtract them from 101 (if the original sequence is in the range 1 to 100) and use these new numbers. These are known as antithetic random numbers. They give a bias in the opposite direction and the results from the two runs can be averaged out.

It can be shown (see Bibliography—Fishman) that the results from the two averaged runs give a smaller variance than would be obtained from a double-length run.

## Subsequent runs

All subsequent runs should be compared against the base run. In order to show the effect of change we must make the changes one at a time, otherwise we will not be able to allocate the benefits to each change. Making one change at a time also gives a better insight into the factors which most influence the performance of the operation.

Usually the total number of runs carried out is small. Some people believe that when a number of factors can take several values a vast number of runs will be needed. Such a situation would occur only if we did not learn anything from each run. After each run we should understand the problem better and possibly be able to discard a number of permutations of factors and values. Typically ten to twelve runs are sufficient to 'home in' on a solution of a particular problem. The case studies in Part Six illustrate this point well.

## Sensitivity analysis

One of the most important responsibilities of the problem solver is to state the limits between which the proposed solutions apply.

For most problems we are unable to find the optimum solution. Even if we did, the solution would only apply to a particular set of circumstances which would probably change anyway, before very long.

Therefore, unless we are able to develop an 'adaptive' model which can optimize for each new set of circumstances, we have to recommend a 'robust' solution which will satisfy an agreed range of expected circumstances. In addition we must state the limits between which we are confident our proposals will apply.

Establishing the robustness and limits of a proposed solution is often referred to as 'sensitivity analysis'. It aims to locate those variables and combinations of factors which are most likely to influence the proposed solution. Sensitivity analysis is often quoted in layman's terms as 'a difference is a difference if it makes a difference'.

For example, in a model of an automated warehouse it was found that the speed of a particular conveyor system could vary between 100 and 200 feet per minute without significantly influencing the total efficiency of the warehouse. Speeding up the conveyor increased the gaps between the packages and meant that larger empty conveyor spaces were moved around at greater speed. Having specified the conveyor speed at 150 feet per minute the designer was confident that the efficiency of operation was 'insensitive' to relatively large changes in this variable.

On the other hand small changes in the acceleration and deceleration of the computer-controlled stacker cranes, which patrolled the aisles and moved the goods in and out of the high bay warehouse, showed that this activity time was extremely sensitive and had a direct influence on the total design. Although the time element was small, the activity occurred frequently, and a small increase in the warehouse throughput would mean an extra crane, an additional aisle and a change in the warehouse configuration.

The designer in such a situation has to be concerned with the robustness of the design to changing circumstances, and the more automated the design the more inflexible, and hence sensitive to design errors, it becomes. The classic solution is to over-design on a 'one for the pot' basis which gives varying levels of slack around the system, but this is a costly way of trying to overcome an ill-considered approach to design. A simulation model will help solve this problem and is particularly valuable for Advanced Manufacturing Technology (AMT) applications. Robots and computer control are very expensive and their use normally entails a significant loss of operating flexibility. There is very little room for error as the company has put most of its eggs into one basket.

These thoughts, it is hoped, will give the reader some ammunition when developing his views on the need to use a simulation model to help assess, design, validate and control projects. We summarize our thoughts as follows.

Before making any firm proposals about our problem, we must check the sensitivity of the results to the assumptions in the model. We should test, for example, whether our conclusions are sensitive to the times of the activities, particularly if there is some doubt about their accuracy. We can easily increase and decrease a time by 10 or even 50 per cent. If such changes make little difference to the results, we have an insensitive system. However, if such changes do influence the results, then we have at least set confidence limits on our results.

We know that if the 'true' time is within certain limits our conclusions are valid. If it is outside, our conclusions may be different. We therefore know which areas to investigate more closely and where to concentrate any further data collection effort. If, on the other hand, we find that parts of our model are insensitive then we should think about simplifying them before any further runs are contemplated.

Any parameter in the model (activity times, number of entities, attribute values, etc.) about which we are not too confident should be the target of some sensitivity analysis. Ask the managers concerned to indicate the factors and the limits they want tested so that they will be reassured.

In this chapter we have described in general terms how simulation models are used to produce solutions to problems. However, we must remember that although the model may be the central part of a project, there are many other factors which influence the success or failure of the total project.

In Chapter 12 we discuss some of these factors and stress that project management is the key to the success of a simulation study.

# 12.

## Management of simulation projects

Because simulation is a trial and error approach to problem solving, the main issue to be faced in managing a simulation project is balancing the expected value of the results that will be produced from a model, against the time and cost involved.

This chapter sets out guidelines for project management which the reader should absorb as an integral part of his modelling approach. It is easy to get carried away by enthusiasm, to a point where the modelling technique becomes an end in itself rather than a means to an end. Frequently questioning whether the nature of the problem, the expected costs and benefits and the best method of approach have changed, is a good discipline.

Modelling expertise has developed rapidly in the last five years. Technological advances have led to significant improvements in hardware and software. There is a very high expectation among users and potential users that computers should be user-friendly, be fully interactive and have sophisticated colour graphics. These expectations continue to grow, spurred on by current developments in, for example, artificial intelligence and expert systems.

It is imperative therefore that we are not blinded by the technology and that we do not lose sight of our goal—solving real problems in the most cost-effective way. It is worth remembering that the main causes of project failure today are poor communications between people, and poor project control.

The use of a model is an iterative process where those involved gain understanding of the problem, get new ideas, constantly review assumptions, explore alternatives and see new methods of approach. This requires good communication between everyone involved in the project which, to be most effective, requires determined leadership.

The ideal leader is someone who can provide the project control, enthusiasm and technical guidance that will exploit the abilities of everyone concerned. It is unfortunate that many of the management training establishments around the world have failed not only to give adequate simulation training to their students, but have also neglected to provide basic training in project control.

In the earlier chapters we have been concerned with helping the reader to develop his ability to build accurate, acceptable simulation models quickly and cheaply. However, to get results it is essential that the modeller also exercises self-control over every stage of the project.

A typical simulation project can be divided into a number of stages as follows:

- problem definition;
- project team selection and training;
- model building and testing;
- experimentation and modification;

- presentation of recommendations;
- implementation;
- review of project.

Each stage requires leadership, technical ability and good communications, which in turn lead to involvement and finally commitment.

## Problem definition

A model is a simplified representation of an existing or proposed real-world system. We need a model:

- because it is risky to experiment by 'trial and error' in the real world;
- because it is the only way of representing a proposed real-world system;
- to act as the focal point for planning, discussion, implementation and control.

To help assess the value of modelling a problem we ask the following questions.

### What questions do we want the model to answer?

The need for a model becomes obvious if we can identify significant questions which cannot be confidently answered in any other way. We list the decisions which will be influenced by the answers the model produces, and ask whether they are urgent and expensive if in error.

This is a salutary exercise which helps to translate a corporate enthusiasm into a precise list of objectives. At some later stage we may well have to balance the time and cost of model complexity with answering all the questions, but at least we rank the questions in order of importance.

We must also be able to explore alternatives and test the sensitivity of proposed solutions.

### In what form should the answers be?

The value of an answer depends upon the form in which it is given. When we discuss the decisions that will be influenced by the model we also assess the most effective way of presenting the information. This may well have considerable impact on our model-building approach and the measures of performance we select. For example, in assessing the time for adding new soaking pits in a steel mill as production expands, the model should measure pit utilization, waiting time for cooling ingots, crane requirements, and the capital investment required.

As described in Chapters 9 and 10, most simulations are now presented to management in a highly visual way—using animated colour graphics. This is a very effective and stimulating way of conveying the options and conclusions to the decision makers. If careful thought is given to this at the beginning of the project, the model can be constructed so that eventual presentations will have maximum impact.

However, we should remember that the outputs from most simulations are concerned with throughput, utilizations, bottlenecks, service levels, etc. While these will be of considerable interest to the intermediate decision makers, we must not forget that the ultimate decision makers (the ones who will spend the money) are primarily interested in the overall financial justification. It is likely that this justification will be the responsibility of the intermediate decision makers but they are likely to involve you to some extent. This aspect of project evaluation is a major subject but is outside the scope of this book. Several useful books on the subject are available and we would refer the reader to the Bibliography (Van Horne, Modigliani).

### What benefits will these answers provide?

What great breakthrough will be achieved if the model answers the listed questions?

We should put a value on these benefits. As there is likely to be some uncertainty, we forecast not only the expected benefit but also the optimistic and pessimistic limits. The benefits may be in terms other than increased throughput, such as improved customer service, flexibility of operation, job satisfaction, reduction in stress levels or accident risk. These measures, and the form in which the answers must be given, should be identified when listing the questions.

### What type of model should be used?

If the expected benefits of using a model are sufficiently attractive, thought must be given to the modelling approach. As mentioned in Chapter 1, models can be classified into two categories:

- 'trial and error' simulation models where we ask questions and observe answers;
- optimizing-type models which either calculate the answer directly, or have an in-built search procedure that finds the best possible answer.

Which approach to use will depend upon the nature of the problem, our understanding of the problem and our technical competence. If uncertain, we should get professional advice, or 'brainstorm' with someone who has experience, to ensure that we are on the right track. If we think that simulation is appropriate, we decide on the first step in the modelling process and set limited objectives within a fixed time. This should be of the order of two to five days. Most models can be assessed and sized in this time.

We formulate the problem as a flow diagram, remembering the form in which we want answers. It may also be useful to try and express the problem in a mathematical form. This helps our thought processes and gives an insight into the conflict which may occur in trying to answer all the questions at once. We may find that we can answer some of the questions but not others.

### Benefits—at what cost?

We have now forecast the likely benefits, decided on a modelling approach and the extent to which we can answer the questions. We are in a position to combine a costed programme of work with the forecast timing of the benefits. Considering the uncertainty in both the cost estimates and forecast benefits, this ought to be a very attractive proposition before the manager is committed to the project.

One of the key factors in successful control of modelling projects is a frequent review to consider to what extent the original problem still exists.

During the problem definition and later stages we continue asking:

- Has the nature of the problem and the urgency of its solution changed?
- Is the model still appropriate? If not, how should it be changed?
- Are the forecast benefits still the same?
- Have the expected costs changed?
- Is a project reappraisal necessary?

The questions must be asked periodically and answered truthfully. The answers may result in reorientating the model, rephasing the project timetable, or even abandoning the project.

## What are the terms of reference?

The purpose of terms of reference is to convey clearly to everyone concerned with the model, what answers are going to be given by whom and when. This is a form of contract and a constant reminder of the objectives, responsibilities and allocated resources.

Should the nature of the problem, or the value of the model, change significantly then the terms of reference will need to be revised. It is recommended that minutes are kept of all project meetings, to record pertinent comments, decisions and responsibility for action.

Frequent short meetings are valuable because they:

- set short-term target dates for completing certain tasks;
- acquaint line management with progress and involve them in discussing any new findings.

## Project team selection and training

The ideal model builders are those who fully understand the details of the problem area and where to get the data; who are trained modellers; who are good friends of the management involved; who have a clear scientific questioning approach; and who are eager to get the answers as quickly as possible. If we happen to be, or have available, such persons then we are lucky. More likely we have to bring together a number of people who can jointly satisfy some or all of these requirements. They must be able to communicate their knowledge and will have to be led. In most cases one or more of the team, and the managers to whom they report, will require training and this must be assessed in estimating both project time and cost.

The purpose of training is to:

- create the model builders;
- give managers an appreciation of simulation and the type of questions that simulation models can answer.

The training of the model builders can either be done by attending a formal training course, which takes the participants step by step through the modelling discipline, or by 'on-the-job' training.

## Formal training

For the approach described in this book the formal course lasts a week and is made up of a series of linked exercises which give comprehensive training in both hand and computer simulation. A synopsis of a one week course is given opposite.

The linked exercises, computer output and notes provide a reference manual to which the modeller can return whenever he needs to refresh his memory.

## On-the-job training

Where the problem must be solved urgently, where resources are scarce and where time is of the essence, on-the-job training may well be preferred. This is where the training takes place during the model building phase and requires a tutor on a day-to-day basis until the technique has been learnt. This type of training has the benefit of using a real-life problem familiar to the participants and has a sense of urgency which encourages rapt attention and a high work rate.

Someone is waiting for the model results and is usually giving every encouragement.

The authors have run many such in-plant courses varying from three days to three weeks depending on the size of the problem, and large models have been operational on a computer within one week.

It is important to start with a model, usually of not more than 50 activities, which describes either the main features or an important part of the problem. This allows the trainees to grasp the flow-charting principles, practice hand simulation and get accustomed to using the computer. When this has been done they can continue to extend the model as necessary under the watchful eye of the tutor. Practice gives everyone confidence.

At the end of each week there should be a formal presentation to the senior members of the organization on the model that has been developed and the questions that it is being designed to answer.

## Appreciation seminars

These aim to give people who have some association with the modelling team an insight into what simulation can and cannot do. This certainly should include those who will make decisions based on the model and those who will provide information and data. In the latter case it helps them to appreciate why we ask certain questions and continually cross-check on the use of resources in activities, timings and queue disciplines.

An appreciation seminar can be given in two hours and a suggested timetable is set out below.

### *Introduction and example (30 min)*

After a brief introduction to the idea of activities, queues, entities and attributes the presenter can discuss the communication problem before undertaking a hand simulation of the beer drinking example (Chapters 1 and 2).

| Time | Day 1 | Day 2 | Day 3 | Day 4 | Day 5 |
|---|---|---|---|---|---|
| 09.30 11.00 | What is simulation? Philosophy of HOCUS system Fundamental concepts: – entities – activities – queues – activity diagrams | Exercise: – drawing activity diagram | Description of entity attributes Use of options | Exercise: – drawing activity diagram | HOCUS graphics. Exercise: – add graphics to model |
| | | | COFFEE | | |
| 11.20 13.00 | Introducing variability into a model: – randomization – distributions Exercise: – drawing activity diagram | Exercise: – hand simulation | Use of options (continued) | Exercise: – coding for computer run | Continuous activities and related options |
| | | | LUNCH | | |
| 14.10 15.40 | Exercise: – hand simulation | A description of the HOCUS computer program Exercise: – coding for computer run | Other facilities: – entity groups – data field selection – condition sets | Exercise: – computer simulation | Other options and facilities |
| | | | TEA | | |
| 16.00 17.30 | Review of exercise Exercise–Model for computer run: – preparation. | Exercise: – coding for computer run – computer simulation | Exercise–Model for computer run: – preparation | Solutions to exercises | Use and abuse of simulation Course review |
| 17.30 18.30 | | Solutions to exercises | | HOCUS program facilities: – menus – user-defined reports | |

### Benefits of modelling approach (5 min)

By reference to the example, the characteristics of hand simulation can be extolled as follows:

- Simple three-step discipline for hand operation of the model.
- We can watch the model advance through time and judge whether it is doing what we want. If necessary we make changes and additions.
- We can observe what happens and gain an understanding of the main influences and where possible changes could be made.
- Anyone can learn to do it.
- It is visual and allows the dynamic behaviour of complex problems to be communicated easily to the observer. It goes straight in through that great integrator of information—the eye.
- Hand simulation is powerful, sure but slow.
- The computer gives the much needed speed.
- It can be transferred direct to the computer.
- The computer output can be validated against the hand simulation to give confidence that the model has been successfully transferred.
- Simulation does not automatically find the best answer, it only gives answers to the questions we ask.

### The need for a formal approach (5 min—optional)

At this point, the activity and queue formats can be shown. These are used to ensure that everyone writes their instructions in a formalized way which they, their colleagues, and the computer can comprehend (Chapter 5).

### Running a model on the computer (45 min)

The graphical displays of a simple model, such as the loading bay (Exercise 5.10) can be shown. The model with say three, four and five bays can be run, to demonstrate the impact on the length of queues. This is guaranteed to encourage questions and discussion. As appropriate the flow chart, the interactive way of running the program and the user-friendly data input can all be displayed. Other models can be demonstrated—production model, hospital model, banking model. It will be quite difficult to limit this session to 45 minutes.

### Ways in which simulation can be used (30 min)

*Existing or new systems*

  (a) To balance resources. What happens if we add or take away certain resources, e.g., machines or operators.
  (b) To check on priorities. Where there is more than one way out of a queue or more than one entity in a queue, which one should be taken? What control should we have? You pay for control, so ensure it is a good investment. All scheduling comes into this category.

(c) To see the effect of changing activity times. Large queues and the activities causing the blockages are easy to find. What will happen if we reduce the activity time? Does the queue move from a place where space is available, to a place where it is not? Are we just queue-chasing around the system? We can find out if reducing an activity time gives any benefit before we pay for it.

*New systems*

(d) To help determine data collection requirements. Money is often wasted on the enthusiastic pursuit of too much data. We can build a model of a proposed system and check its sensitivity to changes of $\pm 10$ per cent, $\pm 25$ per cent or even $\pm 50$ per cent in activity times, expected product mixes, and arrival patterns. If it is extremely sensitive we will have to redesign to reduce vulnerability, and we can specify the form and level of accuracy of any data required. The model will indicate where the new system is sensitive to error and hence requires close project control.

(e) To help design a control system. If we have simulated alternative systems and identified the set of rules which best suit a particular policy, then the flow diagram is a definition of the control system. It can either be adapted from the simulation model or used to specify a specially written program.

(f) To train managers. Just as pilots use flight simulators, because trial and error in the real world could be disastrous, so potential managers could well benefit from making their 'learning mistakes' on a model. There is a good case for having the future manager on the development and commissioning team of a new system. He should confirm the feasibility of the design at the model stage and then he is committed to making it work during the inevitably painful first months of full operation.

(g) To present results. A simulation model is an excellent way of presenting results to decision makers. The justification of the recommendations has to be done in a short time. A visual presentation using the model graphics is a good medium for communication. It helps understanding and encourages involvement, to the point where management see how the model can be used to answer other questions.

## Summary (5 min)

The presenter briefly recaps on the main points of the seminar.

By selecting from the above notes and using the examples in earlier chapters and the case studies, an appreciation seminar lasting about two hours can be prepared in a matter of hours.

The benefit of well prepared and presented appreciation seminars and training courses is that they provide an opportunity for those who have the problem and those who can help to solve it, to get together and communicate in a constructive way. There is nothing like success to breed confidence within an organization and it is unfortunate that many management scientists fail to make the effort to communicate. One of the main reasons for the development of the system described in this book has been to help overcome this deficiency.

## Model building and testing

The watchwords are accuracy, acceptability and speed.

### Accuracy

At the problem formulation stage a decision will have been reached on the boundary of the model and the degree of detail to be incorporated. Accuracy is a measure of the extent to which the model replicates the real world. This reflects the level of detail included and the correctness of the logic.

The objective of the model is to gain understanding and answer specific questions. In order to do this we should build the simplest possible model which will achieve this objective.

If we are unable to build the whole model to start with, then we build a part of the model. In a port, for example, start with no tides, ships coming in at regular intervals and no shift working or breakdowns on the cranes. Add this detail later. The following are the main steps in building and testing a model:

- list the main entity types and their attributes;
- draw the flow diagram of the mainstream entities;
- trace the entities through the diagram;
- decide upon the time units;
- keep the model as simple as possible and add features only as they prove to be necessary;
- check the model carefully by hand simulation;
- in hand simulation use the same random numbers as the computer (Appendix 1) and cross-check results;
- prove that the model replicates an existing or expected situation.

### Acceptability

To help management accept the model we should:

- build the model as close to the problem area as possible, using people who understand and can confirm accuracy. Let them see we are on site, working hard to get answers to their problems;
- use the work place words (if possible!) to describe entities, activities and queues. Make these part of model vocabulary;
- prepare the model in a recognizable form. It may be possible to draw the model on a map of the problem area;
- prepare typical output reports and check that this is the form in which the answers are most useful. We may find that changes are suggested which modify the model logic;
- encourage the managers to trace through the model logic using animated colour graphics;
- discuss the balance between benefits and modelling detail and tailor effort accordingly;
- think of the model as a formal record of the best description of the problem to date.

Acceptability of the model to management is essential and we may have to add certain features to achieve this. We must balance the extra cost against the value of the confidence generated and choose accordingly.

## Speed

Speed is related to:

- the clarity with which the problem is defined and comprehended;
- establishing clear lines of communication;
- the modelling technique used;
- the level of detail involved;
- the work rate of the modellers.

It is particularly true in a modelling project that work expands to fill the time available and therefore those involved need deadlines. These should be set in hours and days rather than weeks. In this way projects are completed in days and weeks rather than weeks and months.

During the building and testing of a model, we gain a greater understanding of the problem and produce answers to some of the questions. These answers will prompt new questions and during this stage we can reassess the accuracy of the estimated costs and benefits.

If there are still questions to be answered at the end of building and testing the model then we move into the experimentation and modification stage.

# Experimentation and modification

Having survived the delirium of building an accurate, acceptable model quickly, the objective is to use it as efficiently as possible to answer the remaining questions.

Questions will be posed as we discuss the results of the experimental runs with management and these in turn may involve modifications to the model. We must beware of overconfidence and discipline ourselves to check carefully the logic of any modifications, however small. We must decide upon an experimental programme and ask the questions in the order which will:

- give the greatest insight into the behaviour of the system;
- test the robustness of any proposed action;
- use the computer efficiently.

We change only one variable at a time so that the effect of change can be attributed to a particular cause. While we should give careful thought to the sequence of experimentation it is the authors' experience that modellers intuitively guide themselves towards the solution. Some ask a few more questions but it is not the mystique which many would have us believe.

We summarize the quantitative results in tables, histograms and graphs. In some cases qualitative interpretation can be made of such things as stress levels, accident proneness, staff acceptability and social benefits. Here we are moving into an area where certain attributes are weighted according to some judgement criteria, and as a result alternative courses of action can be ranked in order of acceptability. Simulation models have proved to be particularly valuable in situations where such factors have some influence on a solution.

Our final task in the experimental stage is to check the robustness of a proposed course of action. Inevitably, the real world is going to differ from the model and therefore it is essential to find out how much the model assumptions must change before the proposed solution is no longer valid. This is often referred to as sensitivity analysis and was discussed in Chapter 11.

This involves running the model with the assumptions being changed through their expected limits.

## Presentation of recommendations

The modelling process falls into three stages:

- the building of the model;
- the dialogue with the model—experimentation;
- the presentation of recommendations.

All three have their special communication problems and it is sad to relate that many well-conducted modelling exercises have failed at the last fence—presenting the results.

We absorb detail, comprehend the dynamic behaviour of the system, evolve solutions, and are anxious to get our message across. To be successful this must be presented in such a way that the maximum impact is achieved in the time available. Therefore we must not only know the message, but also the audience. What method of presentation will have the greatest impact? We must think about this very carefully.

In our view the most practical, cost-effective and professional form of presentation is 35 mm colour slides. Not only is the visual impact good, but also we are forced to keep our text to an absolute minimum—you physically cannot get many words on a slide and this is a very good discipline. It also leads in very nicely to our 'video show' because almost certainly our presentation will involve using colour graphics display. We can very quickly get across all the key aspects of our work:

- the nature of the model; the entities, queues, activities;
- the dynamics of the model and the interactions between the components;
- the detail of the model; the breakdowns, interruptions, erratic supplies, etc.;
- the results from the model.

We can pre-record our graphics presentation and give a quality, punchy 'video show' using our supermicro and colour screen.

Flow diagrams, graphs, plant layout diagrams are all useful in presenting recommendations. The written and spoken word is thus kept to a minimum necessary to support our pictures. Television programmes and advertisements are able to present their message in seconds and we can use this technique. Decision makers are busy people who appreciate effort made to ease their problem of absorbing details.

Having decided on the form of presentation, we:

- rehearse it carefully to make it as professional as possible;
- check that the room has been set up correctly and that all the equipment (projector, supermicro, colour screen, etc.) is in working order;
- stick to our main points;
- remember the questions the model was designed to answer—and answer them;
- avoid temptation to try to impress the audience with our detailed knowledge;
- arrange to go through the presentation with questions afterwards;
- if interrupted try to get back to the main points as quickly and politely as possible;

– do not get lost by chasing details—stick to the script;
– listen to questions and answer the question posed—not a different one.

We must design our presentation with some consideration of our own strengths and weaknesses, and have several trial runs with someone who will give advice on the material and the way it is presented.

## Implementation

When a decision has been taken to go ahead with the recommendations it is necessary to plan and control the implementation programme. The flow diagram can often be used to help prepare the project control network on which due dates can be set. As the project proceeds new factors may arise which require further runs of the model. We use the model to monitor performance against expectation. This allows us to adapt it to the changing realities and use it as an ongoing planning tool.

Some organizations use such a model as a suggestion box where any proposals for improving the performance of an operation can be examined. This allows propositions of some complexity to be explored—such as a change in planning horizon, scheduling rule or staggered working hours by different sections.

If the control rules for a system have been determined then it may be possible to develop the simulation model into the control program.

## Review of project

The purpose of a review is to measure the success of the completed project, list the lessons that have been learnt, and decide how these can be incorporated into the management of future projects. It helps to do this in a structured way, as the cause and manifestation of any deficiency may not be easy to pinpoint.

Earlier in this chapter we urged regular reviews of the problem under study with regard to method, expected costs and benefits. Hopefully, as understanding is gained during the model-building stages readjustments are made to ensure project success. However, these are usually only tactical changes which are limited in their scope by the modelling strategy chosen at the feasibility stage.

An 'end of project review' is an opportunity to review critically every stage in the modelling process. With the benefit of hindsight experiences can be discussed, the factors influencing performance analysed, and the criteria for success in future projects listed. To formulate your own ideas on the criteria influencing the success of a project we suggest you apply the questioning procedure below to a past project.

A review can be conducted under the following headings:

– feasibility and achievement;
– technique;
– work content;
– equipment;
– people.

## Feasibility and achievement

The first step is to compare what was promised at the feasibility stage with what was eventually achieved. The causes of any significant differences can then be explored.

At the feasibility stage the problem was diagnosed and a modelling approach recommended. The time scale, expected costs and benefits were estimated.

Was the problem properly diagnosed? This question can be divided into two parts. Firstly, the nature of the problem and secondly, the human environment in which the problem existed. If the nature of the problem was not adequately diagnosed, why was this? Was it the complexity of the situation, the inexperience of those undertaking the feasibility study, or the information and guidance given by management who commissioned the study? List the lessons learnt and decide what action must be taken to minimize any failings being repeated.

The major cause of project failure or overrun is not wrong diagnosis of the problem but lack of appreciation of the human environment in which it exists. Recommendations involve changes which people may find difficult to accommodate. Many modellers fail to ask the question 'do we intend to change the human environment in which the problem exists?' If the answer is no, then the problem must be solved in that environment, and this may seriously limit the range of possible solutions. If the answer is yes, then both the problem and its human environment must be considered. The pain of change, the speed at which it can take place and the training that should accompany it, must be part of the estimates of costs and benefits. It is the speed at which change can be implemented where most modellers fail. This can usually be attributed to their lack of experience in the management of people, and this is where the line manager's commitment to the project is so important. They are introducing change continuously and should know the problems. They will be responsible for implementation and therefore must endorse the modelling programme at the feasibility stage.

Were they involved and did they endorse the project? If not, who should have been involved? Was the involvement of the line managers lost during the project through lack of communication or disenchantment? If so—why? What steps should have been taken to correct this?

Handling the human beings concerned is a major part of a study. Did the project team do this well? Where did they fail? What must be done to correct the situation?

A project team must start with some goodwill if it is to have any hope of succeeding. It is essential that this fund of goodwill is added to, by the way the team conduct themselves. There will be occasions when they need to draw on this fund to overcome unexpected difficulties. Was goodwill built up? Could they have done better? Did they squander it needlessly? Should they have used it at some point to overcome a difficulty? If the human environment was properly assessed were the benefits of solving the problem clearly identified?

A salutary exercise on any project is to record how the expected benefits and costs change as time progresses and then compare these with the actual results thought to have been achieved. Because of changes that take place in the real world it is seldom that an exact comparison of the forecast and actual benefits can be made but we should at least try to judge the benefits attributable to the modelling exercise.

All too often the benefits diminish and costs increase due to new constraints being discovered, or to human reaction to change. The ability to estimate will improve with experience but the safest project is the one where the potential benefits are many times the costs involved. Trace the causes for the changes in expected benefits and costs. What were the reasons? How can we recognize these sooner in future?

## Technique

The modelling approach was specified at the feasibility stage. Was it the most suitable? While we may start with a flow diagram to help understand the problem it could be that at a certain point in the project a new technique should have been introduced. The modellers may or may not be aware of these alternative approaches.

Simulation, like most techniques, has its devotees and the danger is that it is used beyond its usefulness. Ask of the project:

- Was the right technique used?
- Could we at any point have profitably changed from a simulation to an optimizing-type model?
- Should we have stopped the project earlier?
- What changes should we make before using this technique again?

## Work content

How well was the work content of the project estimated? How accurately was the time required to do this work calculated? The major causes where estimating fails are in:

- data collection effort;
- the validation of the model and error correction;
- meetings and discussions.

Data collection is time-consuming and as the model is developed further information is often required. Delays can be caused by the actual collection of the data, or by waiting for someone else to provide it.

As understanding is gained the model is modified and must be revalidated. The modelling technique described in this book is directed at minimizing this time by a simple, disciplined procedure. However, the validation time required will depend upon the complexity of the model, the understanding and the discipline of the modeller and the speed with which everyone concerned can confirm that the model is accurate.

Validation time should probably be a minimum of 20 per cent of the model-building time with extra allowance depending on the confidence of the feasibility study team.

Meetings and discussions will almost certainly be required to confirm the model, to discuss the results and to prepare for change. Where the changes to the human environment are, or are thought to be, dramatic, these meetings can take several days of effort. Indeed, it is a good idea at the feasibility study stage to list all the interested parties who may be affected by any recommendations, and assess the time needed to explain, discuss and possibly review the model. The whole work programme should be structured to ensure that progress reports go to the right people at the right time.

Simulations of a hospital, an airport, or a new production process are typical examples where many interested parties are involved and may take some time to report back. The time for this communication often exceeds the total modelling effort. If the importance is not appreciated at the estimating stage then the project will almost certainly overrun and tempers will become frayed.

When reviewing the project ask:

— How accurately did we estimate the time required for each stage in the project?
— Where did we make significant errors?
— Why did these happen—naivity, carelessness, poor work rate, human reaction, equipment failure, technique?
— What lessons have been learnt?

The ability to estimate work content and time requirements for a project is something which should improve rapidly with experience. It helps to learn lessons in a structured way by carefully analysing where things went wrong in the past.

## Equipment

Were the computing facilities adequate or not? Assess the effort required to prepare the model for the computer, any problems of getting the model into the computer, the efficiency of running, the speed with which the results are fed back and the form they are in.

Many organizations have computers dedicated to regular commercial functions, and access for scientific work may be irregular. In these circumstances, supermicros are ideal. Although the response time may be marginally slower than on minis or mainframes, the overall level of productivity can be far higher. If the machine is dedicated to the project then there are no problems of access. There is nothing more frustrating than wanting to carry out a simulation and then having to wait to get on to a computer. With the price of supermicros falling almost monthly, no serious simulation project need be held up through lack of computing power. Remember—project time is money and nowadays computers are inexpensive.

## People

This means everyone concerned with the project—managers, modellers, data collectors, computer staff. Whatever the problem or technique adopted, the most significant single factor which discriminates between success or failure is the calibre of the person or team that does the job. This is an obvious statement which is so often repeated, and yet is almost forgotten when it comes to selecting a project team. Some people can do ten times as much work in a day as others. All need motivating and this is the role of the project leader, to see that the tasks are planned and allocated and a high work rate sustained.

At the feasibility study stage the human environment is assessed and allowance made for training. At the review stage judge how well this was assessed. What were the human strengths and weaknesses of the managers and the modellers? What action should be taken to improve the situation? How will future projects be influenced by this action?

## Summary

We know the actual cost, benefit and duration of the project. What was the estimated cost, benefit and duration? With hindsight what should the estimated cost, benefit and duration have been?

At the end of a project you can ask 'where do we stand now in terms of ability and experience?' If all has gone well you will have built up a fund of goodwill and confidence among those for whom you have undertaken the project. They will discuss other problem areas and ask for help. Job satisfaction, promotion and the respect of one's colleagues start from this point.

# Part Five
## The future

# 13.

## Current developments

Computer technology continues to evolve at ever faster rates. Developments in many fields are certain to impact upon the art and science of simulation, and the future is certain to present many new opportunities for development. This chapter reviews some of the recent developments which are relevant to discrete event simulation. Some of these developments, such as improved processing power, will affect all computer applications: others will be of specific relevance to simulation techniques.

An attempt has been made to limit the amount of jargon used but some technical terms have been necessary. Where they are used a brief explanation has been given and, in particular, where acronyms have become established, the full version of the name is given at least on the first occurrence in each case. Although proliferating acronyms are difficult to follow some of the more important and established ones do fulfil a useful purpose, for example Application Program Generators are mentioned in several places but the acronym APG helps to emphasize that the term has a specific and widely understood conventional meaning. It is also more compact.

### Technological advances

Computing in general and computer simulation in particular are certain to benefit during the next decade from the continuing technological revolution. Advances are being made on all fronts as the cost of processing power continues to fall. Ten years ago processing facilities were expensive, bulky and sensitive to their environment. Specially constructed rooms with controlled atmospheres were the province of computer experts who practised their arcane arts well out of the way of ordinary mortals. Now the story is different. Processing power is cheap and plentiful, and microcomputers are at least as powerful as the already outdated minis, if not as powerful as the prematurely senile mainframes of ten years ago. The mystique of computing is diminishing fast along with cost, size and the need for specially controlled environments.

New developments in chip technology allow faster processing to be concentrated in a smaller space. For example, the use of gallium arsenide instead of silicon chips will multiply the processing capability which can be fitted into a given physical volume. Common estimates of the exact multiple by which gallium arsenide processing power exceeds that of conventional silicon chips vary between five and ten. Gallium arsenide transistors require less power to switch and can tolerate higher operating temperatures so that more gates can be fitted on to a chip without it melting. New chips such as these imply cheaper, faster and more reliable computers. Gallium arsenide is already used for Light Emitting Diodes (LEDs) commonly found as winking red lights on the front of electrical equipment. More than 30 different companies are now able to grow large gallium arsenide boules suitable for slicing into fine wafers.

Soon these wafers, transformed into chips, will be found in both analogue and digital circuits, and perhaps also in new hybrid circuits. One possible approach for development in the short term is to raise carrier mobility by improving gallium arsenide lattice structures, for example by creating multi-layer superlattices with layers of gallium arsenide sandwiched between layers of aluminium gallium arsenide. This would be a first step towards sophisticated three-dimensional integrated circuit architecture.

Gallium arsenide is only one of a number of so called 'III–V' compounds which might be suitable for chip manufacture. Other compounds which are made up of one element from Group III and one from Group V of the periodic table may also provide workable alternatives. Indium antimonide for example is currently being assessed by a number of researchers although, at the time of writing, its disadvantages appear to outweigh its advantages.

Another area of interest is superconductivity. Materials are said to superconduct when, under certain conditions, they lose almost all electrical resistance. During 1987 a major breakthrough was reported by Dr Chu at the University of Texas. For the first time a material has been developed which superconducts at temperatures significantly above absolute zero. The compounds previously used have required cooling by liquid helium at less than four degrees above absolute zero. By contrast Dr Chu's barium–yttrium–copper–oxygen compound superconducts at up to 98 degrees above absolute zero. It can therefore be cooled by liquid nitrogen which is much cheaper. Since this initial breakthrough, researchers have claimed to have developed materials which will superconduct at even higher temperatures. The ultimate target is to discover one which will work at room temperature.

It has been long recognized that conventional semiconductor transistors could be replaced by a superconducting equivalent: a so-called Josephson junction, named after its Cambridge inventor, Dr Brian Josephson. The main advantages of this technology would be massive increases in processing speed, potential cost reductions and negligible energy loss.

A further area of potential advancement using this technology involves Superconducting Quantum Interface Devices (SQUID) which exploit the Josephson junction's high sensitivity to magnetic fields. At the time of writing it is not clear whether the most important contribution to computer technology will be directly through Josephson junctions, or SQUID, or some other development such as hybrid superconductor-semiconductor circuits. What is almost certain is that processing speeds are likely to improve again within the next few years, probably by several orders of magnitude.

An entirely independent development involves optical technology. Computers which work on light rather than electricity are on the verge of becoming a reality. All-optical digital circuits already exist, the light equivalent to the old-fashioned electronic transistor being the so-called transphasor. An optical computer's transphasors will be connected up in vast networks to produce a highly sophisticated machine. Its three main advantages over electrical computers will be:

– *Speed of transmission*  Information will be transmitted by photons which, by definition, travel at the speed of light. This is in the order of 200 times faster than the electrons which make up electric currents.

- *Speed of manipulation* The materials used to manipulate light can react in approximately one-tenth of a millionth of a millionth of a second, which again is hundreds of times faster than the conventional electronic equivalent.
- *Simultaneous processing* Light beams can cross each other without interference so that transphasors can be connected by criss-crossing rays. Hundreds or thousands of operations can therefore be carried out in unison without any one of them endangering the integrity of another.

As processing power can be condensed into smaller and smaller volumes, the physical bulk of peripheral devices for input and output is becoming visibly disproportionate. Cathode Ray Tubes (CRTs) take up valuable space because of their undesirable depth. Users might want increased height and width, but they do not want a desk full of display unit. Liquid Crystal Displays (LCDs), gas plasma and electroluminescent display screens can be produced with a negligible depth so that the user is able to use what is effectively a two-dimensional piece of equipment. Such alternative display systems have other advantages: plasma screens for example have low power requirements, they are resilient, they may be much larger in display area than conventional VDUs (and with wider viewing angles), they have good response times even at lower temperatures, and they do not need continuous refresh signals because of their in-built memory.

At present there are still drawbacks with plasma screens: the lack of full colour for example, and to a lesser extent the level of graphics resolution. Nevertheless the ideal flat screen is well on the way. Even if plasma screens fail as cheap and flexible high resolution colour flat screens the old fashioned CRT may still fit the bill. Furnished with multiple cathodes and electrodes, and using a matrix drive and deflection sytem, CRTs may yet provide satisfactory flat screen VDUs.

Other items of hardware can also be expected to become faster and smaller, for example optical technologies are not only making an impact in data processing: optical disks for data storage and optical fibre communications are now commonplace. In the long run any technological development which improves computing will also improve the capabilities for computer modelling, and hence specifically computer simulation.

As a result of all these developments simulation will, in the future, become quicker, more accessible and more widely used.

## Parallel processing

Using conventional technology, advances are already being made in the field of parallel processing by which a number of calculations or other processing functions are performed concurrently. A machine which controls more than one operation at a time obviously enables significant advances to be made, but the problem lies in coordinating the operations carried out. Conventional computers do not need to address this problem: they function serially, along the lines developed by Von Neumann, the founder of modern computer theory. Even conventional multi-tasking systems operate by processing serial instructions. The machine carries out one instruction, and the next, and the next, and the next, . . . It is only ever carrying out one at a time, but because these instructions are executed so quickly, and because the operating system frequently switches from one user to another, the impression is given that the system is simultaneously serving each user. By employing parallel processing, however, it is possible not only to allocate users' tasks so that they really do run simultaneously, but it is also possible to tackle different aspects of the same task simultaneously. Exactly how a task is broken up and allocated is the problem to be addressed. What is relatively simple for specific problems (matrix multiplication for example) is enormously difficult for more general problems.

Established super-computers, such as the CDC Cyber 205 family and the Cray X-MP, employ two pseudo-parallel techniques known as pipelining and chaining. Chaining involves numbers being processed by a chain of arithmetic units, one after another, each one carrying out a single floating point instruction. A stream of numbers is thus processed simultaneously one step at a time. Pipelining is the same technique but applied within a single arithmetic unit. Before it completes one result the unit might already have started on several other sets of operands.

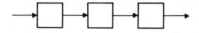

Linear chain

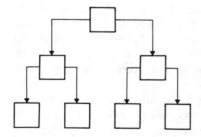

Tree

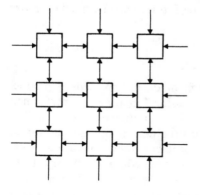

2-Dimensional Array

**Figure 13.1**

Genuinely parallel machines will be much more sophisticated, and furthermore it will be possible to connect them together in linear chains, rings, trees, two-dimensional arrays (meshes) or even multi-dimensional hypercube lattices to provide yet bigger and better capabilities. Figure 13.1 shows three simple interconnection topologies suitable for combining either whole machines or individual chips within a machine.

One way to harness the power of parallel processing is by combining units known as transputers. These units are intercommunicating chips which possess memory and input/output channels, as well as processing power. Using this technology at least one university research team is confident of being able to produce a physically small machine with one gigaflops (capability for one billion floating point operations per second). Conventional super-computers are capable of this sort of performance but they still process the logic of the code in strict serial order, and they cost about 40 times more than the prospective machine envisaged by the research team.

Inmos released the first commercial transputer in late 1985, along with 'Occam', a language designed specifically for concurrent processing. This development opens up the field to many users who are keen to experiment with parallel processing.

The human brain of course manages the problem of parallel processing without any apparent problem, which is why human beings are at the moment so much more clever than computers. Once we develop a method by which computers can also employ sophisticated parallel processing techniques the story may be quite different.

## Fourth generation programming languages

Fourth generation computer languages (or 4GLs as they are often called) are very high level languages: they enable users to create their own suites of computer programs without extensive programming expertise. Such languages allow relatively unsophisticated user-programmers to replace highly skilled conventional programmers, just as conventional high level programmers have largely replaced machine-code programmers. Indeed fourth generation languages are to conventional high level compiled languages what conventional high level compiled languages are to assembler languages.

As with so much recent computer jargon the term 'fourth generation language' means different things to different people. Very broadly the systems described by this term are characterized by some or all of the following features:

- a fast and efficient means to create new applications (but often with built-in exits to native languages for exceptional use where the 4GL is inadequate);
- built-in database (preferably relational);
- screen-based input, sometimes with independently scrolled windows;
- facilities to enable users easily to create and modify screen formats and reports, and thereby add and delete entries to the database and data dictionary;
- *ad hoc* enquiries and query processing employing user-friendly question and answer sessions.

Fourth generation languages are intended to be concise and easy to use. Instructions written in these languages generally produce whole 'macros'—blocks of code in conventional languages. Each statement in such blocks of code will in turn then be converted into a block of machine code. In other words a single statement in the highest level language will generally blossom into a large number of machine instructions.

Most users are interested in producing applications programs, so many commercially available fourth generation languages are specifically Application Program Generators (APGs) which produce either interpretive code or conventional source code for subsequent compilation. In theory, it is possible to create higher and higher level 'languages' in order to allow untrained users to create their own applications with the minimum of 'programming'. Indeed a program generator may be conveniently defined as a software tool which inter-actively translates logic, described in relatively general symbolism, into program code.

Existing APGs are capable of reducing development time scales from years to months, or even weeks. Suites which only a few years ago would have required dozens of man-years to develop, can now be completed in a matter of man-months.

One application amenable to this sort of approach is modelling by simulation. Simulation program generators have existed for several years, although there is still a great deal of scope for development. Conventional simulation packages are essentially pre-determined programs which behave differently for different models only because different data is supplied to them. The data consist largely of flags, the purpose of which is to direct the processing route through the code and to trigger appropriate subroutines. A more sophisticated approach, made possible by simulation program generators, is for the code itself to be created by the model as required.

The distinction between program code and data was a breakthrough when first developed for early electronic computers, but now there is a movement away from that distinction. The 'flags' mentioned are usually considered to be 'data', although in practice they may be argued to be by nature part of the program. One way around this dilemma is to employ a new type of program language: a language which does not recognize data as being in any way different from program code. Such languages belong to the next generation of languages—the fifth generation.

## Fifth generation programming languages

The term 'fifth generation' was originally applied specifically to hardware. In this context the five generations can be differentiated as follows:

*First generation*   computers built of thermionic valves.
*Second generation*   computers employing discrete semiconductors/transistors.
*Third generation*   computers employing integrated circuits (transistors, resistors, capacitors and diodes fabricated in the surface layer of a silicon wafer).
*Fourth generation*   computers using enhanced circuit integration through Very Large Scale Integration (VLSI) technology.
*Fifth generation*   computers employing parallel processing facilities to mimic human thought processes.

With software the same nominal generations are used although there is less agreement as to where one generation finishes and the next begins. Unfortunately it is difficult to make hardware and software developments match up precisely. The five generations of software may be usefully differentiated as follows:

*First generation*   machine code.

*Second generation*   assembly languages (low level symbolic languages).

*Third generation*   higher level conventional procedural languages (such as COBOL, FORTRAN, BASIC, C and APL).

*Fourth generation*   application program generators and non-procedural languages (often integrated with data dictionaries and screen mapping facilities).

*Fifth generation*   genuinely declarative languages allowing the use of artificial intelligence techniques and multi-valued or fuzzy logic.

The need for a distinction between program and data arose largely as a consequence of the fact that computers have been traditionally seen as number crunchers. When the object is to manipulate logical symbols and statements the position is rather different. Fifth generation programming languages are designed to carry out logical inferences upon a body of knowledge. Instead of 'programs' and 'data' what is needed is a collection of rules of deduction along with a knowledge base: one approach is to develop a completely new type of programming language in which symbols rather than numbers are manipulated.

One of the chief characteristics of an ideal symbolic manipulation language is that the order in which the statements appear should not matter. As long as a certain set of instructions (rules) is present the same 'knowledge base' will be processed in the same way to provide the same deductions. Languages with this characteristic are described as 'declarative' in contrast to the more conventional imperative languages, where statement order is of paramount importance, which are 'procedural'.

Languages such as LISP and Prolog are often described as declarative, and indeed they were designed to be so. Nevertheless in order to write successful 'shells' (which are analogous to programs in conventional programming languages), it is necessary to be aware of the order in which statements will be processed—because sometimes it will make a difference to the deduction process. In other words these languages are not truly declarative, they are still procedural. They are merely a first step towards an ultimate goal which can be achieved only when conventional Von Neumann architectures have been superseded. For only then will it be possible to create a useful language which is truly declarative.

Nevertheless languages such as LISP and Prolog provide an initial approach by which exotic areas of research such as artificial intelligence may be tackled. LISP, which is favoured in the USA, is the older of the two; its most important feature is its LISt Processing capability (hence its name). Prolog (PROgramming in LOGic) was developed later (in 1973) and tends to be favoured in Europe and Japan; in fact it is the core language for the Japanese fifth generation project. In essence Prolog is a theorem proving system.

Fifth generation languages permit logical problems to be tackled by enabling a 'shell' along with knowledge base to make valid inferences, so simulating the behaviour of a rational human being. In practice human beings learn by experience—they continually extend the depth and breadth of their knowledge base. This learning characterizes intelligence, and so if a computer could learn in the same way it could reasonably be said to be intelligent. By definition a machine furnished with artificial intelligence would be capable of rational thought. The intelligence required need not be generated by imitating organic brains, nor even necessarily by employing parallel processing. Yet it is difficult to imagine conventionally structured hardware and software being able to provide a genuine power of thought. On the other hand sophisticated game playing conventional computers already exist commercially.

It is relatively easy to program computers to play simple games such as noughts and crosses, and ludo; but a considerable degree of skill is required to play games such as Othello or backgammon well, yet computers are already better than almost all human players of these games and even for chess-playing programs the best development models are comparable in standard to a grand master. In a sense chess-playing computers are simulating the actions of strong chess players. Learning from their mistakes they exemplify in some ways the ambitions of artificial intelligence scientists. If a computer can simulate the role of a chess player, imagine what else it might be capable of doing.

A purely rational machine is not the ultimate goal, however. Genuine intelligence requires rather more than number crunching, theorem proving or other such logical process. For example the ability to recognize patterns is sometimes said to embody the essence of 'intelligence'; many researchers would regard a mechanized system which demonstrated an ability to recognize general patterns even a fraction as well as human beings as demonstrating true artificial intelligence. Good mathematicians reason extensively by analogy; the better they are at generalizing the better mathematicians they are. It would be useful if such a facility could be built into a computer system as a first step towards a more remote goal of building a system with artificial intuition as well as artificial intelligence. A number of projects have such a goal as their objective and a number of tools, such as fuzzy logic and other multi-valued logics, are claimed to provide a suitable way forward. Only time will tell. We are still some way off a simulation system with its own in-built intelligence.

## Expert systems

The possibilities for artificial intelligence (ai) are limitless, especially if machine intelligence is able to learn from an expert, or better still learn from a number of experts. A system with such a capability is called an Expert System (ES). This is simply a piece of software designed to simulate the role of an expert: a medical specialist, weather forecaster, barrister, accountant, mechanic, production controller, project manager or even management consultant. Here again the possibilities are endless. Expert systems are already well established in providing diagnostic advice. Medical expert systems are in some respects far more reliable than many general practitioners and hospital consultants.

The time is not far off when the hypochondriac will be able to amuse himself at home for hours with his very own medical expert system. Those with other hobbies will be able to diagnose electrical and mechanical faults, ask for professional advice or learn a new skill. The expert system will always be there, consistent, always helpful, always patient, ever ready to be of assistance and never asking for additional fees. It will never fall asleep, get drunk, or suffer from absent mindedness. It will also be able to play intellectual games and will learn from its mistakes or from any new information provided for it. It will also be able to justify its reasoning.

At the moment there are many systems which claim to be expert systems because they are able to 'backtrack'. In other words they are able to regurgitate the trail of reasoning which led to a particular inference; but this is not what characterizes a true expert system. A true expert system should be able to present its justification in a manner which is easily understood, as a good teacher does. The original string of logical deductions may appear opaque to users if presented in a raw form; users need to be convinced by a lucid argument.

In the last few years prototype expert systems have scored a number of successes. The first was probably 'Heuristic Dendral' which as early as 1965 deduced molecular structure from a mass spectrogram and other experimental data. 'Mycin' was a medical expert system developed in 1975 which outperformed medical practitioners in its limited field of diagnosis and prognosis. Even more impressive was the performance of 'Prospector' an expert system which predicted the existence of a large deposit of molybdenum at a previously unsuspected site. The 'RI' system used by DEC to configure VAX computers automatically, in response to customer requirements, is said to have made (or saved) millions of pounds already. It has certainly stimulated the other main computer hardware companies to develop their own expert systems for similar purposes. Other systems have independently rediscovered most of the main results in certain branches of mathematics including number theory, Euclidean geometry and differential calculus.

In practice a major difficulty in developing systems is the so-called 'knowledge engineering' aspect. The art of identifying and extracting the knowledge of a human expert turns out to be surprisingly difficult in disciplines less theoretical than pure mathematics.

Typically a user will interact with the expert system in much the same way as people interact with human experts. The user states an objective and the expert system asks pertinent questions. Depending upon the answers provided the system will ask further questions until it has reached a conclusion. It will then be able to provide an answer along with a justification for that answer. A true expert system will even be able to make educated guesses when the available data is incomplete or imprecise; and a really sophisticated expert system will also be able to reason at a meta level. In other words it will be able to analyse its own reasoning processes and change them if it sees fit, if for example its initial approach does not prove fruitful. Systems which have expertise in more than one field will become invaluable when we become accustomed to asking them questions such as: Why does my back ache? Why won't the car start? How much tax should I pay this year? What is the best way to drive to Harpenden? How does a gyroscope work? What do these local government regulations really mean?

Because of advances in chip technology and developments in ai, expert systems will certainly become popular; but other factors will play important roles in enabling such expert systems to gain widespread acceptability. For one thing these systems will be much more user-friendly than the software to which we have traditionally been accustomed.

Software interfaces will need to be friendlier not only for expert systems but also for simulation and for other applications. In particular, integrated systems which combine simulation with expert systems will need to interact with human users in a friendly manner. The question then arises as to how this interaction might be achieved, in so far as it is dependent upon the system architecture. A number of basic possibilities have been identified which together provide a basic taxonomy for simulation–expert system combinations (see Bibliography—O'Keefe). Three basic combination types are named: Embedded, Parallel and Cooperative. The differences may be illustrated by simple diagrams shown in Fig. 13.2.

S = Simulation software   ES = Expert System software

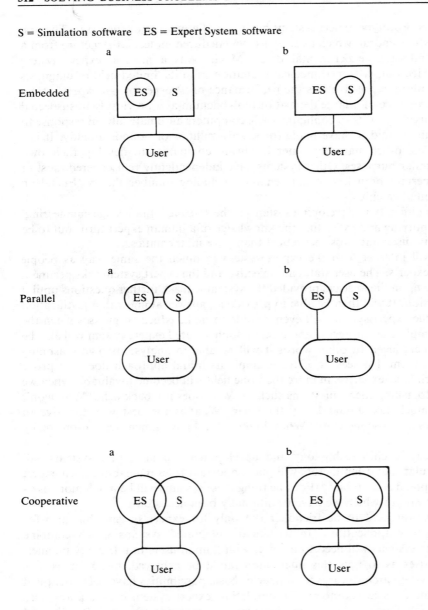

**Figure 13.2**

In addition to these possible combinations an expert system could provide an intelligent front end to a simulation by a configuration topologically identical to that shown in Fig. 13.2, Parallel (b); the operational relationship would however be different.

The pictorial representations are self-explanatory and therefore no further detail is necessary, except for the configuration shown in Fig. 13.2, Cooperative (b). Here cooperating simulation and expert sytems are both embedded in a third software element which handles communications with the user.

Although it is possible to envisage other configurations, the types identified seem to account for the most promising current developments. Of course to the user the expert system would be transparent: he would see only a friendly and helpful user interface.

## Man–machine interfaces

The various media which enable people and computers to communicate with each other are known in the inevitable jargon as Man–Machine Interfaces (MMIs). Conventionally, input has been typed in directly via a keyboard (or indirectly by way of punched cards) while output has been produced in the form of text or graphics, either displayed on a VDU or printed as hard copy. More recently other MMIs have become popular: for example, information may be input by means of a 'mouse', a touch-sensitive screen, or a joystick, and output can be obtained in the form of colour slides or mechanical movement.

Building a simulation model can be made relatively simple by the judicious use of appropriate MMIs. In particular, graphical representations help to validate a model during the development stage, and to interpret results at the end of a simulation run. Statistical analyses of output are easier to comprehend in the form of visual displays of probability density functions. In order to start building a model an ideal medium would be ordinary English language. If the model builder could just describe the system to be simulated in English, rather than a formal programming language, then many of the terrors implicit in model building would vanish.

It is at the development stage that non-expert users need to be able to understand the model under construction. Often they have no interest in computers but do have a keen interest in understanding a complex system and in getting results. They need to see something which is readily comprehensible and clear enough to enable immediate validation, but in order to get the information on to the computer in the first place the user must communicate with it. If the machine could understand ordinary English typescript there would be fewer problems. Natural Language Understanding Systems (NLUSs) enable exactly this sort of communication to take place.

English is a notoriously difficult language to analyse in terms of syntax and grammar, and extensive idiomatic usage complicates matters considerably. The sort of problem to be addressed is neatly encapsulated by a well-known attempt by machine to translate English into Russian and then back into English again. In went the expression 'out of sight, out of mind' and back came the response 'invisible idiot'.

A number of NLUSs are currently under development and their future looks promising. Obviously they are really only specialized applications of artificial intelligence. The understanding of natural language is one of those abilities which superficially appears simple, but upon closer investigation turns out to be astonishingly difficult. Our brains make it seem easy, but only because they are so very clever. So clever in fact that it is only rarely that we become aware of the processes at all: perhaps when we mis-hear a word or notice an ambiguity in what is said. The level of intelligence required is known to be extremely high, and when a NLUS is eventually able to show that it understands natural language as well as we do, then the whole field of artificial intelligence will be accepted as a discipline comparable in size and importance to, say, physics or mathematics.

At the moment the most quickly developing man–machine interface is the familiar VDU. Supplied with high resolution colour graphics and appropriate software, simulation models can be more easily developed, understood and interpreted. Where simulation systems, such as HOCUS, have been used with colour graphics, results have been startling: development times are reduced dramatically because of the useful feedback obtained; non-technical managers are able to understand the model readily (and are therefore more inclined to take notice of it); and meaningful results may be obtained immediately. In practice graphical output is also extremely useful for identifying certain types of error.

In several simulations, problems have been identified which had previously escaped attention in the original model without graphics output. A favourite of this type, easy to see on a graphics display but difficult to deduce otherwise, is the 'deadly embrace' in which activity A is waiting for activity B to stop while activity B is waiting for activity A to stop. Occurring at random times throughout a simulation such deadlocks often go unnoticed without animated graphics output.

It is becoming more and more apparent that the advantages to be obtained from the use of graphics displays are highly significant: not only because of the clarity of exposition, but also because of the resultant close interest shown by non-technical managers and decision makers who are suddenly able to appreciate simulation techniques. In order to capitalize upon this enhanced involvement in the model-building process it is often desirable to design graphical output to mimic the format of existing management information. If performance statistics have customarily been presented to managers in the form of, say, histograms then those managers will be quick to understand performance statistics from a simulation model presented in exactly the same way. Even the smallest variation is a potential cause of confusion.

Using the same graphical representation, modellers are able to develop and validate a simulation model to monitor the simulation in progress, and also interpret the model output. In order to be able to investigate the behaviour of any specific part of the model in detail, sophisticated graphics systems need to take full advantage of windowing facilities along with scrolling and zooming, so that users are able to locate a particular point of interest and observe it in detail. A further useful facility is control over the speed at which the animation runs.

## Modular simulation models

Simulation models which are sufficiently sophisticated to reflect accurately the real world are often large and complex. As a result models tend to be difficult to understand and to explain to others. Furthermore, inconsistencies, omissions and other errors are difficult to detect. One way to minimize these problems is to use a 'top–down' design approach and to ensure that wherever possible the model is built up of discrete modules, any of which may be amended or replaced without confusing the model structure.

To illustrate this approach consider the purchasing function of a typical commercial organization. We may regard 'purchasing' as a single activity in a simple model which is intended to simulate the running of the whole organization. In fact the single activity, 'purchasing', can be broken down into more basic activities which might be classified as follows:

– Order goods
– Check receipt of goods
– Pay for goods

Each of these sub-activities can in turn be broken down, perhaps as follows.

### Order goods

– raise requisition;
– authorize requisition;
– raise purchase order from requisition and price list;
– authorize purchase order;
– dispatch purchase order copy;
– file copy of purchase order in 'orders outstanding' file.

### Check receipt of goods

– Check quantity and type against copy purchase order;
– inspect goods for breakages, etc.;
– raise 'Goods Received Note' (GRN);
– file purchase order and GRN awaiting arrival of invoice.

### Pay for goods

– match invoice against purchase order/GRN;
– raise and authorize cheque;
– make appropriate accounting entries;
– dispatch cheque to supplier.

Clearly it would be possible to break down these functions even further if more detail was required. Also this rather simplistic model would in practice be complicated by problems in real life; a more sophisticated model would need to allow for the activities necessary when faulty goods are delivered or there are discrepancies between the supplier's delivery note and GRN, or between the GRN and copy purchase orders, or between the copy purchase order and corresponding invoice. The position may also be complicated by other factors such as seasonal demand, discounts available, absence of authorized cheque signatories, previous payments on account, hire purchase arrangements, etc.

Sticking to the simplistic model where everything is assumed to go well, and concentrating upon the roles of the purchase order, goods received note, and invoice, the function 'purchase goods' is an activity which, forming part of an activity cycle diagram, might be shown as in Fig. 13.3.

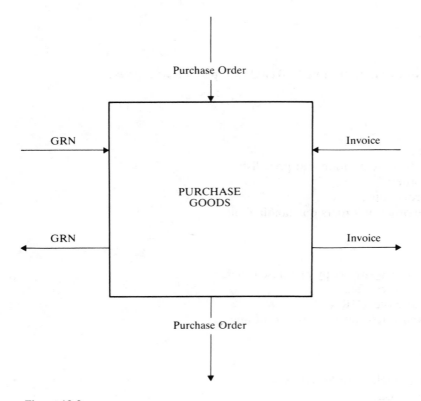

**Figure 13.3**

Treating the activity 'purchase goods' as a module we may depict it as a collection of sub-activities. Notice that the entity inputs and outputs to the module are unchanged, although it is now possible to see what is happening to the entities internally (Fig. 13.4).

At a lower level it is possible to treat any of these three sub-activities as a separate module. Taking, for example, the 'pay for goods' sub-activity, and noting that it is permissible to introduce new and purely internal activities and entities the module may be expanded as in Fig. 13.5.

Again, the expanded module has exactly the same inputs and outputs as the original sub-activity 'pay for goods'. However, the added information reflects the finer detail of what happens; in particular it is apparent that processing invoices may be delayed because the clerk responsible has other duties to perform (preparing the payroll).

Extremely complicated modules can be built up by successively breaking down activities in this way. The requirement that entity inputs and outputs be conserved means that detailed versions of the whole model can be created simply by substituting the fine detail sub-modules for their equivalent 'activities' in the next stage up in the diagram hierarchy.

The nesting approach to the design of complex systems has long been used in the world of

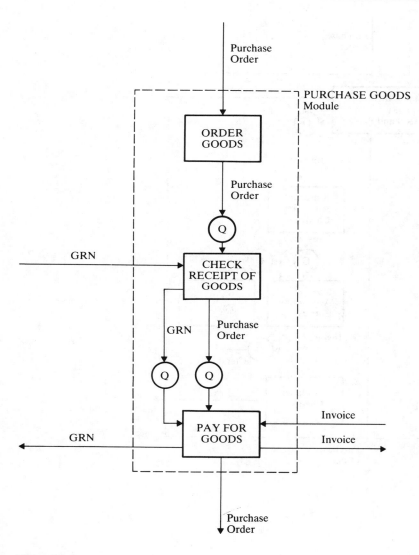

**Figure 13.4**

computing (notably in activity diagrams), but it is only now starting to be widely used in the development of simulation models.

In certain types of application it is likely that the most basic activities will occur repeatedly in a number of different simulations. In such cases it would make sense to use standard activities: pre-written activities which could perhaps be bought off the shelf as development tools. The advantages would be much the same as the advantages of conventional software development tools: speed of development, ease of use and reliability.

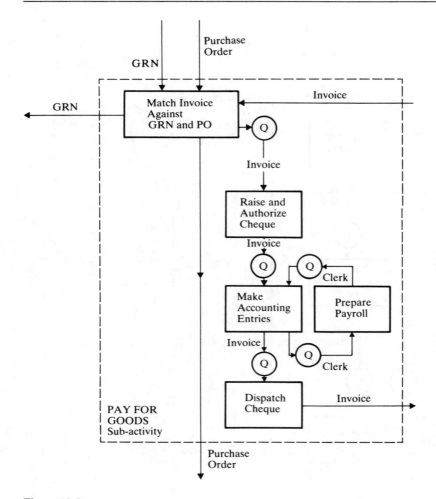

**Figure 13.5**

Certain industries (cigarette manufacture for example) rely upon a small range of different types of machine. Five or six standard activity modules could therefore usefully serve in any one of a large number of possible simulation models for any one of hundreds of different factories.

It is not difficult to foresee enormous possibilities. With supply stimulating demand, as it almost invariably seems to do in the world of computing, more and more basic modelling units will become available. The most basic units could be combined to produce larger standard modules which could also be used repeatedly in many different models. Eventually it could be possible to build a sophisticated model for certain applications in a matter of minutes, simply by assembling pre-produced sub-modules. Even graphical output options could be built into such standard modules in order to enable visual interactive simulations to be created quickly and easily.

As might be expected, this is an area in which considerable research and development is currently taking place. There is a long way to go before the potential of modular simulation models can be fully realized, but as an example we shall describe some preliminary work in the field of Advanced Manufacturing Technology (AMT).

AMT is an area which is particularly well suited to the use of modular simulation because of the degree of generalization built into such systems. The particular area to which a modular approach has been applied is to the production of Flexible Manufacturing Systems (FMS). Flexible manufacturing systems are characterized by some, or all, of the following features: computer controlled machines, automatic materials handling (robotics, wire-guided vehicles, etc.), overall control of the manufacturing process, and the ability to deal with a range of components being processed either sequentially or in parallel. Work at present is being concentrated on specifying the key characteristics which are needed to provide accurate yet simple simulations of such systems.

One current system handles the supply of a pre-defined production schedule to a system. Each batch comprises a number of items with a specified parts list. Each part follows a particular route through the machine shop to be completed. A number of different processes may be performed on each part, and each process can be performed by a number of machines (if required). On each machine, tool-life is monitored, and appropriate action taken when the end of the life is reached.

Transfers between machines can occur in one of two ways. The simpler method requires that the transfer takes a fixed time which depends upon which transfer is taking place. Although simple, this approach can sometimes give surprisingly accurate answers, and can be used to give a preliminary indication of sensitive areas. The other method of transfer is by means of Automated Guided Vehicle (AGV). An arbitrary number of these vehicles run along a network of connections between machines and perform transfers of work pieces. The traverse time of a particular section of track is defined. The AGVs receive tasks to perform from a central controller (such as 'take pallet 91 from workstation 4 to workstation 5'), and are left to get on with their task.

A simulation model to describe this sort of system can require hundreds of activities and queues, and can become extremely complex. There is currently a system which can interactively take an engineer's description of the system to be modelled (in terms of schedules, process plans for each part, machine numbers and types, AGV numbers, track layouts, etc.) and create a HOCUS model which simulates the system defined by the engineer. Although this system is in its infancy a number of the key elements are already in place:

- Information meaningful to an engineer is all that is required to generate the model *automatically*.
- The definition of the system can be changed interactively.
- The individual elements are modelled by use of parameterized building blocks.

The model generates pre-defined modifiable graphics displays and tailored reports automatically.

There are still a number of developments in the modelling of FMS which remain to be completed. The first is the incorporation of production scheduling algorithms into the model; the second is the definition of AGV controlling logic.

Although apparently very different areas, they are both manifestations of an underlying difficulty—the simplification or specification of extremely complex logic. One way of addressing this difficulty is to provide an interface for the model to the actual algorithms in use; another way is to simplify the logic to something which can be handled within the context of a larger simulation.

Both methods have been used to good effect, but it is the authors' opinion that a fundamental change in technique must be made in this area before a really satisfactory method is obtained.

Another difficulty in modular simulation of FMS is an old problem magnified by the complexity of the simulation required—validation of the model. Whole books have been written on the subject of validation of software, and techniques applied formally in the development of software should be applicable to the development of simulation models.

## Viable applications

Applications of interactive models are legion, as indeed are the benefits. Didactic simulation models enable difficult jobs to be learned without the usual attendant dangers and also without the high costs often involved. Such models, along the lines of flight simulators, enable people to develop new skills and to practise existing ones.

They also provide an ideal vehicle for assessing progress and testing reactions to new and unexpected situations. One of the greatest advantages lies in the potential for examining reactions to unusual conditions—conditions which quite often could not be duplicated in the real world without risking the loss of life or the destruction of expensive equipment, or which because of the very nature of things cannot be deliberately duplicated at all. It would be difficult to arrange for two selected galaxies to collide, but relatively easy to simulate such a collision.

On a more mundane level the use of simulation will undoubtedly become more widespread in industry during the next few years. Areas such as risk analysis, capital budgeting, factory design, distribution and production control, as well as Flexible Manufacturing Systems (FMS), and Advanced Manufacturing Technology (AMT) all provide vast scope for new developments.

Figure 13.6 illustrates how various aspects of Computer Integrated Manufacture (CIM) fit together. Notice that the whole system may be 'real' or simulated, or a mix between the two.

Simulation models do not necessarily need to imitate man-made systems. They might just as easily mimic natural forces. Again, the range of possibilities is staggering. We could improve upon existing methods of weather forecasting (and more importantly perhaps be able to investigate the likely changes in climatic conditions on a global scale). We could build models to simulate local or world-wide agricultural trends, or projected population variations. We could even create a model to simulate developments in world economies. But more impressive still simulation models such as these could be interconnected. The output from one

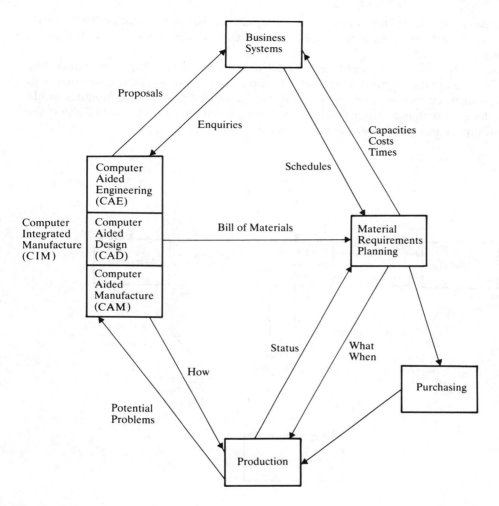

**Figure 13.6**

model could provide the input for another. Complex interactions in the real world could be realistically mirrored by a series of interdependent simulation models, possibly residing on remote systems, but networked together to provide a single super-model.

Clearly there exists an intimate and complicated interdependency between global climatic conditions, local weather, agricultural yields, population fluctuations and macro economic phenomena. Existing simplistic models are not sophisticated enough to allow for the delicate interplay of all factors involved, but the time is not far off when a satisfactory super-model could be created.

A super-model such as this might incorporate a huge number of interdependent sub-models, each of which is perhaps itself an amalgamation of smaller simpler models. A convincing demonstration of the international ecological consequences resulting from a single local event, such as the removal of rain forest, might then justifiably concentrate a few minds in high places.

On a smaller scale we might imagine a model used to simulate a single manufacturing business. One simulation might deal specifically with the purchasing function, another with production and stock control, and another with marketing and sales. These modules would interact with each other and perhaps with a cash management module. Figure 13.7 shows the interplay of inputs and outputs within such a system.

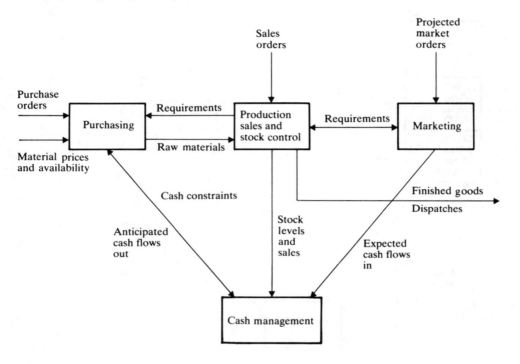

**Figure 13.7**

Consider the purchasing module. Input to this sub-model includes purchase order arrivals, projected material prices and availability forecasts (possibly incorporating a stochastic element). Also input are the projected raw material requirements generated by the production and stock control module. Cash requirements are shown in addition, since cash flow problems would eventually affect the purchasing function.

In practice composite models such as the one for the manufacturing business shown in Fig. 13.7 would be highly complex. This example shows how a number of models may be bolted together. Obviously this whole model could subsequently be built into an even larger one. Perhaps the company buys a second factory. In this case a similar composite model would be used for that. Suppose that the purchasing, production and sales functions were to be operated independently, while the cash management function was centralized. In this case the two models could be merged together to form a larger model for the new configuration. Larger and larger models could be formed by incorporating more and more subsystems. Theoretically there is no reason why models for all such companies should not be coupled together in order, for example, to investigate projected total market demand for raw materials.

Certainly simulation modules can be used as building blocks, but the possibilities are still more extensive. As has already been mentioned other types of software can be accommodated in, or associated with, simulation models as well as expert system user-friendly interfaces and program generators. For many purposes it would be useful to interface operational business software with a simulation model, in order to generate business predictions as early as possible. Using current technology it is easy to foresee a fully robotic factory with integrated software to control and record actual performance and to project future performance by means of a sophisticated simulation model.

Applications which predict the future are often described as Decision Support Systems (DSSs). Their purpose is to provide managers with information upon which to base important decisions. They improve immeasurably the quality of management information available, and enable various options to be explored before an irrevocable decision is made. Merging together computing and management science these DSSs include facilities such as financial models, spreadsheets, fourth generation database management languages, natural language query systems and communications links, all used to enhance managerial productivity. Features which typically characterize them as DSSs include truly interactive operation, supporting utilities such as fault handling, 'what if . . .' facilities, dynamic data management, dynamic colour displays and performance measurement.

Although the vogue expression Decision Support System, and its inevitable acronym DSS, is relatively new, the concept is not. Indeed simulation in the broadest sense has always been a useful support for decision making, even before the advent of the age of electronic computers. Simulations occupy a wide spectrum on a continuum of abstract models of reality used for decision making. Maps are cartographical simulations of geographical reality; mathematical models are theoretical simulations of the physical world; and paintings are pictorial simulations of that same physical world.

Computing is very much a fashion industry and like all fashion industries it is fickle. Salesmen and popular newspapers give grossly distorted views of the true developments and underlying trends. Nevertheless DSSs do have much to commend them, even if it is only that potential users might be encouraged by their stated object of being practical and user-friendly. Decision support systems are intended to give non-technical managers direct access to corporate information held on databases in such a way that they can analyse and display it in order to make decisions. Clearly not all DSSs are simulation models, nor is it true that all simulation models need be DSSs in the restricted technical sense. Nevertheless the area of overlap is great; and if managers who were scared of 'simulation' can be persuaded to accept it under the name of a DSS then everyone will benefit.

# 14.

## Future developments

It is difficult to measure the rate of technological advance using any objective method. Nevertheless it is apparent that scientific and technical disciplines are yielding new knowledge at a rate unparalleled throughout history. Furthermore, it is intuitively apparent that the rate of development is, if anything, increasing.

Since by their nature future discoveries cannot be predicted, nor therefore can their implications be foreseen, it is clearly impossible to foretell what might be possible even ten years from now. As we are becoming conversant with the implications of converging technologies we can sense only vaguely how different the Western world will be for its inhabitants in the next generation.

In this chapter we shall consider some of the possibilities suggested by the course of current research. Which of these possibilities will produce results in the near future, and which are destined to prove false dreams, we shall not know until our speculation has passed into history. Even so it will be surprising if the advances are less spectacular than those envisaged here.

Before dealing with some of the areas which are likely to provide the most dramatic advances it is worth noting that, even with existing technology, simulation systems which are much more sophisticated than any existing system can be envisaged. The following desirable features might be used as a basis for specifying an improved simulation system. It should:

- be suitable for a wide range of problems;
- be easily portable and available on a wide range of machines and operating systems;
- be reliable;
- be cheap to buy;
- be cheap to run;
- be easy to learn;
- employ a very high level fourth generation language to enable new facilities to be introduced;
- require no knowledge of conventional computer languages;
- be user-friendly;
- be easy to integrate with real-life control systems;
- employ screen input validation (for example checking completeness of activity cycles);
- offer built-in debugging facilities including trace capability;
- employ animated high resolution interactive colour graphics with variable animation display speed;
- offer alternative graphical representations (activity cycle diagrams and mimic diagrams);
- employ similar graphic displays for development, running and presentation of results;

- allow users to scroll around the model on screen and to zoom in on selected parts;
- encourage structured top–down design through modularity (possibly with the same module structure used for development and zooming);
- be easy to bolt together with other systems to provide larger integrated models;
- provide statistical facilities for multiple runs, including calculation of means and variances of output measurements (and reduction of confidence intervals to required sizes);
- provide identification of any initial transient period before a steady state is achieved;
- enable breakpoints to be set in order to allow models to proceed repeatedly from specified decision points.

These features are already established although no single simulation package currently provides all of them. Perhaps it would be sensible to develop better systems with more extensive use of these facilities before attempting to build in artificial intelligence or any of the other advances which are looming on the horizon.

## Biotechnology

Biotechnology is likely to provide entirely new capabilities along the path to at least one objective: a computer whose components are interacting three-dimensional arrays of atomic particles. In the short term it is not possible to see how atoms or even molecules could be harnessed for deterministic computing. On the other hand it is well known that protein molecules are able to assemble themselves into pre-determined structures. Instead of crystallizing into potentially infinite arrays as most molecules do, protein molecules form structures of a certain size and shape. Why should new proteins not be designed to assemble themselves into useful biochip structures? One reason is that at the time of writing we are not yet able to produce an organic transistor or logic gate which could be incorporated into such a structure. Yet the problem is almost certainly not insurmountable and the next question will be how to create a sort of viral biocomputer capable of replicating itself in order to form a single supercomputer. The trouble is that biotechnology is such a new discipline that it is not possible as yet to grasp the potentialities opening up. As a first step some firms in the US are attempting to modify naturally occurring proteins in relatively simple ways; for example, by changing a single amino acid.

On another track, it might be possible to gain an insight into alternative methods of information processing by studying the workings of animal central nervous systems. The primary problem is to unravel the complexities of the processes involved; once understood the same methods could be employed in the design of a new generation of computers. Certainly the human brain is capable of much more subtle thought than any computer so far developed. Any 'program' that it uses is very different from the primitive programs written in conventional computer languages. The brain does not process instructions serially; instead it somehow operates upon itself forming and re-forming synapse connections. Each of the 10 billion or so neurons in the human brain connects with up to 10 000 other neurons, and combinations of these connections are responsible for our every thought through the complicated interaction of electrochemical stimuli. Nevertheless, the brain is only a physical organ and if we knew exactly how it worked then we could duplicate the principles involved. It is only a matter of time before we are able to build a primitive brain operating on the same organic principles. Then the race will be on to build one which is bigger in terms of intellectual power, smaller in size and cheap enough to be marketable.

An encouraging indicator is provided by the comparison of communication speeds within electrical computers and organic brains. A transistor in a microprocessor can change state (on–off) in a few millionths of a millionth of a second: but it takes neurons around one-millionth of a second to generate an electrical pulse. In other words the brain's components work over 100 000 times more slowly than those of a computer. It is the brain's massive parallel processing capacity that makes it so powerful. There seems to be no rational reason why it should not be possible to combine the best features of both systems with electrical circuits simulating the structure of the brain.

## Voice recognition

Some advances in Natural Language Understanding Systems (NLUSs) have already been mentioned in Chapter 13, where some of the problems inherent in the interpretation of written English text were addressed. Here the more advanced problem of interpreting human speech will be considered.

The process of understanding spoken language can be divided into two parts. First, it is necessary to determine what the words are, and secondly, to determine what they mean in their current context. Actually this distinction between the two functions is rather artificial. Our brains do not make the distinction since they interpret (and sometimes distort) what is heard in the light of information already processed.

If the topic is 'shoes' then a foot is the thing at the end of a leg, but if the topic is 'distance' then a foot is 12 inches. A little thought will reveal a number of other potential pitfalls which may result from subtleties of language such as intonation and accent, of the use of irony, hyperbole, metaphor, metonymy and other figures of speech.

Researchers are already clocking up successes in voice recognition systems. Clearly an expert system which could understand spoken language would provide an ideal vehicle for communicating with machines. Such a vehicle is simply another example of a Man–Machine Interface (MMI). Development programmes are well under way throughout the world.

Many experts are predicting that elementary 'talkwriters' will be commercially available before the end of the decade. A talkwriter will interpret ordinary human speech and write it down as conventional text—just like a conventional stenographer or audio-typist. In order to write down reliable sentences it will be necessary for the talkwriter to 'understand' what it is hearing and writing. At the moment prototype systems are limited: either they will recognize only a small number of words spoken in a wide range of accents and with a wide range of intonations, or they will recognize a large number of words spoken by a small number of specific people. In order to qualify as a truly friendly man–machine interface, a talkwriter (or more generally a talkinterpreter) will need to be able to understand a wide range of accents, dialects, intonations and idiosyncracies, and will also need an extensive vocabulary.

A friendly MMI will ensure acceptability even for first-time computer users, and in particular voice recognition will enable anyone to develop a simulation model. In order to communicate with the system a user will need only to speak to it. There will be no need for a keyboard, light pen, touch-sensitive screen, or even a mouse. If the user wants to specify any of the simulation parameters he will be able simply to tell the computer what he wants.

Instructions such as 'arrivals at queue number 1 are to be exponentially distributed with mean inter-arrival time 3 minutes' or 'double the capacity of machine X' will be acted upon automatically.

The voice recognition unit will analyse the speech patterns to discern the meaning of the instruction given, and this will then be translated for the simulation software to understand. There will be no need for the user to know anything about computers or computer languages.

Voice recognition systems are in fact already enjoying considerable success, although they are still expensive and there is scope for considerable improvement.

## Visual interactive simulation

Graphic output is easy to assimilate when displayed using high resolution animated colour graphics generated in real time. Although interactive simulation is already a reality, the opportunities provided by future developments will enhance the technique beyond recognition.

The model, or a selected part of it, will be available for immediate inspection using high resolution graphics. Any one of a number of representations is possible, from a logical presentation characterized by an activity cycle diagram all the way to a mimic diagram or animated cartoon presentation. Calling upon a library of established icons and routines the user, or an expert-system aid, will be able to design and format the sort of display required. Implicit conventions are already being established concerning the colour coding of icons to denote their operational status.

One area in which standards could usefully be established is the interpretation of real-time visual animation. There are a number of ways in which such animations could be choreographed. At one extreme the animation could be moved along in discontinuous discrete time intervals reflecting the model processing and at the other it could be scaled to provide a condensed (or expanded) version of the simulated elapsed time.

Here it is necessary to know how long each phase of processing and animation will take in order to ensure a suitable scaling for time intervals. The visual animation must not be left waiting for processing to be completed at any stage. This would suggest that it is necessary to establish the time taken for processing and animating each phase before the simulation is run. In order to employ scaled time animation then it will be necessary either to drop the real-time requirement, or else to arrange that processing and display times be negligible. In the latter case the actual running of the model could be deliberately slowed down to reflect the nominal time elapses, while still permitting real-time interaction. For the moment it will be safe to assume that real-time interaction with colour graphics will become commonplace, with or without time scaling.

Imagine a model which is simulating the production of widgets. A new type of machine is to be introduced and the question is how many such new machines will be needed to maintain present production levels. The simulation model will display on the screen a representation of the machines needed and their relationship with other elements of the model, including perhaps the raw materials being converted into the end product. By asking the model to allow for, say, a set rate of random machine failure it will immediately be possible to observe the effect upon the system. In this way the interrelationships between the various elements of the model are made clear. If queues are seen to build up the user may simply ask for another machine, or may investigate the effect of improving maintenance procedures. Again, the effect will be immediately visible. Output which can be readily assimilated has another advantage: unexpected behaviour can be monitored and explained. Sometimes this will reveal aspects of the systems which had been misunderstood or not considered at all, sometimes it will reveal a fundamental error in the model itself. Such output therefore provides a useful diagnostic facility. Animated graphics also make it easy to monitor warm-up periods, and to assess when a system has reached equilibrium by settling into a steady state.

Traditionally computer modelling, including simulation, has been considered to be a fundamentally simple concept, illustrated in Fig. 14.1.

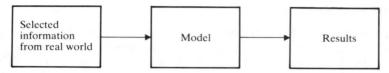

**Figure 14.1**

As long as the problem is tractable in the first place, and as long as the selected information from the real world is adequate, then a satisfactory model will provide a solution. For expert modellers this has proved to be acceptable enough, but in order that less sophisticated users should be able to employ the technique it is necessary for them quickly and easily to interpret the output from the model which they have created. In other words the development process itself requires an element of feedback. Diagrammatically this feedback mechanism is illustrated in Fig. 14.2. Refining input as a consequence of output results is a useful technique even for expert modellers, and has been advocated throughout this book.

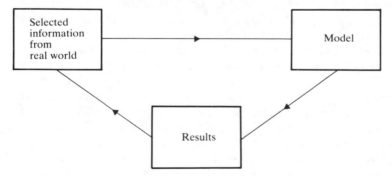

**Figure 14.2**

Interactive simulation models incorporating feedback are likely to benefit from employing the same representation on the same input/output medium as used in creating the model in the first place. A user who has set up a representation of his model will more easily understand model behaviour which is reflected on that same representation.

Traditionally, expert modellers have had to provide a manual feedback by translating model output for the real-world decision maker. Visual interactive simulation can be expected to change all that: the modeller and decision maker will be able to sit at the same terminal and develop the model together, agreeing upon refinements as the model representation takes shape before them in a much contracted timescale.

Sooner or later the services of an expert modeller will inevitably become superfluous. Looking to the future it is possible to conceive of a functional model of a whole factory, created in miniature by computer controlled holograms or automated small-scale physical models. Factory simulations could be made as realistic as, say, existing flight simulations. Games such as Dungeons and Dragons could become so realistic that some individuals may be in even more danger of losing the ability to distinguish between the real world and the artificial world of computer simulation.

In order to save time, holograms of real objects could be created (presumably with much less trouble than is usually involved at the moment) and scaled in magnitude for use in the simulation model. With instant three-dimensional icons, which can be manipulated with the full six degrees of freedom in 3-D space, we shall be in the rarefied atmosphere of a Real Time 3-D Visual Interactive Simulation environment. When that time comes we shall no doubt find it necessary to invent a suitable acronym but for the moment we can get by easily enough with simple VIS (Visual Interactive Simulation) in two dimensions.

VIS is, of course, a special application of Visual Interactive Modelling, an area of interest already sufficiently well established to warrant its own acronym: VIM.

## Fifth generation developments

Fifth generation computing languages are only one aspect of the advances falling within the scope of fifth generation developments.

Some of the developments and possibilities already mentioned in Chapter 13 are basic elements of so-called fifth generation computer systems. In particular the elements generally identified with the fifth generation are:

MMI *Man–Machine Interface* allowing user-friendly interaction by natural written language, speech and pictures.

ES *Expert Systems* applying artifical intelligence techniques to knowledge bases (also known as Intelligent Knowledge Based Systems (IKBSs)).

VLSI *Very Large Scale Integration* concentrating new, cheap processing power into smaller physical units.

Fifth generation machines will need to support very large knowledge bases, allow logical inference options to be executed quickly, utilize parallelism in hardware and software, and provide a reliable, easy to use machine–user interface. They may employ architectures based upon Josephson-junction or gallium arsenide technologies, or upon technologies yet to be developed. Research is being funded by national governments and international agencies. Among the research programmes are Icot in Japan, Alvey in the UK, the MCC and Darpa projects in the US, and Esprit which is supported by the EEC.

How these elements can be combined is illustrated in Fig. 14.3. This diagram is intended to demonstrate that a number of convergent advanced technological innovations can together produce advances which to the user are more significant than the sum of the individual innovations involved.

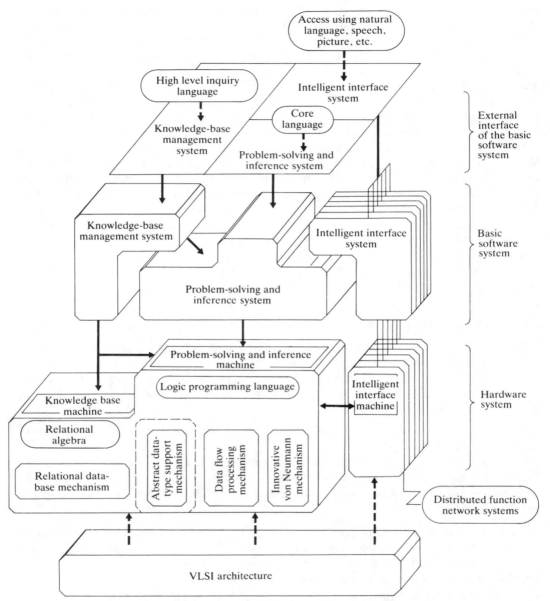

**Figure 14.3** (*Source*: Minutes of International Conference on Fifth-Generation Computer Systems, 19–22 October 1981, JIPDEC.)

As far as the subject of simulation is concerned there are many possible applications of fifth generation systems, and especially for expert systems. It is possible to envisage expert systems being used to validate models, to run the simulation model itself and to communicate with users.

## Intelligent simulation program generators

From what has already been said it is clear that the time is not far off when more sophisticated simulation program generators will reduce development time by another order of magnitude so that a single person will be able to produce large suites of reliable programs within a few weeks or even days. Almost anyone will be able to build a complex simulation model in a short space of time, even without significant training. Input times will be reduced by a user-friendly interface, programming will be simplified by simulation program generators and error identification will be made easy by the use of ever more sophisticated animated colour graphics. Models can then be refined interactively in real time. An animated pictorial representation of the model will allow everyone concerned, whether technical or not, to enter into discussion about the model and to confirm the model's accuracy. This is a very important feature because, for simulation models to be accepted, not only must they be correct but also they need to be seen to be correct. Otherwise non-technical managers have to rely upon a 'black box' providing answers which they are unlikely to trust. The more comprehensible a model is, the better.

All of this is now familiar territory, as is the concept of an expert system; but by bringing together simulation program generators and expert systems it is possible to conceive of a new hybrid: an Intelligent Simulation Program Generator (ISPG).

An intelligent simulation program generator would in essence fulfil the role of present-day human experts who write simulation applications and apply them to specific problems. The ISPG would interact with the user, employing user-friendly human interface mechanisms such as real-time interactive colour graphics, to create a simulation program uniquely appropriate for the specific problem under consideration.

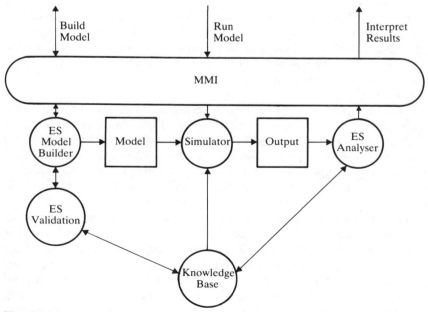

**Figure 14.4**

Such an approach would have a number of advantages: untrained users could build sophisticated models (or rather the ISPG could with help from the user); logical errors and omissions could be spotted, and automatically corrected at an early stage, by the ISPG; and all this would occupy only as much time as it takes for the user to respond to the ISPG's questions about the fundamental entities and attributes.

With the built-in experience of any number of human experts, and the intelligence to employ it sensibly, ISPGs threaten to make traditional simulation experts obsolescent. In the meanwhile human beings will need to build simulation models and interpret their results. Figure 14.4 shows how an ISPG will interact with human users.

## Networks and communications

Imagine the effect of communications links so extensive that any one system within a network may, for a price, access sophisticated simulation systems as well as information and conventional software on any one of a hundred, or a thousand, or ten thousand other machines.

The ability to distribute software is increasing rapidly. Facilities for networking micro-computers are becoming ever more commonplace. As with other facets of technology, standards are being established, prices are coming down, and users are learning about new possibilities. With a combination of Wide Area Networks, Local Area Networks and telephone dial-up facilities it will not be long before every user has access to undreamed of quantities of software even through a conventional telephone line. Distributed database technology is in its infancy, but the concept of a distributed simulation model, with its modules located and maintained separately around the world, might perhaps be feasible. This could even be the route to the super-model discussed in Chapter 13. Value Added Networks are already in place, offering worldwide access to information and services. Of course such software will have to be written by someone, but a new computer-literate generation is already entering industry; and the range and sophistication of software tools available to them is constantly expanding.

In addition to conventional electronic forms of data transmission, media through which information can be speedily transmitted include short-wave and microwave radiation, laser beams and optical fibre—the latter two having the great advantage of not being liable to electromagnetic interference. This is one reason for the increasing interest in creating optical computers which will depend not upon electron but photon movements. If it does nothing else, America's Strategic Defence Initiative (SDI or 'Star Wars') is at least likely to move the relevant technology along considerably within the next few years.

One further development which may also prove significant is the microcomputer packed into a small item such as a credit card. Such a combination, known as a 'smart card', is already being used in France and is expected to be widely available before the end of the 1980s. Smart cards could be plugged into a wide selection of everyday equipment to provide suitable user interfaces: a televison for colour displays; an electronic typewriter for input; and an ordinary telephone for communications. Furnished with sufficient memory and processing power a smart card could provide an easily portable computer system with numerous applications, one of which could very well be a complete simulation package for instant use.

## Possible applications

One use for simulation in the future is the investigation of major disasters. By mimicking in sufficient detail the conditions prevailing at the time of a catastrophe it may be possible to identify its cause. This may sound rather like shutting the door after the horse has bolted, but it may prevent another horse escaping. NASA have in fact pioneered this diagnostic technique in the wake of the 1986 shuttle disaster: different theories about the cause of the explosion were tested by simulating the hypothetical system failures and comparing simulated and observed results.

Another use for simulation which is only just in the first stages of development is in evolutionary modelling. By simulating random mutations in populations of organisms and applying evolutionary pressures it may be possible to learn more about the development of life on earth. Certainly the technique has already shown the relative merits of aggressive and submissive behaviour between members of the same species.

More intriguing is the possibility that simulation can be used for the design of very complicated equipment. If evolutionary pressure can create such an efficient bird wing for example, then why should not simulated evolutionary pressure create an efficient aeroplane wing. All that is necessary is to simulate an obstruction in a fluid flow: by making random changes to the shape of the obstruction, and selecting for those which improve lift while reducing drag, the obstruction will mutate into a wing and will eventually settle down to an optimal design for the given constraints. Obviously the technique is not limited to designing aerofoils: the same idea could be used to generate improved bridges, motor vehicles, houses, ships or manufacturing processes. The list is endless.

Even without simulated evolution, there are enormous possibilities for simulation in manufacturing. It is possible to envisage flexible manufacturing systems (FMS) with robotic capabilities under the control of a single central processor. The system would control, monitor and record performance, schedule throughput, manage work in progress and inventory, and update the accounting records. As well as producing historical results the system could project future performance. Taking into account known existing parameters such as stock levels, machine failures and manning levels a simulation model could be used to investigate likely future production. The output from a large number of stochastic simulation runs may then be used as the input for a statistical software package. In this way it is possible to obtain probability density functions for output variables and hence perform risk and sensitivity analysis. Input parameters can be changed in order to test alternative manufacturing strategies. This sort of analysis does not of course require any further advances in technology: the method has been established for years. It is the ability to interface the various software modules that offers exciting new possibilities.

In order to appreciate the revolutionary significance of the modelling aids currently under development, it will be instructive here to take a look into the future. Imagine the production and stock control module of the hypothetical factory model already mentioned. As we envisaged it before it is part of a larger model: its outputs are used by other models and some of its inputs are generated by other modules. Some inputs are provided by the system which controls and monitors the real factory, and of course the user will be responsible for providing other inputs. In fact the user will have ultimate control over all input variables since hypothetical simulation runs may be useful even if they are not immediately relevant to the existing conditions.

The user's instructions are communicated to the system by some conventional input device or by a voice recognition unit. A typical instruction might be: 'Simulate production over the next month assuming that the production manager is on holiday this week and that the new type X machine is ready by next Tuesday.' An expert system input checker will ensure that the instructions are understood, and if they are not it might ask for clarification. By writing to the screen or perhaps by using a speech synthesizer the system might ask: 'Does that mean that the production manager will be back on Monday morning at the usual time?' A prudent system might well check that the user and the system had in mind the same date and might even name the manager involved. Information such as this would be 'known' to the system through knowledge bases and databases. Once the system thought it had all the information required it would start processing.

Processing times would be negligible although the output could be slowed down and displayed graphically to enable the user to concentrate upon any selected part of the model. By watching animated colour graphics displays users could make on-the-spot decisions in real time which would redirect the subsequent course of the simulation run. Suppose that stock levels appear to be unnecessarily high: the user asks 'Why are we stocking so many finished goods?' After checking with the other modules the system might answer 'Half of the stock shown is obsolete and ought to be reprocessed, and also we need higher than usual stock levels because we are anticipating unusually high demand next month' (one can almost imagine it continuing 'I've told you about that obsolete stock before').

If the user wanted to pursue this he might say 'All right, show the obsolete stock separately and let me see what happens if the advertising campaign is only 50 per cent effective'. The model is changed interactively in real time, and the user sits back to watch the inventory fluctuations in the new presentation and under the new assumptions.

The physical size of the equipment needed to run a system such as this will be limited only by the user interfaces. One can imagine a lightweight flat screen, voice recognition and synthesizer units, and perhaps a range of other devices fitting easily into an executive case. Although the processing power and storage capacities necessary for the whole model will be accommodated in a few cubic centimetres, it may still be necessary for the portable system to communicate with a central unit in order to ensure that all users have access to the latest version of the common knowledge base. Presumably such communication will in the future be possible without the need for physical connection. A medium such as radio transmission might furnish a convenient method of remote communication.

## Finale

In practical terms many of the developments discussed here have been of a speculative nature—but the ideas are not unreasonable, and new advances are being made every day.

Revolutionary advances in technology could be announced at any time in any of a number of fields. Any one of these advances will mean additional scope for more powerful and desirable simulation models.

It will be fascinating to review progress in five years' time. In the meantime for those who are faced with real and pressing complex problems, the practical techniques described in the first four parts of this book show you how to get solutions today.

# Part Six
## Case studies

In this book we describe a method for building simulation models which are accurate, acceptable to management and produced quickly. The approach has been used to solve many hundreds of problems in industry and government, and we illustrate its use with six case studies.

Each has been written by those who carried out the project. They describe their method and experiences, and give a measure of the effort involved and benefits achieved.

At the end of each case study we have written a few comments which highlight the main features of the study.

# Case Study 1.

## Improving safety at sea

*by* **Neil Teller**
*International Maritime Satellite Organization (INMARSAT)*

### Summary

The International Maritime Satellite Organization (INMARSAT) operates a telecommunications network for ships at sea on behalf of its member countries. A simulation model was built to enable the London-based directorate of the Organization to study the effect of growth and technical change in the network. A consultant was used to build the model because the speed of obtaining results and the benefits of exposing INMARSAT staff to a skilled model builder were judged to be of prime importance. The benefits of expert assistance were immediately apparent and appreciated at all levels.

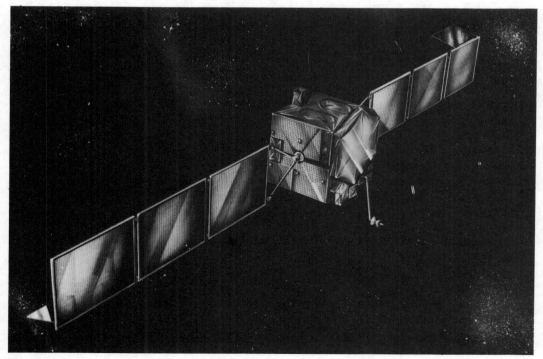

**Figure C1.1**

## Background

INMARSAT's defined purpose is to provide the space segment for global maritime satellite communications, 'thereby assisting in improving distress and safety of life at sea communications, efficiency and management of ship, maritime public correspondence service and radio-determination (position fixing) capabilities'. Figure C1.1 shows a communications satellite. In doing so, INMARSAT has to operate on a sound commercial basis and is funded by capital contributions from its signatories. The overall system comprises:

(a) the coast earth stations (CESs) owned and operated by INMARSAT members. CESs link the space segment with the international and national telephone and telex networks;

(b) the ship earth stations (SESs) owned by shipowners and operated by ship personnel (radio officers);

(c) the space segment, which includes the necessary ground control functions, provided by INMARSAT as an international body;

(d) one CES in each ocean region as a network coordinating station (NCS), controlling the operation and allocating available channels to each CES and SES within the ocean region;

(e) an operations control centre (OCC) in London to coordinate the operation of the whole system.

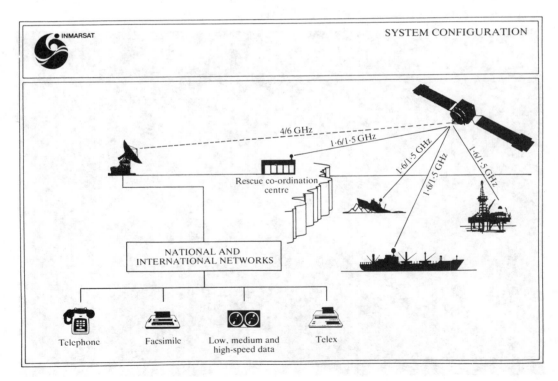

**Figure C1.2**

# The problem

The INMARSAT system consists of three telecommunications regions: the Atlantic, the Indian, and the Pacific Oceans. Each of these ocean regions is served by a dedicated satellite and a number of coast earth stations. Together they provide world-wide telecommunications coverage for ships. The logical arrangement of equipment is shown in Fig. C1.2 and a map showing satellite coverage is shown in Fig. C1.3.

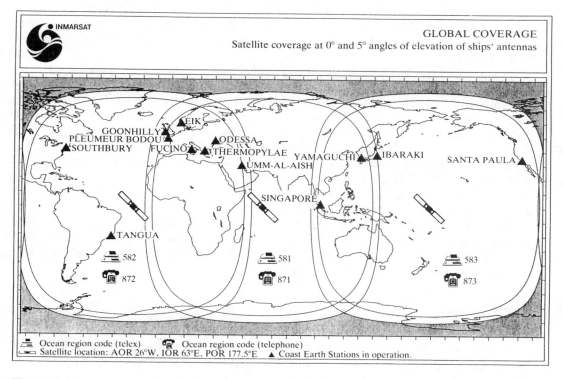

**Figure C1.3**

The technical operation of the system relies to a certain extent upon the data transmission capacity of the radio links that are provided between the coast earth stations (CESs), the network coordination stations (NCSs) and the ships themselves.

The data links carry various signalling messages at different stages during a telephone or telex call. These messages provide the means of communicating call control information between the call processing equipment of the CES, the NCS and the equipment on board the ships.

As the communications traffic in the system grows, the capacity of these data links naturally increases, and especially that on the data link from the NCS to the ships. With the introduction of new coast stations, increasing numbers of ship terminals and new satellite services it was felt that a study should be undertaken to examine the effect of these changes upon the network's capabilities, and explore how the data network might be enhanced.

An earlier study was undertaken to examine the effects of certain technical changes and of increased traffic so as to determine the most cost-effective method of increasing the capacity of the data channels. The predicted costs of the new system were acceptable, but the impact on the performance of the overall system was not satisfactory.

The INMARSAT system is a distributed multi-processor-controlled telecommunications system. Consequently there exists a great deal of interdependency in the behaviour of the main subsystems. A change in one part of the network can have an unexpected and considerably delayed effect elsewhere.

For example, one CES could suffer a complete call processing failure which might cause traffic to be diverted to another CES. This CES could have a resource shortfall and its CPU might overload.

These kinds of effects are rather difficult to study using analytical techniques and it was felt that mathematical models would be too complex for general use within the Organization.

Emphasis was therefore put on the study of data link performance by means of simulating the main call set-up and signalling procedures. By varying, at the modelled CESs, the actual CPU buffer sizes, processing times, time-outs and call processing algorithms, the effects of changes at various points in the network could be quantified.

To get a satisfactory model working quickly P-E were asked to provide a consultant. A small team was established, consisting of two INMARSAT engineers and the consultant. One of the engineers had a mainly mathematical background while the other had worked mainly with systems and had no simulation experience whatsoever.

The models of subsystems were designed and built by one of the engineers and the consultant working together. This method seemed very conducive to producing rapid results. In fact, the final model was operating sufficiently well at the end of three weeks to be able to produce good results.

## The model

The main principle of the model is that it should follow as closely as possible the actual processes used for real-life call set-ups. The overall model is known as RQMAX. During the model's development a certain amount of testing of important subsystems was carried out on additional subsidiary simulation models. These models were built, run at various rates and checked against known mathematical theory. They were then built into the main RQMAX model.

In order to help in understanding the simplified HOCUS flow diagram of RQMAX, which is shown in Fig. C1.4, an outline of a call set-up is described below.

When a radio officer on board a ship wishes to make a telephone call, the SES equipment initiates a radio burst transmission, called a request, to the selected CES. The selected CES can handle this call only if it possesses sufficient resources. The required CES resources in this case are known as voice modems and are used to connect the call to the land-based telephone networks. The next stage of the call is the allocation of a satellite telephone channel between the ship and the selected CES. The control of the satellite resources, which are called channels, lies entirely with the NCS, as described above.

The CES applies to the NCS, via its dedicated data link, for a channel allocation so that the telephone connection between itself and the ship can be set up. If this step is successful, the

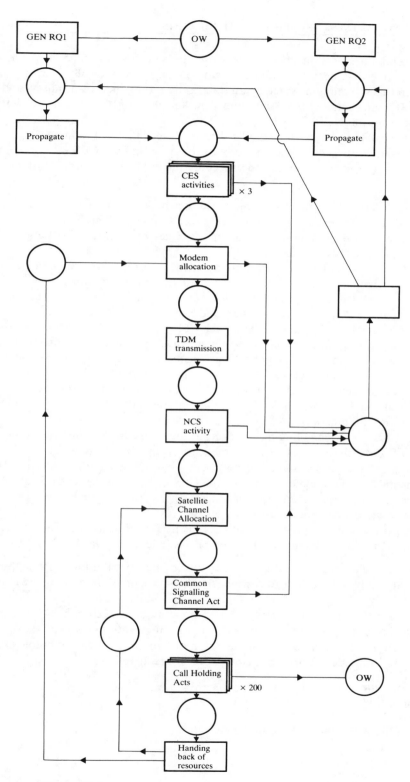

**Figure C1.4**

NCS transmits a signalling message to both the ship and the CES advising them which satellite channel has been allocated to them for the telephone call. The ship and the CES respond to this signalling message by automatically tuning their transmitters and receivers to the correct radio channels. At this point, the telephone call can proceed without further assistance from the NCS.

When the call terminates, there is a further exchange of information relating to the handing back of channels and voice modems to both the NCS and the CES.

In addition to this basic call set-up procedure the model incorporates further details of the operational system:

- When calls fail for one reason or another at the ship's request stage, at the CES stage, or at the NCS stage, the exact failure procedures are simulated. This is because the failure has a direct effect upon the types of signalling messages being transmitted and the subsequent loading of the data channels.
- To add further detail and to help initially in the calibration of the model, an actual ocean region consisting of three CESs can be simulated together with its NCS. The resources available can easily be adjusted to reflect those available at actual CESs, and the satellite channels available in the ocean region under study.
- The processing of calls in the model by the CESs and the NCS is carried out in two distinct stages, which is an approximation to the actual procedures. If a ship's request cannot be serviced due to a lack of voice or telex modem then the call is processed in one particular manner. If, on the other hand, no modems are available then a completely different processing procedure is used. Telex and telephone calls are processed at a CES using technically different methods; these different methods affect the performance of data channels in different ways.
- At the NCS, some signalling messages from the CESs are repeated on to the NCS to ship and CES data channel, while other messages from the CESs terminate at the NCS. In addition, certain types of signalling messages are processed at different time rates to others. For instance, signalling messages from the CES that need to be repeated at the NCS take a shorter time to process than those messages, such as the assignment request, which ask the NCS to assign a satellite channel to the call.
- Holding times and other relevant statistics, such as the time a caller waits before he makes a repeat attempt after his initial call attempt has failed, are available from the model.

When a particular ocean region is to be studied, the distributions of telephone and telex traffic analysed by CES and by direction, ship-to-shore or shore-to-ship, are entered into the model.

To operate the simulation, telex and telephone requests are applied to the model at predetermined inter-arrival rates. These rates conform to negative exponential distributions as in real life. A typical simulation run simulates about an hour of telecommunications traffic.

Some vital statistics regarding the model itself are as follows:

- 15 entity types;
- 3 entity groups;
- 50 queues;
- 37 data fields containing time information;
- 763 activities.

There are 14 different types of signalling message used in the INMARSAT signalling system and 9 are modelled as entity attributes in the RQMAX model.

## History of the project

Much of the statistical data used initially in the model was obtained from the network performance data published regularly by INMARSAT. However, there remained a large amount of data relating to the frequency of unusual and infrequent events in the signalling message procedures that was not available from published information. This area was researched several months before the HOCUS model was developed, since it had been anticipated that such data might be required for a simulation model.

The principle adopted during the building of the model was that a very comprehensive system should be produced. Unnecessary parts could always be removed later. In the event, however, the process of building the model caused the engineers to re-examine their views of what might be worthwhile analysing afterwards. After about three development iterations, the design of the model was considered complete and all efforts were then devoted to the testing of the final version.

The total time taken to produce the 99 per cent tested model was about three weeks and since then the model has been put to regular use by the engineers involved in the project.

The RQMAX model and its derivatives are run on INMARSAT's Prime 750 computer. In a typical run, one hour of real time takes up to 20 minutes of processor time. Since the Prime machine is very heavily used, most runs are submitted as 'phantoms' to be run overnight. Only test and start-up conditions are run interactively, unless spare computer time is available.

## Results

Since engineers had been involved at every stage in the model design process, the results that had been specifically requested were immediately available after a run had taken place.

The results are obtained from 16 histograms and five queue logs as well as the normal activity run counts.

Initially, the results obtained were puzzling, but further analysis of the real-time conditions prevailing in the network revealed that the answers given by the model were very close to reality. The results can never give an exact picture of what is happening because many approximations are being used. However, the model has proved that it can provide an accurate indication of the trends occurring in the network. Learning how to use the model also took a little time, since it was not initially realized just how sensitive the system was to large increases in traffic. This problem was overcome by increasing the calling rate by small increments during successive runs. All these effects occur exactly as they would have done in real life.

The models are run every few months to test a wide variety of network conditions. In general few surprises are found, however a number of hitherto unrealized phenomena have been discovered and, as a result, certain of INMARSAT's network strategies may have to be altered in the future.

## Conclusion

When the project was embarked upon there were a number of unknown factors regarding the performance of the network. These could have been tested in real time by making changes to the network. Such changes are expensive to carry out and carry certain risks to live telecommunications traffic. The simulation exercise produced a model with sufficient realism that it could be relied upon to test any number of changes.

---

## Comments

This case study highlights a number of important points. First, it shows the advantage of using a small, highly skilled multi-disciplinary team of professionals who are able to work closely together. Second, it demonstrates that, as well as simply solving problems, simulation models can enable people to gain a deeper insight into the operation of the real-life system under investigation. Third, this study emphasizes that the objective of building a model is not always to improve profitability through operational efficiency. One of the principal objectives here was to reduce the risk of danger at sea. Finally, the case study shows how quickly useful results can be obtained from a well thought out model. This model was 99 per cent complete after only three weeks.

# Case Study 2.

## At the forefront of technology

*by* **John Wood**
*Lucas Electrical Ltd*

**Summary**

This case study deals with the introduction of 'Just in Time' techniques into an established manufacturing environment. This was achieved over a one-year period as part of a business redesign in Lucas Instrumentation at Ystradgynlais in South Wales (see Fig. C2.1).

**Figure C2.1**

Benefits achieved to date as a result of the redesign are substantial and include:

– product integration;
– inventory reduced by 60 per cent;
– lead time reduced from 5 days to 5 hours;
– improved product quality;
– productivity increased by 35 per cent;
– de-centralized structure;
– indirect manning reduced;
– increased flexibility—facilities and people;
– workforce committed to work with change.

Most of these benefits are attributable to the introduction of 'Just in Time' techniques, known familiarly as JIT or, in Japan, as Kanban.

There were four major phases to the project, viz: business analysis, detailed analysis of the then current operation, business redesign, and implementation. These are outlined in Fig. C2.2.

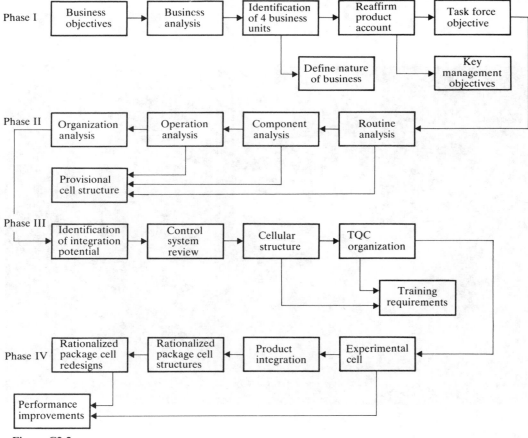

**Figure C2.2**

## Phase 1—Business analysis

The analysis indicated a broad European customer base, with 2500 varieties of product. The products fitted into three families, each having its own characteristics:

- high volume, low variety, frequently scheduled;
- low volume, very high variety, generally infrequently scheduled;
- high and low volume.

The analysis considered the current market-place, product viability, market share growth opportunities, competition and trends in vehicle instrumentation systems over a five-year period.

Each product group was analysed and measured against key ratios. This resulted in identifying areas to be investigated by a systems task force. Other areas were identified and these were pursued by site management.

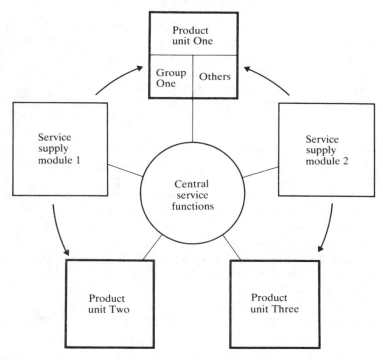

**Figure C2.3**

## Phases 2 and 3—Analysis and redesign

Three businesses were identified within the overall business. At an operational level each of the business units is supported internally by an electronics manufacturing unit (PCB assembly, thick film substrate manufacture and production) and a print and spray unit. These two were classified as the service business units and operated on a supplier–customer relationship similar to other external suppliers. The overall business structure can be seen in Fig. C2.3. It shows the traditional central service with which manufacturing industry is familiar.

A multi-disciplinary task force was formed to analyse the business. It encompassed skills as diverse as business analyst to quality supervisor to work study engineer. The task force of 12 full-time representatives quickly expanded to between 20 and 40 full-time personnel as we studied the then current operation and considered its redesign. One particular product group business was quickly identified as the first area for detailed redesign, this business representing 50 per cent of turnover with good market potential in volumes of up to 8000 units per week.

Manufacture was fragmented across three factory areas and a routing (work flow) analysis showed the excessively high work movement. From this we identified the relationship of value-added activity to non-value-added. Transportation and delays which add cost but no value predominated and reorganization of the manufacturing facilities was obviously necessary.

We examined the structure of the bill of materials (BOM) and the manufacturing procedures in use. We found that generally we dedicated our products early in the manufacturing cycle. Simple reshaping of the procedures pushed the operations that dedicated product by type towards the end of the manufacturing cycle. This gave clear performance gains and some early indication of how to modify our organizational structures.

Each element of the manufacturing routine was examined in detail and a workstation audit produced. This allowed new tooling, equipment and handling facilities to be identified and ordered to meet the redesign criteria.

In conducting the detailed analysis of the operation, lead and response times in days, and for some areas in weeks, were identified. These times were important criteria for improvement in the redesign.

We operated functionally and with a high level of central control which gave rise to an individualistic approach with responsibility and accountability very vague. Problems occurring in manufacture could not be resolved fast enough, and due to the high raw material availability in some instances problems never were resolved.

Reorganization was necessary and the objectives clear: devolve those skills necessary in support of operational improvement into the business units to create a 'cellular' operation embracing team work, flexible working and continuous improvement. A number of cells would form a module and a number of modules constitute a business.

The redesign of the first product group identified the following operating improvements and benefits:

- responsibility for business performance can be identified at business level;
- Kanban should be introduced;
- integrated manufacture;
- reduction in non-value-added activity;
- improved control;
- reduction in indirect support;
- productivity improvement of 25 per cent;
- inventory reduction of 60 per cent;

- stock turn improvement to 36;
- lead time improvements from 5 days to 5 hours.

With the level of improvement identified it was necessary to simulate the redesign to optimize these benefits. Initially, this was attempted manually but, although we could test the design statically, we found it impossible to monitor under dynamics of change. The use of HOCUS, however, allowed the dynamic testing and optimization of cell, module and business performance. The HOCUS package became an even more important tool when implementation commenced, as it allowed sensitivity measurement to take place with true shop floor dynamics. This work still continues, allowing further gains to be achieved in cell performance.

Having qualified the bottom–up design, work commenced on identifying the bottom–up and top–down control system needs of the business, devolving the strategy and plans for system integration, development and implementation. Having identified the organizational structure and formalized the necessary changes in working practices to achieve labour flexibility and team work, we could begin to re-examine the functional structures within the business. Development of skills changed responsibilities within cells and reduced the external support service requirements.

To enable the business to move towards a true 'Just in Time' development plan, certain key activities had to be developed. With lead and response time reductions being so dramatic, supplier and customer development programmes were crucial to support the JIT strategy.

In fact change of this magnitude necessitated the development of training plans for all levels of personnel within the business.

## Phase 4—Implementation

The key features of this phase were:

- product integration;
- production rationalization;
- experimental cell;
- supplier development;
- customer development;
- simulation;
- control system—top–down/bottom–up;
- payment scheme review;
- training.

Product integration took four months to complete. The first product unit business was sited in Factory 1, the second and third in Factory 2 and the Service Supply Modules in Factory 3.

Immediate benefits were achieved: reduced transportation, storage and delays; improved quality; reduced WIP; better communications; floor space saving and easier identification of problems.

Recognizing the nature and order of change being proposed, it was thought necessary to set up an experimental cell where Kanban, statistical process control (SPC), problem-solving skills, and team work could be demonstrated.

A particular product unit was chosen for the experiment with the following objectives:

- to develop awareness;
- to demonstrate new job roles and the team approach;
- to establish a vehicle to sell the approach within the business;
- to encourage feedback from the shop floor and from management.

Agreement was reached with the unions that within the cell all personnel would operate flexibly and develop practices as required for a period of six months.

The cell was redesigned to work with Kanban and optimized using HOCUS. The area was reconstructed, without 'work storage' conveyors. The classic 'U' shaped line was introduced, supported by sub-cell operations. Raw material stores were brought on-line, piecework removed and the operators trained on Kanban and SPC.

Although a simple tool to use, Kanban does demand rigid discipline by all who work with it in order to sustain the high levels of control it offers. A Lucas-developed Kanban training package was used to train all cell personnel. The manufacturing systems engineers trained the team and then joined the team when the system went 'live'. The systems engineers supported the teams for approximately six months, guiding, encouraging and policing the maintenance of Kanban discipline.

The cell was structured with key skills and resources being introduced to ensure quick responses and resolution to problems. The key elements, team work and continuous improvement, were not easy to introduce. Many lessons were learnt and most certainly mistakes made. The most important lesson was that management cannot say 'Yes' and then walk away. Their involvement, participation and support is essential.

It is interesting to note that although initially everyone claimed to wish to participate in a team approach, in practice we found that at first some were only prepared to go part of the way. Although it is necessary to emphasize the need to find the right blend of skill, attitude becomes the predominator in achieving a successful team. The perfect blend of skill and attitude is rarely found, but those individuals with real commitment to make teams work and change happen, generally sway the dissenters into following the team approach.

We were surprised at the effectiveness of Kanban. Bottlenecks and scrap generators were clearly identified, known to the whole team and dealt with accordingly. With the cell structure designed to incorporate additional skill levels, the response to problems and the solving of them was much enhanced. However, we could see that still more could be achieved and so a continuous improvement (quality circle) activity was developed.

The results were astounding, not only in business performance terms, but in enhancing the commitment of our people. They quickly adopted the business as 'theirs'. They realized they could be involved, play a real part and influence the performance of 'their business'. This experiment achieved:

- operation within four months;
- work-in-process reduced by 84 per cent in four weeks;
- raw materials stock reduced by 40 per cent;
- productivity improved by 22 per cent;
- stock turn increased to 15;
- lead times reduced;

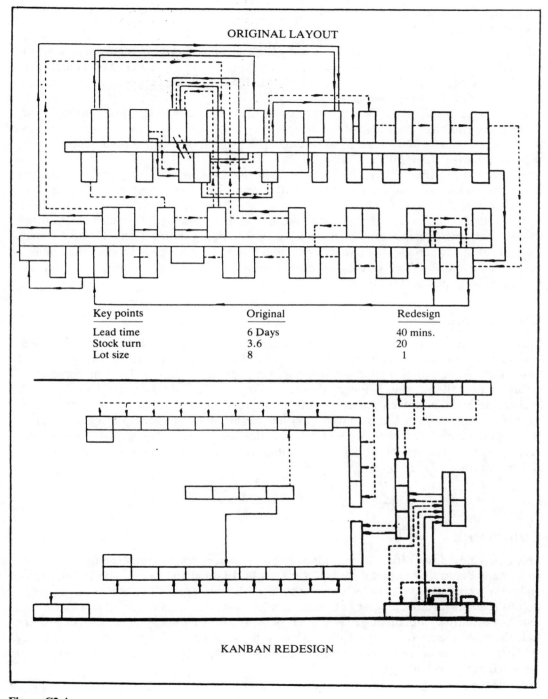

ORIGINAL LAYOUT

| Key points | Original | Redesign |
|------------|----------|----------|
| Lead time | 6 Days | 40 mins. |
| Stock turn | 3.6 | 20 |
| Lot size | 8 | 1 |

KANBAN REDESIGN

**Figure C2.4**

– improved product quality;
– changeover time reduced from 30 to 5 min.

Of course, this was only an experiment, but all of our objectives were met. Agreement was reached with the unions to proceed with full implementation. The agreement incorporated flexible working, removal of restrictive practices and lines of demarcation, and the continued development of the team approach.

Following the success of the experimental cell, further cells were implemented. It was decided that although the whole of the first product unit business was to be redesigned using Kanban, it would be advantageous to redesign a cell within the other product units as well, thereby initiating change in each major business unit.

The second cell (Fig. C2.4) again incorporated the 'U' shaped facility, the old conveyor line being unnecessary. In the four months of redesign and implementation, 100 metres of conveyor were disposed of.

The overall benefits of redesign have already been discussed. Full implementation has commenced, with final assembly being achieved from a kitting station where all non-standard elements of the 24 varieties built are placed into a box and are bar-code labelled. Assembly is by unit build and work delivered by a computer-controlled conveyor, allowing a 'one on one' build capability and WIP control.

## Conclusion

This case study demonstrates the structured Lucas Industries approach to business redesign. Although not all facets have been covered here, the detailed analysis and simulation required to support the activities undertaken is obvious. The approach to 'Just in Time' manufacturing embraces all of the elements highlighted. It is not simply building to order or having materials available to build, it is much deeper if a real JIT approach is to be adopted. The methodology has been adopted across Lucas Industries in the pursuit of manufacturing excellence, but no matter how sound our concepts and technologies are, success depends on management developing and training the workforce, and stimulating its involvement in the performance and effectiveness of their operations.

---

## Comments

This case study deals with powerful innovatory techniques which are currently revolution-izing manufacturng processes throughout the world. In order to achieve their full potential, and remain competitive, manufacturers must take full advantage of the latest techniques. To do this requires investment, and as ever investment involves risk. Simulation helps to reduce risk significantly by obtaining reliable predictions about proposed systems, and also to fine tune the performance of newly installed systems. By using simulation to carry out sensitivity analysis, Lucas Industries is confidently optimizing their production capability to remain at the forefront of technology.

# Case Study 3.

## Manufacturing with robots

*by* **John Gorman** (Salford University)
*for Mather and Platt Ltd*

**Summary**

The Rotating Machinery Division of Mather and Platt Ltd manufactures a range of electric motors. Motors are designed around customer specifications and in general each motor, and hence each set of stator and rotor laminations, is different.

The purpose of the project was to design a flexible manufacturing cell (FMC) for the production of these laminations utilizing new technology methods. A number of models were developed to assess the alternatives available and to aid in the development of the cell.

The overall study lasted 18 months and was carried out by the author with input from Mather and Platt and Salford University. The result was a specification of the new machines and materials handling units, and the operating strategy of the cell to produce stator and rotor core packs with acceptable lead times. In addition to this a model was constructed to determine the manning levels and operating capacity of a number of existing machines required for the manufacture of some smaller motors. The project was carried out under the auspices of the Teaching Company Scheme operating at Salford University.

## Background

Mather and Platt, Park Works, Manchester is part of Wormold, Australia. There are two divisions at Park Works: Fire Engineering Division and Rotating Machinery Division (RMD). In addition to these there is also a foundry.

This project was concerned with RMD which designs and manufactures centrifugal pumps capable of delivering between 1 cubic metre/hour and 60 000 cubic metres/hour, and electric motors with outputs of 15 kW to 4500 kW to be sold separately or coupled to a pump. A photograph of the plant is shown in Fig. C3.1.

Both products are customer specified and are aimed at the very high quality, high technology end of the market. The pumps and motors are used for power stations, oil installations, water supply, sewage disposal, chemical plants, mining and quarrying, and industrial processes of all kinds.

The Department of Aeronautical and Mechanical Engineering at Salford University operates a multi-host Teaching Company Scheme in which several large and medium sized companies in the North-West participate in collaborative projects involving FMS design, CADCAM, Design for Assembly, CAPM, QA and Simulation.

**Figure C3.1**

## The problem

From initial investigations, a cell emerged as potentially suitable for the production of these laminations. The cell consisted of a CNC laser cutting machine, a CNC notching press, a high technology robot and two low technology robots. The laser is used to profile the outside diameter of the stator and a centre hole with keyway. In this form the stator is then passed to the notching press for the following operations:

– stator notch and separation of the finished stator from the rotor blank;
– rotor notch.

In most cases the laminations are complete at this stage, but a few motor types require a second laser operation to open out the centre hole to the finished rotor shaft hole diameter. The process is shown diagrammatically in Fig. C3.2.

The robots are used to load and unload the machines. The high technology robot is coupled to the laser and the two low technology robots are coupled to the notching press. Pallets are required and since the stator and rotor core packs are built during the process, stator and rotor fixtures are also required.

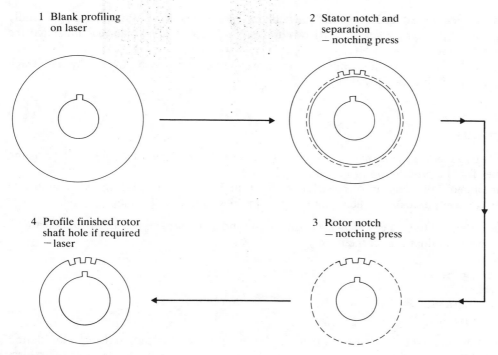

1 Blank profiling on laser

2 Stator notch and separation — notching press

4 Profile finished rotor shaft hole if required — laser

3 Rotor notch — notching press

**Figure C3.2**

The proposed cell will not cater for all the motor types and in addition to the above machines, a number of existing machines need to be kept to manufacture some smaller motors in the traditional way.

The main questions to be answered are:

(a) Can one laser and one notching press cope with the anticipated demand and provide built core packs with acceptable lead times? On a 'static' basis the machines can do this, but what happens in the 'dynamic' situation when they are coupled to each other with robotic handling devices to form an interdependent cell?

(b) If they cannot cope, what modifications are required to remedy this, without the purchase of additional expensive machines and the associated materials handling units?

(c) What are the maximum permissible cycle times for the robots?

(d) What effect do different operating capacities have on the lead times?

(e) How many pallets, stator fixtures and rotor fixtures are required?

(f) What operating/manning levels are required to run the existing machines to provide acceptable lead times on the smaller motors, and can the number of these machines cope, or are additional machines required?

Questions (a) to (e) are related to a system which does not in effect exist and therefore the answers are difficult to ascertain. The concept of using simulation to answer these questions was suggested by staff at Salford University, who had experience in using and developing simulation techniques. HOCUS was particularly mentioned as a powerful, user-friendly package, highlighted by a survey carried out at Salford University which recommended the purchase and installation of HOCUS at the university.

Question (f) would, without simulation, require experimentation with the real system which was neither desirable, nor feasible.

## The model

Basically two models were constructed; one of the proposed cell, and the other of the existing machines for the production of the smaller motors.

A simplified flow diagram of model 1 is shown in Fig. C3.3. The full model contains 24 activities (5 continuous), 25 queues and 6 main entities (9 in all). The main entities are:

- Order; 10 attributes (4 clocks, 4 cycle times, 1 to indicate motor types and 1 to indicate the number of laminations in the order);
- Laser;
- Notching Press;
- Pallets;
- Stator Fixtures;
- Rotor Fixtures.

The flow diagram shows the routes taken by orders through the cell, and the interrelationships of the various entities; pallets, laser, notching press, stator fixtures and rotor fixtures. The logic of the model is such that priority is given to orders already in the system over those waiting in the order store ready for processing.

A number of clocks are placed on the orders to determine the time spent in various parts of the cell, and one clock monitors the lead time of each order from receipt of the order to finish core packs.

Smaller models of the laser and notching press with their associated robots were constructed and run. The results from these are incorporated into the total model of the cell.

A flow diagram of model 2 is not shown, but briefly the full model contained 43 activities (6 continuous), 41 queues and 9 main entities (10 in all). The main entities are:

- Order; 14 attributes (6 clocks, 6 cycle times, 1 to indicate motor type and 1 to include the number of laminations in the order);
- Stator;
- Grinder;
- Men;
- Five Production machines (2 blanking presses and 3 notching presses).

This model incorporates the various routines of the smaller motors with the existing machines required for their production. Again a number of clocks are placed on the orders to determine lead time and time spent in various parts of the system.

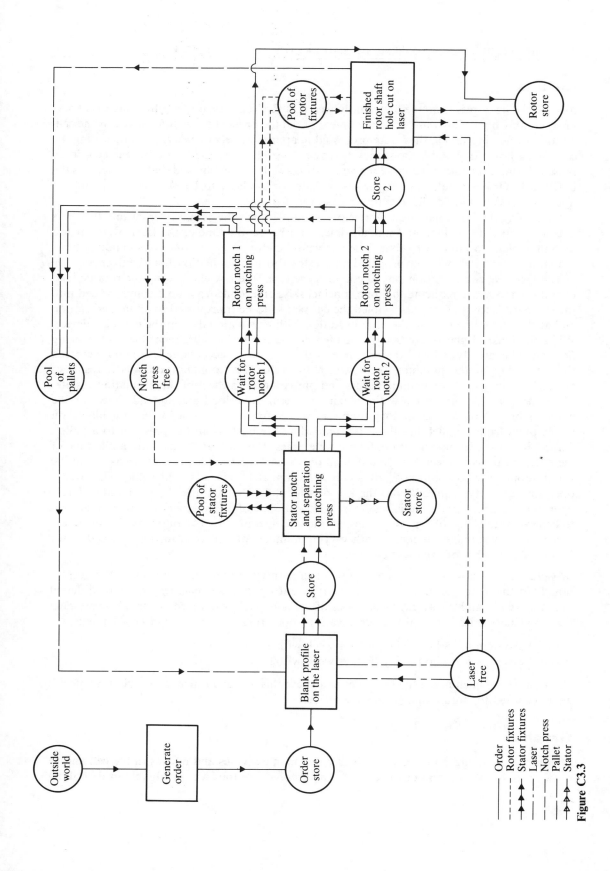

**Figure C3.3**

Outside world

Generate order

Order store

Blank profile on the laser

Store

Laser free

Stator notch and separation on notching press

Pool of stator fixtures

Stator store

Wait for rotor notch 1

Wait for rotor notch 2

Rotor notch 1 on notching press

Rotor notch 2 on notching press

Notch press free

Pool of pallets

Pool of rotor fixtures

Finished rotor shaft hole cut on laser

Store 2

Rotor store

——— Order
------ Rotor fixtures
▲▲▲ Stator fixtures
—·—· Laser
—··— Notch press
—— Pallet
▲▲ Stator

## Results

*Model 1*   The results from the first run showed that the lead time for the built core packs was unacceptably high. This was due to the time spent in the order store waiting to access the cell, although when in the cell, they were processed in approximately one day. Even operating the cell for 24 hours/day and 7 days/week had very little effect on the lead time: the cell, in its present form, just could not cope. Further scrutiny of the results showed that the laser was the bottleneck. Orders would wait in the order store for the laser to become available and the notching press would lie idle awaiting blanks for the laser.

Examining the laser operation more closely revealed that the actual laser cutting time was adequate but that the load and unload times, and hence idle time of the laser, were far too high in comparison to cutting time. The problem therefore was to reduce this handling time. A number of options were investigated and tested through simulation for effectiveness.

The resulting configuration was to coil feed the laser, thereby eliminating the robotic load operation and hence reducing the time considerably, and to incorporate a conveyor bed into the standard laser system. This enabled the cut blanks to be transported to an unload station and at the same time to load the cutting station with new material from the coil feed device. While the finished blanks are being unloaded by the robot the subsequent blanks are being profiled. This greatly reduced the idle time of the laser to an acceptable level, and increased the utilization of the notching press within the cell. This configuration was a result of discussions with the laser manufacturers and presentation to them of the simulation results.

The next area of interest was the maximum permissible load and unload times for the notching press. Two low technology robots were used for this task: one loading the blanks on to the press from a pallet and the other unloading the parts from the press on to a pallet/ fixture. Running the model with different cycle times showed that the maximum idle time of the notching press between load and unload operations is seven seconds. This was put to the robot suppliers who confirmed, after consideration, that this was achievable. The overall operating capacity required from the cell was identified by running the model at different operating capacities and examining the average lead time of the core packs. It was found that to achieve a lead time of four days the cell must be operated for 14 hours/day, 7 days/week.

Similarly by running the model with varying numbers of pallets, rotor fixtures and stator fixtures the number of each was determined.

*Model 2*   As with Model 1, this model was run with varying modifications and the outputs noted. In this case the model was run at different operating capacities and with different manning levels, and the average lead times of the core packs examined. Thus it became clear that to achieve a lead time of four days various operating strategies could be adopted:

– run the system for 8 hours/day, 6 days/week with 1 man;
– run the system for 5 hours/day, 5 days/week with 2 men.

The number of machines needed in order to achieve this was confirmed, and various strategies were recorded for future management scrutiny.

## Graphics

Graphics were used, in model 1, to display the main activities and queues in the cell and to show visually the progress of the orders. The graphical output was invaluable in describing the process to personnel not directly involved in the simulation (management, shop floor, etc.). It was also very useful in promoting confidence in both the simulation model and in some ways the proposed cell itself. The order store was the key queue and this queue could be seen building up and dying away as time progresses at different operating levels.

Although the graphics proved very useful in many ways, in this application they were of limited use to the simulator himself. The author relied on the many output reports available to determine the performance of the cell in detail.

The interactive input program was used with great effectiveness and proved to be a major benefit. It was found that a model could be read from a drawn activity cycle diagram and input via the input program directly into the computer.

## Conclusions

The study proved very successful as is apparent from the results. The initial cell, if installed without the simulation study, would have caused many problems in lead time of core packs, efficiency of cell, etc. The 'static' performance of the individual machines is very different to the 'dynamic' performance of the cell. Simulation allowed a picture of this 'dynamic' situation to be drawn.

In general the study provided the following benefits:

(a) The general configuration of the cell (particularly the laser) to maximize efficiency and provide acceptable lead times was determined.
(b) The specific robotic requirements in terms of cycle times were determined. This enabled confident discussions with robotic suppliers about our needs.
(c) The number of pallets, stator and rotor fixtures were determined. The number required, highlighted from the simulation, was far less than indicated from intuition. This provided a direct measurable saving.
(d) The operating capacity (and in the case of model 2 the manning levels and number of various machines) required to provide acceptable lead times was determined. Since the operating capacity and manning levels were known, accurate financial statements were compiled and published with confidence. The capital investment required in this project is considerable and any additional confidence that could be provided at the justification stage was invaluable.

## Comments

The project as a whole took approximately 18 months, including financial justification, preliminary technical investigations, detailed technical design and the simulation exercise. HOCUS was used as a tool to aid development of the cell, not only to verify it, and as such it was profitably used at intervals throughout the study. This timescale was more or less what was expected from estimates made at the beginning of the project.

In general the simulation promoted confidence in the feasibility of the real cell. All concerned in the project were talked through the activity cycle diagram and asked to comment on its accuracy. They could ask 'what if' questions and modify the diagram accordingly, and then monitor the results. This gave them a much better appreciation of the cell.

When constructing the various activity cycle diagrams all the facts about the system to be simulated must be known. No vague areas must exist: if they do they must be clarified. In other words building the activity cycle diagram teaches the simulators more about the system.

It was felt by Mather and Platt and Salford University that HOCUS (indeed simulation generally) proved very effective throughout the project and that it would certainly be used in future projects.

# Case Study 4.

## Educating tomorrow's managers

*by* **Sheila Stone**
*The Open University*

**Summary**

The Open University provides distance learning for adults at graduate, undergraduate and continuing education levels (Fig. C4.1 depicts graduation day). This case study describes how simulation is taught using HOCUS in practical work connected with the course PT611— Structure and Design of Manufacturing Systems. The model is of a gears manufacturing system comprising 11 computer numerical controlled (CNC) machines and two manual operators divided between seven workstations.

**Figure C4.1**

## Background

The Open University, sponsored by the Scientific and Engineering Research Council, offers two MSc programmes entitled: 'Manufacturing' and 'Industrial Applications of Computers'. These programmes comprise a set of teaching modules to help update industry. They have been designed for distance learning, thus enabling a student to combine work and study conveniently. It is expected that in most cases the employer will provide active support in the form of finance and/or study time. The courses aim to train engineers and managers engaged in manufacturing in the new technologies available to them.

This case study describes how HOCUS is used as part of the teaching strategy in one of the core modules, PT611—Structure and Design of Manufacturing Systems. The module comprises three blocks of work: Structure, Choice, and Design.

The Design block is made up of three units: Concept Design, Computers and Manufacturing Systems Design, and Detailed Design; together with a software workbook and audio visual material.

The Concept Design Unit deals with the initial stages in the design of a manufacturing system (concept stage leading to a feasibility study). The next unit concentrates on the use of the computer and various types of software as tools which can help improve design at both feasibility and detailed design stages. It gives an overview of software currently available and looks in depth at the use of modelling and simulation as well as the use of geometrical graphics packages. The software workbook includes exercises to give the student practical experience in using some of the software suggested.

Modelling and simulation are important tools for use in both feasibility and detailed design stages. Some modelling and simulation can be done manually using mathematical equations or other types of analytic manipulation. However, the computer provides a much more flexible tool for this purpose, allowing the designer to conduct a more thorough investigation of the proposed systems than other methods permit.

The aims of the simulation and modelling part of the unit are:

- to provide a guide to the use of models and simulation in manufacturing system design;
- to facilitate the design of a manufacturing system, through the application of software packages within a systems methodology.

After studying this part of the unit the student is expected to be able to:

- state how to approach the creation of a model or simulation;
- recognize the need for model credibility, and state how to go about establishing it;
- explain the importance of communications between interested parties when software packages are being employed in the design of a manufacturing system;
- use a model already provided to understand some design problems;
- either provide a solution or state what the next step should be to resolve the problem.

The unit investigates queueing theory and various other models derived from theory. Many of the scheduling problems that are encountered in modern manufacture can be analysed using this theoretical basis.

Three software packages have been chosen to give the student practical experience in relevant computer use. They were selected because:

- they are able to make a positive contribution to the design of a manufacturing system;
- they illustrate the different types of software available to the designer;
- they use different assumptions;
- they illustrate the different uses of computer hardware; a standalone microcomputer, a mini, and a mainframe computer;
- they are suitable for distance teaching.

## The OU approach

Initially the student is led through the construction of simple algebraic models for calculating the time taken to machine parts, assuming constant arrival and machining rates, via a series of self-assessment questions (SAQs). The student starts with the assumption that a batch of parts is waiting to be machined at a constant rate and develops a very simple mathematical model to include parts arriving at a constant rate and being added to the initial batch. The machining rate is still constant and this is greater than the arrival rate. Besides a model to calculate the time taken the student develops several others as well.

This modelling exercise provides the student with an introduction to mathematical models and how assumptions play an important part in their construction. These models can be used to assess whether a system under consideration can achieve what is required of it; to provide the student with an insight into the problem areas needing investigation with more sophisticated methods; and finally to provide a set of criteria with which to compare results from later models and thus help to establish the credibility of more complex and opaque models.

The next group of models uses the assumption that arrival and machining rates have a Poisson distribution instead of being constant. This statistical distribution allows for consideration of some variation in both areas. The distribution adequately represents the variations in behaviour expected in many queueing situations over long periods of time.

Two different pieces of software based on this theory are used—Queue[1] and GMS[2]. Queue is a simple discrete simulation of the analytical model using the Poisson distribution for single and multi-channel service at a single workstation. It has the advantage over the analytical model that the user can replace the standard Poisson distribution with another distribution if preferred. The behaviour at a single workstation is simulated.

The second software package, GMS, assumes a Poisson distribution applied to the manufacturing system as a whole, with constant travelling time between workstations. Both packages are data driven, and do not allow the student to incorporate different logic. The results they give are means (averages) so only the behaviour taken over a long period, not minute by minute, can be assessed.

When a new model is created its credibility needs to be assessed. In part this can be done by comparing new and previous results. Any unexpected disagreement should be investigated in order to understand its cause. This helps to prevent errors creeping in and being perpetuated in later modelling.

The models used by the student so far cannot answer questions such as:

- what happens in detail while the manufacturing system is working?
- how does the scheduling logic affect the system?
- how will breakdowns affect the system?

To answer this type of question the student needs to use detailed simulation, and HOCUS is the software package chosen for this purpose.

HOCUS was chosen because:

– it has animated colour graphics;
– models are constructed using methods which are easily described to a distant learner;
– it does not require any prior knowledge of computer programming;
– results are obtained in a variety of ways via reports;
– the behaviour of the system can be followed without using the animation facility.

This last point is very important as our students would not have access to a graphics terminal. The animation side of HOCUS is demonstrated on video.

## The case study

To demonstrate how these various models help in the design of a manufacturing system, the same case study is used for all the modelling and simulation exercises. It concerns the manufacture of three types of gears, and is based on a real-life problem which one of our consultants had encountered.

The manufacturing system (Fig. C4.2) consists of a set of seven workstations linked by a conveyor, 11 CNC machines and two manually operated workstations (4 and 7).

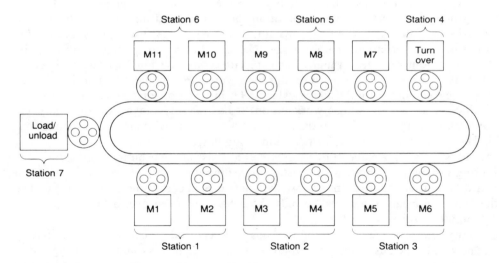

**Figure C4.2**

Each machine or operator has a four-place rotary buffer to hold parts unloaded from or waiting to be loaded on to the conveyor. There are three different parts being machined at these workstations using two different process routes. The data about the stations and process routes are given in Table C4.1.

Table C4.1 Process times and routes for Parts A, B, C

| Workstation | Machines/operators | Process time (min) |
|---|---|---|
| **Process route for Part A:** | | |
| 7 | LOAD | 1.67 |
| 3 | M5, M6 | 3.00 |
| 4 | TURNOVER | 1.67 |
| 6 | M10, M11 | 11.62 |
| 7 | LOAD/UNLOAD | 1.67 |
| **Process route for Parts B and C:** | | |
| 7 | LOAD | 1.67 |
| 1 | M1, M2 | 5.65 |
| 2 | M3, M4 | 5.93 |
| 3 | M5, M6 | 4.37 |
| 4 | TURNOVER | 1.67 |
| 5 | M7, M8, M9 | 7.92 |
| 7 | UNLOAD | 1.67 |

The objective of the investigation is to ensure that the proposed system can produce 2200 parts (Part A, 700; Part B, 700; Part C, 800) in an 80-hour week (double shift).

## Initial modelling

Before students are allowed to touch the computer they use the models they have originally developed using the assumption of constant arrival and machining rates. This can be considered as the system working under 'ideal' conditions, i.e., with no scheduling problems. This gives additional information about the system's boundary conditions. Workstations are treated in isolation to determine the utilization of each one necessary to produce the output required (Table C4.2). They are required to identify which workstations form queues naturally if a constant arrival rate is equal to the maximum machining rate of the previous workstation.

Table C4.2 Time taken to produce required output

| Workstation | | Hours | Utilization (%) |
|---|---|---|---|
| 1 | $(5.65*(700 + 800)/2)/60$ | = 70.625 | 88.3 |
| 2 | $(5.93*(700 + 800)/2)/60$ | = 74.125 | 92.7 |
| 3 | $((4.37*(700 + 800) + 3*700)/2)/60$ | = 72.125 | 90.2 |
| 4 | $(1.67*(700 + 700 + 800)/60)$ | = 61.233 | 76.5 |
| 5 | $(7.92*(700 + 800)/3)/60$ | = 66.000 | 82.5 |
| 6 | $(11.62*700/2)/60$ | = 67.783 | 83.8 |
| 7 | $(1.67*2*(700 + 700 + 800)/60)$ | = 122.466 | 153.0 |

It is clear from Table C4.2 that workstation 7 cannot fulfil its target within the allotted time. Normally this would mean going back to reassess the time taken at that workstation. However, because this is a teaching exercise the students use these figures with two other models to confirm that the problem really exists, thus checking the credibility of their initial model.

It can also be seen that to obtain the required output two machines have utilizations of over 90 per cent. Again in a real-life situation one would check the reliability of the machines for such high utilization. If the machines could not achieve this utilization then clearly there could be a scheduling problem. To assess the degree of severity of the problem one can determine whether a queue naturally forms at each of the workstations if the previous one is working at its maximum rate. It can be shown that queues do not naturally occur at workstations 1, 3, 4, 7. The problem at workstation 1 can be alleviated when the lack of performance at 7 is resolved. More worrying is the lack of a natural queue forming at workstation 3 which requires very high utilization.

This initial modelling provides the student with a better understanding of the problem and some guide to what type of experimenting is needed. It is essential that an experimental design is formulated before the computer is used to prevent unproductive experimentation with the model. An experimental design will keep one in touch with the real system being modelled thus avoiding ending up with a non-implementable solution.

*Using the first two pieces of software*   The next stage in the experimentation is to look at the behaviour in non-ideal conditions. For this the student uses Queue and examines the behaviour at each workstation when using firstly, the Poisson distribution, and secondly, his own distribution. It is found that not assuming constant inter-arrival times increases utilization and in some cases long queues form. The software confirms that workstation 7 has the highest utilization.

GMS is used to look at the behaviour of the system as a whole. Again this shows that workstation 7 is the bottleneck and that output is far below what is required. At this stage the student is given revised values for the manual workstations. Workstation 7 is revised to 0.67 minutes and workstation 4 to 1.33 minutes. The data are altered on the computer and the program re-run. Except for the conveyor, the utilization of the other workstations seems to be quite close to that of workstation 2 thus indicating a well balanced system. However, it is a system which is still not achieving its target output.

The GMS software assumes that the system is closed. Therefore among the data required is the number of parts in circulation in the system, which so far has been set at 25. When this is changed to 50, the required output is at last achieved.

The rest of the section of the unit on the use of GMS discusses the assumptions made in the model and how they affect the assessment of the result. One assumption in the model is that queue lengths are not limited at each workstation.

In reality, this is not true and such an assumption has a profound influence on our conclusions about whether the conveyor can cope. Also we have no control over the scheduling rules used. Nor can a model concerned with runnng in equilibrium take account of how starting up, breakdowns, etc., affect the system. This can only be assessed by detailed simulation.

## HOCUS simulation model

Students are not expected to create a complete model for detailed simulation for themselves. The aim of this part of the unit is to enable students to understand what is required when creating a HOCUS model and how to use the model created. This should enable them to know whether they wish to learn more about creating their own models.

Alternatively, they should be more able to brief a consultant to create the model and assess its relevance to their system.

The student is taken through the initial steps in creating a model, starting with a subsystem—workstation 4. The student works through a set of instructions and SAQs to obtain the activity diagram for the workstation, Fig. C4.3, which he then tests using hand simulation. The next SAQ requires him to repeat this modelling exercise with respect to workstation 2. It is suggested that he does this by identifying the differences between workstation 2 and workstation 4 and then adapts the earlier model.

In the software workbook there is an explanation of the complete model which the student will use.

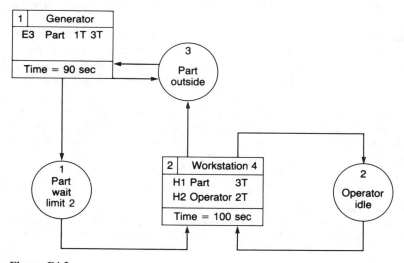

**Figure C4.3**

## Students' use of HOCUS

Students are first taken through a practical demonstration of how to use HOCUS interactively. For this practical demonstration the original values for the manual stations are used. This is done so that comparison with earlier results can be made. Also this allows activity times to be changed as part of the demonstration.

During the demonstration reports are used to check that the logic of the behaviour of the model is as expected. The model simulates one hour and the results are compared with those gained using GMS. The output per hour is less than that given by GMS. This is to be expected because the present model is being used in start-up conditions. It therefore does indicate that the model is credible.

The students are then provided with a second model with an extra machine and activity at each workstation which could be incorporated into the system if required. In a Tutor Marked Assessment students are asked to use HOCUS and GMS to establish a method for making the system viable or show that it never will be. This requires them to explore scheduling and possibly add machines which need to be paid for by extra output.

## Conclusions

This is a new course and as yet I am unable to report on the response from the first students. I hope that the combination of software and their initial modelling will make the students realize that the computer allows the setting up of a 'laboratory' to do experiments on a set of models. These models provide a deeper understanding of the behaviour and problems of the final manufacturing system before any commitment is made to capital investment in manufacturing equipment. This laboratory should allow the testing of ideas and incorporation of changes, even at the last minute, so that their effect can be assessed before further costly work is done.

The use of computerized models allows the effect of any changes in one aspect of the design to be easily tested in other parts of the system. Modelling and planning need to use the most up-to-date data available and this means that information used in the model can change radically during the course of the design. When the model or plan has been computerized, the effects of any changes take little time to assess, and costly mistakes can thus be prevented.

Personally I enjoyed modelling with HOCUS. I found it easy to follow and to express my ideas about the system. I hope the students enjoy it as well. My main regret is that, because of cost, students only see the animation part on video. The use of animation would make the task of teaching that much easier.

## References

1. Rasmussen, E. H., 'Queue Simulation', *BYTE*, **9**(3), 157–174, 1984.
2. Kay, J. J., and A. J. Walmsley, 'Computer Aids for the Optimal Design of Operationally Effective FMS', *Proceedings of the First International Conference on Flexible Manufacturing Systems (FMS)*, Kempston, Bedfordshire: IFS (Publications), pp. 463–480, 1982.

---

## Comments

This case study illustrates how simulation packages are used to teach the principles of discrete event simulation. Students are assured of the validity of the technique by comparing their simulation results for elementary models with results obtained analytically.

Having established the advantages of simulation over formal mathematical models in all but the simplest of cases, the students are introduced to further real-life complications. With this carefully structured approach novices are quickly able to appreciate and use the power of simulation.

The study emphasizes that simulation packages are useful for didactic, as well as practical, applications.

# Case Study 5.

## More lager, please

*by* **Roddy MacKenzie**
*Scottish & Newcastle Beer Production Ltd*

### Summary

Scottish & Newcastle Breweries plc, employing a total of 21 000 people throughout the UK, is one of the principal companies managed and resident in Scotland. Its main activities are the production, wholesale and retail sale of beer, the sale of wines and spirits, and the ownership and operation of hotels. Beer production is the responsibility of Scottish & Newcastle Beer Production Ltd which operates three brewing complexes—Fountain Brewery in Edinburgh, Tyne Brewery in Newcastle and the Royal Brewery in Manchester.

The Edinburgh brewery is one of the largest and most fully automated brewery complexes in the world. The use of simulation to solve management problems was initiated by the Industrial Engineering Department based in the Edinburgh brewing complex. This model of the brewery is in regular use to ratify capital investment strategies and to test operational alternatives to improve plant efficiency.

The case study describes an investigation which evaluated proposals to re-allocate the use of existing tanks and utilize new tanks in the brewery in order to increase the proportion of lager processed. The model was to include the operation of current process developments. These included the installation of a new packaging line, a new filter, brewhouse modifications to increase throughput and a new filter to separate residual yeast/beer slurries.

## Background

The Group's products include McEwan's Export, McEwan's Lager, Younger's Tartan, Younger's Scotch Bitter, Newcastle Brown Ale and Exhibition Ale. The Group also have a franchise agreement to brew and sell the Harp Lager brands.

The production process utilizes basic raw materials such as water, barley, maize, sugar and hops. These materials are blended, heated and filtered through a series of specialized vessels to produce a sweet fermentable liquid called wort. The addition of yeast converts wort sugars to alcohol which is then matured before filtration and packaging in cans, kegs or bottles.

The process essentially involves the transfer of a liquid product from one specialized tank to another. It is complicated by the number of different beer qualities, variable process times, shift cycles, downtime levels and a limited number of processing routes through the system. The interaction of these parameters can make the effects of major process changes difficult to predict.

When the brewery was planned to undergo a major re-development it was decided that a simulation model of the plant was needed to study the effects of the proposed plant changes. Figure C5.1 shows the construction of a brewery.

The HOCUS simulation system was selected from a number of simulation packages as it offered a readily understandable format for model construction and experimentation, and effective support and training facilities. On completion of an in-house training course involving production/industrial engineers, brewers and line managers a complete model of the production process was developed.

**Figure C5.1**

The model provided management with an insight to the potential bottlenecks of the new plant and a detailed assessment of capacity. Subsequent studies have identified energy saving measures which eliminated the requirement to purchase an additional warm water overflow tank. Proposals to centralize bright beer filtration in the complex were initially evaluated on the model. Other applications have examined manning and fork truck utilization.

The simulation expertise gained from the brewery model has been used to assist in the development of simulation models of management problems in the Tyne and Manchester brewing centres. In the Tyne brewery a model was used to evaluate alternative plant configurations for a new brewhouse. In Manchester a more elaborate model was constructed to simulate the evolution of $CO_2$ from the process. This model identified process changes which would increase the volume of the $CO_2$ recovered from the process.

## The problem

The rapid growth in consumer demand for lager products and the re-allocation of ale and lager brewing throughout the group led to the formulation of a series of options which would increase the volume of lager processed in the Edinburgh brewing complex.

Proposals ranged from the purchase of new tank capacity to a combination of new tanks and spare tanks from another part of the process. The alternative uses of the additional tanks were to be tested against different permutations of the existing tank population. The development was designed as a two-stage process matching the programmed lager increase. The following options were evaluated by the simulation:

*Option 1*
*Stage 1* Split the existing tank population between ale unitanks and lager fermentation tanks to meet stage 1 lager demand.
*Stage 2* Add new lager fermentation/maturation tanks to meet stage 2 lager demand.

*Option 2*
*Stage 1* Add new lager fermentation/maturation tanks to the existing plant configuration to meet stage 1 lager demand.
*Stage 2* Purchase additional lager fermentation/maturation tanks and split the tank population as option 1, stage 1.

*Option 3*
*Stage 1* Add surplus tanks from another part of the process and re-use as lager fermenters.
*Stage 2* Add new lager maturation tanks and swap existing lager fermentation with ale fermentation. The additional stage 1 tanks to be used for minor ale qualities.

The problem was further complicated as the model was to include the operation of current plant developments. These developments included:

- the completion of an additional packaging line which would be supplied direct from the brewery buffer tanks instead of first being transferred to buffer tanks located in the packaging area;
- a high capacity filtration unit which was nearing completion (the model previously had been used to help justify the purchase of this unit and considerable data were available on operational capacity);
- a yeast filter was to be installed which would remove a significant delay factor during peak production;
- a new lager quality was to be introduced with a longer processing time;
- production management had requested that a number of proposed options to increase the brewhouse throughput be evaluated with the new tanks.

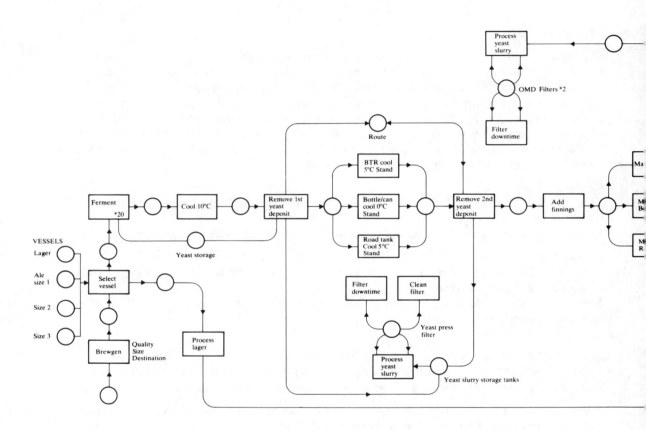

**Figure C5.2**

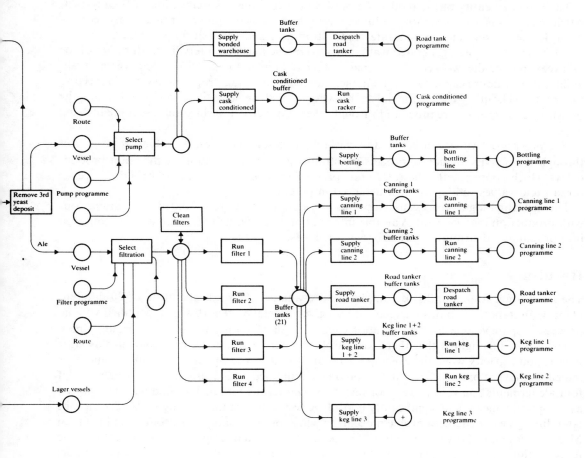

## The model

The model simulates a continuous process 24 hours a day, 7 days per week. It consists of 228 entities, 10 entity groups, 122 queues, 60 timetables/distributions, 6 databases, 276 discrete activities (100 identical) and 42 continuous activities. A summary of the main activities is shown in Fig. C5.2.

The principal entity of the model is a brew which contains a specification of the product. Attributes are set which identify volume, strength, brew type, process route, yeast requirement, fermentation time, cooling rate, maturation time and yeast slurry generated.

The number of brews generated was controlled by the mashing interval, the duration of the midweek break, the weekend maintenance break, brewhouse downtime and vessel availability. If brewhouse capacity was available, the weekly brewing programme was advanced to the next week in order to maximize brewhouse and vessel utilization. On leaving the brewhouse the brews were processed through a series of activities which represent the brewing logic.

The process activities can be fixed or variable duration activities. As the brew progresses through the activity sequence, process constraints and the interaction of the plant produce delays which contribute to the total brew processing time. This interaction produces vessel turnaround values similar to those achieved in practice.

The operating logic, process assumptions and parameters were validated from discussions with production management. Variable information (e.g., fermentation times) was compiled into probability distributions from brewing records.

## Results

The study took four months to complete and evaluated the peak operation of 20 different plant permutations. Senior management was given a detailed report which identified volume processed, spare vessel capacity, filtration capacity, delay factors and vessel turnaround times.

The report highlighted that there was surplus ale fermentation capacity and surplus lager maturation capacity when the existing plant configuration was operated at peak output. This indicated that the present ale volumes could be maintained and lager significantly increased if four ale fermentation vessels were converted to lager fermentation. This finding was reported as an option which could significantly boost lager output from the existing tanks. Six months later during peak demand a problem occurred which put the main lager production facility in Manchester temporarily out of action. The decision was taken temporarily to convert four ale fermentation vessels to lager fermentation. As had been predicted by the simulaton model lager output from the Edinburgh brewery was increased to the desired level while ale capacity was maintained.

This strategy along with other measures to boost lager output enabled the Group to meet peak output without the loss of sales.

## Conclusion

The model assisted senior management in selecting the most appropriate plant configuration and development strategy for the programmed increase in lager production. The ability to experiment with the process parameters generated new options which in the case of the ale fermentation conversion made a major contribution to the company meeting demand when the main lager production unit was out of action.

---

## Comments

This case study highlights the cost-effectiveness of a well conducted simulation exercise. By testing the effect of proposed developments it was possible to plan for the future with confidence.

All too often intuitive decisions are taken on the appropriate utilization of a piece of equipment without appreciating the dynamics of the total system and the consequent effects. In complex queuing problems where mistakes can be expensive it pays to buy understanding and confidence. The cost of a simulation study is usually a small fraction of the bill for making a mistake at the design stage.

In this example expenditure on simulation bought confidence—not only the confidence to select robust development paths, but also the confidence to deal with contingencies quickly and efficiently as they arose.

# Case Study 6.

## Designing a better conveyor system

*by* **Brian Hargrave and Malcolm Steeksma**
*Logan Fenamec (UK) Ltd*

### Summary

Established in Kingston-upon-Hull, North Humberside, in 1956, Logan Fenamec (UK) Ltd have carried out advanced conveyor system design for many well known national and international companies.

A major oil company, which was an established customer, commissioned the design of a new barrel handling installation early in 1985 through a firm of engineering consultants in London. Work began in 1985 on the two-year project which was to include a simulation study.

As conveyor systems were becoming more complex, it was thought necessary to introduce computer modelling as a design tool to study the interaction of the various elements present in the system. For this study the HOCUS simulation program was used and a model built within three months.

Experience gained through building the model has led to a greater understanding of conveyor systems' operational characteristics, not only on the project in question, but over a wide area of general applications. The study therefore also forms the basis of research into creating standard modules for conveyor applications.

## The problem

The empty barrel store comprises a multi-level live storage system together with a system of powered belt and roller conveyors which route the barrels into and out of the barrel store. Barrel store controls are shown in Fig. C6.1.

The conveyor system accepts barrels from the loading dock and transports them via a buffer store to primary inspection. Barrels may be old or new and the inspection time varies. From primary inspection the barrels may be routed direct to filling but the majority are fed to storage.

Efficient control and use of the live storage system often necessitates recirculating barrels. Barrels may be re-assigned to another storage lane. The conveyor system is able to transport barrels from any lane at any level back into the store at the re-assigned location.

Barrels from the store are routed to one of several filling heads and are handled in batches. A batch may be made up of a number of barrels from different locations within the store. In

**Figure C6.1**

some instances it may be necessary to route the barrels to filling via secondary inspection. From secondary inspection barrels may merge with those from storage to filling and those from primary inspection direct to filling. The whole of the conveyor system is in fact a shared resource and satisfies a multi-functional role.

Due to the complexity of the system and its functional interdependencies it was decided to use simulation to evaluate the performance of the real system and compare this with the contractual requirements specification. The specification dictated several functional requirements for the store in terms of overall barrel movement into and out of the store. The model was to simulate individual barrel movement from off-loading through inspection tasks to storage or to filling.

Barrel output from the store to filling and for recirculation was to be modelled using instruction sets down-loaded by the supervisory computer system. The effect of simulated information was to be similar to the *real* data generated. The model was to test for significant queues, monitor filling head activities and idle time, and evaluate the capability of the system to handle concurrent tasks.

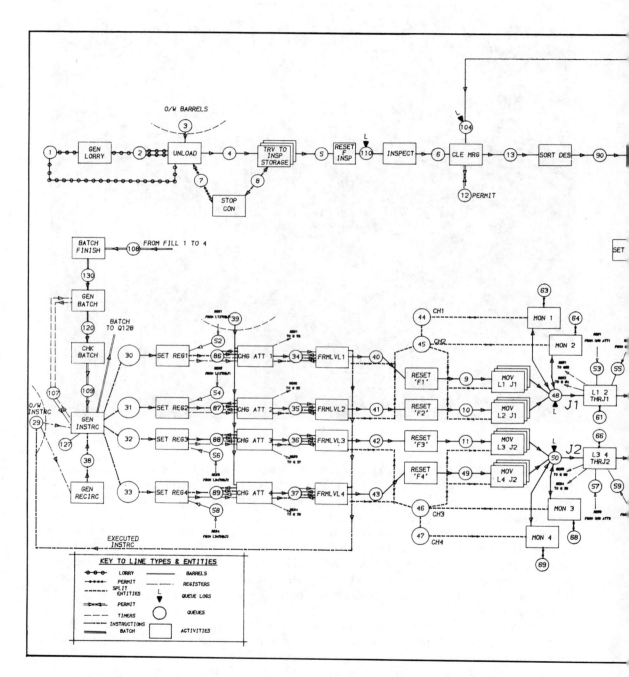

**Figure C6.2**

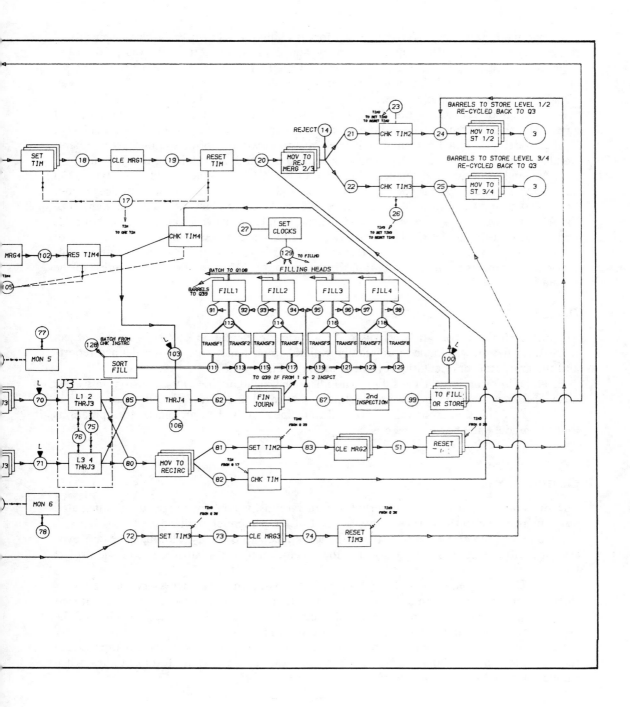

## The model

The flow diagram was considered essential for checking the logic of the various elements in the conveyor system with plant management and consultants. Attention was paid to the definition of entity life cycles and the routes through the model were described using an approach similar to hand simulation. This ensured that all logic operations could be checked visually as well as by detailed reference to attributes and other data.

Any initial objections to the defined logic were quickly corrected and eventually full agreement, that the model reflected the operational characteristics of the plant, was achieved.

The model was built for formal computer operation without prior use of extensive hand simulation as it was thought too complex and time consuming for long simulation runs.

In the final form the model which is outlined in Fig. C6.2, consisted of 38 entity types, 130 queues, 29 data fields, 267 activities, 4 queue logs and 8 histograms. The model was run on a Prime 450 Series 1 computer used by the company for CAD (computer aided design). The simulation time unit was one second and the run simulated between one and four hours. It was found that the model reached a steady state after about three hours and comparison of output was based upon this run time. Each computer run took about 20 minutes with various user-defined reports giving a continuous display on the VDU to monitor the progress of the simulation.

## Results

The output from the program was used for a formal presentation of results to the project team. Information was made more readily available by extensive use of user-defined reports and the graphical representation of queue logs and histograms.

Essential information such as filling head idle time was highlighted by the histograms while areas of limited accumulation were constantly monitored and recorded in the queue logs.

Further graphical analysis was performed to define exactly the time phases for operations that the model had shown to be critical.

## Conclusions

The study was performed over a period of four months, which was longer than anticipated but primarily due to the part-time involvement of the personnel involved.

In some respects the benefits of the study are difficult to quantify, although the conveyor system performance was verified against the specification to the satisfaction of the project team.

Particular attention was paid to multi-use of conveyor elements, a necessary feature due to the physical constraints within the building. The simulation was able to monitor the traffic at points of potential interference and enable decisions to be made on the feasibility of the layout before any commitment to manufacture was made.

Significant advances were made during the building of the model in the general approach to tackling material handling problems. This will lead to savings in future studies when simulation could be readily applied.

## Comments

In any complex system the temptation to draw intuitive conclusions from simply applied theory is a dangerous one. The sheer mass of data needed to verify a single move is simply outside the scope of manual analysis. Only by employing simulation to model the complete dynamic picture can we be confident that our beliefs are based on proven facts, backed up by results that can inspire confidence in the observer.

The expense of simulation cannot be overlooked. However, if correctly managed it can be justified by the avoidance of hugely expensive design errors before they are cast in concrete.

# Appendix 1.

## Tables of random numbers

These random numbers are generated by the HOCUS program and should be used when the hand and computer simulations are to produce identical results.

Each distribution has its own stream of random numbers. Stream 1 is used for distribution 1, stream 2 for distribution 2, etc.

The values in each table should be taken in strict order, reading from left to right along successive rows.

*Note*   The distribution number may not be the same as the data field number used in the 'time data' of the activities. The distribution number ignores any timetables while the data field number includes them.

## Stream 1

| | | | | | | | | | |
|---|---|---|---|---|---|---|---|---|---|
| 89 | 42 | 85 | 26 | 53 | 66 | 49 | 13 | 97 | 13 |
| 20 | 21 | 5 | 5 | 34 | 60 | 70 | 49 | 68 | 82 |
| 43 | 52 | 61 | 93 | 33 | 57 | 66 | 4 | 98 | 27 |
| 45 | 61 | 9 | 33 | 27 | 40 | 94 | 19 | 9 | 31 |
| 100 | 100 | 24 | 96 | 1 | 69 | 11 | 70 | 37 | 70 |
| 82 | 9 | 47 | 76 | 75 | 98 | 17 | 12 | 81 | 60 |
| 40 | 46 | 53 | 4 | 93 | 48 | 70 | 21 | 93 | 7 |
| 34 | 26 | 65 | 64 | 49 | 47 | 2 | 98 | 38 | 55 |
| 46 | 59 | 58 | 98 | 58 | 48 | 76 | 88 | 83 | 32 |
| 31 | 66 | 59 | 59 | 62 | 78 | 33 | 87 | 92 | 14 |
| 76 | 46 | 60 | 22 | 18 | 43 | 59 | 80 | 18 | 28 |
| 47 | 25 | 29 | 18 | 39 | 44 | 25 | 64 | 23 | 24 |
| 62 | 59 | 4 | 77 | 48 | 100 | 47 | 3 | 86 | 53 |
| 40 | 26 | 73 | 59 | 79 | 42 | 23 | 47 | 93 | 39 |
| 88 | 76 | 14 | 6 | 72 | 70 | 100 | 37 | 57 | 21 |
| 89 | 28 | 59 | 86 | 49 | 38 | 56 | 33 | 74 | 43 |
| 79 | 72 | 48 | 57 | 72 | 58 | 3 | 37 | 23 | 15 |
| 4 | 9 | 25 | 45 | 95 | 14 | 18 | 46 | 75 | 35 |
| 73 | 32 | 69 | 87 | 99 | 32 | 1 | 41 | 49 | 80 |
| 43 | 63 | 72 | 78 | 82 | 82 | 37 | 21 | 51 | 84 |
| 24 | 13 | 41 | 64 | 70 | 3 | 52 | 12 | 75 | 93 |
| 50 | 22 | 56 | 63 | 99 | 53 | 57 | 91 | 63 | 18 |
| 81 | 67 | 35 | 76 | 47 | 24 | 42 | 3 | 54 | 63 |
| 10 | 63 | 42 | 40 | 87 | 88 | 99 | 21 | 91 | 56 |
| 99 | 56 | 73 | 46 | 18 | 22 | 3 | 30 | 4 | 90 |
| 9 | 20 | 66 | 20 | 75 | 2 | 20 | 82 | 20 | 45 |
| 76 | 10 | 3 | 2 | 30 | 15 | 100 | 94 | 70 | 91 |
| 91 | 92 | 56 | 76 | 61 | 73 | 77 | 7 | 52 | 67 |
| 60 | 23 | 82 | 63 | 44 | 91 | 22 | 58 | 91 | 39 |
| 23 | 81 | 99 | 24 | 6 | 11 | 54 | 60 | 95 | 8 |
| 88 | 36 | 65 | 26 | 29 | 7 | 29 | 59 | 75 | 39 |
| 53 | 7 | 9 | 3 | 25 | 25 | 15 | 69 | 4 | 40 |
| 27 | 60 | 74 | 64 | 23 | 37 | 47 | 74 | 24 | 63 |
| 47 | 19 | 62 | 28 | 15 | 47 | 84 | 70 | 28 | 11 |
| 32 | 29 | 15 | 24 | 89 | 70 | 59 | 1 | 62 | 93 |
| 45 | 42 | 81 | 23 | 83 | 26 | 64 | 76 | 34 | 62 |
| 22 | 84 | 37 | 74 | 61 | 84 | 87 | 92 | 1 | 91 |
| 31 | 40 | 36 | 19 | 24 | 44 | 55 | 89 | 33 | 3 |
| 81 | 74 | 65 | 86 | 57 | 32 | 86 | 28 | 94 | 91 |
| 34 | 56 | 91 | 74 | 28 | 66 | 17 | 59 | 47 | 65 |

## Stream 2

| | | | | | | | | | |
|---|---|---|---|---|---|---|---|---|---|
| 43 | 78 | 84 | 33 | 72 | 91 | 44 | 2 | 56 | 38 |
| 40 | 33 | 4 | 69 | 89 | 50 | 67 | 71 | 33 | 67 |
| 12 | 69 | 62 | 40 | 12 | 47 | 19 | 75 | 13 | 30 |
| 67 | 70 | 69 | 47 | 27 | 57 | 58 | 9 | 68 | 33 |
| 25 | 12 | 54 | 49 | 85 | 23 | 38 | 11 | 94 | 9 |
| | | | | | | | | | |
| 75 | 51 | 50 | 7 | 43 | 8 | 10 | 43 | 50 | 10 |
| 58 | 63 | 65 | 48 | 72 | 72 | 28 | 77 | 27 | 44 |
| 97 | 89 | 48 | 16 | 36 | 63 | 75 | 94 | 37 | 37 |
| 41 | 44 | 14 | 53 | 38 | 75 | 38 | 89 | 87 | 24 |
| 91 | 21 | 94 | 71 | 54 | 11 | 77 | 68 | 80 | 92 |
| | | | | | | | | | |
| 17 | 92 | 1 | 15 | 26 | 40 | 5 | 29 | 94 | 80 |
| 24 | 71 | 42 | 49 | 57 | 48 | 63 | 3 | 68 | 12 |
| 45 | 67 | 40 | 43 | 37 | 49 | 38 | 44 | 48 | 59 |
| 23 | 93 | 73 | 29 | 41 | 47 | 29 | 8 | 93 | 79 |
| 60 | 51 | 57 | 38 | 53 | 18 | 19 | 88 | 75 | 50 |
| | | | | | | | | | |
| 86 | 87 | 58 | 96 | 6 | 13 | 6 | 95 | 65 | 100 |
| 6 | 67 | 91 | 25 | 97 | 41 | 94 | 96 | 13 | 31 |
| 31 | 90 | 54 | 59 | 31 | 88 | 3 | 24 | 61 | 95 |
| 84 | 92 | 36 | 96 | 16 | 59 | 71 | 60 | 78 | 67 |
| 93 | 77 | 32 | 11 | 87 | 14 | 45 | 56 | 30 | 58 |
| | | | | | | | | | |
| 88 | 24 | 68 | 26 | 94 | 2 | 44 | 41 | 40 | 98 |
| 98 | 84 | 71 | 16 | 26 | 17 | 10 | 29 | 25 | 70 |
| 54 | 34 | 72 | 68 | 49 | 2 | 87 | 28 | 70 | 96 |
| 34 | 87 | 81 | 4 | 91 | 96 | 35 | 51 | 1 | 89 |
| 3 | 100 | 66 | 95 | 16 | 82 | 66 | 60 | 46 | 77 |
| | | | | | | | | | |
| 63 | 13 | 2 | 92 | 95 | 60 | 21 | 31 | 28 | 74 |
| 99 | 4 | 27 | 66 | 40 | 54 | 47 | 34 | 88 | 68 |
| 19 | 76 | 77 | 50 | 52 | 82 | 73 | 78 | 71 | 72 |
| 52 | 72 | 27 | 13 | 7 | 59 | 85 | 85 | 18 | 71 |
| 21 | 70 | 12 | 34 | 57 | 55 | 94 | 13 | 78 | 21 |
| | | | | | | | | | |
| 90 | 92 | 79 | 71 | 61 | 42 | 87 | 77 | 88 | 36 |
| 42 | 31 | 29 | 38 | 19 | 89 | 39 | 70 | 71 | 99 |
| 62 | 27 | 51 | 27 | 99 | 58 | 24 | 81 | 88 | 14 |
| 21 | 61 | 30 | 89 | 77 | 54 | 31 | 57 | 13 | 94 |
| 98 | 65 | 66 | 1 | 82 | 72 | 90 | 56 | 87 | 71 |
| | | | | | | | | | |
| 58 | 26 | 32 | 23 | 84 | 14 | 79 | 61 | 15 | 77 |
| 22 | 65 | 22 | 49 | 32 | 89 | 43 | 49 | 46 | 38 |
| 78 | 53 | 44 | 42 | 28 | 13 | 83 | 64 | 85 | 16 |
| 7 | 1 | 85 | 100 | 30 | 26 | 11 | 79 | 19 | 15 |
| 62 | 10 | 10 | 32 | 40 | 25 | 9 | 39 | 94 | 30 |

## Stream 3

| | | | | | | | | | |
|---|---|---|---|---|---|---|---|---|---|
| 98 | 14 | 84 | 41 | 90 | 16 | 38 | 91 | 15 | 64 |
| 61 | 45 | 2 | 32 | 43 | 40 | 64 | 93 | 99 | 52 |
| 81 | 86 | 63 | 86 | 91 | 37 | 71 | 46 | 29 | 32 |
| 88 | 79 | 29 | 61 | 27 | 74 | 22 | 99 | 27 | 34 |
| 51 | 24 | 84 | 3 | 69 | 76 | 65 | 52 | 52 | 47 |
| 68 | 93 | 53 | 37 | 11 | 18 | 4 | 75 | 20 | 60 |
| 77 | 80 | 78 | 92 | 52 | 97 | 86 | 33 | 61 | 81 |
| 59 | 52 | 31 | 68 | 23 | 79 | 47 | 89 | 37 | 18 |
| 36 | 29 | 70 | 9 | 19 | 2 | 100 | 90 | 90 | 16 |
| 51 | 76 | 30 | 83 | 47 | 44 | 21 | 48 | 68 | 69 |
| 58 | 37 | 42 | 8 | 34 | 38 | 50 | 79 | 69 | 33 |
| 2 | 17 | 54 | 80 | 75 | 53 | 2 | 42 | 13 | 100 |
| 28 | 75 | 76 | 9 | 27 | 97 | 30 | 84 | 11 | 64 |
| 6 | 60 | 72 | 100 | 3 | 52 | 36 | 70 | 93 | 19 |
| 32 | 26 | 100 | 69 | 34 | 66 | 37 | 39 | 92 | 79 |
| 84 | 46 | 57 | 6 | 63 | 88 | 55 | 57 | 56 | 58 |
| 33 | 63 | 33 | 94 | 22 | 24 | 86 | 54 | 4 | 46 |
| 58 | 70 | 83 | 73 | 67 | 61 | 87 | 2 | 47 | 56 |
| 95 | 53 | 3 | 6 | 33 | 85 | 40 | 79 | 6 | 54 |
| 42 | 90 | 93 | 43 | 91 | 46 | 53 | 91 | 8 | 33 |
| 51 | 35 | 94 | 88 | 19 | 1 | 36 | 70 | 5 | 4 |
| 47 | 45 | 85 | 68 | 53 | 81 | 62 | 68 | 86 | 22 |
| 27 | 1 | 9 | 59 | 50 | 80 | 33 | 53 | 87 | 29 |
| 58 | 11 | 19 | 68 | 95 | 5 | 72 | 81 | 10 | 22 |
| 6 | 45 | 59 | 45 | 13 | 43 | 28 | 90 | 88 | 64 |
| 16 | 6 | 37 | 65 | 15 | 19 | 22 | 80 | 35 | 4 |
| 22 | 99 | 50 | 29 | 51 | 93 | 94 | 73 | 6 | 46 |
| 47 | 60 | 98 | 23 | 43 | 91 | 69 | 48 | 91 | 77 |
| 43 | 21 | 72 | 63 | 69 | 27 | 47 | 12 | 44 | 3 |
| 20 | 58 | 25 | 45 | 8 | 99 | 33 | 65 | 61 | 34 |
| 92 | 47 | 94 | 16 | 93 | 76 | 45 | 96 | 2 | 33 |
| 31 | 55 | 49 | 74 | 13 | 53 | 62 | 70 | 38 | 57 |
| 97 | 94 | 28 | 91 | 76 | 79 | 1 | 87 | 52 | 65 |
| 96 | 3 | 97 | 51 | 40 | 61 | 78 | 44 | 97 | 77 |
| 63 | 1 | 17 | 77 | 75 | 75 | 22 | 12 | 12 | 49 |
| 70 | 10 | 83 | 22 | 85 | 1 | 94 | 46 | 95 | 91 |
| 23 | 46 | 6 | 24 | 3 | 95 | 99 | 5 | 91 | 86 |
| 25 | 66 | 51 | 64 | 32 | 83 | 12 | 39 | 36 | 30 |
| 34 | 29 | 4 | 14 | 4 | 20 | 35 | 30 | 45 | 39 |
| 89 | 63 | 29 | 91 | 52 | 84 | 1 | 18 | 41 | 95 |

## Stream 4

| | | | | | | | | | |
|---|---|---|---|---|---|---|---|---|---|
| 52 | 50 | 83 | 48 | 8 | 41 | 33 | 80 | 73 | 89 |
| 82 | 57 | 1 | 96 | 98 | 30 | 61 | 16 | 64 | 37 |
| 50 | 2 | 64 | 33 | 70 | 27 | 24 | 17 | 44 | 34 |
| 10 | 88 | 89 | 75 | 26 | 91 | 87 | 89 | 86 | 36 |
| 76 | 36 | 14 | 57 | 54 | 30 | 93 | 93 | 9 | 86 |
| 61 | 35 | 56 | 67 | 79 | 28 | 97 | 7 | 89 | 11 |
| 95 | 96 | 90 | 36 | 31 | 21 | 44 | 89 | 94 | 18 |
| 21 | 16 | 15 | 19 | 10 | 95 | 20 | 85 | 36 | 100 |
| 31 | 14 | 26 | 64 | 100 | 29 | 62 | 91 | 94 | 7 |
| 11 | 31 | 65 | 95 | 39 | 77 | 66 | 29 | 57 | 47 |
| 99 | 83 | 83 | 1 | 41 | 36 | 95 | 28 | 44 | 86 |
| 79 | 63 | 66 | 12 | 92 | 57 | 40 | 81 | 58 | 89 |
| 11 | 83 | 11 | 75 | 16 | 45 | 22 | 25 | 73 | 69 |
| 89 | 27 | 72 | 71 | 64 | 57 | 42 | 32 | 93 | 58 |
| 4 | 1 | 43 | 100 | 15 | 13 | 56 | 90 | 10 | 8 |
| 81 | 5 | 55 | 16 | 20 | 63 | 5 | 20 | 47 | 15 |
| 60 | 58 | 75 | 63 | 48 | 7 | 77 | 13 | 95 | 62 |
| 85 | 51 | 12 | 86 | 3 | 35 | 71 | 80 | 34 | 17 |
| 7 | 14 | 70 | 15 | 50 | 12 | 10 | 98 | 35 | 40 |
| 91 | 4 | 54 | 76 | 95 | 78 | 62 | 26 | 87 | 7 |
| 14 | 46 | 20 | 50 | 43 | 100 | 28 | 98 | 71 | 9 |
| 96 | 7 | 100 | 21 | 80 | 46 | 14 | 7 | 48 | 75 |
| 100 | 68 | 47 | 51 | 52 | 58 | 78 | 78 | 3 | 62 |
| 82 | 35 | 57 | 31 | 99 | 13 | 9 | 11 | 20 | 55 |
| 10 | 90 | 53 | 95 | 11 | 3 | 91 | 20 | 30 | 51 |
| 70 | 99 | 73 | 37 | 36 | 77 | 24 | 29 | 42 | 34 |
| 44 | 93 | 74 | 93 | 61 | 32 | 41 | 12 | 24 | 23 |
| 75 | 44 | 19 | 97 | 33 | 100 | 66 | 19 | 11 | 82 |
| 35 | 70 | 16 | 14 | 32 | 95 | 10 | 39 | 71 | 35 |
| 19 | 47 | 39 | 55 | 58 | 44 | 73 | 18 | 43 | 47 |
| 95 | 3 | 8 | 61 | 25 | 10 | 2 | 14 | 15 | 30 |
| 20 | 80 | 69 | 10 | 7 | 17 | 85 | 70 | 5 | 16 |
| 32 | 60 | 5 | 54 | 53 | 100 | 78 | 93 | 16 | 17 |
| 71 | 45 | 65 | 12 | 3 | 67 | 25 | 30 | 82 | 59 |
| 29 | 36 | 68 | 54 | 69 | 77 | 53 | 67 | 37 | 28 |
| 82 | 94 | 34 | 21 | 86 | 89 | 9 | 31 | 76 | 5 |
| 24 | 27 | 90 | 99 | 74 | 1 | 56 | 62 | 35 | 33 |
| 72 | 79 | 59 | 87 | 37 | 53 | 41 | 14 | 88 | 43 |
| 60 | 56 | 23 | 28 | 78 | 14 | 59 | 82 | 70 | 63 |
| 16 | 17 | 47 | 50 | 65 | 43 | 93 | 97 | 88 | 61 |

## Stream 5

| | | | | | | | | | |
|---|---|---|---|---|---|---|---|---|---|
| 6 | 87 | 83 | 55 | 26 | 66 | 28 | 69 | 32 | 14 |
| 2 | 69 | 100 | 60 | 52 | 21 | 58 | 38 | 29 | 23 |
| 19 | 19 | 64 | 80 | 50 | 17 | 77 | 88 | 60 | 37 |
| 31 | 98 | 49 | 89 | 26 | 8 | 51 | 79 | 45 | 38 |
| 2 | 48 | 44 | 10 | 38 | 83 | 20 | 34 | 66 | 25 |
| 54 | 77 | 59 | 98 | 47 | 38 | 91 | 38 | 59 | 61 |
| 14 | 13 | 2 | 80 | 10 | 45 | 2 | 45 | 28 | 55 |
| 83 | 79 | 98 | 71 | 97 | 11 | 92 | 81 | 35 | 81 |
| 26 | 99 | 81 | 19 | 81 | 56 | 25 | 91 | 98 | 99 |
| 71 | 86 | 1 | 7 | 31 | 10 | 10 | 9 | 45 | 25 |
| 40 | 28 | 24 | 94 | 49 | 34 | 41 | 78 | 19 | 38 |
| 57 | 10 | 79 | 43 | 10 | 62 | 78 | 20 | 2 | 77 |
| 95 | 90 | 47 | 41 | 6 | 93 | 13 | 65 | 36 | 75 |
| 72 | 94 | 72 | 42 | 26 | 62 | 48 | 94 | 92 | 98 |
| 76 | 76 | 86 | 32 | 97 | 61 | 74 | 41 | 27 | 37 |
| 78 | 64 | 54 | 27 | 77 | 38 | 54 | 82 | 39 | 73 |
| 86 | 54 | 17 | 31 | 73 | 90 | 69 | 72 | 86 | 77 |
| 12 | 31 | 42 | 100 | 39 | 8 | 56 | 59 | 20 | 78 |
| 18 | 75 | 37 | 25 | 67 | 39 | 79 | 17 | 64 | 27 |
| 40 | 17 | 14 | 9 | 100 | 10 | 70 | 61 | 65 | 82 |
| 77 | 57 | 46 | 12 | 68 | 98 | 20 | 27 | 36 | 15 |
| 44 | 69 | 15 | 73 | 7 | 10 | 67 | 45 | 10 | 27 |
| 73 | 35 | 84 | 42 | 54 | 36 | 23 | 3 | 19 | 94 |
| 5 | 60 | 96 | 95 | 3 | 21 | 46 | 40 | 29 | 88 |
| 14 | 34 | 46 | 45 | 9 | 63 | 53 | 50 | 72 | 38 |
| 23 | 92 | 9 | 9 | 56 | 35 | 25 | 78 | 49 | 64 |
| 67 | 88 | 97 | 57 | 71 | 71 | 88 | 52 | 42 | 1 |
| 3 | 28 | 40 | 70 | 24 | 9 | 62 | 89 | 30 | 87 |
| 26 | 19 | 61 | 64 | 95 | 62 | 72 | 66 | 97 | 67 |
| 17 | 36 | 52 | 65 | 9 | 88 | 12 | 70 | 26 | 60 |
| 97 | 59 | 23 | 6 | 58 | 44 | 60 | 33 | 28 | 28 |
| 9 | 4 | 89 | 45 | 100 | 81 | 8 | 71 | 71 | 75 |
| 67 | 27 | 82 | 17 | 29 | 21 | 55 | 99 | 79 | 68 |
| 46 | 87 | 32 | 73 | 66 | 74 | 72 | 17 | 67 | 42 |
| 95 | 72 | 18 | 31 | 62 | 80 | 84 | 22 | 62 | 6 |
| 94 | 77 | 85 | 21 | 87 | 76 | 24 | 16 | 57 | 19 |
| 25 | 8 | 75 | 74 | 45 | 7 | 12 | 18 | 80 | 80 |
| 20 | 92 | 67 | 10 | 41 | 22 | 70 | 88 | 39 | 57 |
| 86 | 84 | 43 | 41 | 51 | 8 | 83 | 33 | 95 | 86 |
| 44 | 71 | 66 | 8 | 77 | 2 | 85 | 77 | 35 | 26 |

## Stream 6

| | | | | | | | | | |
|---|---|---|---|---|---|---|---|---|---|
| 60 | 23 | 82 | 63 | 44 | 91 | 22 | 58 | 91 | 39 |
| 23 | 81 | 99 | 24 | 6 | 11 | 54 | 60 | 95 | 8 |
| 88 | 36 | 65 | 26 | 29 | 7 | 29 | 59 | 75 | 39 |
| 53 | 7 | 9 | 3 | 25 | 25 | 15 | 69 | 4 | 40 |
| 27 | 60 | 74 | 64 | 23 | 37 | 47 | 74 | 24 | 63 |
| 47 | 19 | 62 | 28 | 15 | 47 | 84 | 70 | 28 | 11 |
| 32 | 29 | 15 | 24 | 89 | 70 | 59 | 1 | 62 | 93 |
| 45 | 42 | 81 | 23 | 83 | 26 | 64 | 76 | 34 | 62 |
| 22 | 84 | 37 | 74 | 61 | 84 | 87 | 92 | 1 | 91 |
| 31 | 40 | 36 | 19 | 24 | 44 | 55 | 89 | 33 | 3 |
| 81 | 74 | 65 | 86 | 57 | 32 | 86 | 28 | 94 | 91 |
| 34 | 56 | 91 | 74 | 28 | 66 | 17 | 59 | 47 | 65 |
| 78 | 98 | 82 | 7 | 96 | 41 | 5 | 6 | 98 | 80 |
| 55 | 61 | 72 | 13 | 87 | 67 | 55 | 56 | 92 | 38 |
| 48 | 51 | 29 | 63 | 78 | 9 | 92 | 92 | 45 | 66 |
| 76 | 23 | 52 | 37 | 34 | 13 | 4 | 44 | 30 | 30 |
| 13 | 49 | 59 | 100 | 98 | 73 | 61 | 31 | 77 | 92 |
| 39 | 12 | 71 | 14 | 75 | 82 | 40 | 37 | 6 | 39 |
| 29 | 35 | 4 | 34 | 84 | 65 | 49 | 36 | 92 | 13 |
| 89 | 31 | 75 | 41 | 4 | 42 | 78 | 95 | 43 | 57 |
| 41 | 68 | 73 | 73 | 92 | 97 | 12 | 56 | 1 | 20 |
| 93 | 30 | 30 | 26 | 34 | 74 | 19 | 84 | 72 | 80 |
| 46 | 2 | 22 | 33 | 55 | 14 | 69 | 28 | 35 | 27 |
| 29 | 84 | 34 | 59 | 6 | 29 | 83 | 70 | 39 | 21 |
| 17 | 79 | 39 | 95 | 7 | 24 | 16 | 80 | 14 | 25 |
| 77 | 85 | 44 | 82 | 76 | 93 | 26 | 27 | 56 | 94 |
| 89 | 83 | 21 | 21 | 81 | 9 | 34 | 91 | 60 | 79 |
| 31 | 13 | 62 | 44 | 15 | 17 | 58 | 60 | 50 | 93 |
| 18 | 68 | 6 | 15 | 57 | 30 | 35 | 93 | 24 | 99 |
| 16 | 24 | 66 | 75 | 59 | 32 | 52 | 23 | 9 | 73 |
| 99 | 15 | 37 | 51 | 90 | 79 | 18 | 51 | 42 | 25 |
| 98 | 28 | 9 | 8i | 94 | 45 | 31 | 71 | 38 | 34 |
| 2 | 94 | 59 | 80 | 6 | 43 | 32 | 5 | 43 | 19 |
| 20 | 28 | 100 | 35 | 29 | 81 | 19 | 4 | 51 | 25 |
| 60 | 8 | 69 | 8 | 55 | 82 | 15 | 78 | 86 | 85 |
| 7 | 61 | 36 | 20 | 87 | 64 | 40 | 1 | 37 | 34 |
| 25 | 89 | 59 | 49 | 16 | 13 | 68 | 75 | 25 | 27 |
| 67 | 4 | 74 | 32 | 45 | 92 | 99 | 63 | 91 | 71 |
| 12 | 11 | 62 | 55 | 25 | 2 | 8 | 84 | 20 | 10 |
| 71 | 25 | 85 | 67 | 89 | 61 | 77 | 56 | 82 | 92 |

## Stream 7

| | | | | | | | | | |
|---|---|---|---|---|---|---|---|---|---|
| 14 | 59 | 82 | 70 | 63 | 16 | 17 | 47 | 50 | 65 |
| 43 | 93 | 97 | 88 | 61 | 1 | 51 | 82 | 60 | 93 |
| 56 | 53 | 66 | 73 | 8 | 97 | 82 | 30 | 91 | 41 |
| 74 | 16 | 68 | 17 | 25 | 42 | 80 | 59 | 63 | 42 |
| 53 | 72 | 3 | 18 | 7 | 90 | 75 | 15 | 81 | 2 |
| | | | | | | | | | |
| 40 | 61 | 65 | 59 | 82 | 57 | 78 | 1 | 98 | 62 |
| 50 | 46 | 27 | 68 | 68 | 94 | 17 | 57 | 96 | 30 |
| 8 | 6 | 64 | 75 | 70 | 42 | 37 | 72 | 33 | 44 |
| 17 | 69 | 93 | 30 | 42 | 11 | 49 | 93 | 5 | 83 |
| 91 | 95 | 71 | 31 | 16 | 77 | 99 | 70 | 22 | 81 |
| | | | | | | | | | |
| 22 | 19 | 6 | 79 | 65 | 30 | 32 | 77 | 69 | 44 |
| 12 | 2 | 3 | 5 | 45 | 70 | 55 | 98 | 92 | 53 |
| 61 | 6 | 18 | 72 | 85 | 90 | 97 | 46 | 61 | 86 |
| 38 | 27 | 71 | 84 | 49 | 72 | 61 | 18 | 92 | 77 |
| 20 | 26 | 72 | 95 | 59 | 57 | 11 | 43 | 63 | 95 |
| | | | | | | | | | |
| 73 | 82 | 51 | 47 | 91 | 88 | 53 | 6 | 21 | 88 |
| 40 | 44 | 1 | 69 | 23 | 55 | 52 | 89 | 68 | 8 |
| 66 | 92 | 100 | 27 | 11 | 56 | 24 | 15 | 93 | 99 |
| 40 | 96 | 71 | 44 | 1 | 92 | 18 | 55 | 21 | 100 |
| 38 | 44 | 36 | 74 | 8 | 74 | 87 | 30 | 22 | 31 |
| | | | | | | | | | |
| 4 | 79 | 99 | 35 | 17 | 96 | 3 | 85 | 66 | 25 |
| 41 | 92 | 44 | 78 | 61 | 38 | 72 | 22 | 34 | 32 |
| 19 | 69 | 59 | 25 | 57 | 93 | 14 | 53 | 51 | 60 |
| 53 | 8 | 73 | 23 | 10 | 37 | 19 | 100 | 49 | 55 |
| 21 | 23 | 33 | 44 | 4 | 84 | 78 | 10 | 56 | 12 |
| | | | | | | | | | |
| 30 | 78 | 80 | 54 | 97 | 52 | 28 | 76 | 63 | 24 |
| 12 | 77 | 44 | 85 | 92 | 48 | 81 | 31 | 78 | 56 |
| 59 | 97 | 83 | 18 | 6 | 26 | 55 | 30 | 69 | 98 |
| 9 | 17 | 51 | 65 | 20 | 98 | 97 | 20 | 51 | 31 |
| 15 | 13 | 79 | 85 | 10 | 77 | 91 | 75 | 92 | 86 |
| | | | | | | | | | |
| 2 | 71 | 51 | 95 | 22 | 13 | 76 | 69 | 55 | 22 |
| 87 | 53 | 29 | 16 | 88 | 9 | 55 | 71 | 5 | 93 |
| 37 | 60 | 36 | 44 | 83 | 64 | 8 | 11 | 7 | 70 |
| 95 | 70 | 67 | 96 | 92 | 87 | 66 | 91 | 36 | 7 |
| 26 | 44 | 20 | 84 | 48 | 85 | 46 | 33 | 11 | 63 |
| | | | | | | | | | |
| 19 | 45 | 87 | 20 | 88 | 51 | 55 | 86 | 18 | 48 |
| 26 | 70 | 43 | 24 | 87 | 18 | 24 | 31 | 70 | 74 |
| 14 | 17 | 82 | 55 | 50 | 61 | 28 | 38 | 42 | 84 |
| 39 | 38 | 81 | 69 | 99 | 96 | 32 | 36 | 46 | 34 |
| 99 | 78 | 4 | 26 | 2 | 20 | 69 | 35 | 30 | 57 |

# Stream 8

| | | | | | | | | | |
|---|---|---|---|---|---|---|---|---|---|
| 69 | 95 | 81 | 77 | 81 | 41 | 12 | 36 | 8 | 90 |
| 64 | 5 | 96 | 52 | 15 | 91 | 48 | 5 | 26 | 78 |
| 25 | 69 | 67 | 19 | 87 | 87 | 35 | 1 | 6 | 44 |
| 95 | 25 | 28 | 31 | 24 | 59 | 44 | 49 | 23 | 43 |
| 78 | 84 | 33 | 72 | 91 | 44 | 2 | 56 | 38 | 40 |
| 33 | 4 | 69 | 89 | 50 | 67 | 71 | 33 | 67 | 12 |
| 69 | 62 | 40 | 12 | 47 | 19 | 75 | 13 | 30 | 67 |
| 70 | 69 | 47 | 27 | 57 | 58 | 9 | 68 | 33 | 25 |
| 12 | 54 | 49 | 85 | 23 | 38 | 11 | 94 | 9 | 75 |
| 51 | 50 | 7 | 43 | 8 | 10 | 43 | 50 | 10 | 58 |
| 63 | 65 | 48 | 72 | 72 | 28 | 77 | 27 | 44 | 97 |
| 89 | 48 | 16 | 36 | 63 | 75 | 94 | 37 | 37 | 41 |
| 44 | 14 | 53 | 38 | 75 | 38 | 89 | 87 | 24 | 91 |
| 21 | 94 | 71 | 54 | 11 | 77 | 68 | 80 | 92 | 17 |
| 92 | 1 | 15 | 26 | 40 | 5 | 29 | 94 | 80 | 24 |
| 71 | 42 | 49 | 57 | 48 | 63 | 3 | 68 | 12 | 45 |
| 67 | 40 | 43 | 37 | 49 | 38 | 44 | 48 | 59 | 23 |
| 93 | 73 | 29 | 41 | 47 | 29 | 8 | 93 | 79 | 60 |
| 51 | 57 | 38 | 53 | 18 | 19 | 88 | 75 | 50 | 86 |
| 87 | 58 | 96 | 6 | 13 | 6 | 95 | 65 | 100 | 6 |
| 67 | 91 | 25 | 97 | 41 | 94 | 96 | 13 | 31 | 31 |
| 90 | 54 | 59 | 31 | 88 | 3 | 24 | 61 | 95 | 84 |
| 92 | 36 | 96 | 16 | 59 | 71 | 60 | 78 | 67 | 93 |
| 77 | 32 | 11 | 87 | 14 | 45 | 56 | 30 | 58 | 88 |
| 24 | 68 | 26 | 94 | 2 | 44 | 41 | 40 | 98 | 98 |
| 84 | 71 | 16 | 26 | 17 | 10 | 29 | 25 | 70 | 54 |
| 34 | 72 | 68 | 49 | 2 | 87 | 28 | 70 | 96 | 34 |
| 87 | 81 | 4 | 91 | 96 | 35 | 51 | 1 | 89 | 3 |
| 100 | 66 | 95 | 16 | 82 | 66 | 60 | 46 | 77 | 63 |
| 13 | 2 | 92 | 95 | 60 | 21 | 31 | 28 | 74 | 99 |
| 4 | 27 | 66 | 40 | 54 | 47 | 34 | 88 | 68 | 19 |
| 76 | 77 | 50 | 52 | 82 | 73 | 78 | 71 | 72 | 52 |
| 72 | 27 | 13 | 7 | 59 | 85 | 85 | 18 | 71 | 21 |
| 70 | 12 | 34 | 57 | 55 | 94 | 13 | 78 | 21 | 90 |
| 92 | 79 | 71 | 61 | 42 | 87 | 77 | 88 | 36 | 42 |
| 31 | 29 | 38 | 19 | 89 | 39 | 70 | 71 | 99 | 62 |
| 27 | 51 | 27 | 99 | 58 | 24 | 81 | 88 | 14 | 21 |
| 61 | 30 | 89 | 77 | 54 | 31 | 57 | 13 | 94 | 98 |
| 65 | 66 | 1 | 82 | 72 | 90 | 56 | 87 | 71 | 58 |
| 26 | 32 | 23 | 84 | 14 | 79 | 61 | 15 | 77 | 22 |

## Stream 9

| | | | | | | | | | |
|---|---|---|---|---|---|---|---|---|---|
| 23 | 32 | 81 | 84 | 99 | 66 | 6 | 26 | 67 | 15 |
| 84 | 17 | 95 | 16 | 70 | 81 | 45 | 27 | 91 | 63 |
| 94 | 86 | 67 | 66 | 66 | 77 | 87 | 72 | 22 | 46 |
| 17 | 34 | 88 | 45 | 24 | 76 | 8 | 39 | 82 | 45 |
| 4 | 96 | 63 | 25 | 76 | 97 | 29 | 97 | 96 | 79 |
| 26 | 46 | 72 | 19 | 18 | 77 | 65 | 65 | 37 | 62 |
| 87 | 79 | 52 | 56 | 27 | 43 | 33 | 69 | 63 | 4 |
| 32 | 32 | 30 | 79 | 44 | 74 | 82 | 63 | 32 | 6 |
| 7 | 39 | 5 | 40 | 4 | 65 | 74 | 95 | 12 | 67 |
| 11 | 5 | 42 | 55 | 100 | 43 | 88 | 31 | 98 | 36 |
| 4 | 11 | 89 | 65 | 80 | 26 | 22 | 77 | 19 | 49 |
| 67 | 95 | 28 | 67 | 81 | 79 | 32 | 76 | 82 | 29 |
| 27 | 21 | 89 | 4 | 64 | 86 | 80 | 27 | 86 | 97 |
| 4 | 61 | 71 | 25 | 72 | 82 | 74 | 42 | 91 | 57 |
| 63 | 76 | 58 | 57 | 22 | 53 | 48 | 44 | 98 | 53 |
| 68 | 1 | 48 | 67 | 5 | 38 | 52 | 30 | 4 | 3 |
| 94 | 35 | 85 | 6 | 74 | 21 | 35 | 7 | 49 | 39 |
| 20 | 53 | 59 | 55 | 83 | 3 | 93 | 71 | 65 | 21 |
| 62 | 17 | 4 | 62 | 35 | 45 | 57 | 94 | 78 | 73 |
| 36 | 72 | 57 | 39 | 17 | 38 | 4 | 100 | 79 | 80 |
| 31 | 2 | 52 | 59 | 65 | 93 | 88 | 42 | 96 | 36 |
| 38 | 16 | 74 | 84 | 15 | 67 | 76 | 100 | 57 | 37 |
| 66 | 3 | 34 | 7 | 60 | 49 | 5 | 3 | 83 | 25 |
| 100 | 56 | 49 | 51 | 18 | 53 | 93 | 60 | 68 | 21 |
| 28 | 12 | 19 | 44 | 100 | 5 | 3 | 71 | 40 | 85 |
| 37 | 64 | 51 | 99 | 37 | 68 | 31 | 74 | 77 | 84 |
| 57 | 67 | 91 | 13 | 12 | 26 | 75 | 10 | 14 | 12 |
| 15 | 65 | 25 | 65 | 87 | 44 | 47 | 71 | 8 | 8 |
| 92 | 15 | 40 | 66 | 45 | 34 | 22 | 73 | 4 | 94 |
| 12 | 90 | 6 | 5 | 11 | 65 | 70 | 80 | 57 | 12 |
| 7 | 83 | 80 | 85 | 86 | 82 | 91 | 6 | 81 | 16 |
| 65 | 1 | 70 | 87 | 75 | 37 | 1 | 72 | 39 | 10 |
| 7 | 94 | 90 | 70 | 36 | 6 | 62 | 24 | 35 | 72 |
| 44 | 54 | 2 | 18 | 18 | 100 | 60 | 65 | 6 | 73 |
| 57 | 15 | 22 | 38 | 35 | 89 | 9 | 44 | 61 | 20 |
| 43 | 12 | 90 | 18 | 90 | 26 | 85 | 56 | 79 | 76 |
| 28 | 32 | 12 | 74 | 29 | 30 | 37 | 44 | 59 | 69 |
| 8 | 43 | 97 | 100 | 58 | 1 | 86 | 88 | 45 | 11 |
| 91 | 93 | 20 | 96 | 46 | 85 | 81 | 38 | 96 | 81 |
| 54 | 86 | 41 | 43 | 26 | 38 | 53 | 94 | 24 | 88 |

# Stream 10

| | | | | | | | | | |
|---|---|---|---|---|---|---|---|---|---|
| 77 | 68 | 80 | 92 | 17 | 92 | 1 | 15 | 26 | 40 |
| 5 | 29 | 94 | 80 | 24 | 71 | 42 | 49 | 57 | 48 |
| 63 | 3 | 68 | 12 | 45 | 67 | 40 | 43 | 37 | 49 |
| 38 | 44 | 48 | 59 | 23 | 93 | 73 | 29 | 41 | 47 |
| 29 | 8 | 93 | 79 | 60 | 51 | 57 | 38 | 53 | 18 |
| 19 | 88 | 75 | 50 | 86 | 87 | 58 | 96 | 6 | 13 |
| 6 | 95 | 65 | 100 | 6 | 67 | 91 | 25 | 97 | 41 |
| 94 | 96 | 13 | 31 | 31 | 90 | 54 | 59 | 31 | 88 |
| 3 | 24 | 61 | 95 | 84 | 92 | 36 | 96 | 16 | 59 |
| 71 | 60 | 78 | 67 | 93 | 77 | 32 | 11 | 87 | 14 |
| 45 | 56 | 30 | 58 | 88 | 24 | 68 | 26 | 94 | 2 |
| 44 | 41 | 40 | 98 | 98 | 84 | 71 | 16 | 26 | 17 |
| 10 | 29 | 25 | 70 | 54 | 34 | 72 | 68 | 49 | 2 |
| 87 | 28 | 70 | 96 | 34 | 87 | 81 | 4 | 91 | 96 |
| 35 | 51 | 1 | 89 | 3 | 100 | 66 | 95 | 16 | 82 |
| 66 | 60 | 46 | 77 | 63 | 13 | 2 | 92 | 95 | 60 |
| 21 | 31 | 28 | 74 | 99 | 4 | 27 | 66 | 40 | 54 |
| 47 | 34 | 88 | 68 | 19 | 76 | 77 | 50 | 52 | 82 |
| 73 | 78 | 71 | 72 | 52 | 72 | 27 | 13 | 7 | 59 |
| 85 | 85 | 18 | 71 | 21 | 70 | 12 | 34 | 57 | 55 |
| 94 | 13 | 78 | 21 | 90 | 92 | 79 | 71 | 61 | 42 |
| 87 | 77 | 88 | 36 | 42 | 31 | 29 | 38 | 19 | 89 |
| 39 | 70 | 71 | 99 | 62 | 27 | 51 | 27 | 99 | 58 |
| 24 | 81 | 88 | 14 | 21 | 61 | 30 | 89 | 77 | 54 |
| 31 | 57 | 13 | 94 | 98 | 65 | 66 | 1 | 82 | 72 |
| 90 | 56 | 87 | 71 | 58 | 26 | 32 | 23 | 84 | 14 |
| 79 | 61 | 15 | 77 | 22 | 65 | 22 | 49 | 32 | 89 |
| 43 | 49 | 46 | 38 | 78 | 53 | 44 | 42 | 28 | 13 |
| 83 | 64 | 85 | 16 | 7 | 1 | 85 | 100 | 30 | 26 |
| 11 | 79 | 19 | 15 | 62 | 10 | 10 | 32 | 40 | 25 |
| 9 | 39 | 94 | 30 | 19 | 16 | 49 | 25 | 95 | 13 |
| 54 | 26 | 90 | 23 | 69 | 1 | 24 | 72 | 5 | 69 |
| 42 | 60 | 67 | 33 | 13 | 27 | 39 | 30 | 99 | 24 |
| 19 | 96 | 69 | 80 | 81 | 7 | 7 | 51 | 90 | 55 |
| 23 | 51 | 73 | 14 | 28 | 92 | 40 | 99 | 86 | 99 |
| 56 | 96 | 41 | 18 | 91 | 13 | 100 | 41 | 60 | 91 |
| 28 | 13 | 96 | 49 | 100 | 36 | 93 | 1 | 4 | 16 |
| 55 | 55 | 5 | 23 | 63 | 70 | 14 | 62 | 97 | 25 |
| 17 | 21 | 39 | 10 | 19 | 79 | 5 | 90 | 22 | 5 |
| 81 | 39 | 60 | 1 | 39 | 98 | 45 | 74 | 71 | 53 |

## Reference

Smith, C. S., 'Multiplicative Pseudo-Random Number Generators with Prime Modulus', *Journal of the Association for Computing Machinery*, **18** (4), 586–593, 1971.

# Appendix 2.

## Random arrivals

If entities arrive randomly into a system, the time for the 'generate' activity is a *negative exponential distribution* (see Bibliography—Moore). The coordinates of the distribution depend on the *rate of arrival* of entities.

The cumulative distributions for rates of arrival, varying from 1 arrival per 60 time units to 300 arrivals per 60 time units, are given in the next three pages (see Figs A2.1–A2.4). We illustrate their use in the following example:

*Example*  Cars arrive at a garage at the rate of 25 per hour. If the time units in the model are minutes, we use the distribution marked 25/60. In hand simulation we sample direct from the graph. In computer simulation we specify coordinates which represent the curve accurately [e.g., (0, 1), (1, 31), (2, 55), (3, 71), (4, 80), (5, 87), (6, 92), (8, 96), (13, 100)].

If this is distribution 3 in our model, we use random numbers from Stream 3 in Appendix 1, and sample as follows:

| Random number | Time (minutes) |
|:---:|:---:|
| 98 | 10 |
| 14 | 0 |
| 84 | 4 |
| 41 | 1 |
| 90 | 6 |
| 16 | 0 |
| 38 | 1 |
| 91 | 6 |
| 15 | 0 |
| 64 | 2 |
| 61 | 2 |
| 45 | 2 |
| 2 | 0 |
| 32 | 1 |
| 43 | 1 |
| 40 | 1 |
| 64 | 2 |
| 93 | 6 |
| 99 | 11 |
| 52 | 2 |

These times are then used in the 'generate' activity. Another example is given in Exercise 4.8.

*Note* The coordinates of the cumulative distribution for *any* rate of arrival can be calculated from the formula:

$$p = 1 - e^{-\lambda t}$$

where $p$ is the probability,
  $\lambda$ is the rate of arrival,
  $t$ is the inter-arrival time.
In the above example $\lambda = 25/60$ (25 arrivals per 60 time units).
For $t = 3$, $p = 1 - e^{-1.25} = 1 - 0.2865 = 0.7135 = 0.71$ rounded, thus the coordinates are (3, 71); see Fig. A2.3.
For $t = 6$, $p = 1 - e^{-2.5} = 1 - 0.0821 = 0.9179 = 0.92$ rounded, thus the coordinates are (6, 92); see Fig. A2.3.

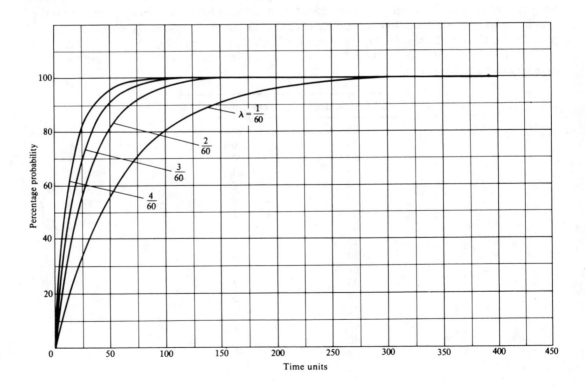

**Figure A2.1**

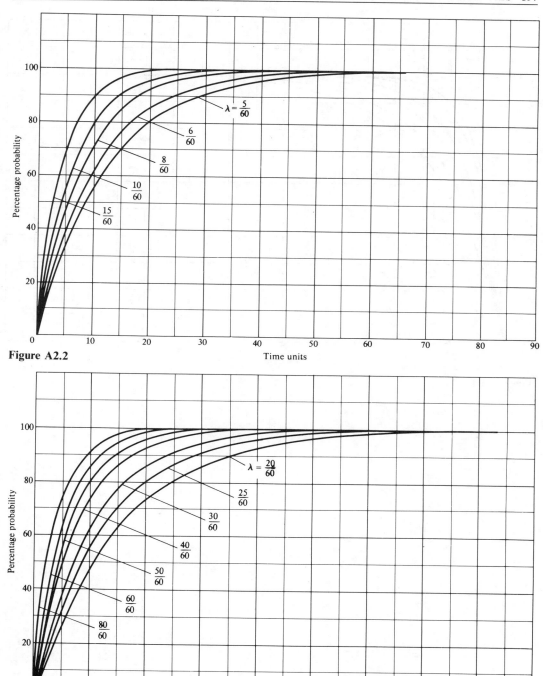

**Figure A2.2**

**Figure A2.3**

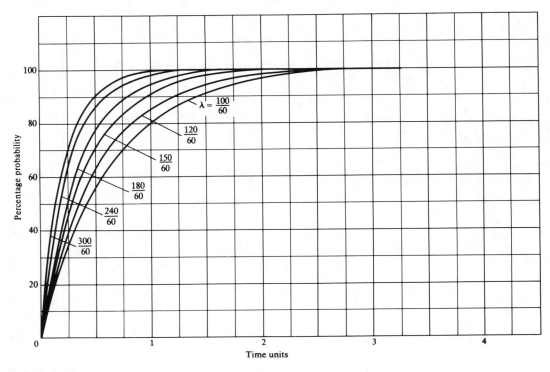

**Figure A2.4**

# Appendix 3.

## List of options

The options described in Chapter 7 are summarized on the following pages in alphabetical order.

### Key

| | | |
|---|---|---|
| Percentage of attribute | ✓ | mandatory |
| | Op | optional |
| | | |
| Attribute | ✓ | mandatory |
| | Op | optional |
| | | |
| Percentage of quantity | ✓ | mandatory |
| | Op | optional |
| | | |
| Activities | C | option can be used in continuous activity |
| | D | option can be used in discrete activity |

Any restrictions on numerical values are indicated using conventional mathematical notation.

| Option | Name | Percentage of attribute | Att | Percentage of quantity | Activities | Details on page |
|---|---|---|---|---|---|---|
| =A | equal all | √ (>1) | | | CD | 160 |
| AA | Add All | √ (≠0) | √ | | D | 153 |
| AC | Arithmetic Calculation | √ (>0) | √ | | D | 153 |
| AI | Arithmetic Insert | | √ | √ (≠0) | D | 155 |
| AJ | Arithmetic Join | | √ | √ (≠0) | D | 155 |
| AP | Add Part | √ (≠0) | √ | | D | 153 |
| AR | Arithmetic Reset | | | √ (0–100) | D | 155 |
| AS | Arithmetic Shortfall | | √ | √ (≠0) | D | 155 |
| BA | Book All | √ (≠0) | Op | | D | 154 |
| BD | (Book) Divide | √ (≠0) | Op | | D | 154 |
| BM | (Book) Multiply | √ (≠0) | Op | | D | 154 |
| BP | Book Part | √ (≠0) | Op | | D | 154 |
| CC | Check Contents | | √ | Op (0–100) | CD | 149 |
| CE | Check Empty | | √ | | CD | 149 |
| CL | Check Less than or equal to | | √ | √ (1–100) | CD | 149 |
| CM | Check More than or equal to | | √ | √ (1–100) | CD | 149 |
| CX | Check not equal to | | √ | √ (0–100) | CD | 149 |
| DD | Direct Data | { • 1–N* | { √ • | | CD | 146 |
| DE | Direct Entry | { √ (>0) Op(>0) | { Op √ | | CD | 146 |
| DI | Data Insert | | √ | √ (>0) | CD | 146 |
| DJ | Data Join | | √ | √ (≠0) | CD | 146 |
| DV | Denominator Value | √ (>0) | √ | | CD | 159 |
| EA | End check contents —Always satisfied | | • | | D | 150 |
| EC | End check Contents —equal | | √ | √ (0–100) | D | 150 |
| EE | End check contents —Empty | | √ | | D | 150 |
| EL | End check contents —Less than or equal | | √ | √ (1–100) | D | 150 |
| EM | End check contents —More than or equal | | √ | √ (1–100) | D | 150 |
| EX | End check contents —not equal | | √ | √ (0–100) | D | 150 |
| FC | Flow Control | √ (≠0) | √ | | C | 173 |
| FQ | Fixed Quantity | √ (>0) | √ | | D | 135 |
| FR | Flow Rate | | √ | √ (≠0) | C | 173 |
| G1–G9 | Greater than or equal to | √ (>0) | √ | | CD | 141 |
| GD | Get Data | { • 1–N* | { √ • | | D | 144 |

| Option | Name | Percentage of attribute | Att | Percentage of quantity | Activities | Details on page |
|---|---|---|---|---|---|---|
| GI | (Get) Insert data | | √ | √ (>0) | D | 144 |
| GJ | (Get) Join data | | √ | √ (≠0) | D | 144 |
| HE | Histogram of Existing values | Op (>0) | Op | | CD | 157 |
| HS | Histogram | Op (≠0) | Op | | CD | 156 |
| I1–I9 | Insert | | √ | √ (>0) | CD | 141 |
| IC | Initial Contents | √ (>0) | Op | | D | 148 |
| IE | Initial Empty | | • | | D | 148 |
| IL | Initial Less than or equal to | √ (>0) | Op | | D | 148 |
| IM | Initial More than or equal to | √ (>0) | Op | | D | 148 |
| IX | Initial not equal to | √ (>0) | Op | | D | 148 |
| J1–J9 | Join | | √ | √ (≠0) | CD | 141 |
| KA | Key Amount | √ (>0) | √ | | C | 174 |
| KP | Key Pass | | √ | √ (≠0) | C | 174 |
| KS | Key Space | √ (>0) | √ | | C | 174 |
| L1–L9 | Less than or equal to | √ (>0) | √ | | CD | 141 |
| LE | Lower Extent of attribute | √ (>0) | √ | | CD | 137 |
| LL | Lower Limit of attribute | √ (>0) | √ | | CD | 137 |
| LQ | Lower limit of Quantity | √ (>0) | √ | | D | 135 |
| M1–M9 | Match | √ (>0) | √ | | CD | 139 |
| MQ | Match with match Quantity | √ (>0) | √ | | CD | 138 |
| MX | Must not match | √ (>0) | √ | | CD | 138 |
| NI | No Interruption | | | | D | 181 |
| NV | Numerator Value | √ (>0) | √ | | CD | 159 |
| PI | Present time Insert | | √ | √ (>0) | CD | 143 |
| PJ | Present time Join | | √ | √ (≠0) | CD | 143 |
| PL | (Present time) Less than or equal to present time | | √ | √ (>0) | CD | 152 |
| PM | (Present time) More than or equal to present time | | √ | √ (>0) | CD | 152 |
| PX | (Present time) not equal to present time | | √ | √ (>0) | CD | 152 |
| QC | Queue Contents | | | √ (>0) | CD | 162 |
| QE | Queue Empty | | | | CD | 162 |
| QI | Queue size Insert | | √ | √ (>0) | D | 163 |
| QJ | Queue size Join | | √ | √ (≠0) | D | 163 |
| QL | Queue size Less than or equal to | | | √ (>0) | CD | 162 |
| QM | Queue size More than or equal to | | | √ (>0) | CD | 162 |
| QX | Queue size not equal to | | | √ (>0) | CD | 162 |
| R9 | Run stop | | | | CD | 167 |

| Option | Name | Percentage of attribute | Att | Percentage of quantity | Activities | Details on page |
|---|---|---|---|---|---|---|
| RD | Revise Data field | $\begin{cases} \bullet \\ 1\text{–}N* \end{cases}$ | $\begin{cases} \checkmark \\ \bullet \end{cases}$ | | CD | 147 |
| RE | Revise Entry point | $\begin{cases} \checkmark\,(>0) \\ \text{Op}\,(>0) \end{cases}$ | $\begin{cases} \bullet \\ \checkmark \end{cases}$ | | CD | 147 |
| RI | Revise Insert | $\checkmark\,(>0)$ | $\checkmark$ | | CD | 147 |
| RJ | Revise Join | $\checkmark\,(\neq0)$ | $\checkmark$ | | CD | 147 |
| =S | equal Some | $\checkmark\,(>1)$ | | | CD | 160 |
| S1–S9 | Special subroutine | | Op | | CD | 168 |
| SD | Search Data | $\begin{cases} \bullet \\ 1\text{–}N* \end{cases}$ | $\begin{cases} \checkmark \\ \bullet \end{cases}$ | | CD | 146 |
| SE | Search Entry | $\begin{cases} \checkmark\,(>0) \\ \text{Op}\,(>0) \end{cases}$ | $\begin{cases} \bullet \\ \checkmark \end{cases}$ | | CD | 146 |
| SI | Search Insert | | $\checkmark$ | $\checkmark\,(>0)$ | CD | 146 |
| SJ | Search Join | | $\checkmark$ | $\checkmark\,(\neq0)$ | CD | 146 |
| TD | Timetable Data | $\begin{cases} \bullet \\ 1\text{–}N* \end{cases}$ | $\begin{cases} \checkmark \\ \bullet \end{cases}$ | | D | 147 |
| TE | Timetable Entry | $\begin{cases} \checkmark\,(>0) \\ \text{Op}\,(>0) \end{cases}$ | $\begin{cases} \bullet \\ \checkmark \end{cases}$ | | D | 147 |
| TH | Test and Hold | | $\checkmark$ | $\checkmark\,(\neq0)$ | D | 132 |
| TI | Timetable Insert | $\checkmark\,(>0)$ | $\checkmark$ | | D | 147 |
| TJ | Timetable Join | $\checkmark\,(\neq0)$ | $\checkmark$ | | D | 147 |
| TR | TRansfer | | $\checkmark$ | $\checkmark\,(\neq0)$ | CD | 130,171 |
| TT | Total Transfer | | $\checkmark$ | $\checkmark\,(\neq0)$ | D | 133 |
| U1–U9 | User-defined reports | | | | CD | 165 |
| UC | User Control | | | | CD | 167 |
| UE | Upper Extent of attribute | $\checkmark\,(>0)$ | $\checkmark$ | | CD | 137 |
| UL | Upper Limit of attribute | $\checkmark\,(>0)$ | $\checkmark$ | | CD | 137 |
| UQ | Upper limit of Quantity | $\checkmark\,(>0)$ | $\checkmark$ | | D | 135 |
| UR | Unit Rate | | $\checkmark$ | $\checkmark\,(\neq0)$ | CD | 143,172 |
| VV | Variable Value | $\checkmark\,(>0)$ | $\checkmark$ | | CD | 158 |
| X1–X9 | not equal to | $\checkmark\,(>0)$ | $\checkmark$ | | CD | 141 |
| XC | eXtra Correlation | $\checkmark\,(\neq0)$ | $\checkmark$ | | D | 164 |
| XR | eXtra Reset | | $\checkmark$ | $\checkmark\,(0\text{–}100)$ | CD | 142 |
| XS | eXtra Set | | $\checkmark$ | $\checkmark\,(0\text{–}100)$ | CD | 142 |
| 01–22 | output report | | | | CD | 165 |

N* = number of data fields.

*Note* New options are being added all the time. A complete up-to-date list is given in the HOCUS manual, available from P-E International plc, Park House, Wick Road, Egham, Surrey, United Kingdom.

# Appendix 4.

## Error diagnostics

There are two types of input error diagnostic, cautionary and fatal, and one type of processing error:

- C-type are cautionary errors in the input data. Parts of the data are rejected or modified, but the model as a whole is accepted. C-type errors do not stop the simulation run but give a warning that the results may be subject to error.
- F-type are fatal errors in the input data. The model as specified is not valid. However, all the input data is checked before the current verification run is stopped.
- P-type are either fatal or non-fatal processing errors during the simulation run. Fatal errors cause the run to stop immediately, and return control to the user. Program systems errors cause the printing of the data structure and release the program.

Each diagnostic consists of three asterisks followed by a code number.

With the exception of some initial condition diagnostics, C-type and F-type errors are printed below the line containing the error. If the input listing is not requested and an input error is found, then, in most cases the contents of the invalid line are printed, followed on the next line by the error diagnostic. The exceptions occur when an error on a line cannot be diagnosed until the next line is read. In these cases the diagnostic is printed first followed by the contents of the line after the invalid line. The diagnostics of this nature are marked in the list of errors with an asterisk (*).

In addition to the code number, P-type diagnostics give the simulation clock time at which the error occurred, together with other relevant information.

A list of diagnostics and their causes is given in the following pages.

## C-type errors

| Number | Cause | Action |
|--------|-------|--------|
| *General input errors* | | |
| C5 | Integer is larger than the maximum allowed by the computer. | The value is set to the maximum integer allowed. |
| C10 | Invalid number of bit-planes specified. | Default value 2 is taken. |
| *Entity description* | | |
| C100 | Number of attributes is negative, non-numeric, not right-justified or greater than 20. | The number of attributes is set to 20. |
| C105 | Attribute maximum given to an attribute outside the range specified by the number of attributes. | Number of attributes extended. |
| C110* | Number of entity types read is not equal to the number declared on the model size header. | Number of entity types read is accepted. |
| C115 | Entity colour left blank. | Colour 8 specified. |
| *Entity group description* | | |
| C150* | Number of entity groups read is not equal to the number declared on the model size header. | Number of entity groups read is accepted. |
| C155 | Entity group contains no entities. | No action. |
| *Queue description* | | |
| C205* | Number of queues read is not equal to the number declared on the model size header. | Number of queues read is accepted. |
| C210 | More than 20 queues are marked for tracing. | Only first 20 queues are traced. |
| C215 | Queue is logged but is not used in any activity. | No action. |
| C220 | More than 20 queues are marked as Outside World queues. | Only first 20 queues are checked. |
| C225* | Outside World queue is not used as a source queue. | No action. |
| C230 | Queue colour left blank. | Colour 1 specified. |
| C235 | Queue colour is not a fixed display colour. | No action. |
| C240 | Queue size colour left blank. | Colour 8 specified. |
| *Data field description* | | |
| C300* | Number of data fields read is not equal to the number declared on the model size header. | Number of data fields read is accepted. |

## C-type errors (cont.)

| Number | Cause | Action |
|---|---|---|
| **Activity description—header** | | |
| C400 | Either or both coordinates are negative, non-numeric or not right-justified. | Activity assumed to have no coordinates or graphics information. |
| C405* | Number of activities read is not equal to the number declared on the model size header. | Number of activities read is accepted. |
| C410 | Activity box colour is not a fixed display colour. | No action. |
| C415 | Activity text colour is not a fixed display colour. | No action. |
| C417 | Activity icon is not a fixed display colour. | No action. |
| C420 | Activity box colour left blank. | Colour 1 specified. |
| C425 | Activity text colour left blank. | Colour 0 specified. |
| C430 | Icon colour left blank. | Colour 1 specified. |
| C435 | Activity time colour left blank. | Colour 8 specified. |
| C440 | Type 1 activity height left blank. | Value 2 specified. |
| C445 | Activity would fall outside map area. | Activity not displayed. |
| C450 | Listing direction left blank. | Listing down assumed. |
| C455 | Activity offset left blank. | Offset specified as five steps. |
| **Activity description—conditions** | | |
| C500 | Alternative queue has a size limit. | No action. |
| C502 | More than one condition has an entity name identical to the correlation entity in the activity header. | This may be correct. The first of the identically named entities satisfied is used. |
| C505* | Number of conditions read is not equal to the number declared on the activity header. | Number of conditions read is accepted. |
| C508 | Number of conditions declared on the activity header is negative, zero, blank, non-numeric or not right-justified. | The number of conditions is treated as one. |
| C528 | Obsolete option code used. | Converted to equivalent new version. |
| C530 | Match follower option is not the first option in the condition. | No action. |
| C532 | An option is used twice for the same attribute in the same condition. | No action. |
| C535 | HS option follows an option which does not alter the value of the attribute. | Histogram option ignored. |

## C-type errors (cont.)

| Number | Cause | Action |
|--------|-------|--------|
| C538 | This option refers to a percentage of the attribute maximum but no maximum is specified. | No action. |
| C540 | UQ, LL or UL option may conflict with the match or minimum quantity. | No action. |
| C550 | Percentage has been specified with option that does not require it. | No action. |
| C554 | The code in the attribute column is invalid for this output report option. | Treated as blank. |
| C555 | Invalid attribute letter used with HS or S1–S9 option. | Attribute letter ignored. |
| C556 | The report referred to in a report option cannot use editing lists. | Code ignored. |
| C557 | The output report option code cannot be used with a continuous activity. | Entry ignored. |
| C558 | Invalid output report option. | Entry ignored. |
| C559 | Report 23 cannot be called from a report option. | Option ignored. |
| C560 | Queue is used by a continuous activity but is liable to be re-ordered by another activity. | No action. |
| C565 | Source and destination position in a continuous activity are not identical. | Destination position set to source position. |
| C575 | This queue is not used in the model. | No action. |
| C580 | The activity was too complex for detailed checking and run switch 22 was set. | Options are not checked for compatibility. |

Histogram description

| Number | Cause | Action |
|--------|-------|--------|
| C700 | Entity name is not declared in the list of entity type or groups. | Histogram ignored. |
| C705 | Attribute letter is not valid or is out of range for the entity type specified. | Histogram ignored. |
| C710 | Lower boundary is blank, non-numeric or not right-justified. | Lower boundary set to 10. |
| C715 | Interval size is negative, zero, blank, non-numeric or not right-justified. | Interval size set to 10. |
| C717 | The number of intervals is less than 1. | Number of intervals set to 10. |
| C720* | Number of histograms read is not equal to the number declared on the model size header. | Number of histograms read is accepted. |
| C730* | HE or HS option has been used in an activity but no histogram has been set up. | No action. |

## C-type errors (cont.)

| Number | Cause | Action |
|--------|-------|--------|
| **Queue logs** | | |
| C750* | Number of queue logs read is not equal to the number declared on the model size header. | Number of queue logs read is accepted. |
| **Initial condition description** | | |
| C802 | Queue size limit is exceeded. | No action. |
| C805 | More than 12 entities are marked for tracing. | Only first 12 entities traced. |
| C840 | Remainder code (R) is used but all members are already allocated. | Entry ignored. |
| C854 | More than 15 attributes are marked for tracing. | Only first 15 attributes traced. |
| **Initial conditions—modification data** | | |
| C856 | Modifications would result in more than 15 attributes being marked for tracing. | Entry ignored. |
| C860 | Request to trace entity already traced or untrace entity not traced. | No action. |
| C865 | Not all entities marked for tracing were previously untraced, or vice versa. | Entry ignored. |
| C875 | Modification would result in more than 12 entities being traced. | Entry ignored. |
| **Join description** | | |
| C900 | Join colour not fixed display colour. | No action. |
| C905 | Join colour not specified. | Colour 1 specified. |
| C910 | Number of joins read is not equal to the number declared on the model size header. | Number of joins read is accepted. |
| **Feature description** | | |
| C950 | Feature colour is not specified. | Colour 1 specified (text background colour is defaulted to zero). |
| C955 | Line feature type left blank. | Type 0 specified. |
| C960 | Number of features read is not equal to the number declared on the model size header. | Number of features read is accepted. |
| C965 | Text past specified length in text feature definition. | Excess text ignored. |
| C970 | More than one colour line has been defined. | The last one read is used. |

## F-type errors

| Number | Cause |
|--------|-------|

### General input errors

| | |
|--------|-------|
| F5 | First line of model is not a run header (R in column 1) or is an invalid run header (does not have one and only one of switches 1, 4, 11 and 12 set). The program continues to read data until it finds a valid run header or an end flag. |
| F7 | The line following the run header is not a model name line (N in column 1). |
| F10 | Monitor header missing. The program continues to read data until it finds a run header or an end flag. All lines will be printed but not validated until the next run control command is recognized. |
| F15 | Model data too large for program to store. The program continues to read data until it finds a run header or an end flag. Data will be printed but not validated until the next run control line is recognized. |
| F20 | Invalid identifier in column 1. |
| F25 | Data out of sequence. The data is printed but the contents are not stored or validated. |
| F30 | A re-run is requested by switch 11 or 12 without the run having first been stored. The program continues to read data until it finds a run header or an end flag. |
| F35 | Modification data expected but not found. The program continues to read data until it finds a run header or an end flag. |
| F40 | Insufficient room for graphics data. |

### Entity description

| | |
|--------|-------|
| F100 | First character of entity name is blank. Name must be left-justified. |
| F105 | Number of entity members is negative, zero, non-numeric or not right-justified. |
| F110 | Attribute maximum value is negative, non-numeric or not right-justified. |
| F115 | No entity description continuation line, although the number of attributes is greater than 10. |
| F120 | Display mnemonic incorrect. |
| F125 | Entity icon colour not an animation colour. |
| F130 | Icon shape definer not valid. |
| F135 | Icon shape definer and mnemonic both specified. |
| F140 | Icon has colour defined by both single value and attribute. |
| F150 | Entity group name contains no asterisks. |
| F155 | Entity group mnemonic not left-justified character string. |
| F160 | Column 13 of entity group definition not left blank. |
| F165 | Entity group icon shape definer not valid. |
| F170 | Entity group icon shape definer and display mnemonic both specified. |
| F175 | Entity group icon too small. |

### Queue description

| | |
|--------|-------|
| F200 | Queue size limit is negative, non-numeric or not right-justified. |
| F202 | Queue map coordinates are invalid. |
| F205 | Queue log is not blank or L, or queue trace is not blank or T. |
| F210 | Outside World is not blank or W. |
| F215 | Spare queue is not blank or S. |
| F220 | A size limit has been placed on a spare queue. |
| F225 | Queue display type invalid. |
| F230 | Queue size colour not an animation colour. |
| F235 | Queue entity attitude invalid. |
| F240 | Queue display size is negative, zero, non-numeric or not right-justified. |
| F245 | Invalid queue colour identifier. |

## F-type errors (cont.)

| Number | Cause |
|---|---|
| | |

### Date field description

| | |
|---|---|
| F300 | Number of distribution coordinate pairs or timetable entries is negative, zero, non-numeric, not right-justified or not a valid standard distribution code. |
| F305 | Distribution time, distribution probability or timetable entry is negative, non-numeric or not right-justified. |
| F310 | Fewer continuation lines found than expected from the number of distribution coordinates or timetable entries field. |
| F315 | Lowest distribution probability not 1. |
| F320 | Highest distribution probability not 100. |
| F325 | Distribution probabilities not in ascending sequence. |
| F330 | Number of data field entries does not agree with number specified *or* entry for standard distribution is invalid. |

### Activity description—header

| | |
|---|---|
| F400 | Number of identical activities (columns 57 and 58) is negative, zero, non-numeric or not right-justified. |
| F405 | Data column 20 is not blank. |
| F410 | Match or minimum quantity (columns 21–25) is negative, non-numeric or not right-justified. |
| F415 | Constant is non-numeric or not right-justified. |
| F420 | Data field number is negative, zero, non-numeric, not right-justified or is greater than the number of data fields input, or data options used in a continuous activity. |
| F425 | Correlation percentage is non-numeric, not right-justified or exceeds maximum permitted size. |
| F430 | Correlation entity is missing (or column 39, the first character, is blank) but correlation attributes and/or percentage are valid. |
| F435 | Correlation entity name is not a valid entity type or group. |
| F440 | Correlation attribute is out of the range for the entity name or is an invalid attribute letter, or an attribute is specified without a percentage. |
| F445 | Function is negative, zero, non-numerical or not right-justified. |
| F450 | Alpha percentage is negative, non-numeric or not right-justified. |
| F455 | Beta percentage is negative, non-numeric or not right-justified. |
| F460 | Function number, alpha or beta percentage used in a continuous activity. |
| F465 | Invalid activity display type. |
| F470 | Invalid activity box colour identifier. |
| F472 | Invalid activity text colour identifier. |
| F473 | Invalid icon colour identifier. |
| F474 | Activity end time colour is not an animation colour. |
| F476 | Activity height is not a blank or digit. |
| F478 | Active entity list code is not R or D or blank. |
| F480 | Identical activity offset is negative, non-numeric or not right-justified. |
| F490* | Insufficient room defined for icons. |
| F495 | Graphics data supplied but no icons defined. |

### Activity description—conditions

| | |
|---|---|
| F500 | No activity header data for the condition. Activity condition data read before activity header. |
| F505 | In-switch clock is not a valid attribute letter, or the switch is not a plus (+) or a minus (−) which matches the + or − on the literal header (columns 38 and 39). |

## F-type errors (cont.)

| Number | Cause |
|--------|-------|
| F510 | Source queue position not E, H, T, I or Z. |
| F515 | Source queue number is negative, zero, non-numeric, not right-justified or exceeds the highest queue number. |
| F520 | Entity name is not declared in the list of entity types or groups. |
| F525 | In-switch clock is not a valid attribute for the entity. |
| F536 | LQ or FQ option used with a match or minimum quantity. |
| F540 | Destination queue number is negative, zero, non-numeric, not right-justified or exceeds the highest queue number. |
| F545 | Destination queue position is not H, T, Z or a valid attribute letter within the range for the entity. |
| F550 | Destination or alternative queue has already been defined as an ordered queue (queue position designated by an attribute letter) and is now specified as a non-ordered queue (queue position designated as H, T, or Z), or vice versa. |
| F555 | Alternative queue number is negative, zero, non-numeric, not right-justified or exceeds highest queue number. |
| F560 | Alternative queue position is not H, T, Z or a valid attribute letter within the range for the entity. |
| F565 | Alternative queue specified but the destination queue has no size limit. |
| F570 | Out-switch clock is not a valid attribute letter, or is out of range for the entity, or the switch is not a plus (+) or minus (−) which matches the + or − on the literal header (columns 38 and 39). |
| F575 | Option percentage is zero, non-numeric or not right-justified, or is negative when the option does not permit negative values. |
| F576 | Variable percentage not permitted with HE, HS, QA, QS or database options. |
| F580 | Option attribute is not a valid attribute letter, or is out of range for the entity. |
| F581 | With a data option, entries have been made in both the percentage of attribute and attribute columns. |
| F585 | A histogram cannot be specified on an attribute which is used as a clock and manipulated by an option. |
| F590 | A matching master has been set up but not used in this activity. |
| F595 | Alternative condition field (columns 26 and 27) is not valid. |
| F600* | No conditions for the activity. |
| F604 | There are no compulsory conditions in the activity. |
| F605* | Alternative condition ('OR' in columns 26 and 27) specified in last condition of the activity. |
| F606 | Error in formulation of condition set. |
| F620* | Correlation entity name on the activity header is not in any of the conditions. |
| F630 | Error in formulation of option. |
| F631 | Extent options have been specified but not used. |
| F633 | Data options out of order. |
| F635 | More than one FC option in the same condition. |
| F637 | Attribute for split entity has more than one transfer option in the same condition. |
| F640 | Sign of percentage with FR option incorrect. |
| F642 | FR option used before an FC option. |
| F643 | KP option used before KA or KS option. |
| F645 | C1–C9, G1–G9, L1–L9, X1–X9, I1–I9 or J1–J9 option appears before the corresponding M1–M9 option. |
| F646 | Matching follower options not in the same order as matching masters. |
| F647 | VAR or SUP used before the variable percentage has been defined by VV or NV and DV options. |

## F-type errors (cont.)

| Number | Cause |
|---|---|
| F648 | The VV, NV or DV option conflicts with similar options already specified. |
| F649 | MX option used before M1–M9 option. |
| F650 | CC or XR option requires a percentage between 0 and 100, *or* AR option requires a percentage less than or equal to 100. |
| F652 | Arithmetic options out of sequence. |
| F654 | Invalid output report option. |
| F655 | In a continuous activity, source queue position is not E or I. |
| F660 | In a continuous activity, destination queue is not the same as source queue. |
| F665 | In a continuous activity, the destination queue position is not E or I. |
| F670 | In a continuous activity, an alternative queue must not be used. |
| F673 | In a continuous activity, a TR option is used before the condition in which the correlation term entity is located or in the same condition before a match follower option. |
| F675 | Option percentage is in the wrong column. |
| F676 | ZP, ZQ, ZS or ZT options have been used without a valid reference option (ZR) in a different condition but for the same queue. |
| F677 | A source queue position option must be the first option of the condition. |
| F678 | There are conflicting source queue position options. |
| F679 | The percentage entry for a ZX or ZY option is not valid. |
| F680 | Two option percentages given. |
| F681 | A percentage has been entered for an option in which it is not allowed. |
| F683 | In a continuous activity, UL, LL or FC option used after a TR option. |
| F685 | This option is not permitted in a continuous activity. |
| F687 | In a continuous activity, this option alters the value of an attribute already used (in the correlation term or with an FC option) to calculate the rate for the activity. |
| F690 | This option is only permitted in a continuous activity. |
| F695 | Illegal information has been coded in continuation data. |
| F700 | More than 100 continuous activities use the same split entity from the same queue. |
| F705 | Queue number in a condition is non-numeric or not right-justified. |
| F707 | Invalid option code associated with alternative queue in a continuous activity. |
| F708 | An alternative queue in a continuous activity may not be used for a split entity. |
| F710 | Queue used by a queue size option does not have a queue size limit specified by the user. |
| F715 | Queue size option used before a queue has been specified. |
| F725 | The previous queue specified for use with a queue size option has no queue size option. |
| F731 | End Check option is not permitted in condition line. |
| F732 | End Check option without Alternative Queue on same line. |
| F733 | Alternative Queue without End Check option on same line. |
| F734 | End Check option EA with non-variable Alternative Queue. |
| F739 | The identical condition option ( = A or = S) must not have H or T as source queue position. |
| F740 | The identical condition option ( = A or = S) must have a positive entry greater than 1 in the percentage of attribute column. |
| F741 | The number of identical conditions is more than the number of members of the type or group. |
| F742 | The condition contains options not allowed with identical condition options. |
| F743 | Identical condition options are not allowed with alternative conditions or condition sets. |
| F744 | Identical condition options ( = A or = S) must be the last options in a condition. |
| F745 | Activity too complex to check. |
| F746 | The defined activity is too complex and therefore detailed checking is impossible—use run switch 22 to bypass checking. |
| F750 | This option is not permitted in continuation data. |

## F-type errors (cont.)

| Number | Cause |
|--------|-------|

### Queue logs

| | |
|--------|-------|
| F755 | Number of queue logs read is not equal to the number of logs requested in the queue description data (L in column 18). |
| F760 | Queue number is non-numeric or not right-justified. |
| F765 | Queue number is negative, zero or exceeds the number of queues. |
| F770 | Queue log is not specified in the queue description data (L in column 18). |
| F775 | Number of intervals is non-numeric, not right-justified, less than 1 or greater than 10. |
| F780 | Lower boundary is negative, zero, non-numeric or not right-justified. |
| F785 | Interval is negative, zero, non-numeric or not right-justified. |

### Initial conditions

| | |
|--------|-------|
| F800 | Entity name is not declared in the list of entity types. |
| F805 | Number of members is negative, zero, blank, non-numeric or not right-justified. |
| F810 | Queue number is negative, zero, blank, non-numeric, not right-justified or exceeds the highest queue number. |
| F812 | The total number of entity members allocated is less than the total number of entity members declared on the entity description. |
| F815 | Entity members allocated to an ordered queue but the entity does not have appropriate attribute for the queue. |
| F820 | Number of entity members allocated is greater than the number declared on the entity type description, *or* the entity type has been declared more than once on the entity description. |
| F825 | Attribute initial value is negative, zero, non-numeric, not right-justified or higher than the maximum on the entity type. |
| F826 | Serial input is non-numeric or not right-justified. |
| F830 | Initial value given to attribute not declared on the entity type description. |
| F835 | No continuation data, although the number of attributes defined for the entity type is greater than 10. |

### Modification data—initial conditions

| | |
|--------|-------|
| F845 | Entity name is not declared in the list of entity types. |
| F850 | Number of members to be modified is negative, zero, blank, non-numeric, not right-justified or greater than the number declared. |
| F855 | First member to be modified is negative, zero, blank, non-numeric, not right-justified or not consistent with the number modified or the number declared. |
| F860 | Queue number is negative, zero, blank, non-numeric not right-justified or greater than the number of queues declared. |
| F865 | Trace is not blank, T, a valid attribute letter or '/'. |
| F870 | Initial attribute value given to an attribute not declared on the entity type description. |
| F872 | Ordered queue specified for an entity which does not have the required attribute. |
| F875 | Initial attribute value is negative, non-numeric, not right-justified or greater than the maximum declared for the entity type. |
| F880 | No continuation data, although the number of attributes defined for the entity type is greater than 10. |
| F885 | Continuation data contains invalid information. |
| F890 | Initial attribute value in continuation data given to an attribute not declared for this entity type. |
| F895 | New value for attribute is non-numeric, not right-justified or greater than the maximum declared for the entity type. |

## F-type errors (cont.)

| Number | Cause |
| --- | --- |
| F900 | No modifications made to initial conditions—data are read but no change requested. |

### Modification data—general

| | |
| --- | --- |
| F905 | Invalid identifier in column 1. |

### Modification data—data fields

| | |
| --- | --- |
| F910 | Data field number is negative, zero, blank, non-numeric, not right-justified or greater than the number of data fields declared. |
| F915 | Data field type (D or T) is not the same as originally specified. |
| F920 | Number of data field entries differs from the number in the original data field. |
| F925 | Data field entry is negative, blank, non-numeric or not right-justified. |
| F930 | Number of data field entries in the continuation data is inconsistent with the number of original entries, or the continuation data is invalid, i.e., the identifier has changed or the data field number has not been left blank. |
| F935 | For the distribution either the first probability is not 1 or the last probability is not 100. |

### Modification data—activities

| | |
| --- | --- |
| F940 | Activity number exceeds the number of activities. |
| F945 | Neither activity name nor number specified. |
| F950 | Activity name does not match with any in the model. |
| F955 | Time data entry beyond those previously used by the activity. |
| F960 | Constant is non-numeric or not right-justified, or data field term is negative, non-numeric or not right-justified. |
| F965 | Data field number is greater than the number of data fields declared. |
| F970 | Correlation entity name is not a valid entity type or group, or correlation percentage is non-numeric, not right-justified or not 'DATA'. |
| F975 | Correlation attribute is not a valid attribute letter for the entity. |
| F980 | Function number, alpha and beta entry invalid. |
| F985 | Match or minimum quantity is negative, non-numeric, not right-justified. |

### Graphical joins

| | |
| --- | --- |
| F1000 | Invalid activity specifier in join data. |
| F1005 | Invalid queue specifier in join data. |
| F1010 | Invalid join colour. |
| F1015 | Invalid join line type. |
| F1020 | Number of join coordinates is not a blank or a digit between 2 and 9. |
| F1025 | .Invalid activity location specification. |
| F1030 | Invalid join coordinate specification. |
| F1035 | Invalid queue location specification. |
| F1040 | Join specified linking unconnected activity and queue. |
| F1045 | Too many joins between this activity and queue. |
| F1050 | Joins between same activity and queue have different specification. |
| F1055 | Repeated join cannot be calculated. |

### Graphical features

| | |
| --- | --- |
| F1100 | Invalid feature type. |
| F1105 | Map or display specifier not M or D. |
| F1110 | Coordinate specifier invalid. |
| F1115 | Invalid feature colour. |

## F-type errors (cont.)

| Number | Cause |
|--------|-------|
| F1120 | Invalid radius for circle feature. |
| F1125 | Invalid line feature type. |
| F1130 | Invalid text feature height. |
| F1135 | Invalid text feature width. |
| F1140 | Invalid number of text characters. |
| F1145 | Invalid colour modifier. |

## P-type errors

| Number | Cause | Action |
|--------|-------|--------|
| P1 | Invalid identifier in expert command. | Command ignored. |
| P2 | Control time in a command is negative or non-numeric. | Command ignored. |
| P3 | Run control switch is negative, zero, non-numeric or two successive commas specified. | Switch ignored. |
| P4 | Run control switch not a valid number. | Switch ignored. |
| P5 | An entity has been put in a queue which exceeds its size limit. | Warning only. |
| P6 | A function is requested but the user has not provided coding for the subroutine FUNC. | Value of function is zero. |
| P7 | Attribute in the activity correlation term contains a negative value. | Control returned to user. |
| P8 | Attribute in an option contains a negative value. | Control returned to user. |
| P9 | Attribute clock is switched off, when already switched off. | Current simulation clock time added to elapsed time already held. (If a histogram is used a warning is printed with the histogram results.) |
| P10 | Attribute clock is switched on, when already switched on. | Attribute set to current simulation clock time. (If a histogram is used a warning is printed with the histogram results.) |
| P11 | The transfer quantity calculated using beta is outside the constraints imposed by the activity and the chosen entities. | The quantity is either set to the minimum acceptable value if less than the minimum constraint, or set to the maximum acceptable value if greater than the maximum constraint. |
| P13 | Activity end time exceeds the maximum integer allowed. | Set to maximum integer. |

## P-type errors (cont.)

| Number | Cause | Action |
|---|---|---|
| P14 | Activity duration is negative. | (a) If run switch 5 is not set on the run header—control returned to user. (b) If run switch 5 is set on the run header—activity duration set to zero and simulation continues. |
| P15 | Control time in command exceeds the maximum integer allowed. | Command ignored. |
| P16 | End flag (* in column 1) read before run switch 9. | Control returned to user. |
| P17 | Histogram or queue log report requested (monitor switch 14 or 18) but no valid histograms or queue logs set up. | Monitor switch 14 or 18 ignored |
| P18 | Attribute used by data option or 'DATA' in correlation term does not contain a valid data field number. | Option ignored or correlation term set to zero. |
| P19 | Initial state of model was not stored. | Initial state of model not restored. |
| P20 | Insufficient space to store initial state of model when run switch 10 is set. | Initial state of model not stored. |
| P21 | When calculating the variable percentage the DV option is found to be zero. | Entity does not satisfy condition. |
| P22 | Matching quantity found to be negative. | Entity not accepted. |
| P23 | Quantity to be copied into an attribute exceeds the maximum for that attribute. | Entity not accepted. |
| P24 | The number of zero time advances has exceeded 50 (or the maximum set in the monitor header data). If there is no error in the logic increase the maximum on the monitor header card. | Control returned to user. |
| P25 | In calculating the variance of a histogram the numbers involved have become too large to process correctly. | Warning only. |
| P26 | Run switch cannot be set except at the start of a run or re-run. | Run switch ignored. |
| P27 | Transfer rate for a continuous activity is greater than the maximum integer allowed. | Set to maximum integer. |
| P28 | Cumulative quantity for an activity has exceeded 30 million. | 30 million deducted. |
| P29 | More than one special subroutine (S1–S9) used in the same activity. | Only the first is used. |
| P30 | Simulation clock time has exceeded the maximum integer allowed. | Control returned to user. |

## P-type errors (cont.)

| Number | Cause | Action |
|---|---|---|
| P31 | Transfer quantity has exceeded the maximum integer allowed. | Control returned to user. |
| P32 | Special subroutine (S1–S9) requested but the user has not provided coding for the subroutine SPECL. | Option ignored. |
| P33 | Attribute value in a BD option is zero, when ending an activity. | Calculation total set to zero. |
| P34 | Attribute value in a BD option is zero, when checking if an activity can start. | Entity not accepted. |
| P36 | Transfer rate for split entity has exceeded the maximum integer allowed. | Rate set to maximum integer. |
| P37 | When routing to variable alternative queue, either the attribute value is negative, greater than the number of queues in the model or the queue position is incompatible with the rules for priority. | The alternative queue in question is not used. |
| P39 | Value of attribute after switching off clock (thereby adding simulation clock time) exceeds its maximum value. | Attribute value set to maximum. |
| P40 | Value of attribute after use of transfer or alteration option is negative or exceeds its maximum value. | Attribute value set to zero or maximum. |
| P41 | No activities are running and none can start. The probable cause is a fault in the model logic, or in setting the initial conditions. However, in some types of simulation this may be achieved deliberately to provide a natural end to the run. | Control returned to user. |
| P42 | An error has occurred indicating that there is a fault in the program. Please inform software supplier immediately. | Control returned to user. |
| P43 | In queue log storage, time × size value is too large for storage available. | Value is set to zero. |
| P44 | A value in a queue log has become too large to store. | Queue log is printed and re-set to zero. |
| P45 | The variance in a queue log has become too large to store. | Variance set to zero. |
| P46 | Attribute value in a DV option is zero. | Attribute value assumed to be 1.0. |
| P47 | Run switch cannot be set before the simulation begins. | Run switch ignored. |
| P48 | The total in the accumulator exceeds the accumulator maximum. | Accumulator total set to maximum. |

## P-type errors (cont.)

| Number | Cause | Action |
|--------|-------|--------|
| P49 | A continuous activity is about to start, but the duration is found to be zero. This may be caused by the interruption of another continuous activity changing the net rate of transfer for a a split entity, so that the attribute value is already equal to or on the wrong side of a limit. | Activity starts but runs for zero time. |
| P50 | There have been more than 1100 zero time advances at the same decimal time, i.e. in stopping or starting continuous activities. | For the last 100 advances, switches 1 and 2 will be switched on. Control returned to user. |
| P51 | Data Base operation. DD option is not permitted with a distribution. | Operation abandoned. |
| P52 | Data Base operation. Move option (DM) requires Number option (DN) to be specified also. | Operation abandoned. |
| P53 | Data Base operation. Length of list (DL option) exceeds specified length of Move (DM option). | Operation abandoned. |
| P54 | Data Base operation. Length of access instruction (options DE, DL, DM, DN) exceeds length of timetable. | Operation abandoned. |
| P55 | Data Base operation. Pass (DP) option requires several attributes (DS) option to be specified also. | Operation abandoned. |
| P56 | Data Base operation. Length of list (DL option) exceeds specified length of Pass (DP option). | Operation abandoned. |
| P57 | Data Base operation. Length of access instruction (DL, DP, DS options) exceeds number of attributes available. | Operation abandoned. |
| P58 | Data Base operation. If Number (DN) and several attributes (DS) options are both specified, their values must be the same. | Operation abandoned. |
| P59 | Data Field Revision. Entry Point (RE option) exceeds length of data field specified (RD option). | Operation abandoned. |
| P60 | Data Field Revision. After applying RJ option, a value in a data field would be negative. | Value set to zero. |
| P61 | Data Base operation. RD option is not permitted with a distribution. | Operation abandoned. |
| P62 | Data Base operation. Move option (RM) requires Number option (RN) to be specified also. | Operation abandoned. |
| P63 | Data Base operation. Length of list (RL option) exceeds specified length of Move (RM option). | Operation abandoned. |
| P64 | Data Base operation. Length of access instruction (options RE, RL, RM, RN) exceeds length of timetable. | Operation abandoned. |

## P-type errors (cont.)

| Number | Cause | Action |
|---|---|---|
| P65 | Data Base operation. Pass option (RP) requires several attributes (RS) option to be specified also. | Operation abandoned. |
| P66 | Data Base operation. Length of list (RL option) exceeds specified length of Pass (RP option). | Operation abandoned. |
| P67 | Data Base operation. Length of access instruction (RL, RP, RS options) exceeds number of attributes available. | Operation abandoned. |
| P68 | Data Base operation. If Number (RN) and several attributes (RS) options are both specified, their values must be the same. | Operation abandoned. |
| P69 | Entry point or data field number is found to be negative or zero when using options DI, DJ, RI or RJ. | Operation abandoned. |
| P71 | Edit list (L) requested but list does not exist. | Full report given. |
| P72 | Duplication or contradiction in edit list codes after a switch number. | Full report given in most cases. |
| P73 | Edit list is too long, contains duplicates, zeros or values too large. | Any usable entries in the list accepted. |
| P74 | Invalid character, or character in invalid position. | Character ignored. |
| P75 | Edit list not permitted. | Edit list ignored. |
| P76 | Invalid entry in brackets. | Entry ignored. |
| P77 | Error in use of minus sign. | Edit list accepted as far as possible. |
| P78 | Edit list has no valid values. | No output given. |
| P79 | Edit list specified twice for the same model components. | The first list found is accepted. |
| P80 | User report not yet created. | Entry ignored. |
| P81 | An Outside World queue has become empty. | Control returned to user. |
| P94 | Icon colour defined by entity attribute is non-animation colour. | Colour is set to 8. |
| P95 | Attempt to display graphics when none has been defined. | Command ignored. |
| P96 | Attempt to display graphics on non-graphics terminal. | Command ignored. |
| P97 | Entry point or data field number is found to be negative or zero when using TD, TE, TI, TJ. | Check satisfied but no updating done. |
| P98 | Entry number less than or equal to zero or greater than number of entries in timetable. | Check satisfied but no updating done. |
| P99 | TJ makes timetable negative. | Timetable set to zero. |

# Bibliography

Ames, W. F. and R. Vichnevetsky (eds), *IMACS Transactions Vol III. Modelling and Simulation in Engineering*, North-Holland, Amsterdam, 1985.

Anderson, V. L. and R. A. McLean, *Design of Experiments—A Realistic Approach*, Marcel Dekker, New York, 1974.

Bell, C. B., 'Visual Interactive Modelling in Operational Research: Successes and Opportunities', *J. Opl. Res. Soc.*, **36** (11), 975–982, 1985.

Bell, M. Z., 'Why Expert Systems Fail', *J. Opl. Res. Soc.*, **36** (7), 613–619, 1985.

Bell, P. C. and D. C. Parker, 'Developing a Visual Interactive Model for Corporate Cash Management', *J. Opl. Res. Soc.*, **36** (9), 779–786, 1985.

Burger, J. and Y. Jarny (eds), *Simulation in Engineering Sciences*, North-Holland, Amsterdam, 1985.

Carter, L. R. and E. Huzan, *A Practical Approach to Computer Simulation in Business*, Allen and Unwin, London, 1973.

Christy, D. P. and H. J. Watson, 'The Application of Simulation: A Survey of Industry Practice', *Interfaces*, **13**, 5 October 1983, 47–52.

Clementson, A. T., 'Towards Modular Simulation', Paper presented at the 1985 OR Conference.

Clementson, A. T. and G. K. Hutchinson, 'The Simulation of Flexible Manufacturing Systems', Paper presented at the 1985 OR Conference.

Clocksin W. F. and C. S. Mellish, *Programming in Prolog*, Springer-Verlag, Berlin, 1981.

Conolly, B., *Queueing Systems*, Ellis Horwood, Chichester, 1975.

Corcoran, D. W. J., *Pattern Recognition*, Penguin, Harmondsworth, 1971.

Crookes, J. G. and B. Valentine, 'Simulation in Microcomputers', *J. Opl. Res. Soc.*, **33** (9), 855–858, 1982.

Crookes, J. G., D. W. Balmer, S. T. Chew and R. J. Paul, 'A Three-Phase Simulation System Written in Pascal', *J. Opl. Res. Soc.*, **37** (6), 603–618, 1986.

Davies, R. M., 'An Interactive Simulation in the Health Service', *J. Opl. Res. Soc.*, **36** (7), 597–606, 1985.

Doukidis, G. I. and R. J. Paul, 'Research into Expert Systems to Aid Simulation Model Formulation', *J. Opl. Res. Soc.*, **36** (4), 319–325, 1985.

Durham, A., ' "Over the Horizon" features', *Computer Weekly*, *passim*, 1985 and 1986.

Feigenbaum, E. A. and P. McCorduck, *The Fifth Generation*, Pan Books, London, 1984.

Fishman, G. S., 'Variance Reduction in Simulation Studies', *Journal of Statistical Computation and Simulation*, **1**, 173–182, 1972.

Heginbotham, W. B., 'Simulation in Manufacturing', North-Holland, Amsterdam, 1985.

Henriksen, J. O., 'The Integrated Simulation Environment (Simulation Software in the 1990s)', *Operations Research*, **31** (6), Nov.–Dec. 1983.

Hinde, C. J., 'Artificial Intelligence and Expert Systems', Paper presented at the 1985 OR Conference.

Van Horne, J. C., *Financial Management and Policy*, Prentice-Hall, Hemel Hempstead, 1977.

Kleijnen, J. P. C., *Statistical Techniques in Simulation* (2 vols), Marcel Dekker, New York, 1974.

Klein, J. H., 'The Abstraction of Reality for Games and Simulations', *J. Opl. Res. Soc.*, **36** (8), 671–678, 1985.

Law, A. M., *Statistical Analysis of Simulation Output Data, Operations Research*, **31** (6), Nov.–Dec. 1983.

Mathewson, S. C., 'Simulation Program Generators: Code and Animations on a PC', *J. Opl. Res. Soc.*, **36** (7), 583–589, 1985.

Modigliani, F. and M. Miller, 'The Cost of Capital, Corporation Finance and the Theory of Investment', *American Economic Review*, **XLVIII**, 261–297.

Moore, P. G., *Statistics and the Manager*, Macdonald, London, 1966.

O'Keefe, R. M., 'Simulation and Expert Systems—A Taxonomy and Some Examples', Paper presented at the 1985 OR Conference.

Paul, R. J. and G. I. Doukidis, 'Further Developments in the Use of Artificial Intelligence Techniques which Formulate Simulation Problems', Paper presented at the 1985 OR Conference.

Peck, S. N., 'Intermediate Generality Simulation Software for Production', *J. Opl. Res. Soc.*, **36** (7), 591–595, 1985.

Preedy, D. K. and R. G. A. Brittlestone, 'OR and the Boardroom for the 90s', *J. Opl. Res. Soc.*, **36** (9), 787–794, 1985.

Simons, G. L., *Towards Fifth Generation Computers*, NCC, 1985.

Taha, H. H., *Operations Research, an Introduction*, Collier MacMillan, London, 1971.

Taylor, A. J., 'The Verification of Dynamic Simulation Models', *J. Opl. Res. Soc.*, **34** (3), 233–242, 1983.

Tocher, K. D., *The Art of Simulation*, English Universities Press, London, 1963.

Virjo, A., *A Comparative Study of some Discrete-Event Simulation Languages*, Finnish State Computer Centre, Planning Dept AV., 1972.

Withers, S. J. and R. D. Hurrion, 'The Interactive Development of Visual Simulation Models', *J. Opl. Res. Soc.*, **33**, 973–975, 1982.

'Seeking the Mind in Pathways of the Machine', *The Economist*, 29 June 1985, 83–88.

# Glossary of simulation terms

*Activity*   A task in which one or more entities are engaged and which directly or indirectly changes the state of the model.

*Activity condition*   A requirement that must be satisfied before an activity can start.

*Activity life cycle*   A flow diagram which shows the behaviour of an entity as a sequence of active and idle states.

*Analytical model*   A model which describes a situation in mathematical terms. Analytical models often offer a technique for finding an optimum solution.

*Animation colour*   A colour, used for parts of a graphical display, which can change during a simulation.

*Antithetic random numbers*   A complementary stream of numbers created by subtracting from 101 a stream of random numbers between 1 and 100 (inclusive).

*Attribute*   A numerical property or characteristic of an entity.

*Boundary of model*   The interface of the model with the outside world.

*Clock switch*   A signal to switch an entity clock on or off so that elapsed times can be recorded.

*Command file*   A sequence of expert commands and special control commands which perform a series of changes to the state of a simulation without user intervention.

*Continuous process*   A process during which the resources are consumed continuously at a definable rate until either all the resources are exhausted or the activity is interrupted.

*Correlation term*   An attribute value which is used to modify an activity duration.

*Data field*   A list of values in a timetable or the coordinates in a cumulative distribution.

*Destination queue*   The queue to which an entity is sent at the end of an activity.

*Discrete process*   A process which has a pre-calculated end time, and which cannot be interrupted.

*Discrete time advance*   The movement of the simulation clock from one event to the next.

*Entity*   A resource or object whose behaviour is described in the model.

*Entity group*   A number of entity types which are treated in a similar manner in the model.

*Entity trace*   A mechanism for printing the path of an entity around its activity life cycle as time advances.

*Error diagnostic*   A facility in a computer program which prints out a message when input data is unacceptable or the model cannot be advanced exactly as instructed.

*Expert command*   An instruction issued to the HOCUS Interactive program which is equivalent to answering a series of questions to establish the user's intention.

*Fixed colour*   A colour, used for parts of a graphics display, which cannot change during a simulation.

*Flow diagram*   A diagram which uses symbols to describe the behaviour of a system as a sequence of events.

*Generator*   An activity which feeds entities into the model at required intervals from the outside world.

*Graphical display*   A window on the graphics map, being the portion visible on a graphics terminal at any one time.

*Graphical feature*   An element of a graphical presentation of a model which is not logically required but which improves the presentation.

*Graphical join*   A series of connected straight lines joining an activity to a queue on a graphical display.

*Graphical map*   A square area (of 100 by 1000 pixels) on which a graphical presentation is laid out.

*HOCUS*   An acronym which stands for Hand Or Computer Universal Simulator.

*Icon*   A graphical representation of an entity.

*Initial condition*   A datum specifying where an entity is located at the start of the simulation.

*Input program*   The program in the HOCUS suite which controls the transfer of a hand simulation to the computer.

*Interactive program*   The program in the HOCUS suite which allows the user to control the progress of a simulation and produce reports.

*Matching*   The situation in which the values of the attributes of two or more entities must have defined values before an activity can start.

*Mixed colour*   A colour which is neither a fixed nor an animation colour. It can be used as a fixed colour provided that it is not overwritten during the simulation.

*Model*   A representation of a real-life system which is used to examine the reaction of the system when subjected to a particular set of conditions.

*Ordered queue*   A queue in which the entities are ranked according to a single defined attribute.

*Queue*   Where entities wait when not involved in activities.

*Random number*   A number taken from a specified range (usually 1–100) in such a way that every number has an equal probability of occurring, and its occurrence is random in nature (i.e., it simulates events such as rolling an unbiased dice or spinning a roulette wheel).

*Save file*   The form in which a verified model is saved. It is the description of the simulation which is accessed by the interactive program.

*Sensitivity analysis*   The testing of a solution to a problem by changing the variables involved.

*Source queue*   The queue from which an entity is taken to start an activity.

*Split entity*   A special type of entity used where the logic of the simulation requires the same entity to be in more than one activity at a time.

*User-defined report*   A report whose contents are defined by using the HOCUS report generator rather than one of the 23 standard reports.

*Verifier program*   The program in the HOCUS suite which checks the proposed simulation model for errors and inconsistencies. If the model is acceptable it creates a save file for the interactive program to access.

*Zero time iteration*   A cycle of the START—TIME—END phases performed without advancing the simulation clock. This occurs when the model has zero time activities.

# Index